ANGLO-SOVIET RELATIONS, 1917-1921

Volume I

Intervention and the War

ANGLO-SOVIET
RELATIONS, 1917-1921

Intervention
and the War

BY RICHARD H. ULLMAN

PRINCETON, NEW JERSEY
PRINCETON UNIVERSITY PRESS
1961

Publication of this book has been aided by the
Ford Foundation program to support publication, through university presses, of works in the
humanities and social sciences.

Printed in the United States of America by
Princeton University Press, Princeton, New Jersey

To

GEORGE F. KENNAN

in gratitude and appreciation

PREFACE

THIS volume and the one that will follow it comprise an account of how the British government—the politicians, the civil servants, and the military and naval officers—dealt with the problem of Russia during the critical period between the Bolshevik Revolution in November 1917 and Britain's *de facto* recognition of the Soviet government in March 1921. These three and one-half years witnessed London's initial, hesitant attempts to understand and to reach an accord with the Bolsheviks and, that failing, to take military action against them as an adjunct to a desperate phase in the war against Germany. They saw the continuation in peacetime of the intervention born in war, and its ultimate failure with the realisation that the Soviet regime could be overthrown only by a costly military campaign which the Great Powers could not or would not undertake. This period included the British government's efforts to impose a policy on their allies and associates, first in order to collaborate with the Bolsheviks, then to make war upon them, and finally to move towards peace with them. And it contained—in the negotiations which proceeded throughout 1920 and into 1921—Britain's first prolonged attempt to come to terms with the Revolution.

The fact that Allied policy towards Russia in these years so largely *originated* in London, and not in Paris, Washington, or Tokyo, makes it important that there should appear a study devoted specifically to the formulation and conduct of British policy. There exist several satisfactory general works on Allied intervention in Russia. In addition, Mr. George F. Kennan and Mr. James W. Morley have contributed authoritative studies of American and Japanese policies during the period preceding the beginning of intervention in August 1918; Mr. Kennan hopes to extend his account of American-Soviet relations to the spring of 1920, when the last American troops left Siberia. Yet there exist no studies of the making of British policy, either before the beginning of intervention in Russia or afterwards. It is my hope that the present volume and its successor will fill this gap.

This first volume covers only the initial twelve months of the troubled Anglo-Soviet relationship. These were the months which remained of the war with Germany; after the Armistice, the problem of Russia was altogether different from what it had been during the war. In the following pages the events of this first year of Anglo-Soviet relations are discussed in considerable detail, because it is only by examining this detail that one can understand how British policy was actually made. London's response to Bolshevism was far from coherent; nothing could be further from the truth than the picture presented by Soviet historians of a deliberate British effort, from the moment of the Bolshevik Revolution, to stifle the infant Soviet government. Far from being deliberate, British armed intervention in Russia came about through a combination of widely disparate circumstances and a sequence of day-to-day decisions which at first had little to do with hostility to the revolutionary regime. These decisions were taken by a British government wholly absorbed in the events of the last year of a terrible war. They were taken on the basis of information from Russia that was often inadequate and sometimes wrong; not infrequently they were taken on sheer conjecture alone, or in contradiction to the advice of the most able British representatives in Russia.

Through the materials which have been available to me, it has been possible to show for the first time not only the nature of the information upon which the British government acted in reaching their decisions concerning Russia, but also the ways in which the government interpreted that information and related it both to the general strategy of the war and to the often delicate relations which existed between Britain and the other Allied and Associated Powers. Also for the first time, it has been possible to show something of the behaviour in Russia of the British representatives, civil and military, through whom London maintained contact both with the Bolsheviks and with those Russian elements which sought to overthrow them. In a situation as fluid as that created by the Revolution, the actions of these representatives exerted an influence upon British policy that was wholly disproportionate to their status in the government's service. For this reason they play such an important part in the narrative which follows.

British official publications give virtually no information concerning British policy in Russia during 1918. Because of the wide range of documentary materials which have been available to me from other sources, however, I hope that I have been able to overcome this handicap. The most important single source from which this study is drawn is the collection of the papers of Lord Milner in the Library of New College, Oxford. Milner was a member of the War Cabinet and, during 1918, Secretary of State for War. The immensity of my debt to the Warden and Fellows of New College, my old college, will be apparent on every page of this book.

The second invaluable source for this narrative has been the papers of Sir William Wiseman in the Library of Yale University. Officially, Wiseman was the chief British intelligence agent in the United States. Unofficially, because of his intimate friendship with Colonel House, he became the most important channel of communication between the British and American governments during the last eighteen months of the war. Fortunately for the historian, Wiseman lived not in Washington but in New York, where he could confer daily with House. Therefore the British Embassy in Washington had to send him copies of their important telegrams to and from London on all subjects, and these telegrams are in his papers. During the prolonged Anglo-American-Japanese negotiations over intervention in Siberia, the Foreign Office repeated to Washington all their important correspondence on this subject with the British Embassy in Tokyo. The Wiseman Papers are thus an indispensable source for documenting these negotiations.

The third important source of documentary material for this account has been the National Archives of the United States at Washington. There, in the Supreme War Council Records, are to be found the complete minutes of the meetings of the Council and also of the Council's Permanent Military Representatives. In addition, these records contain many staff papers prepared for the Council, among them important memoranda from the British War Office on all aspects of intervention in Russia. The Supreme War Council Records, however, are only the most important of the many different sorts of papers relevant to this study to be found in the National Archives; the records of the State, War, and Navy Departments also provided me with much valuable material.

Although a few important documents (and clarifications of many details) were found in the other collections of papers cited in the bibliography to this volume, it is largely from these three major sources that I have drawn this study of British policy towards Russia during the last year of World War I. The materials from these sources are so rich and so varied—a wealth that will be apparent to the reader—that I am convinced that when British archives for this period are eventually opened to the historian, they will be found to contain no information which will appreciably alter the substance of the present account.

Finally, it should be stated that neither this volume nor its sequel will attempt to describe systematically the course of British domestic politics or to trace the development of British public opinion toward Russia. Except in those instances in which these factors seem to have had a direct influence upon policy, they will be sketched in only as a background to the pattern of military and diplomatic events. This is logical enough: domestic politics have been treated at length elsewhere; opinion about Russia, on the other hand, is a subject so complicated and so intimately connected with domestic politics that its treatment could fill whole volumes in itself.[1] Moreover, during the period covered by this first volume, public opinion may be said to have played no part in the formation of the government's policy. For policy towards Russia was dictated entirely by the demands of the war with the Central Powers, and the British public were given relatively little information from which they could be expected to form an opinion. During the period from the Bolshevik Revolution to the Armistice, there was not a single important Parliamentary debate on the subject of Russia.

✧

It is my pleasure to acknowledge my indebtedness to the many individuals and institutions who have contributed in so many ways to the writing of this book.

First, I wish to express my gratitude to Mr. George F. Kennan, who from the outset has taken an unfailing interest in this study. Not only has he contributed innumerable useful suggestions and criticisms, but he has placed at my disposal the research materials he himself has gathered—a generosity all too rare in the world of scholarship. But I am perhaps most indebted to him for the example of the two volumes of his *Soviet-American Relations, 1917-1920*, which have thus far appeared: *Russia Leaves the War* and *The Decision to Intervene*. Only someone who has worked through the same thickets

---

[1] The only attempt so far at a study of British opinion towards Russia during this period is Stephen R. Graubard's *British Labour and the Russian Revolution, 1917-1924*, Cambridge, Massachusetts, 1956.

can realise how carefully he has weighed his evidence and how resolutely he has faced up to the hard problems involved. His account of
the making of American policy has been an inspiration to me in my
attempt to chronicle the course of British policy.

Next I must thank the Rhodes Trust and the Warden, Mr. D. N.
Chester, and Fellows of Nuffield College, Oxford, for enabling me
to spend the first year of my research in such agreeable surroundings.
The remaining year and a half were spent as a Research Fellow in
the stimulating company of the Warden, Mr. F. W. D. Deakin, and
Fellows of St. Antony's College, Oxford; to them and to the Social
Science Research Council of New York, who during that period
contributed most generously towards the completion of my work,
I am exceedingly grateful.

To Sir Robert Bruce Lockhart, Sir Reginald Leeper, and Mr. C.
H. Ellis, who shared with me their memories and impressions of the
events with which this study deals, I owe a special debt of gratitude.
I must also thank those who have made available to me the documentary materials upon which this study is based. My greatest debt,
as I have said, is to the Warden, Sir William Hayter, and Fellows
of New College for allowing me to use the Milner Papers. I am
similarly indebted to the Library of Yale University, to the Foreign
Affairs, Modern Army, and Naval Records Branches of the National
Archives in Washington, and to the Manuscripts Division of the
Library of Congress. The staffs of all of these institutions provided
me with immensely helpful assistance.

I should also like to acknowledge my indebtedness to the following:

to Mrs. Woodrow Wilson for permission to have access to and to
quote from the papers of the late President Wilson;
to the Beaverbrook Foundations for permission to quote from *War
Memoirs of David Lloyd George*, published by Odhams Press,
Ltd.;
to Cassell and Company Ltd. for permission to quote from *My
Mission to Russia and Other Diplomatic Memories*, by Sir George
Buchanan, 1923;
to Chatto & Windus Ltd. for permission to reproduce the map of
Transcaspia which appeared on page 132 of *St. Antony's Papers,*

[xi]

No. 6: Soviet Affairs, Number Two, edited by David Footman, 1959;

to Harcourt, Brace & Company, Inc., for permission to quote from *Russian-American Relations, March 1917-March 1920*, compiled and edited by C. K. Cumming and W. W. Pettit, 1920;

and to Sir Robert Bruce Lockhart for permission to quote from his *Memoirs of a British Agent*, published by Putnam, 1933.

I wish especially to thank three people who have painstakingly read this study in manuscript form and who have made innumerable invaluable contributions to it. They are Professor Max Beloff of All Souls College, Oxford; my former colleague Anthony C. E. Quainton; and my wife Yoma Crosfield Ullman, who, in addition, has given me enormous assistance in seeing this book through the press. Finally, I am grateful to my friend William H. Josephson for wise counsel which has sustained me at every step of the way.

❖

Although the Gregorian calendar was not adopted in Russia until 14 January 1918, I have used it, in order to avoid confusion, to refer to all dates previous to its adoption. Similarly, I refer to the March and November Revolutions—the terms usually used in London during the period here considered in referring to these events—instead of the designations of February and October which were and still are used in Russia.

Cambridge, Massachusetts   R.H.U.
March 1961

CONTENTS

PREFACE   vii

I.   BRITAIN, BOLSHEVISM, AND THE WAR   3

II.   FIRST CONTACTS WITH COUNTER-REVOLUTION:
THE COSSACKS OF THE DON   40

III.   THE BOLSHEVIKS MAKE PEACE   58

IV.   RATIFICATION AND THE THREAT OF INTERVENTION   82

V.   SEMENOV, VLADIVOSTOK, AND THE MYTH OF
CO-OPERATION   128

VI.   EMBROILMENT   168

VII.   LONDON–TOKYO–WASHINGTON: THE CRUCIAL
NEGOTIATIONS   191

VIII.   THE BEGINNING OF INTERVENTION: THE NORTH   230

IX.   THE BEGINNING OF INTERVENTION: SIBERIA   258

X.   THE BEGINNING OF INTERVENTION: REPERCUSSIONS
IN MOSCOW   285

XI.   THE DEFENCE OF INDIA:
THE CAUCASUS AND TRANSCASPIA   302

EPILOGUE: INTERVENTION AND THE WAR   330

SELECTED BIBLIOGRAPHY   337

INDEX   345

ILLUSTRATIONS

Plates   *facing page*

Ambassador Sir George Buchanan   16

Foreign Secretary Arthur Balfour

R. H. Bruce Lockhart

Chicherin and Litvinov   17

General Sir Henry Wilson

Lord Robert Cecil

Murmansk from the harbour, 1918   48

Docks at Archangel

Major-General F. C. Poole and his second-in-command
   disembarking at Archangel

Allied diplomats at Archangel with members of the
   Provisional Government of Northern Russia   49

The 25th Middlesex Battalion in a parade at Vladivostok   272

Major-General Alfred Knox in his headquarters at
   Vladivostok   273

Admiral Aleksandr V. Kolchak

Kolchak's headquarters at Omsk

Major-General L. C. Dunsterville's column of Ford cars
   on a road in Persia   304

Dunsterville inspecting an Armenian soldier

[xv]

Illustrations

facing page

British troops advancing toward Turkish positions north
of Baku   305

British troops taking up positions for the defence of Baku

Maps   *page*

Southern Russia   41

Eastern Siberia and Manchuria   97

Northern Russia   110

Urals and Central Siberia   268

Transcaspia   312

ANGLO-SOVIET RELATIONS, 1917-1921

Volume I

Intervention and the War

CHAPTER I

BRITAIN, BOLSHEVISM, AND THE WAR

Now even the most hardened European diplomats . . . have to reckon with the Soviet government as a fact, and to establish certain relations with it.—*Trotsky, before the Central Executive Committee, 21 November 1917*

. . . it is to our advantage to avoid, as long as possible, an open breach with this crazy system.—*Balfour, in a memorandum to the War Cabinet, 9 December 1917*

ON 12 November 1917, a Foreign Office official in London wrote the obituary of the Bolshevik Revolution which, five days before, had swept the Russian Provisional Government from its nervous eight months of office. "It is still too soon to speculate on the immediate future of Russia," stated the official in a memorandum for the guidance of his superiors, "though it may be taken for granted that the Bolshevik Government is probably already on its last legs. It never had any support outside a few of the big towns where it was controlled by fanatical but not always dishonest intellectuals."[1]

In a more leisurely style, the writer went on to dissect the corpse:

Bolshevism is essentially a Russian disease; it is Tolstoyism distorted and carried to extreme limits. But in the present case it has been fastened on and poisoned by the Germans for their own purposes. It is not yet possible to say which of the Bolshevik leaders have taken German money; some undoubtedly have, while others are honest fanatics.

Russia would be saved, the report confidently continued, by the armies which Prime Minister Kerensky was even then leading against the capital. Bolshevism could lead only to a reaction against itself as the Russian people began to comprehend the depths of anarchy into which they were being dragged: "even if the Bolshevik coup has

---

[1] Intelligence Bureau, Foreign Office, "Weekly Report on Russia xxix," CRW/29, 12 November 1917. U.S. National Archives, Petrograd Embassy 800 file (sent to U.S. Ambassador David R. Francis by Ambassador Walter Hines Page, in London).

done harm temporarily, in the long run it will do good." Salvation would come in the form of a combination of the staunchly monarchist generals, Kornilov and Kaledin, with the socialist lawyer and Prime Minister, Kerensky, "each expressing one aspect of the best in Russian character: discipline and Tolstoyan brotherhood and humanity."

If the bulk of this first analysis of the November Revolution was simply naïve rhetoric, its concluding remarks contained a truth that British generals and politicians, in the fourth year of an all-consuming war, found impossible to admit: public opinion in Britain and in Russia, the memorandum stated, was concerned with two wholly different things—in Britain with winning the war, in Russia with preserving the fruits of the March Revolution.[2] Indeed, much of the anguish which preceded (and resulted in) the November days and the tangle of indecision and recrimination that followed was due simply to the fact that leaders in London, and in other Allied capitals, could not understand that for the average Russian the great battles on the plain of Flanders were as remote as if they were on another planet. Long before the advent of Bolshevism, Russia had left the war.

That the Russians were no longer fighting, however, had been only too apparent throughout the previous year. The summer of 1916 had seen Russia's greatest victory, when Brusilov had driven his Seventh Army deep into the Carpathians. But Brusilov's relentless campaign had cost Russia over a million men, and had broken the spirit of her army. During the winter that followed, the number of deserters, most of whom were living quietly at home, was estimated at a million.[3] Incomplete statistics (Russian records were very imperfect) showed that in the course of the war Russia had lost nearly two million killed, five million wounded, and two-and-one-half million prisoners, a total far exceeding the losses of any other belligerent, and as much as the other Allies combined.[4]

Throughout the wasting stalemate on the Western Front, the British and French never quite gave up hope in the Russian steamroller that had seemed so formidable in 1914. Britain, in particular, had backed this hope with huge cash loans, totalling, during the

[2] *idem.*
[3] C. R. M. F. Cruttwell, *A History of the Great War, 1914-1918*, Second Edition, Oxford, 1936, pp. 287-88.
[4] *ibid.*, pp. 630-32.

war years nearly £600 million.[5] But the Allies, hard-pressed them-selves, were not nearly so willing to supply the Russians with the munitions they needed if the steam-roller was to have any effect, and too many times the Russian forces launched massive attacks with little or no artillery support, sometimes even without rifles for all of the charging infantry.

Of all the Western politicians, David Lloyd George was probably most aware of the futility of appealing to the Russians for offensives and then not supporting them with sufficient material assistance.[6] "Had we sent to Russia half the shells subsequently wasted in these ill-conceived battles and one-fifth of the guns that fired them," he wrote, referring to the useless war of attrition on the Western Front, "not only would the Russian defeat have been averted, but the Germans would have sustained a repulse by the side of which the capture of a few blood-stained kilometres in France would have seemed a mockery."[7]

Accordingly, almost the first action Lloyd George took when he became Prime Minister in December 1916 was to make definite the arrangements for the long-discussed inter-Allied conference with the Russians at Petrograd. The object of this conference, held during the first three weeks of February 1917, was to secure, finally, an adequate flow of munitions to the Eastern Front and to help the Russians implant in their armies the efficiency without which the war material would do little good. The British delegation to Petro-

---

[5] The war-debt figures are given in Paul N. Apostol, "Credit Operations," in Alexander M. Michelson et al., *Russian Public Finance During the War*, New Haven, Conn., 1928, p. 320. The French contribution during the war was considerably smaller, some £160 million.

The effect of these massive British loans on Anglo-Russian relations during the war was characterised bitterly, but not unfairly, by Constantin Nabokov, the Chargé d'Affaires of the Russian Embassy in London, in his book, *The Ordeal of a Diplomat*, London, 1921, pp. 59-60: "*Russia became entirely dependent on Great Britain for the prosecution of the war.* Russia was unable to repay by material means for the sacrifices in war material, tonnage, and capital which Great Britain made to supply our armies. Russia paid *only* with the rivers of blood of her sons who died in battle. Russia was always *asking*. Britain was always *giving*. This condition of affairs undoubtedly had an overwhelming influence upon the psychology of British public opinion and of the Government. During the whole time of my tenure of office in London I cannot recall a case of Great Britain requesting us to do a *reciprocal* service of a material order."

[6] As Minister of Munitions and Secretary of State for War, Lloyd George in 1915 and 1916 repeatedly pleaded for greater aid to the Russians. His appeals are set forth in his *War Memoirs* (all references here are to the two-volume second edition, London, 1938), vol. I, pp. 261-73, 461-65, 563.

[7] *ibid.*, vol. I, p. 284.

grad was particularly impressive. Led by Lord Milner, who had played so important a part in the building of the Union of South Africa and who had recently become a member without portfolio of the War Cabinet, it included General Sir Henry Wilson, who, it was recognised, had the most capable mind (if not the most tactful tongue) in the British Army, and five other generals. But the conference accomplished little more than securing an estimate of Russia's needs. Round after round of official banquets and receptions allowed the Russians—in particular the Tsar—to escape serious talk about the total disorganisation of their Empire. Milner is said to have abandoned all hope from the very beginning, and the six-foot five-inch Wilson contented himself with a detailed and discouraging tour of the front and pleasant reminiscences with the Empress, with whom, at Darmstadt thirty-six years before, he had often played tennis.[8]

The Allied delegations had scarcely left Russia when the Empire dissolved in Revolution and the Tsar abdicated. From the beginning of its short life, the Provisional Government was caught between the same forces that had crushed the Imperial regime—domestic clamour for peace and the obsession of the Western Allies that victory in the west depended upon continued Russian pressure in the east. This obsession coloured all Allied reaction to Russian events, and was typified by *The Times*, which, echoing the opinion of the government,[9] saw the Revolution as a purifying influence that would lead to renewed prosecution of the war: ". . . the army and people," it remarked confidently, "have joined hands to overthrow the forces of reaction which were stifling the national aspirations and strangling the national efforts."[10] But as time passed and it was seen how misplaced these hopes had been, the jubilation of the press turned to vituperation, and it was darkly hinted that the chaos and defeatism in Russia had been brought about by German money. A Labour member of Parliament could charge with justice that

---

[8] The best account of the Petrograd conference is by Lloyd George, *ibid.*, vol. I, pp. 928-51. Some of the recollections of Milner and Wilson are gathered in John Evelyn Wrench, *Alfred Lord Milner, the Man of No Illusions, 1854-1925*, London, 1958, pp. 320-29, and in Major General Sir C. E. Callwell, *Field Marshal Sir Henry Wilson, His Life and Diaries*, London, 1927, vol. I, pp. 301-27. See also Robert D. Warth, *The Allies and the Russian Revolution*, Durham, North Carolina, 1954, pp. 18-22.

[9] For the government's initial reaction, see Lloyd George, *War Memoirs*, vol. I, pp. 969-71.   [10] *The Times*, 19 March 1917.

All the German gold in the world has not done as much harm in Russia to the cause of the Allies as the insulting series of articles in the Times directed against the leaders of the Revolution, as the policy of the Government, or as speech after speech delivered from that box—speeches such as that with which the Prime Minister greeted the Russian Revolution when he told us that the purpose of it was to get on with the war. . . .[11]

This is not the place to examine the complex relations that existed during the summer and autumn of 1917 between the Provisional Government, recognised by Russia's allies on 24 March (12 days after the Revolution), and the unrecognised but increasingly powerful Soviet of Workers', Soldiers', and Peasants' Deputies, and the effect of these relations on Russian foreign policy.[12] It was not a creditable episode for Allied diplomacy. Allied insistence on a renewed war effort inevitably increased the gap between the Provisional Government and the mass of the Russian population. As it became more and more clear that the Soviet's call for a democratic peace "without annexations or indemnities" expressed a deep-felt Russian need, the government of Prince Lvov and Foreign Minister Paul Milyukov pressed the Allies for a joint restatement of war aims. But any restatement coming at this time had necessarily to be vague and misleading: Milyukov had no intention of relinquishing the territorial concessions, particularly control of the Straits, which had been promised Russia in the secret treaties of 1915 and 1916. The pious exchange of notes that resulted from the Russian government's appeal could hardly have satisfied anyone on the Left.[13] When the Soviets finally voted 13 May to reverse their position and participate at least to a limited extent in the Provisional Government, their price was the resignation of Milyukov, who was succeeded by M. I. Tereschenko, a wealthy young sugar manufacturer of liberal views. Lvov remained as premier, becoming more of a figurehead than ever. The leading figure not only in the new Cabinet, but in the whole subsequent course of the Provisional Government, was the socialist lawyer, Alexander Kerensky, who took over the Ministry of War.[14]

[11] 96 HC Deb. 5s (26 July 1917), col. 1518.

[12] Warth, *Allies and the Russian Revolution*, is almost entirely devoted to the period of the Provisional Government, and is an extremely detailed and well-documented study. See pp. 23-158.

[13] Cmd. 8587 (Misc. No. 10, 1917). *Note from the Russian Provisional Govt. and the British Reply respecting the Allied War Aims.*

[14] The internal politics of this shift in the Provisional Government are well described in W. H. Chamberlin, *The Russian Revolution, 1917-1921*, New York, 1935, vol. i, pp. 148-50.

The reorganised Cabinet now included 6 socialists out of 16; even before its accession, however, the Allied governments had started sending prominent (and firmly pro-war) socialists from their own countries to tour Russia and revive the Russian will to finish the war. Among them were France's Albert Thomas and Britain's Arthur Henderson, a member of the War Cabinet. At home they carried the label of "socialist," but in the distorted spectrum of Russian politics at the time their socialism seemed far to the Right indeed.

Thomas, when he arrived in Petrograd on 22 April, brought with him a letter recalling the French Ambassador, Maurice Paléologue, whose attachments to the old regime had been too conspicuous. Henderson, an undoctrinaire and shrewdly practical trades unionist, carried a similar message from Lloyd George when he arrived on 2 June. Lloyd George later explained this move as follows:

Our Ambassador there, Sir George Buchanan, had rendered very fine service, but the very fact that he had established excellent relations with the Imperial Government, and with the Provisional Government which replaced it, made him an object of suspicion and distrust to the new Administration which had now been set up under Kerensky, with the support of the Soviet. It was urged by the Foreign Office that he should be supplemented or replaced by someone whose known sympathies with Labour and Socialist movements would ensure him the confidence of the Russian Government.[15]

Sir George Buchanan had, indeed, rendered very fine service. A lean, frail man of sixty-four with white hair and a small, immaculately-trimmed moustache, he looked the schoolgirl's ideal of a British diplomat. The son of an ambassador, he had spent his whole life in the Foreign Service, and his appointment to St. Petersburg in 1910 was the culmination of an unusually successful career.[16] In Russia he scrupulously avoided any appearance of interference in domestic politics, but was careful to keep in touch both with the Court and with all of the leading politicians of the Duma. He was particularly friendly with Sazonov, and during the latter's tenure as Minister for

---

[15] Lloyd George, *War Memoirs*, vol. II, pp. 1121-22. Lloyd George is, of course, incorrect in saying that the new government had been set up under Kerensky.

[16] For excellent descriptions of Buchanan see two long introductions to books by his daughter, Meriel Buchanan: Sir George Arthur's preface to her *Dissolution of an Empire*, London, 1932, and Bernard Pares' introduction to her *Diplomacy and Foreign Courts*, London, 1928. Both Pares and Arthur knew Buchanan intimately.

Foreign Affairs (he resigned in July 1916) the Anglo-Russian Entente was at its strongest. Although he was himself a firm upholder of constitutional monarchy, the British Ambassador had nevertheless a warm feeling and real sympathy for the Tsar, and fully appreciated how extraordinarily difficult were the circumstances in which he ruled. This warm feeling drove Buchanan in January 1917 to seek an audience to warn Nicholas that unless he changed his policy and replaced his ministers with men who retained the confidence of the people as well as the Court, his Empire was doomed. The Tsar instituted no changes.[17]

The British Ambassador was an equally warm friend to the Provisional Government which followed. Thomas Masaryk, the Czech leader and a true liberal if there ever was one, came to Russia in May 1917 and later recorded his very high opinion of Buchanan, calling him "a loyal friend of the Provisional Government and Liberal circles generally," and noting that "he had remarkable influence in the Petrograd of that time."[18]

It was just after Masaryk's visit that Henderson came to Russia, bringing Buchanan's recall. But it did not take long for Henderson to realise that he was far beyond his depth in the morass of Russian revolutionary politics, and sessions with both the Petrograd and the Moscow Soviets convinced him that his socialism was far removed from theirs. Inquiries assured him that the Provisional Government, to a man, wished Buchanan to remain, and in a letter to Lloyd George only twelve days after his arrival Henderson noted the absence of the "slightest hint of dissatisfaction" with the Ambassador except from "the extremists, who, in their present temper, would probably treat in the same way any representative our country appointed who dared to do his duty."[19] So Buchanan stayed. Henderson remained another month, and, according to Buchanan, the two

[17] Buchanan describes this interview in his memoirs, *My Mission to Russia and other Diplomatic Memories*, London, 1923, vol. ii, pp. 41-50. The Court around the Tsar were furious at the Ambassador's *démarche*—Protopopov, the incompetent Minister of the Interior of whom Buchanan especially complained, even insisting that the British Embassy be watched—but Nicholas shrank at anything so drastic as making public his distrust of an ally's representative. See Warth, *Allies and the Russian Revolution*, p. 18.

[18] T. G. Masaryk, *The Making of a State: Memories and Observations*, London, 1927, p. 135.

[19] Mary Agnes Hamilton, *Arthur Henderson*, London, 1938, p. 127. See also Warth, *Allies and the Russian Revolution*, pp. 69-71.

worked together "on the most cordial terms," holding the same views on many important questions.[20]

Among the questions on which the tradition-minded, conservative Ambassador and the Secretary of the Labour Party agreed was that Allied socialists, including a strong British delegation, should take part in a proposed meeting at Stockholm of socialists from all the belligerent nations for a discussion of war aims.[21] The conference had the strong support of the Petrograd Soviet, and the Provisional Government, again caught in the conflict of domestic and international demands, tried to convince the Russian population that it was wholly sympathetic to the proposal, while assuring the Allied governments that it was opposed to it.[22]

Buchanan noted in his diary on 2 August his opinion that "it would be a mistake to leave the Germans a clear field at Stockholm, especially as it would render our attitude open to misconstruction here."[23] It was becoming increasingly important, the Ambassador thought, to convince the Russian extreme Left that the Allies did not wish Russia to remain in the war only for imperialist reasons. The Allied governments, however, were unanimously opposed to any dealings with the German socialists. When Arthur Henderson returned to England, he paid for his public support of the conference by being forced to resign his seat in the War Cabinet.[24]

Because the French and British socialists could not participate, the Stockholm conference was never held. This was a bitter blow to the prestige of the Russian moderate socialist parties—the Mensheviks and the Socialist-Revolutionaries (S-R's)—who had so hopefully heralded the possible outcome of talks between the Allied and German socialists. The Bolsheviks, scornful of the project from the very beginning, won increasing popular support for their programme of unilateral action for bread and peace, not words.

The prospects for the Stockholm conference did not finally collapse

[20] Buchanan, *Mission*, vol. ii, p. 146.

[21] For an authoritative account of the circumstances surrounding the proposed Stockholm conference, see Arno J. Mayer, *Political Origins of the New Diplomacy, 1917-1918*, New Haven, Conn., 1959, pp. 125-27, 192-208, 214-41.

[22] Warth, *Allies and the Russian Revolution*, p. 77.

[23] Sir George Buchanan, *Mission*, vol. ii, p. 161.

[24] Lloyd George, *War Memoirs*, vol. ii, pp. 1127-38. The influence of the Stockholm proposals on the British labour movement is ably detailed in S. R. Graubard, *British Labour and the Russian Revolution, 1917-1924*, Cambridge, Massachusetts, 1956, pp. 25-36.

until late in the summer. By then Kerensky had succeeded Lvov as Premier of the Provisional Government. The preceding months had seen a series of disasters: the already-weakened Army, goaded by Kerensky (who was still Minister of War) into an attack that would satisfy the Allies, began on 1 July an offensive that ended in a catastrophic rout and virtually destroyed it as a fighting force.[25] In the capital the reaction to the defeat was a spontaneous popular uprising not initially organised by the Bolsheviks but soon led by them. The government met the challenge of the "July days" with seeming success: on the 19th the last strongholds of the armed Bolshevik forces, the Fortress of Peter and Paul and their headquarters in the Kshesinskaya Palace directly across the Neva from the British Embassy, were occupied without resistance or bloodshed.[26] But although the Provisional Government had triumphed, it failed to take the step that was necessary to make its victory anything more than momentary: vigorous action against the Bolshevik leaders. As it was, Lenin and Zinoviev escaped; and while Trotsky, Kamenev, and others were arrested, they were soon released.[27] To many responsible Russians, disgusted by the government's inability to act decisively, the only solution was a dictatorship. When Kerensky announced on 31 July that General Brusilov had been replaced as Commander-in-Chief by General Lavr Kornilov, it seemed that a dictator was in sight.

Some who looked to Kornilov were within the British establishment in Russia. Brigadier-General Alfred Knox, the Military Attaché, was a particularly ardent supporter of this stocky son of a Siberian Cossack. Kerensky has charged Knox with subsidising and distributing a Kornilovist pamphlet.[28] Whether this is true or not, it is certainly true that Knox, who had returned to England in late August, urged the War Cabinet on 7 September to press Kerensky to give Kornilov a free hand with the Army and indicated that a coup was in the offing.[29] Kerensky also alleges that at about this same time, a messenger arrived in Russia with a letter for Kornilov from Lord Milner, expressing approval of a military dictatorship in Russia and giving Milner's blessing to Kornilov's plans to establish one.[30]

---

[25] Warth, *Allies and the Russian Revolution*, pp. 111-13.
[26] Chamberlin, *Russian Revolution*, vol. 1, p. 177.   [27] *ibid.*, vol. 1, p. 183.
[28] Alexander F. Kerensky, *The Catastrophe*, New York, 1927, p. 315.
[29] Major-General Sir Alfred Knox, *With the Russian Army, 1914-1917*, London, 1921, vol. 11, p. 677. See also Lloyd George, *War Memoirs*, vol. 11, p. 1538.
[30] Kerensky, *Catastrophe*, p. 315. Milner's papers, in New College, Oxford, contain no trace of this letter.

When, on 9 September, Kornilov ordered the troops under his command to march on the capital to unseat the government, one of the few units which proved faithful to him was a British armoured-car squadron, under Commander Oliver Locker-Lampson, whose members were furnished with Russian uniforms for the occasion. Warth speculates that Knox arranged for their participation, "since it is scarcely conceivable that their commander would have done so upon his own initiative and without the knowledge or consent of the British authorities."[31]

Buchanan admitted that all of his sympathies, too, were with Kornilov, whom he believed to be not a reactionary but simply a genuine patriot interested only in the renewed prosecution of the war. But the Ambassador always discouraged the idea of a military coup, as he felt that Russia's best hope of salvation lay in close co-operation between Kornilov and Kerensky.[32] Buchanan called a meeting of the Allied ambassadors at the British Embassy on the 11th, and the diplomats decided to offer to mediate the dispute.[33] A similar decision was reached in London by the War Cabinet on the following day, and Buchanan was directed to inform Kerensky "that the British Government viewed with the greatest alarm the probabilities of civil war, and urged him to come to terms with General Korniloff not only in the interest of Russia herself, but in that of the Allies."[34] The mediation, refused by Kerensky because it meant placing Kornilov, the usurper, on a par with the legitimate government, was unnecessary: the Petrograd population, united under the leadership of the Soviet, blocked the rail and road entrances to the city and flooded the advancing troops with revolutionary propaganda. Without a shot being fired, the threat of counter-revolution collapsed.[35] But Kornilov's defeat strengthened the Soviet, particularly its Bolshevik faction, and not the Provisional Government.[36]

[31] Warth, *Allies and the Russian Revolution*, p. 123.
[32] Sir George Buchanan, *Mission*, vol. II, p. 185.
[33] As reported by U.S. Ambassador Francis: Francis to Secretary of State, telegram 1734, 11 September 1917. *Papers Relating to the Foreign Relations of the United States, 1918, Russia*, vol. I, Washington, 1931, pp. 187-88. Hereafter this series of publications will be referred to simply as *Foreign Relations*.
[34] Lloyd George, *War Memoirs*, vol. II, p. 1539.
[35] Francis to Secretary of State, telegram 1738, 12 September 1917, *Foreign Relations, 1918, Russia*, vol. I, pp. 188-89. Warth, *Allies and the Russian Revolution*, p. 129.
[36] Foreign Minister Tereshchenko explicitly pointed this out in a telegram to his Ambassador in Washington, 13 September 1917 (copy given to the State Department), *Foreign Relations, 1918, Russia*, vol. I, p. 193. His opinion was shared by subsequent

In London, the Prime Minister remarked to a confidant, the news-paper magnate George Riddell, that he felt that Kornilov's failure was "a serious blow for the Allies," and again reiterated his low opinion of Kerensky, whose policies had brought only indecision and inefficiency.[37] Across the Atlantic, Sir William Wiseman, the intelligence agent who served as the channel of communication be-tween the War Cabinet and President Wilson and Colonel House, told House that the British government had begun to look upon Russia as a hopeless problem.[38] A fortnight later, in early October, Lloyd George gave to Bernard Pares, an English Russian-specialist just returned from Petrograd, the impression that "he had simply lost all interest in Russia as a working factor in the success of the Allies." With a shrewd insight into the nature of the Prime Minister's mind, Pares commented on this attitude: "There was no quick and ready way which could be devised by a brilliant tactician to turn Russia into an asset for the war."[39]

Military authorities in the field echoed London's despair. General Maude, the British commander in Mesopotamia—the one front on which British and Russian forces had joined hands—cabled on 21 September that the time had come when he should cease to depend on the Russians and asked that his Persian flank be reinforced by troops from India. Until this time, Maude had constantly hoped and planned for Russian co-operation and had refused to accept the view of the Indian Army Chief of Staff, expressed as early as April, that his hopes were unwise.[40] At the end of September, when it was pro-

commentators on the Russian Revolution. See Chamberlin, *Russian Revolution*, vol. 1, pp. 216-17; E. H. Carr, *The Bolshevik Revolution, 1917-1923*, vol. 1, London, 1950, pp. 92-93; it is of course the official Soviet view—see *History of the Communist Party of the Soviet Union (Bolsheviks), Short Course*, London, 1943, pp. 184-85.

[37] Lord Riddell, *Lord Riddell's War Diary*, London, n.d. (1933), entry for 14 September 1917, p. 272.

[38] Entry for 16 September 1917. House Diary. Edward M. House MSS, Yale University Library.

[39] Bernard Pares, *My Russian Memoirs*, London, 1931, p. 480. Opinions of the sort that Lloyd George expressed in September had been voiced long before by others. On 15 May, Milner wrote privately to Buchanan: "The work which our Mission tried to do at Petrograd, and which was, of course, based on the hypothesis that Russia would continue to be an effective member of the Alliance, is all as dead as Queen Anne." (Wrench, *Milner*, p. 328.)

[40] *History of the Great War Based on Official Documents: The Campaign in Mesopotamia, 1914-1918*, vol. IV, compiled at the request of the Government of India under the direction of the Historical Section of the Committee of Imperial Defence by Brig.-General F. J. Moberly, London, 1927, p. 44. (Hereafter referred to as *Official History: Mesopotamia Campaign*.)

posed that Britain take over responsibility for Russian troops in this theatre, the British liaison officer with the Caucasus Headquarters cabled gloomily:

British gold may keep the Russian troops in Persia, but it will not make them fight. The old Russian army is dead, quite dead. Our efforts, therefore, to resuscitate it stand useless.[41]

The most ominous sign of all was that German divisions, withdrawn from Russia because they were no longer needed, were beginning to appear on the Western Front.[42]

In Petrograd, meanwhile, the British Ambassador busied himself with yet another appeal for a renewed Russian effort, and convoked a meeting of his Allied colleagues to draft a note for presentation to Kerensky. The document they produced (unsigned by the American Ambassador, who had not received instructions from his government), bluntly threatening that unless the Provisional Government acted to restore discipline and fighting spirit both at the front and in the rear, the Allied governments would be forced to question "the utility of the considerable sacrifices in arms, munitions, material of every kind accorded without counting to Russia,"[43] was needlessly tactless: Kerensky did not have to be told the extent to which he had lost control. The harassed Premier instructed his diplomatic representatives to protest vigorously against the tone of the communication; as a result, Buchanan and his Italian colleague received instructions to apologize. Joseph Noulens, the Radical politician who had replaced Paléologue in July, refused to join in the apology, saying that his government stood by the contents of the note.[44]

The Provisional Government's last month was spent in a futile search for a way to counter the growing influence of the Soviet. Throughout the summer, Kerensky and Tereshchenko had pressed Britain and France for an inter-governmental conference for the revision of war aims, and hopes for such a conference were probably the only factor which kept the moderate socialists from advocating the obviously appealing policy of a separate peace. The British government, too, had urged an inter-Allied conference, but for one

[41] *ibid.*, p. 37.

[42] *The Times*, 10 October 1917, cites three by number.

[43] The text of the note is given in Francis to Secretary of State, telegram 1582, 9 October 1917. *Foreign Relations, 1918, Russia*, vol. i, pp. 207-8.

[44] Francis to Secretary of State, telegram 1949, 4 November 1917, *ibid.*, p. 219.

purpose only: to establish (as Lloyd George wrote to President Wilson on 3 September) more effective unity in Allied strategy. The conference, said the Prime Minister, would meet at the end of November—as soon as the results of the autumn campaigns became clear.[45]

It seems that no-one ever bothered to make clear to the Russians that the conference would not consider war aims. In the terrible autumn of 1917, after Passchendaele and Caporetto, the Allied governments were concerned only with the detailed conduct of war in the west. Russia had nearly ceased to be a factor in Allied military thinking. On 8 October, however, Kerensky declared to the Russian people that at the forthcoming conference, Russia would be represented "by a person enjoying the full confidence of the democratic organisations," who would endeavour, "in addition to coming to an agreement with our Allies regarding our common war aims, to effect an agreement with them on the basis of the principles announced by the Russian revolution."[46] The government named Tereshchenko and General Alekseyev, the Army's new chief of staff, as its delegates; the Soviet, assuming that "democratic organisations" meant themselves, named Michael Skobelev, who had been Minister of Labour in August and September, and instructed him to go to Paris to appeal for "peace without annexations or indemnities."[47] Skobelev was hardly acceptable in the West: "We do not understand in what capacity the Soviet representative intends to come to Paris," the Foreign Office told Nabokov in London. "One thing is certain. He will not be admitted to the Allied Conference."[48] As if to underline this statement, Andrew Bonar Law, the Chancellor of the Exchequer, told the House of Commons on 29 October that the conference would consider only the prosecution of the war and not war aims.[49]

In Petrograd, Tereshchenko planned to leave for Paris on 8 November and Sir George Buchanan arranged to accompany him. Nearly broken in health, the Ambassador had not been away from his post since the start of the war. He, for one, was a dissenter from the Allied policy concerning the conference. As he later put it:

[45] Lloyd George, *War Memoirs*, vol. II, p. 1415.
[46] Text of declaration enclosed in Francis to Secretary of State, unnumbered despatch, 26 October 1917, *Foreign Relations, 1918, Russia*, vol. I, pp. 212-14.
[47] Warth, *Allies and the Russian Revolution*, p. 150.
[48] Nabokoff, *Ordeal*, p. 166.
[49] 98 HC Deb. 5s cols. 1187 and 1447.

I, personally, thought that it would be a mistake on our part either to veto the discussion of peace terms or to raise difficulties about Scobeleff attending it. Such a discussion, as I pointed out, need not commit us in any way, while we could count on Tereschenko keeping the latter in his place. I had a twofold reason for wishing to humour the Socialists. In the first place, though Russia could not be expected to play more than a passive rôle, it was incumbent on us to try and keep her in the war so that her vast resources should not be exploited by Germany, and, in the second, I was afraid that if we drove the more moderate Socialists into opposition we should promote the triumph of Bolshevism.[50]

Though the Ambassador did not know it, the time for negotiation had ended. On 3 November he entered in his diary:

The arrival this afternoon of a guard of cadets of the military school for the protection of the Embassy indicates the approach of a storm.[51]

Four days later, the storm had come. In the early morning of the 7th, the cruiser *Aurora* and three destroyers, whose crews had already declared for the Bolsheviks, drew up the Neva and discharged sailors onto the Palace Quay, which ran from the Winter Palace to the British Embassy, half a mile up-stream. Two of the destroyers lay directly by the Embassy, at the meeting of the great Troitski bridge and Suvorov Square.[52] In the afternoon, the Ambassador walked out alone down to the Winter Palace Square and watched detachments of Red Guards, organised by Trotsky's Military Revolutionary Committee, surrounding a government building. That evening, when it became clear that the Winter Palace, where the members of the government had been meeting, would not surrender, the *Aurora* began an hour's bombardment with blank cartridges, reinforced with real but poorly aimed shells from the ancient batteries in the Fortress of Peter and Paul across the Neva. As Buchanan and his wife and daughter stood at the huge windows in the front of the Embassy and watched the flashes of the gun muzzles across from them, they noticed that the trams ran as usual across the bridge.[53] By 2 o'clock the following morning, the Bolsheviks had succeeded in capturing the Winter Palace. The Revolution came to the British Embassy when the eight military cadets sent by the Provisional Government to guard

---

[50] Sir George Buchanan, *Mission*, vol. II, p. 199.
[51] *ibid.*, p. 203.
[52] Meriel Buchanan, *Diplomacy and Foreign Courts*, p. 234.
[53] Sir George Buchanan, *Mission*, vol. II, pp. 205-7.

Ambassador Sir George Buchanan

Foreign Secretary Arthur Balfour

R. H. Bruce Lockhart (a sketch made in 1934)

Georgi V. Chicherin and Maxim Litvinov
(photographed in the court of the Foreign Office,
Moscow, 1924)

General Sir Henry Wilson,
Chief of the Imperial General Staff

Lord Robert Cecil, Under-Secretary of State
for Foreign Affairs

the building celebrated the new order of things by appropriating a case of claret and a case of whisky and becoming sick in the hall. When some were seen at the windows, Red Guards threatened to shoot them, and they had to be smuggled out in disguise.[54]

The first contact between the British and the Bolshevik authorities (and the last for some time) came on the 8th, when General Knox, at the earnest pleading of Lady Georgina Buchanan, took the Ambassador's car and motored down to the Smolny Institute, an aristocratic girl's finishing school converted by the Bolsheviks into their headquarters, to demand the release of a battalion of women soldiers, captured as they defended the Winter Palace. After a heated interchange with the secretary of the Military Revolutionary Committee, Knox obtained their release.[55]

That same day, in Smolny, after a prolonged ovation from the delegates of the second All-Russian Congress of Soviets, Lenin read a "Decree on Peace" proposing "to all belligerent peoples and their Governments the immediate opening of negotiations for a just and democratic peace," without "annexations" or "indemnities." By annexations, the Soviet decree meant not only territory captured during the war, but also all colonial territories. The "Workers' and Peasants' Government" proclaimed that it henceforth abolished secret diplomacy and on its part expressed "the firm intention to conduct all negotiations absolutely openly before the entire people." As a first step in this direction, Lenin promised the publication of the secret treaties. Finally, he made clear that the appeal for an immediate armistice was addressed in particular "to the class conscious workers of the three most advanced nations of the world and the three mightiest states taking part in the present war—England, France, and Germany."[56] It was the first of a long list of appeals expressing the faith of the Bolsheviks in the power of the working classes of all nations.

Also on the 8th, acting in his capacity as Dean of the Diplomatic Corps, the British Ambassador called a meeting of all his colleagues.

---

[54] *ibid.*, p. 212; Meriel Buchanan, *Diplomacy and Foreign Courts*, pp. 235-36.

[55] Knox, *Russian Army*, vol. II, p. 712.

[56] The text of the "Decree on Peace" is printed in *Dokumenty vneshnei politiki SSSR* (Documents on the Foreign Policy of the U.S.S.R.), vol. I, Moscow, 1957, pp. 11-14. A translation appears in Jane Degras, ed., *Soviet Documents on Foreign Policy*, London, 1951, vol. I, pp. 1-3. The "Decree" was published, but never formally communicated to foreign governments.

According to the American Ambassador, the meeting was called simply to consider measures for the safety of the various foreign colonies, and no mention was made of any new government or the recognition of one if and when it became established. The session's only result was a decision that each head of mission should act according to the dictates of his own judgement.[57]

The next few days were filled with rumours of counter-revolution. Kerensky, who had left the city on the morning of the 7th in a car commandeered from the American Embassy, was many times reported to be nearing the capital at the head of a column of loyal troops. But he managed only to enlist the support of about 700 Cossacks, who were forced, on the 12th, to retreat before a much larger Red force massed outside Petrograd. On the following day, Buchanan wrote in his diary:

Kerensky has again failed us, as he did at the time of the July rising and of the Korniloff affair. His only chance of success was to make a dash for Petrograd with such troops as he could get hold of; but he wasted time in parleying, issued orders and counter-orders which indisposed the troops, and only moved when it was too late. The Bolsheviks . . . are now confident of victory.[58]

The Ambassador also recorded that no-one at the Embassy or in the Petrograd British colony had yet been injured.[59] The Embassy, at least, was more or less under the protection of the Bolsheviks. In another trip to Smolny, Knox had secured a guard of Polish soldiers, and in addition, officers of the British Military Mission began to sleep on the premises. Although a warning came on the night of the 12th that the premises were to be attacked, and although a Russian petty officer was shot dead in front of the building by workers to whom he refused to surrender his sword, no incidents directly involving the Embassy occurred.[60] The Foreign Office was, of course, concerned about Buchanan's safety. In reply to a cable saying that he was remaining at his post, Arthur Balfour, the former Conservative Prime Minister who was Foreign Secretary in Lloyd George's Coalition, assured the Ambassador on the 9th that the government had com-

[57] Francis to Secretary of State, telegram 1968, 9 November 1917, *Foreign Relations, 1918, Russia*, vol. I, p. 228.
[58] Sir George Buchanan, *Mission*, vol. II, pp. 212-13.
[59] *ibid.*, p. 213.
[60] *ibid.*, p. 213.

plete confidence in him and that he was at liberty to leave Petrograd for Moscow or any other place he thought desirable.[61]

In London, the Bolshevik Revolution was seen at first as just another black event in an autumn of unmitigated gloom. The four-month campaign in the mud of Passchendaele, just ended, had cost 400,000 British casualties to the enemy's 250,000. When the news from Russia reached the West, Lloyd George was at Rapallo conferring with the French and Italian premiers on how Italy could best recover from the débâcle that began at Caporetto. Lord Milner, in London, noted in his diary on 8 November that there was "very bad news both from Italy and Russia" which put "a new and worse complexion on the war."[62]

The British press took up from the start a set of positions which, for each newspaper, remained remarkably the same throughout the following four years. *The Times*, blaming Kerensky for failing to use sufficient strength against "anarchy," proclaimed its faith in what it confidently believed (and continued to believe) to be the "real Russia," which would never consent to make a separate peace.[63] The arch-Tory *Morning Post* found that Russia had been betrayed by "Russian Jews of German extraction" and in German pay, and maintained that Britain could never have any dealings with them. The *Post* hinted at Allied intervention from the very beginning:

It remains only for the Allied nations to reach by some means the heart of the Russian people themselves and those elements in Russia which are true to the cause of the Allies. We think this is a task in which the U.S. and Japan might exercise their new-found power of friendly co-operation.[64]

The liberal newspapers, the *Manchester Guardian* and the *Daily News*, blamed the November upheaval not on Germany but on Britain, citing British hostility to the Provisional Government's many appeals for a revision of Allied war aims. The conservative press's repeated abuse of the Kerensky regime, and the government's refusal to allow British socialists to go to Stockholm, were also condemned.[65]

Curiously, about the only organ whose initial reaction to the Bolshevik Revolution was substantially different from the position

---

[61] *ibid.*, p. 209.
[62] Milner diary, partial typed transcript in Milner MSS, New College, Oxford.
[63] *The Times*, 9 November 1917.
[64] *Morning Post*, 9 November 1917.
[65] *Manchester Guardian*, 9 November 1917; *Daily News*, 9 November 1917.

it later took was George Lansbury's left-Labour, more or less pacifist weekly, *The Herald* (which later became the *Daily Herald*). H. N. Brailsford's sharply anti-Bolshevik article, "Russia, Peace and Bread,"[66] the *Herald's* first mention of the Russian events, was perhaps the most intelligent of the initial commentaries. The month of November, Brailsford wrote, with the Italian disaster and the Russian Revolution, was "likely to stand in our memories as the blackest of the war." If Brailsford erred, it was in attributing to the Bolsheviks any intention at all of following democratic procedures:

On any reading of sane democracy, the Maximalists have acted ill. If it is really a fact . . . that the elections for the Constituent Assembly were to be held about November 25, the Maximalist stroke is inexcusable. They had only to be patient for a month and the will of Russia, whatever it might be, would have been declared through universal suffrage . . . no humane man would have plunged Russia into chaos when democratic order was in sight after a month's delay. This stroke is a piece of reckless and uncalculating folly. One hesitates to believe, however, that the leaders of this movement, Lenin and Trotsky, are corrupt, though some of their lieutenants may well be so. . . . Their real crime against Russia is that they have followed Korniloff in perpetuating an epoch of violence.

Brailsford, too, blamed the British press:

From May onwards it has been clear that the mind of the Russian people was bent on securing an early general peace. At first our Press pretended to see in this demand an amiable but childlike idealism. Then it fell into the other extreme of attributing it to German bribes. It has never to this day faced the plain fact that Russia is physically unable to continue the war without self-destruction. . . .

Meanwhile, in Russia, the new regime began the search for an armistice.[67] The first move, on the evening of 20 November, was a telegram to General Dukhonin, who, in the absence of Kerensky, had assumed the command of the remnants of the Russian armies, at General Staff Field Headquarters (the Stavka) at Mogilev, directing him to propose to his German military counterpart a three months' armistice.[68] On the 21st, Trotsky, as People's Commissar for

---

[66] *The Herald*, 17 November 1917.

[67] For a fully detailed account of the Bolshevik efforts to secure an armistice, see George F. Kennan, *Soviet-American Relations, 1917-1920*, vol. 1, *Russia Leaves the War*, Princeton, 1956, pp. 85-98.

[68] The text of the telegram is in *Dokumenty vneshnei politiki*, vol. 1, pp. 15-16; translation in Degras, *Soviet Documents*, vol. 1, pp. 3-4.

Foreign Affairs, sent a note to the Allied missions in Petrograd, formally notifying them of the establishment "of a new government of the Russian Republic in the form of a Council of People's Commissars," drawing their attention to the Decree on Peace issued on the 8th, and asking them to regard it as "a formal proposal for an immediate armistice on all fronts and for the immediate opening of peace negotiations." The note ended with an expression "of the profound respect of the Soviet government for the people of your country, who, like all other peoples exhausted and racked by this unparalleled butchery, cannot do otherwise than ardently desire peace." The Allied governments were not mentioned.[69]

On the same day, at the meeting of the Central Executive Committee of the Soviet of Workers' and Peasants' Deputies, at which the steps towards an armistice were approved, Trotsky made a speech examining probable reactions to the Soviet peace move. Of all nations, he thought the most hostile would be Britain, "whose upper bourgeoisie risk losing less than anybody else from the war, and hope to gain most. The drawn-out nature of the war is not in the least inconsistent with British policy." Trotsky closed his speech by announcing that on the next day he would begin publication of the secret treaties, taken from the archives of the Tsarist and Provisional Governments. They were, he assured his listeners, "even more cynical in their contents than we supposed."[70]

Reporting all this to the Foreign Office, Buchanan suggested that no reply should be given to Trotsky's note, but that the government should make a statement in the House of Commons that, while they were ready to discuss peace terms with a legally constituted government, they could not do so with one that had broken the engagements taken by one of its predecessors under the agreement of 5 Sep-

---

[69] *Dokumenty vneshnei politiki*, vol. 1, pp. 16-17. Like all of the notes in this volume which originally bore the signature of Trotsky, the printed copy bears no signature, but is signed simply "People's Commissar for Foreign Affairs"; notes despatched after Chicherin took over at the Narkomindel, on the other hand, are all printed as signed with the Commissar's name. And this volume was published in 1957! A translation of the note of 21 November is in Degras, *Soviet Documents*, vol. 1, p. 4.

[70] *ibid.*, pp. 5-8. In the House of Commons on 29 November 1917, after a flurry of questions and an evasive reply by Lord Robert Cecil as to whether or not the documents published by the Bolsheviks were genuine ("Some of them may be authentic and some not," said Cecil), an enraged Tory (J. M. Hogge) indignantly asked: "Do we understand that these documents have been published without reference to the Foreign Office?" (99 HC Deb. 5s col. 2191.)

tember 1914.[71] On the following day, the 22nd, on the instructions of their governments (as the signatories, with Russia, of the Treaty of London barring a separate peace), the British, French, and Italian ambassadors ordered their military representatives at the Stavka to protest to General Dukhonin against the armistice appeal.[72] When Dukhonin received their protests on the 23rd he had already been dismissed as commander, having the previous day told the Soviet authorities he was unable to execute their orders. He was carrying on, however, until the arrival of his Bolshevik successor, Ensign Krylenko. The Allied protest was in the strongest possible terms, warning rather threateningly that "any violation of the treaty by Russia will be followed by the most serious consequences."[73]

The Bolsheviks were obviously angered by the tone of this communication. Since Dukhonin had published it to his troops Trotsky moved rapidly to counteract its charge that Russia had betrayed her allies. In an appeal broadcast "To All Regimental, Divisional, Corps, and Army Committees, to All Soviets of Workers', Soldiers', and Peasants' Deputies, to All, All, All!" on 24 November, he pointed out that the Soviet proposal was for an armistice on *all* fronts. In any case, he added, revolutionary Russia would not be bound by dead treaties. "Soldiers! Workers! Peasants!" his appeal continued, "Your Soviet government will not allow the foreign bourgeoisie to wield a club over your head and drive you into the slaughter again. Do not be afraid of them." Finally, he exhorted soldiers to "Elect your delegates for the negotiations," and informed them that "Your Commander-in-Chief, Ensign Krylenko, starts for the front today to take charge of the armistice negotiations."[74] Krylenko had indeed left; by the afternoon of the 27th he could report to Petrograd that the Germans were ready to begin negotiations and that formal talks would begin at Brest-Litovsk on 1 December (later changed to the 2nd).[75]

[71] Diary entry, 21 November; Sir George Buchanan, *Mission*, vol. ii, p. 223.

[72] Francis to Secretary of State, telegram 2007, 22 November 1917; *Foreign Relations, 1918, Russia*, vol. i, p. 245.

[73] The text of the protest is printed in the article "Nakanune peremiriya" (On the Eve of the Armistice), *Krasnyi Arkhiv* (The Red Archives), Moscow-Leningrad, 1922-41, vol. 28, 1927, No. 4, p. 201. See Kennan, *Russia Leaves the War*, pp. 90-91, 93.

[74] *Dokumenty vneshnei politiki*, vol. i, pp. 23-24. Some excerpts are translated in James Bunyan and H. H. Fisher, *The Bolshevik Revolution, 1917-1918: Documents and Materials*, Stanford University, 1934, pp. 245-46.

[75] *Dokumenty vneshnei politiki*, vol. i, pp. 25-28; Bunyan and Fisher, *Bolshevik Revolution*, pp. 256-58.

Just as this news was reaching Smolny, the Allied military attachés were summoned to the old General Staff Headquarters and handed another note from Trotsky, who again stated that the Bolsheviks were striving for a general, not a separate, armistice, but added that they might be forced by the Allies to a separate peace if they continued to "close their eyes before the facts." Pressing the Entente Powers for a definite answer as to whether they would support the Bolshevik initiative for an armistice, and warning them that their refusal would in no way alter Soviet policy, he concluded:

As long as Allied Governments answer with bare "no recognition" of us and our initiative we will follow our own course appealing to the peoples after the governments. Should the results of the appeal bring separate peace, which we do not want, responsibility will fall completely upon the Allied Governments.[76]

In the British Embassy, both the Ambassador and General Knox were becoming increasingly convinced that an attempt to hold Russia to her agreement could do the Allies only harm. "It appears quite clear," Knox cabled the War Office on the 25th, "that whatever happens politically in Russia, the bulk of the Russian Army refuses to continue the war."[77] Accordingly, he felt that the only course was to issue a statement releasing Russia from the obligations she had undertaken in 1914.[78] Buchanan agreed. The Allies, he wrote in his diary, should *"faire bonne mine à mauvais jeu."*[79] On 27 November, after receiving Trotsky's second note, he sent a long telegram to the Foreign Office:

I share the view, already expressed by General Knox, that the situation here has become so desperate that we must reconsider our attitude. In my opinion, the only safe course left to us is to give Russia back her word and to tell her people that, realizing how worn out they are by the war and the disorganisation inseparable from a great revolution, we leave it to them to decide whether they will purchase peace on Germany's terms or fight on with the Allies, who are determined not to lay down their arms till binding guarantees for the world's peace have been secured.

[76] The text was transmitted by Francis in telegram 2034 to Secretary of State, 27 November 1917, *Foreign Relations, 1918, Russia*, vol. I, p. 250.
[77] Lloyd George, *War Memoirs*, vol. II, p. 1540.
[78] Knox, *Russian Army*, vol. II, p. 727.
[79] Sir George Buchanan, *Mission*, vol. II, p. 225.

At the back of the Ambassador's mind, however, lay the rather naïve hope that they still might be able to induce Russia to go on with the war:

It has always been my one aim and object to keep Russia in the war, but one cannot force an exhausted nation to fight against its will. If anything could tempt Russia to make one more effort, it would be the knowledge that she was perfectly free to act as she pleased, without any pressure from the Allies.

Applying pressure to Russia, Buchanan felt, might force her into an alliance with Germany, which would be catastrophic for Britain:

There is evidence to show that Germany is trying to make an irreparable breach between us and Russia, so as to pave the way for the German protectorate which she hopes eventually to establish over the latter. *For us to hold to our pound of flesh and to insist on Russia fulfilling her obligations, under the 1914 Agreement, is to play Germany's game.* Every day that we keep Russia in the war against her will does but embitter her people against us. If we release her from those obligations, the national resentment will turn against Germany if peace is delayed or purchased on too onerous terms. For us it is a matter of life and death to checkmate this latest German move, for *a Russo-German alliance after the war would constitute a perpetual menace to Europe, and more especially to Great Britain.*

He was not, he maintained, "advocating any transaction with the Bolshevik Government."

On the contrary, I believe that the adoption of the course which I have suggested will take the wind out of their sails, as they will no longer be able to reproach the Allies with driving Russian soldiers to the slaughter for their Imperialistic aims.[80]

While waiting for London to consider his suggestions, the Ambassador felt it necessary to issue a public statement setting forth the British attitude towards the Bolshevik government and explaining why his government had made no reply to the Soviet armistice proposals. His statement, made on 29 November, was the first that an Allied representative had made in Russia since the November revolution, and it was the only Allied reply of any kind to the repeated

[80] *ibid.*, pp. 225-26 (italics added).

Bolshevik armistice invitations.[81] Trotsky's note (of the 21st, proposing a general armistice), Buchanan pointed out, was delivered at the British Embassy fully nineteen hours after Dukhonin had received the order to open immediate negotiations with the enemy. The Allies had therefore been confronted with an accomplished fact on which they had not been consulted. Besides—and here the statement was perhaps needlessly contentious—it was impossible for the Ambassador to reply to notes addressed to him by a government which his own government had not recognised. Governments like the British, whose authority came directly from the people, had no right to make a decision of such importance without first making sure that it would meet with the complete approval and support of their electorate. They could not, therefore, return an answer off-hand.

Smolny's reply, issued the next day, was surprisingly mild, stating only that if the orders to Dukhonin and the notes to the Allied embassies, which were despatched simultaneously, arrived at different times, the difference was simply due to "secondary technical reasons" and had no relation to Soviet policy. Reiterating its senders' desire for a general rather than separate armistice, it did not even make the easy propaganda it could have done had it pointed out that the British statement evaded the issue: would the Allies join the peace discussions?[82] But this question was asked directly in a note to the Allied embassies delivered the day before, informing them that military operations on the Russian front had ceased and that negotiations with the Germans would begin on 2 December.[83]

✧

Meanwhile, in Paris, there had assembled the most distinguished diplomatic gathering the war had yet seen. Representatives of eighteen governments convened to discuss the co-ordination of their war efforts. This was the conference to which Tereshchenko and Buchanan

[81] Issued in Russian, the statement was published in *Izvestiya* on 1 December 1917 and is printed in *Dokumenty vneshnei politiki*, vol. 1, p. 31. It was summarised in *The Times*, 3 December. A translation is in C. K. Cumming and W. W. Pettit, eds., *Russian-American Relations, March, 1917 - March, 1920, Documents and Papers*, New York, 1920, pp. 51-52.

[82] The text, from *Izvestiya*, 1 December 1917, is printed in *Dokumenty vneshnei politiki*, vol. 1, pp. 30-31, and is translated in Degras, *Soviet Documents*, vol. 1, p. 14.

[83] *Dokumenty vneshnei politiki*, vol. 1, pp. 31-32 (where it is dated 30 November, the day it appeared in *Izvestiya*); the American Embassy's translation, transmitted by Francis as telegram 2040 to Secretary of State, 29 November, is in *Foreign Relations, 1918, Russia*, vol. 1, p. 253.

should have gone. The original purpose for which the gathering was called had been to establish a Supreme War Council, composed only of the Great Powers. But when the smaller nations had heard of the forthcoming assembly, they had asked to be included. Paul Cambon, the French Ambassador in London, told President Wilson's personal representative, Colonel Edward M. House, that he was afraid the lesser powers would utilise the occasion to voice their political aspirations, and thus obscure the main object of the conference, which was the successful prosecution of the war. Of course, no Russian delegation was sent, but delegates were well aware that the Russians desired from them a new declaration of their aims in continuing the war. This, said Cambon, was quite unnecessary: "the object of the war was to beat Germany; all other objects would be discussed after that."[84] Before the conference opened, House noted in his diary:

I find it will be useless to try to get either the French or British to designate terms. Great Britain cannot meet the new Russian terms of "no indemnities and no aggression" and neither can France. Great Britain at once would come in conflict with her Colonies and they might cease fighting, and France would have to relinquish her dream of Alsace and Lorraine.[85]

To avoid embarrassing discussion, only two plenary sessions were held, each lasting but a few minutes. All important work was done at private meetings of Colonel House and the British, French, and Italian premiers and foreign ministers (Lloyd George and Balfour, Clemenceau and Pichon, Orlando and Sonnino), and their military advisers. To the first of these meetings, on 30 November, Balfour brought Buchanan's telegram urging that Russia be released from her treaty obligations and recommended the adoption of this policy by the Allies. This brought violent objection from Sonnino and equally firm opposition from Clemenceau, who declared that "if M. Maklakoff [the Provisional Government's Ambassador in Paris] and all the celestial powers asked him to give Russia back her word, he would refuse."[86] Several days of discussion proved that no agreement on a Russian policy was possible. "It was decided finally," House cabled President Wilson on 2 December,

[84] Charles Seymour, *The Intimate Papers of Colonel House*, New York, 1928, vol. III, p. 235.
[85] House diary, entry for 16 November 1918; House MSS.
[86] Lloyd George, *War Memoirs*, vol. II, p. 1543.

that each Power should send its own answer to its Ambassador at Petrograd, the substance of each answer to be that the Allies were willing to reconsider their war aims in conjunction with Russia and as soon as she had a stable government with whom they could act.[87]

That evening, House and Balfour had a long conference, and the British Foreign Secretary wrote out a telegram to Buchanan which, House noted, "goes far in the direction I have been urging."[88] Balfour wanted to bring it up for approval at the inter-Allied conference the next morning, but House urged him not to, thinking that it would only have provoked discussion and that Sonnino and perhaps the French would bring pressure upon him to modify it. Balfour agreed to despatch the telegram without submitting it to the conference, "believing [House wrote] that he betrayed no confidence in doing so" because of the resolution that had been previously adopted.[89] Nor did the Foreign Secretary consult the Foreign Office, or his colleagues in the Cabinet, before sending the cable.[90]

The tone of Balfour's telegram was hardly in keeping with Buchanan's recommendations. Of the Bolshevik theory that a treaty concluded while the autocracy was in power could have no binding force on the democracy that succeeded it, the Foreign Secretary wrote:

I doubt whether this doctrine, inconsistent as it clearly is with any kind of stability in international agreements, will commend itself to a Russian government which can claim with justice to represent the Russian people.

The British government, however, based their claims not on an appeal to treaties, but on "deeper principles" accepted by the Soviet government themselves. Buchanan had reported that the Bolsheviks wanted

a democratic peace: a peace which repudiates the idea of squeezing plunder out of conquered enemies under the name of war indemnities: or adding by force of arms reluctant populations to great empires.

---

[87] Seymour, *Intimate Papers*, vol. III, pp. 290-91.
[88] House diary, entry for 3 December 1917; House MSS.
[89] *idem.*
[90] In sending a copy of Balfour's telegram to the President, House prefaced it with the remark that it would be cabled to Petrograd provided that the British government agreed. This remark, along with the text of Balfour's telegram, is printed in *Foreign Relations, 1918, Russia*, vol. I, pp. 256-57. But on the copy of the telegram (with the prefatory remark) which House kept for his own papers, he wrote: "Balfour afterwards told me he sent this despatch without consulting London." House MSS, drawer 2, no. 10.

This, Balfour continued, "speaking broadly, is also the kind of peace which His Majesty's Government desire to see secured for the world," and while they were always ready to discuss these aims, they could not do so "until Russia has established a stable government acceptable to the Russian people, a consummation which has not been reached."

In the meantime, Balfour told Buchanan, he was at liberty to point out to the Bolsheviks that the very worst way to obtain the sort of peace that both they and the British government desired was the way they had chosen, separate negotiations:

When arms have failed, rhetoric is not likely to succeed. So far as His Majesty's Government are aware of, no responsible German statesman has ever said a word indicating agreement either with the ideals of the provisional government [so Balfour referred to the Soviet regime] or with the Allied declaration of policy. Their attitude is not likely to become more accommodating nor will Russian aims be nearer of accomplishment if the Russian Army is permitted to become negligible as a fighting force. The only peace which could be secured by substituting argument for action is one which would be neither democratic nor durable nor Russian. It would be German and imperialistic.

To put these views before the Russian people, Buchanan resorted to a device that would soon characterise "open diplomacy": the press conference. On 8 December, before 25 journalists "representing papers of every shade of opinion save the Bolsheviks,"[91] Harold Williams, a British linguist-cum-journalist who served as *de facto* press attaché of the Embassy, read out a long statement whose first paragraphs reiterated, at greater length, the text of Balfour's telegram.[92]

The last half of the statement was devoted to another matter: the bitter attacks on Britain that were appearing in the official Soviet press. Perhaps the bitterest of these was an appeal, issued in the name of the Sovnarkom by Lenin and Stalin (as Commissar for Nationalities) on 3 December, inciting the peoples of the East, "in whose lives and property, in whose freedom and native land the rapacious European plunderers have for centuries traded," to "Overthrow these robbers and enslavers" of their countries. British rule in India, in particular, was singled out as a target for revolution; the peoples of

[91] Diary entry for 10 December 1917. Sir George Buchanan, *Mission*, vol. II, p. 238.
[92] The text of the statement is printed in *ibid.*, pp. 233-37.

India were urged to struggle for the freedom that the coming of Soviet power had given the eastern peoples of Russia.[93]

Buchanan was particularly exasperated by Lenin's incendiary appeal. "It is an unheard-of thing," said the British statement, "for a man who claims to direct Russian policy to use such language of a friendly and Allied country." Briefly, the statement sketched out the methods of the British Raj and the steps that were being taken to prepare the Indians for self-government. It then turned to the British colony in Russia:

The position of Englishmen in this country is not an enviable one at the present moment. They are singled out for attacks, or regarded with suspicion. Our propaganda bureau, which was started with the object of making our two countries better known to each other, is even accused of being in league with counter-revolutionaries. There is not the slightest foundation for such a charge, unless it is a crime to defend one's country against the calumnies and misrepresentations of German agents. . . .

I wish the Russian people to know that neither myself nor any agency under my control have any wish to interfere in the internal affairs of this country. During the seven years that I have been Ambassador here I have worked heart and soul to bring about the closest understanding between Russia and Great Britain; but, though I have associated, as it is my duty, with members of all parties, I have ever since the February revolution maintained a strictly neutral attitude. Prior to that date I did, it is true, endeavour to use all my influence with the ex-Emperor in favour of some form of Constitutional Government, and I repeatedly urged him to concede the legitimate wishes of the people. Now that his sovereign rights are vested in the Russian people, the latter will, I trust, pardon my transgression of the strict rules of diplomatic etiquette.

The statement ended with a warning. The Soviet leaders, it said, "are creating, no doubt unintentionally, the impression that they set more store by the German than by the British proletariat." This could only

[93] *Dokumenty vneshnei politiki,* vol. 1, pp. 34-35; Degras, *Soviet Documents,* vol. 1, pp. 15-17. This appeal was taken extremely seriously in London. Steps were taken to prevent its publication—in Britain, of course, where this was simply a matter of censorship—but also abroad. In Washington, the British Ambassador summarised it for the State Department, noting that it "would seem to be one of the first results of [Bolshevik] negotiations with Germany," and adding: "You will of course realise that this is a most serious matter and the British Government have instructed me to approach the United States Government with a view to all vigilance being exercised against the publication of this appeal in the newspapers, and the prevention of its transmission by cable and, as far as possible, by post." (Sir C. Spring-Rice to Acting Secretary of State, 8 December 1917, U.S. National Archives, State Department file 861.00/782½.)

estrange, rather than attract, the sympathies of the British working classes; like the appeals of the French in the wars that followed their Revolution, it would only steel the resolve of the British people to fight the war to the end.

The Ambassador's statement was clearly reasoned, moderate, and sympathetic throughout; it was, in fact, characteristic of the best of a diplomatic service that was (at its best) understanding, chivalrous, and humane. But the statement's central point—that the British government would not discuss terms of peace with the revolutionary regime—was wholly antithetic to the mood that had swept Russia. Buchanan's own comment on its reception unwittingly revealed the void that divided the new diplomacy from the old:

This reply has been severely criticized by the *Novaya Jizn* [Maxim Gorky's newspaper] and by some of the Bolshevik papers as showing that we will not meet the wishes of the Russian democracy. My statement, on the other hand, has met with warm approval in diplomatic circles and has evoked a cordial expression of thanks from the Russian colony in London.[94]

Unfortunately, diplomats and émigrés had little sway in the Russia of December, 1917.

❖

Buchanan released his statement to the press after exactly a month's confrontation with the vexing realities of Bolshevik power. Quite early he had come to the conclusion that although the new government could not be accorded official recognition it was nevertheless necessary to establish relations of some sort with it for the conduct of everyday affairs.[95] The Foreign Secretary had agreed that unofficial relations were necessary to safeguard the interests of Allied citizens, and had instructed the Ambassador that British *consuls* should be used for any dealings with the Soviet authorities.[96] Trotsky, in his speech of 21 November, had boasted of these informal contacts. Allied diplomats, he said,

have to reckon with the Soviet government as a fact, and to establish certain relations with it. These relations are being formed empirically, in practice; the agents of the European Powers are compelled to approach

[94] Diary entry, 10 December 1917; Sir George Buchanan, *Mission*, vol. II, p. 238.
[95] Buchanan to Balfour, telegram 1812, Petrograd, 16 November 1917, 8:10 p.m. A copy of this telegram is in the Papers of Sir William Wiseman in the Yale University Library.
[96] Diary entry, 20 November 1917; Sir George Buchanan, *Mission*, vol. II, p. 238.

us with all sorts of questions concerning current matters, such as questions of leaving or entering the country, etc.[97]

These were haphazard relations, necessarily of a temporary nature. But before the British government could make any specific decisions regarding a future policy towards Russia, it was necessary that they form some notion of the nature and purposes of the Bolshevik regime which ruled so much of the country. During the first uneasy month of Anglo-Soviet relations, little thought had been given to the nature of Bolshevism. On 9 December, therefore, the Foreign Secretary broached this subject in a memorandum to the War Cabinet.[98]

Some of his colleagues, he said, had suggested that after their recent proclamations the Bolsheviks could be regarded only as avowed enemies of Britain, and that to regard them in any other way would show lamentable blindness to facts and inability to act with decision. Balfour announced his complete dissent from this view which, he believed, was founded on a misconception:

If, for the moment the Bolsheviks show peculiar virulence in dealing with the British Empire, it is probably because they think that the British Empire is the great obstacle to immediate peace; but they are fanatics to whom the constitution of every State, whether monarchial or republican, is equally odious. Their appeal is to every revolutionary force, economic, social, racial, or religious, which can be used to upset the existing political organisations of mankind. If they summon the Mohammedans of India to revolt, they are still more desirous of engineering a revolution in Germany. They are dangerous dreamers, whose power . . . depends partly on German gold, partly on the determination of the Russian Army to fight no more; but who would genuinely like to put into practice the wild theories which have so long been germinating in the shadow of the Russian autocracy.[99]

Instead of breaking with the Bolsheviks, as some of his colleagues had recommended, Balfour thought Britain should "avoid, as long as possible, an open breach with this crazy system." And he added: "if this be drifting, then I am a drifter by deliberate policy." Needless to say, nothing in Balfour's memorandum even remotely hinted at the prospect of recognising the Bolshevik regime. It is doubtful whether

[97] Degras, *Soviet Documents*, vol. i, p. 5.
[98] "Notes on the Present Russian Situation," 9 December 1917; printed in Lloyd George, *War Memoirs*, vol. ii, pp. 1545-47.
[99] *ibid.*, pp. 1545-46.

at this stage it ever even occurred to any member of the government or any member of the British establishment in Petrograd that Britain might recognise the usurpers.[100] But a definite break in relations, the Foreign Secretary thought, would not only endanger British subjects in Russia, but would drive Russia into the hands of Germany and "hasten the organisation of the country by German officials on German lines." Nothing, he thought, could be more harmful both to the immediate conduct of the war and to post-war Anglo-Russian relations.

Germany, he continued, could possibly gain two advantages by removing Russia from the war. By transferring troops from the Russian front, she might greatly augment her forces in the west. And by exploiting the immense resources of Russia—minerals, cereals, oil, and even manpower—she might avoid the strangling effects of the Allied blockade. Balfour thought there was little the Allies could do to prevent the transfer of troops to the Western Front.[101] But his policy of "drifting" could keep Germany from making use of Russia's resources. His memorandum continued:

Russia, however incapable of fighting, is not easily overrun. Except with the active goodwill of the Russians themselves, German troops (even if there were German troops to spare) are not going to penetrate many hundreds of miles into that vast country. A mere armistice between Russia and Germany may not for very many months promote in any important fashion the supply of German needs from Russian resources.[102]

Britain's business, Balfour concluded, was to make those "many months" as long as possible. Nothing would be more fatal than to

[100] Lord Robert Cecil, the Under Secretary of State for Foreign Affairs, surely echoed the thoughts of his colleagues when, on 23 November, in answer to a journalist's question as to whether the Allies were likely to recognise "the present Russian Government," he replied that he "could not imagine such a step possible." (Kennan, *Russia Leaves the War*, p. 94, quoting *New York Times*, 24 November 1917.)

[101] Balfour was correct. In fact, the transfer of German troops had already begun. When the Bolshevik delegates met the Germans at Brest-Litovsk on 2 December, one of the proposals they put forth was that no such transfers should take place. They thought that their insistence upon this condition would earn them the gratitude of Russia's allies. Hoffmann, the German commander on the Eastern Front, agreed to this condition with the provision that it would not apply to forces already being moved or with orders to go. He could make this agreement because before the negotiations had begun the Germans had already issued orders for the transfer of the bulk of their forces in the East to the Western Front. See John W. Wheeler-Bennett, *The Forgotten Peace: Brest-Litovsk, March 1918*, London, 1939, p. 89.

[102] Lloyd George, *War Memoirs*, vol. ii, p. 1547.

give the Bolsheviks a motive for "welcoming into their midst German officials and German soldiers as friends and deliverers."

❖

In this memorandum of 9 December Balfour confined himself to generalities, and referred to only one specific measure the government could take to help avoid a breach with the Bolsheviks and also to help protect the Embassy staff and British colony in Petrograd. He asked his colleagues to reverse a decision they had reached while he was absent in Paris a few days before and allow the return to Russia of two Bolsheviks, Georgi V. Chicherin and P. Petrov, who had been interned in Britain.[103]

Chicherin and Petrov were part of the vast Russian émigré community of socialists of every shade that had gathered in London to escape the persecutions of the Tsarist regime. During its brief spell of authority, the Provisional Government set up a repatriation committee in London with the object of bringing back to Russia all of the émigrés who wanted to come, no matter how violent their politics. Chicherin and Petrov soon took control of this committee, and used their control to facilitate the repatriation of Bolsheviks.[104] Nabokov, the Chargé d'Affaires in London, warned the Provisional Government that by being so indiscriminate it was bringing about its own destruction. But he was not permitted to interfere in the work of the repatriation committee, and had to endure the humiliation of watching Chicherin send messages to the Petrograd Soviet, in private cipher, through Embassy channels.[105]

Chicherin and Petrov did not confine their work to the repatriation programme, but like many other Russians in London spent considerable time addressing workers' meetings and writing articles and manifestoes denouncing the war in general and, often, British imperialism in particular. Such behaviour, in the last years of the Great War, was clearly seditious. In late August or early September (exactly when is unclear) the two men were arrested and interned in Brixton Prison on a charge of "anti-Ally and pro-German activities" which were considered to be a danger to the realm. Chicherin did not help his case by objecting, at the time of his arrest, that he "opposed Im-

---

[103] *ibid.*, p. 1546.
[104] Nabokoff, *Ordeal*, pp. 99-100.
[105] *ibid*, p. 103.

perialism in its totality, alike in its British, German, and other representatives."[106] Kerensky forced Nabokov to protest against the arrest.[107]

The November Revolution found the pair—who, in comparison
with many of their Bolshevik colleagues, were moderate, reasonable
men—still in prison. When Trotsky got around to considering their
case, he was indignant, and on 26 November he addressed a note of
protest, written in his characteristic vein, to the British Embassy. Both
Chicherin and Petrov, he wrote, were "well known in Russia as irre-
proachable, self-denying idealists, the former activities of which stood
above all suspicion." If the British government objected to their
behaviour, they should not be imprisoned, but immediately returned
to Russia, where they could "work with honour for the benefit of their
people." Trotsky continued with a threat:

> In order to reinforce this request, I take the liberty to call your attention,
> Mr. Ambassador, to the fact that many Englishmen live in the Russian
> Empire, who do not hide a bit their counter-revolutionary way of think-
> ing, and openly enter into political relations with counter-revolutionary
> elements of the Russian Bourgeoisie. The public opinion of the revolu-
> tionary democracy of our country will not stand for it, that Russian
> revolutionary fighters of merit have to suffer in concentration camps in
> England, at the same time as counter-revolutionary British citizens are in
> no way oppressed in the territory of the Russian Republic.

The note ended in a particularly insolent[108] fashion:

> Permit me, Mr. Ambassador, to express my assurance that my insistent
> request will meet full sympathy of the labour party of the people, the
> freedom lovers of your country.[109]

Trotsky made good his threat four days later (30 November) by
issuing an order that no British subject would be allowed to leave

---

[106] *The Times*, 4 December 1917.

[107] Nabokoff, *Ordeal*, p. 107.

[108] Trotsky, it should be noted, had little love for England. In April 1917, sailing
from New York to Russia (under the Provisional Government's repatriation pro-
gramme) on a Norwegian ship, he was forcibly removed by British naval police at
Halifax, Nova Scotia. Although he had all the necessary travel documents, including
a Russian entry permit and a British transit visa, he was interned for a month among
German prisoners of war (whom, by constant harangue, he practically converted into
Bolsheviks). His release came only through the insistence of Milyukov. (See I.
Deutscher, *The Prophet Armed—Trotsky: 1879-1921*, London, 1954, pp. 246-47; also
Sir George Buchanan, *Mission*, vol. II, p. 121.)

[109] The only copy of this Note that I have been able to find is among the papers of
the American Ambassador, David R. Francis, in the Missouri Historical Society, St.
Louis, Missouri.

Russia until the two men were released. That night he told a cheering crowd that "if the comrades [continued] to remain in concentration camps through the ill will of the British government," the Soviet regime would start interning Englishmen. And he added:

Our Allies and enemies abroad must understand that the times of Tsars and of Kerensky with Milyukov are over, that every Russian citizen, be he even a political emigrant or a revolutionary soldier in France, now finds himself under the protection of the governmental authority of the Russian revolution.[110]

Buchanan advised the government to release Chicherin and Petrov. "Our position is becoming very difficult," he noted in his diary on 4 December, "as while it is impossible for our Government to yield to threats, it is very hard on our subjects, who have come here from the provinces on their way home, to be put to the expense of remaining on indefinitely." He did not, moreover, want to see Trotsky retaliate by arresting the members of the British propaganda bureau in Petrograd. "There is, after all," he wrote,

something in Trotsky's argument that, if we claim the right to arrest Russians for making a pacifist propaganda in a country bent on continuing the war, he has an equal right to arrest British subjects who are conducting a war propaganda in a country bent on peace.[111]

The government took the Ambassador's advice. Although the Cabinet had decided on 29 November that no notice should be taken of Soviet demands for the release of the two prisoners, they resolved on 10 December that Balfour should be given discretion to handle the case as he chose.[112] It will be remembered that the Foreign Secretary's memorandum, written on the previous day, advocated their release. Accordingly, on the 14th, the Embassy told Smolny that the government would reconsider the cases of the two men, with a view to their repatriation. Immediately, the ban on Britons leaving Russia was lifted. *The Times* Petrograd correspondent reported that this step was very satisfying to the British community.[113]

---

[110] Reported in Francis to Secretary of State, telegram 2049, 1 December 1917. *Foreign Relations, 1918, Russia*, vol. 1, p. 276.

[111] Sir George Buchanan, *Mission*, vol. 11, p. 228.

[112] From memorandum by Captain E. Abraham, War Cabinet Secretariat, "Policy of the War Cabinet Relative to Revolutionary Governments at Petrograd," dated 23 February 1918; Milner MSS, box B.

[113] *The Times*, 17 December 1917. It seems that the ban might not have been lifted at all points simultaneously. On 20 December the American consular official on the

But as soon as this particular problem of "contact" between the two governments had been eased, another cropped up to take its place. The Bolsheviks were acutely conscious that they had not been recognised by any foreign power. Their attitude toward this fact was very complex. They did not really expect to be recognised, and so they continually expressed their disdain and contempt for the forms and methods of "bourgeois" diplomacy. Yet at the same time they insisted that these forms and methods be observed; observation of them, after all, would imply recognition of the Soviet regime as the *de facto* government of Russia. Their insistence on forms was never plainly stated, however; conventional usage was always disdained, and each form was given a new revolutionary utility.

This was to be true time and time again of Soviet diplomatic representation abroad. And it was also true in December 1917 for the problem at hand—diplomatic couriers. In a note sent on 14 December, Trotsky complained that "certain" (in fact, all) of the Allied and neutral embassies had refused to visa the passports of Soviet diplomatic couriers, on the ground that the Council of People's Commissaries was not recognised as the government of Russia. "The question of recognition is one of form," Trotsky wrote,

and the government of the Soviets treats with entire indifference this detail of the diplomatic ritual. Non-recognition does not free, however, from the necessity to reckon with the Soviet government as with a fact. Statements to the effect that "unrecognised government" cannot have diplomatic couriers are unfounded if only because the Soviet government considers necessary diplomatic relations not only with the governments *but also with the revolutionary socialist parties which are striving for the overthrow of the existing governments.*[114]

Henceforth, Trotsky concluded, the various embassies themselves would not be allowed to use couriers, nor to claim diplomatic immunity, unless their governments granted similar privileges to the Soviet government. This statement—a request for governments to allow within their borders agents who would plot their overthrow—shows perhaps more clearly than any other the nature of the

Russian-Finnish frontier at Torneo (where he was stationed along with British and French officers to aid Allied nationals in crossing) reported that the British still could not obtain exit permits; other foreigners, he said, had little trouble (U.S. National Archives, Department of State file 861.00/843).

[114] Reported in Francis to Secretary of State, telegram 2107, Petrograd, 15 December 1917; *Foreign Relations, 1918, Russia*, vol. I, p. 303 (italics added).

"Soviet mind" in the months immediately following the Revolution.

The incredible thing is that Trotsky at least half expected his request to be fulfilled. In a conversation with a British officer, he explained that he was entirely within his rights—that since Sir George Buchanan was accredited by a government which did not recognise the Soviet government to one which no longer existed, the Ambassador was actually only a private individual not deserving of diplomatic privileges. Buchanan, always a realist, pointed out to London that he was indeed at Trotsky's mercy.[115]

The reply which Buchanan was instructed to give only made Trotsky even more furious: the British government was quite prepared to grant visas to Soviet couriers, but since the Bolshevik government had no accredited representative in London, it would have no occasion to send a courier there.[116] This was, perhaps, Balfour's idea of humour. In any case, it was little more than humour, because, in view of Trotsky's threatened reprisals against the British community in Petrograd, the Ambassador was very soon authorised to issue the requested visas unconditionally.[117]

❖

Long before this, the Foreign Office, deeply concerned about the safety of the British mission, had informed Buchanan that he should withdraw the Embassy whenever he felt necessary, leaving the protection of British interests in the hands of Consuls.[118] Throughout the turbulent weeks since the November Revolution the Ambassador had maintained his outward appearance of complete calm and imperturbability. He continued to take his long daily walk alone, dismissing those who warned him by saying that it bored him to be constantly told that his throat was going to be cut. Once, however, he was nearly involved in a street fight near the Embassy, and, after that, his wife and daughter insisted upon walking with him, maintaining that there was less danger of his being assaulted if a woman were present.[119]

However calm he may have appeared, the anxieties and pressures of years of war and revolution were fast closing in. The Ambassador

---

[115] Sir George Buchanan, *Mission*, vol. ii, p. 241.

[116] Diary entry, 22 December 1917; *ibid.*, vol. ii, pp. 241-42.

[117] Diary entry, 28 December 1917; *ibid.*, vol. ii, p. 243.

[118] Reported to the State Department in a memorandum from the British Embassy, 13 December 1917; U.S. National Archives, State Department file 861.00/805.

[119] Meriel Buchanan, *Dissolution of an Empire*, p. 263. Also Knox, *Russian Army*, vol. ii, p. 728.

had had only a single fortnight's holiday since the outbreak of war in August 1914. Now, in December 1917, his health—never very good—broke completely, and from the 10th he was confined for much of the time to his bed. Because of his health the Foreign Office called him home on leave, and he planned a departure in early January.[120]

He was well enough, however, to attend the Embassy's annual celebration on Christmas night. It was the last of a long line of receptions given in the great building, a palace which Catherine the Great had built for her favourite, Sergei Soltikov. By some quirk, the electricity had not been cut off that night, and the massive crystal chandeliers blazed with light. Unlike previous years, when the Embassy's Christmas entertainment had been a gathering point for Petrograd society, only a few Russian friends were present. The crowd of over a hundred was composed mostly of members of the Embassy staff and of the various military missions. Each officer is reported to have carried a pistol in his pocket, and rifles and cartridge cases were hidden throughout the building.[121]

Regardless of the fears and uncertainty that all must have felt, and despite the bursts of gunfire which still echoed sporadically through the dark streets of the capital, the party was a merry one. After a concert and a variety show organised by Colonel Thornhill, the chief of military intelligence in Russia, the entire company sat down to a vast Christmas dinner. Despite the terrible shortages of food, the Embassy chef managed to provide a sumptuous feast.

The festivities too severely taxed the Ambassador, however, and he paid for his exertions with a relapse; his doctor insisted that he leave Russia at the earliest possible moment. The 7th of January was chosen. It was decided that, besides the Buchanan family, General Knox, Admiral Stanley (the Naval Attaché), and five other ranking officers would also leave Russia. By this time the peace negotiations at Brest-Litovsk had progressed a long way; there seemed no reason for keeping a military mission in the capital.

The Ambassador spent his last fortnight in Russia confined to the Embassy where he had lived almost continuously for the preceding eight years. On 6 January—his last day in the capital—he journeyed out to pay a sorrowful farewell visit to his old friend, the Grand Duke

---

[120] Diary entry, 18 December 1918; Sir George Buchanan, *Mission*, vol. II, p. 239..
[121] Both Sir George and his daughter have described this evening. See *ibid.*, vol. II, p. 243, and Meriel Buchanan, *Dissolution of an Empire*, p. 273.

Nicholas Michailovich, who had only recently returned from exile (imposed by the Tsar) near Kherson, and who was to be executed the following summer by the Bolsheviks.

The next morning, long before the late mid-winter dawn, the small party set out. This time there was no electricity, and their departure was made even more depressing by the long shadows cast by the candles on the dark Embassy staircase. Outside, the snow was deep, and the drive to the Finland Station, past scowling Red Guards, was slow and cold.

Trotsky managed to make things unpleasant right up to the final moment. Though he granted the Ambassador and his family immunity from customs procedures, he would not make the same concession for the military officers. Neither had the Commissariat of Foreign Affairs reserved any special accommodations on the train to the Finnish frontier. But the old Russia had not quite died—a gift to the station-master of two bottles of very old brandy from the Embassy cellars produced a private sleeping car. Despite the bitter cold and the early hour, many of the Ambassador's Allied colleagues, as well as the Embassy staff and several friends from the British colony, came down to see the party off. It was more than a decade later, under conditions not much more cheerful, before another British Ambassador set foot on Russian soil.

Almost exactly a year before, Sir George Buchanan had boarded another train. Then it was to make the short trip to the palace at Tsarskoe Seloe, to warn the Tsar of impending disaster.

CHAPTER II

FIRST CONTACTS WITH
COUNTER-REVOLUTION: THE COSSACKS
OF THE DON

Less than a fortnight after the Bolshevik Revolution, the Chief of the Imperial General Staff, General Sir William Robertson, addressed a grave warning to the War Cabinet. "If Russia makes a separate peace," he wrote on 19 November, "or if the greater part of the enemy's forces now on the Eastern front are able to come West, there may not be adequate prospect for obtaining decisive results in the coming year." And if victory were not possible in 1918, he implied, the Allies—particularly the Italians and the French—might be too war-weary to make a great offensive in 1919, despite the addition of American forces to the Allied armies.[1]

In the late autumn of 1917, with the fortunes of the Allies at ebb-tide, there were few people who cared to dispute these views of the C.I.G.S. Thus, even before the Bolsheviks had formally concluded an armistice with the Central Powers, there began a desperate search for some means of filling the gap that would be left by the probable withdrawal of Russia's armies. One possible source of strength in the east was the Rumanian Army. Although most of Rumania was in enemy hands, the Army was still intact, basing itself on the northeastern provincial town of Jassy. Since its great defeat in late 1916, the Rumanian Army had been made into an immeasurably better fighting force by a French military mission under General Berthelot.[2] To keep this force in the field, however, it was essential that it have free access to the food supplies of the Ukraine and have friendly forces at its rear.

When Rumania had entered the war in August 1916 the Allied governments had undertaken to give her all possible support. After

[1] Memorandum, "Future Military Policy," 19 November 1917; Milner MSS, box AE-2.
[2] Cruttwell, *Great War*, p. 297.

[40]

SOUTHERN RUSSIA

Simbirsk (Ulyanovsk)

Samara (Kuibyshev)

URAL MTS.

MOSCOW

Mogilev

Warsaw Brest-Litovsk

Kiev Kharkov

U K R A I N E

Dnieper R.

Donets R.

Don R.

Volga R.

Astrakhan

Novocherkassk

Rostov

NORTHERN CAUCASUS

Krasnodar

Novorossisk

CAUCASUS MOUNTAINS

Tiflis

TRANSCAUCASUS

Batum

TURKEY

CASPIAN SEA

Baku

Krasnovodsk

BLACK SEA

Odessa

Jassy

AUSTRIA-HUNGARY

RUMANIA

BULGARIA

the Bolshevik Revolution the King of Rumania told the British and French ambassadors in Jassy that if their governments would continue to give their support, despite the collapse of Russia, he would try, with a portion of his troops, to force a passage through Russia in an effort to effect a junction with the Cossacks of South Russia and ultimately, if possible, with British forces in Mesopotamia. But if he did not receive the necessary assurances, he would abdicate or even come to terms with the Central Powers.[3]

The Rumanian question was raised at the War Cabinet on 21 November. The question was complex and was made much more difficult by the absence of any precise information as to the strength of independent Russian forces in southwest Russia. It was known only that the Cossack general, A. M. Kaledin, had some troops under his command at Novocherkassk, on the Don, and had proclaimed his opposition to the Bolsheviks and his loyalty to the Allies.[4]

In the Cabinet there was a strong element, including Balfour, who wished to accord Kaledin implicit recognition as an independent leader by advising the Rumanians to co-operate with him. The Cabinet could reach no decision, however, and it was decided to seek the advice of Colonel House, who had come to London for preliminary discussions before the Paris conference of early December. In a long talk with House, Balfour pleaded earnestly that the Allies should offer their support to Kaledin. Although House favoured making Rumania the rallying point for all forces in South Russia willing to stay in the war, he was nevertheless afraid that any overt step to support one Russian faction against the Bolsheviks would simply strengthen the Soviet determination to make peace, and might be used by them to inflame anti-Allied feeling in Russia. House felt that the most the Allies could do would be to advise the Rumanians to co-

[3] Reported in telegram 161 from Vopicka, the U.S. Minister to Rumania, to Secretary of State, 17 November 1917; Woodrow Wilson mss, series ii, Library of Congress, Washington, D.C.

[4] In the midsummer of 1917 the peoples of the Cossack communities of the Don had reasserted their old autonomous privileges and traditions and had elected Kaledin "ataman." In September Kaledin had publicly announced his support of Kornilov, and although he did not actually take part in the latter's abortive uprising, his support was sufficient to cause Kerensky to name him as a traitor. From thenceforth Kaledin had carried on without regard to Petrograd as the head of a virtually independent government on the Don, and had gathered about him dissident groups of officers who yearned for the restoration of days gone by. See George Stewart, *The White Armies of Russia: A Chronicle of Counter-Revolution and Allied Intervention,* New York, 1933, pp. 27-28; also Kennan, *Russia Leaves the War,* pp. 161-64.

operate with whatever forces, loyal to the Allies, were nearest them, and he strongly advised against specifically naming any of them. Lloyd George agreed with House, and this policy was adopted by the Cabinet on 22 November.[5]

Accordingly, that evening Balfour cabled the British Minister in Jassy, telling him of the decision and emphasising that Britain had no desire to interfere with Russian internal affairs; the government's sole preoccupation, he said, was with the safety of the Rumanian army and with the successful prosecution of the war. But Balfour also asked the Minister to despatch an agent to Kaledin to inquire whether the Cossack leader was willing to co-operate with the Rumanian Army and to learn the size of the forces at Kaledin's disposal.[6]

Meanwhile, emissaries from the Don began to come to the British Embassy in Petrograd to appeal for Allied support. On 23 November Buchanan received the first of these callers, the wealthy banker, Prince Shakhovski. The Prince told him that Generals Kaledin and Alekseyev were at Novocherkassk, along with Savinkov, the Socialist-Revolutionary Minister of War under Kerensky who had been one of Kornilov's staunchest supporters. Rodzianko, the former President of the Duma, and Kornilov himself were reported to be on their way there. Their object, said Shakhovski, was to form a governmental council with Kaledin as military dictator and Alekseyev as commander-in-chief. After gathering local forces they would march on Petrograd and Moscow and unseat the Bolshevik regime. But they lacked financial support. Shakhovski proposed a complicated scheme whereby a Cossack bank would be established, its capital guaranteed by the mineral wealth of South Russia. Immediate financial support would come through the purchase of shares in the bank by the Allies.

Buchanan was quite circumspect with his caller, who wanted to bring to Alekseyev and Kaledin an assurance of Allied support. The Ambassador said he could give no reply because his government could not interfere in Russian internal affairs. He asked the banker not to say he had been received at the Embassy, but to tell the Cossack leaders that, having made inquiries, he had reason to believe that the

[5] House diary, entry for 21 November 1917; House MSS. See also Lloyd George, *War Memoirs*, vol. II, p. 1540.

[6] Balfour to Sir G. Barclay, Jassy, telegram 457, 22 November 1917, 9:30 p.m.; Milner MSS, box D-2.

Allies would welcome any strong, stable, and legally-constituted government which was prepared to keep Russia in the war.[7]

Meanwhile, the British military attaché at Jassy, without yet having heard from the agent sent to Novocherkassk, telegraphed the War Office that *if* it were found that Kaledin was well-disposed toward the Allies, a fully accredited British and French mission should be sent to his headquarters with full power to take independent action and authorisation to guarantee British financial support up to £10 million.[8] This advice can only be regarded as rash. Very little was known about the Cossacks; although Kaledin might have been found to be well disposed, he might also have been found to be powerless. In effect the military attaché was recommending a blind commitment without regard to the overall Russian situation.

Not only were there no reports on Kaledin from British agents, but there was wide disagreement among reports from Russian sources. On 29 November General Knox reported that a trustworthy Russian, just returned from the Don, had brought news of the formation of a South-Eastern Union composed of representatives of all the important Cossack communities of South Russia. But Knox's informant also said that the Union had no strength. Cossacks were scattered throughout the Russian Army and it was difficult to withdraw and regroup them without arousing Bolshevik suspicion. Another great difficulty would be supplying them with ammunition.

Knox himself suggested that if the Cossacks could be united and if money were available, the Allies might use them against the Turks to reinforce the Georgians and Armenians on the Caucasian Front. Also, by occupying the Donets Basin, the Cossacks might keep the enemy from getting any coal, iron, or oil from Russia or grain from Siberia. Knox reported that the Union was most anxious to have a British representative and recommended the despatch of one of his officers, Captain Noel, who was stationed at Tiflis.[9] Buchanan, reporting on yet another interview between an Embassy official and an emissary from the Don, also recommended that Captain Noel be sent to Novocherkassk. The Ambassador said that he, personally, would

[7] Buchanan to Balfour, un-numbered telegram, Petrograd, 23 November 1917, 9:42 p.m.; Milner MSS, box D-2.

[8] Lloyd George, *War Memoirs*, vol. II, p. 1542.

[9] Knox to Director of Military Intelligence, transmitted in Buchanan to Foreign Office (repeated to Balfour in Paris), telegram 1896, Petrograd, 29 November 1917, 8:50 p.m.; Milner MSS, box D-2.

keep clear of all contact with the Alekseyev-Kaledin group because Trotsky was already suspicious enough of his behaviour.[10] London quickly approved of Noel's mission (although an officer had already been sent out from Jassy), and he set out for the Don.

At this point the situation suddenly shifted from cautious investigation to impulsive action; the reasons for this shift are still only partially clear. The Allied leaders were by then in Paris for the conference on the co-ordination of war efforts. Although no reports had been received from the British agents on the Don, the question of supporting pro-Ally groups there and also in Transcaucasia was raised on 1 December at a meeting of the British, French, and Italian premiers and their advisors. Colonel House, who also attended, reported to Washington that the inclination of all the others was to support these movements, and that they decided to send a combined Anglo-French military mission from Rumania to Kaledin's headquarters. House himself was against giving any encouragement to the various anti-Bolshevik movements:

Personally I consider it dangerous for the reason that it is encouraging internal disturbances without our having any definite program in mind or any force with which to back up a program.

This was a sound principle. But House conceded: "if they are not given money or encouragement they may go to pieces."[11]

Balfour, too, was not pleased with the decision reached at the meeting. The next day, after reflecting overnight on the scanty intelligence on the Don movement that had been transmitted by Buchanan and Knox, he telegraphed the Foreign Office that upon further consideration he thought it undesirable to despatch a mission to Kaledin at that time. After all, he said, a British officer had already been sent to Novocherkassk from Jassy. Until that officer's report on Kaledin had been received, an "ostentatious act" such as the despatch of a military mission would clearly be premature. The Bolsheviks would take it as a definite commitment to support Kaledin in opposition to themselves, and might take retaliatory measures against Allied representatives in Petrograd.[12]

[10] Buchanan to Foreign Office (repeated to Balfour in Paris), telegram 1917, Petrograd, 30 November 1917, 9:20 p.m.; Milner MSS, box D-2.
[11] House to Secretary of State, un-numbered telegram, Paris, 2 December 1917; *Foreign Relations, 1918, Russia*, vol. II, Washington, 1932, pp. 583-84.
[12] Balfour to Foreign Office, Paris telegram 1408, 2 December 1917, 10:30 p.m.; Milner MSS, box D-2.

Advice of this kind, coming from the Foreign Secretary, should certainly have prevented any precipitate action. Yet on the following morning, 3 December, with Balfour still in Paris, Lloyd George (who had returned to London the previous evening) and the rest of the War Cabinet decided to guarantee to Kaledin all the financial support he needed, without regard to expense.

This was an astonishing decision. Some of the factors which lay behind it are revealed in a telegram to Buchanan sent that evening by Lord Robert Cecil, Minister of Blockade and Under Secretary of State for Foreign Affairs, who was actually in charge of the day-to-day business of the Foreign Office. The War Cabinet had considered the Russian situation, Cecil told the Ambassador, and had decided that every effort should be made to keep Russia from making a separate peace. The Cabinet believed that the only way to do this was to strengthen by every means those Russian elements genuinely friendly to the Entente, of whom the chief were Kaledin, Alekseyev, and their supporters. Though there had been some talk of a coalition of Bolsheviks, Social Revolutionaries and even Mensheviks, the Cabinet did not consider that such a "combination of talkers and theorists" under Bolshevik influence would be any improvement. If, on the other hand, a southern bloc could be formed consisting of the Caucasus, the Cossack regions, the Ukraine, and the unoccupied parts of Rumania, it would probably be able to set up a reasonably stable government and would, through its command of oil, coal, and corn, effectively control the whole of Russia. "You are therefore authorised," the telegram closed, "to take whatever steps you regard as possible with a view to carrying out this policy either directly or through such agents as you select. No regard should be had to expense and you should furnish to Cossacks or Ukrainians any funds necessary by any means you think desirable."[13]

The Chief of the Imperial General Staff, General Sir William Robertson, sent a similar message to the military attaché in Jassy, recommending that the attaché himself, possibly with his French colleague, go to Kaledin. And he stated: "You are authorised to grant Kaledin financial support up to any figure necessary."[14]

[13] Cecil to Buchanan, Petrograd, telegram 2407, 3 December 1917, 7:15 p.m.; Milner MSS, box D-2.

[14] C.I.G.S. to Brig.-Gen. C. R. Ballard, Jassy, transmitted in telegram 479, Foreign Office to Sir G. Barclay, 3 December 1917, 7:30 p.m.; Milner MSS, box D-2.

The wisdom of this policy received what seemed to be early confirmation in a glowing telegram from Oliver Wardrop, the Consul General in Moscow (and also the world's leading authority on Georgian literature), who was assured, again by an "absolutely reliable informant" just arrived from Novocherkassk, that Alekseyev had organised there a well-trained force of 50,000 Cossacks and 200,000 infantry, all ready for service. Their signal to march, Wardrop said, would be the anticipated Bolshevik dissolution or terrorisation of the Constituent Assembly which was still scheduled to convene in Petrograd in early January. Alekseyev, according to Wardrop's informant, was confident that Ukrainian forces would join the seven Cossack governments of the South-Eastern Union and that Rumanian and Caucasus troops would also co-operate, the total force being more than sufficient to re-establish constitutional democratic (not, Alekseyev insisted, monarchic) government.[15]

In Petrograd, however, both Knox and Buchanan were stunned by what they believed to be the folly of the government's decision. On the basis of information they had now begun to receive from the British officers sent to the Don and relying on their own experienced judgement, both sent strong telegrams of protest emphasising that naïve estimates like Wardrop's gave an "entirely false idea" of Kaledin's strength. Alekseyev and Kaledin, Knox cabled the Director of Military Intelligence, had nothing except two companies and a promise of three more. "I consider any alliance between the South-Eastern Union and Ukraine on the basis of continuance of the war to be fantastically unlikely," Knox said. There were no Ukrainian troops, he continued, except a few mutinous regiments at Kiev. The Ukrainians had no more desire to fight than the people of the rest of Russia. The Don group had only pestered the Embassy with emissaries asking for money. "These are all talkers," Knox said, "not men who will risk their lives." It was obvious, he felt, that the British could not advertise their connection with such a movement, "as we should be at once arrested and properly so." He concluded bitterly:

I am afraid position in Russia is not at all understood at home. No Russian, Cossack or otherwise, will fight unless compelled to by foreign force. To ask us to intrigue with Cossacks while we are here in the power

[15] Wardrop to Balfour, telegram 52, Moscow, 4 December 1917, 7:58 p.m.; Milner MSS, box D-2.

[47]

of the Rebel Government is merely to get our throats cut to no purpose.[16]

Knox was a realist who respected only power. When he supported Kornilov it was because the Cossack general, as commander-in-chief, seemed to be the only man in Russia with any degree of power at his disposal. Later, in Siberia, he was to back Admiral Kolchak for the same reason.[17] But in December 1917, as he wrote afterwards in his memoirs:

I did not believe in the power . . . of any . . . organisation in Russia to force its soldiers to continue the war against the Central Powers, and failed to see any use in supporting any organisation without that power. It seemed, too, to be at least irregular for us to enter into relations with groups openly opposed to the Government, such as it was, from which, as diplomats, we claimed protection. . . . Nothing more was to be hoped from the corps of officers, who were powerless, and it was useless as well as cruel to reproach them with Russia's treachery and to try to exact our pound of flesh. . . .[18]

Buchanan's telegram, sent at the same time, made the same points. He quite agreed with the government's opinion that a combination of Bolsheviks, Mensheviks, and Social Revolutionaries (even if possible) would be worth little so far as Allied purposes were concerned. But the forces at the disposal of Kaledin and Alekseyev were not sufficient to enable them to engage in any serious enterprise, and it would be "useless to found exaggerated expectations on overtures made to us by their emissaries." Buchanan gave the same warning as Knox: "Constant visits which these emissaries, whose discretion cannot be relied on, pay to Embassy will end by seriously compromising us." The Ambassador urged that any dealings with anti-Bolshevik factions be handled through the Legation in Rumania. He concluded:

His Majesty's Government do not I fear realise how very precarious our position here is. If Trotsky can prove our complicity in a counter-revolutionary plot he will not hesitate to arrest either Military Attaché or myself, and such a step apart from personal inconvenience to ourselves would cause His Majesty's Government grave embarrassments.[19]

[16] Knox to D.M.I., transmitted in Buchanan to Balfour, telegram 1963, Petrograd, 5 December 1917, 9:10 p.m.; Milner MSS, box D-2.
[17] For Knox's relations with Kolchak, see below, Chapter IX.
[18] Knox, *Russian Army*, vol. II, p. 727.
[19] Buchanan to Balfour, telegram 1964, Petrograd, 5 December 1917, 9:12 p.m.; Milner MSS, box D-2.

Murmansk from the harbour, 1918

Docks at Archangel, 1918

Major-General F. C. Poole (left) and his second-in-command, Brigadier-General R. G. Finlayson, disembarking at Archangel after the Allied landing of 2 August 1918

Allied diplomats in the residence of the American Ambassador at Archangel, with members of the Provisional Government of Northern Russia just after its reorganisation in October 1918

Front row, l-r: Serbian Minister Spaleikovich, Minister of Justice Gorodetskii,   Minister of Commerce and Industry Mefodiev; *rear row, l-r:* Minister of Posts
Italian Chargé Torretta, Prime Minister and Minister for Foreign Affairs   and Telegraphs Zubov, Chinese Chargé Chen-Yi-Chi, Brazilian Chargé Kelsch;

The Ambassador was not exaggerating the danger he was in. Only a few days before, Trotsky had told a French officer (unnamed in all accounts, but surely Captain Jacques Sadoul, a socialist lawyer attached to the French Military Mission and an old friend of Trotsky) that he was particularly angry with Buchanan for his dealings with Kaledin's movement, and had a good mind to arrest him.[20]

As if to emphasise the dissenting views of Knox and Buchanan, the officer sent to the Don by the military attaché in Jassy cabled from Novocherkassk on 7 December the brief message: "Cossacks absolutely useless and disorganised."[21] Captain Noel, sent from Tiflis, made clear in his reports that Kaledin was primarily concerned with the Cossack territories themselves. The Cossacks were battle-weary and demoralised. Their chief preoccupation was the restoration of order in their own region. They could not be expected to take active measures outside these areas.[22]

As we have seen, the War Cabinet was not only interested in supporting the Cossacks, but was also hoping for the formation of a "southern bloc," comprising the Cossacks, the Ukraine, the Rumanians, and the Caucasus. Before we continue the story of British involvement with the Cossacks—regarded as the most important group in South Russia—we should look briefly at the other elements which London hoped to include in the "bloc."

In the Ukraine, too, the downfall of Tsarism had produced strong separatist tendencies. During the rule of the Provisional Government, a body called the Ukrainian Central Rada had been established at Kiev, proclaiming itself the autonomous political authority for the region. But the Rada's control was loose and ill-defined. Although it was composed of rather extreme socialists, their Ukrainian nationalism was stronger than their socialism, and after the November revolution they refused to accept the authority of the central Soviet regime. A very uneasy situation resulted, with the soviets of several Ukrainian cities recognising the Rada, while that of Kharkov recognised the Bolsheviks. In December, the Bolsheviks established

[20] Diary entry, 3 December 1917; Sir George Buchanan, *Mission*, vol. II, p. 227. Knox, *Russian Army*, vol. II, p. 728.

[21] The message was transmitted by Ambassador Barclay, Jassy, to Balfour, telegram 756, 9 December 1917, 7:30 p.m.; Milner MSS, box D-2.

[22] Noel's reports were summarised in Knox to D.M.I., Buchanan telegram 1970, Petrograd, 6 December 1917, 9:5 p.m., and in General Shore to D.M.I., telegram 118, Tiflis, 4 December 1917. Both in Milner MSS, box D-2.

their own Ukrainian government at Kharkov, and began military operations against the Rada.[23]

The large French military mission in Rumania, under General Berthelot, had great hopes for the Rada as a loyal pro-Ally government. On 6 December, however, Knox telegraphed from Petrograd that the Rada had decided to join the Brest-Litovsk armistice negotiations and commented that he had always thought the French had been deluded in their hopes.[24] Ukrainian leaders told the Allies that their dealings with the Germans were only a means of gaining time to consolidate their authority, but the British, in particular, were sceptical. A Foreign Office memorandum, written in mid-December, said:

> Such assurances at the present moment can hardly be accepted at their face value. In the first place the influence of the Rada over the Ukrainian people is not established on very firm foundations, their territorial claims in Russia are disputed, and the success of their nationalist propaganda in the eastern districts they claim is still uncertain . . . there may be an anti-nationalist reaction headed by the Soviets in many of the towns the Rada claims as supporting its programme. In the second place there is always a danger that any recognition on the part of the Allies might be used by the Ukrainians simply to get better terms out of the Germans, while the Germans on their part might use it in order to complicate still further the relations between Britain and Russia.[25]

In the Caucasus, a somewhat similar pattern of events had taken place, but because of the great differences among the peoples comprising the region, anything like a Transcaucasian union was from the outset an even shakier edifice than a Ukrainian state. Nevertheless, on 28 November, a government calling itself the Transcaucasian Commissariat was founded at Tiflis. Composed entirely of socialists of one sort or another, it included three Georgians, three Azerbaijanis, three Armenians, and two Russians. The next day, by seizing the arms of the Bolshevik garrison at Tiflis, the Transcaucasian Commis-

---

[23] For details of the complex Ukrainian situation in 1917, see John S. Reshetar, Jr., *The Ukrainian Revolution, 1917-1920*, Princeton, 1952, pp. 47-142, and Richard Pipes, *The Formation of the Soviet Union: Communism and Nationalism, 1917-1923*, Cambridge, Mass., 1954, pp. 53-75, 114-26.

[24] Knox to D.M.I., in Buchanan to Balfour, telegram 1970, Petrograd, 6 December 1917, 9:5 p.m.; Milner MSS, box D-2.

[25] Intelligence Bureau, Department of Information, Foreign Office, "Weekly Report on Russia, XXXIII," 18 December 1917, U.S. National Archives, Petrograd Embassy 800 file (transmitted to Francis by Ambassador Page in London).

sariat became a *de facto* authority. Its members agreed that Trans-caucasia could not recognise the Petrograd regime, but would have to govern itself until the Constituent Assembly convened on an all-Russian basis.[26]

The first important act of the Transcaucasian Commissariat was to enter into negotiations with the Turks for an armistice. On 5 December the Commander of the Russian forces in the Caucasus informed the French and British consuls in Tiflis that he had accepted a Turk-ish offer for an armistice along the entire front. He apologized for his action, but stated that the political conditions prevailing in Russia left him no other choice—had he not acted, the Bolsheviks would have gained control of his troops. The Commissariat had insisted, he said, that among the armistice terms be included the condition that there should take place no strategic regrouping of forces which might injuriously affect the British army in Mesopotamia. In order to ensure Turkish compliance with this condition, he wanted to hold his forces in place after the armistice; this would be possible, he said, only with Allied financial assistance.[27]

Before this, on 22 November, the War Office had authorised the British commander in Mesopotamia to supply any Russian forces which came forward to the Persian frontier.[28] On 3 December, before the armistice, at the same meeting at which it was decided to support Kaledin, the War Cabinet also decided to meet any reasonable demands for money made by the Russian Caucasus Army and the Cossack division which was in Persia.[29] On the 8th, after the armistice, General Shore, the chief of the British Military Mission with the Caucasus Army, telegraphed that even at that late date it might be possible to reverse the defeatist tendencies in both the Caucasus and the Ukraine by telling the Transcaucasian Commissariat and the Ukrainian Rada that Britain would give them financial support if they would join the South-Eastern Union (with the Cossacks) and continue opposition to the enemy.[30] Here, in other words, was a

[26] Firuz Kazemzadeh, *The Struggle for Transcaucasia, 1917-1921*, Oxford, 1951, pp. 54-60.
[27] U.S. Consul, Tiflis, to Secretary of State, 5 December 1917, *Foreign Relations, 1918, Russia*, vol. II, pp. 585-86. See also Kazemzadeh, *Transcaucasia*, pp. 81-82.
[28] *Official History: Mesopotamia Campaign*, vol. IV, p. 87.
[29] From memorandum, "Policy of the War Cabinet Relative to Revolutionary Governments at Petrograd," cited above, Chapter I, footnote 112.
[30] Shore to War Office, telegram 160, Tiflis, 8 December 1917; Milner MSS, box G-1.

proposal for just the same great southern bloc that had seemed so appealing to the Cabinet, and which General Knox, on the 5th, had called so fantastically unlikely.

Despite the protests of Knox and Buchanan, the War Cabinet acted quickly to implement its decision. By 14 December, when it laid down the general rule that

Any sum of money required for the purpose of maintaining alive in South East Russia the resistance to the Central Powers, considered necessary by the War Office in consultation with the Foreign Office, should be furnished, the money to be paid in instalments so long as the recipients continued the struggle.[31]

the Cabinet had already approved two advances of £10 million, one to be distributed by British representatives in Rumania to whatever Russian forces could be persuaded to continue resistance on the Ukrainian and Rumanian fronts, and a similar sum to be dispensed by British agents on the Don to support Kaledin and Alekseyev. In addition, an unspecified sum (but certainly smaller than these) was put at the disposal of Sir Charles Marling, Minister at Teheran, to open a credit to support loyal forces in the Caucasus, particularly the Armenians.[32]

Naturally, these arrangements were kept as secret as possible.[33] When the Petrograd press reported the presence of British officers at

[31] Memorandum, "Policy of the War Cabinet Relative to Revolutionary Governments at Petrograd," *loc.cit.*

[32] *idem.* See also the telegrams from the American ambassadors in Jassy (13 December) and London (18 and 21 December), *Foreign Relations, 1918, Russia*, vol. II, pp. 591-92, 595-96.

[33] The exact manner in which these sums were provided remains a mystery, but a surprising amount of information about a portion of them was revealed three years later in the reports of a lawsuit in London. Apparently the method chosen was that suggested to Buchanan by Prince Shakhovski—working through a prominent Russian financier named Jaroshinski the British government tried secretly to get a controlling interest in some of the largest Russian banks and commercial houses. (This was before the Bolshevik nationalisation of banks, which took place on 27 December 1917.) The Embassy in Petrograd seems to have given Jaroshinski some funds directly—approximately £500,000—to be sold for rubles: other sums were placed (in sterling) to Jaroshinski's account in London by the Foreign Office. It is not clear from the law report exactly how much passed through Jaroshinski himself, although it probably amounted only to a few million pounds.

(The lawsuit was reported in the Law Report, King's Bench Division: Isidore Martinovitch Kon v. Hugh Ansdell Farran Leech: *The Times*, 4 and 5 November 1920. Leech was the Foreign Office agent involved, having given the plaintiff a guarantee for payment in London.)

Novocherkassk, the Embassy issued a statement denying they were there, and adding:

If some British railroad experts have passed through several sectors of General Kaledin, this was exclusively for the purpose of securing the shipment of foodstuffs for the Rumanian army and the civil population of Rumania.[34]

Britain's allies were also given only the scantiest information, but it was soon seen that there was a danger that British and French missions in South Russia would duplicate each other's work. On 21 December the War Cabinet expressed concern not only at the lack of co-ordination among the Allies, but also at the dangerous inconsistency in British policy whereby the Embassy was attempting to conciliate the Bolsheviks in Petrograd while military officers were supporting their enemies in the provinces. Accordingly, it was decided to consult the French.[35]

The next day Milner and Cecil left for Paris with a memorandum to submit to Clemenceau and Pichon.[36] The Allies should make clear to the Bolsheviks, the memorandum said, that they had no desire to take any part in Russian internal politics. The Bolshevik impression that the Allies favoured a counter-revolution was a "profound mistake." To counteract this impression, the British government had decided to send Sir George Buchanan on leave for reasons of health;[37] the Ambassador's long residence in Petrograd had "indelibly associated him, in the minds of the Bolsheviks, with the policy of the Cadets." Yet far from removing the inconsistency of attempting to woo both the Bolsheviks and their enemies, the memorandum went on to declare:

But we feel it necessary to keep in touch as far as we can with the Ukraine, the Cossacks, Finland, Siberia, the Caucasus, etc., because these various semi-autonomous provinces represent a very large part of the strength of Russia. In particular, we feel bound to befriend the Ukraine, since upon the Ukraine depends the feeding of the Roumanians, to whom we are bound by every obligation of honour.

[34] Francis MSS, press item in folder "December 21-24, 1917." Quoted in Kennan, *Russia Leaves the War*, p. 170, n. 7.
[35] Noted in the memorandum, "Policy of the War Cabinet Relative to Revolutionary Governments at Petrograd," *loc.cit.*
[36] The text of the British memorandum is printed in Lloyd George, *War Memoirs*, vol. II, pp. 1550-51, and in *Foreign Relations, 1918, Russia*, vol. I, pp. 330-31.
[37] The Ambassador's health had already broken down. See above, Chapter I.

The memorandum then turned specifically to southern Russia, and set forth two very extensive goals for Allied policy there: to prevent the Germans and Austrians from obtaining raw materials—particularly the wheat of the Ukraine—and to erect a barrier, in the form of independent or autonomous Georgian and Armenian states,

. . . against the development of a Turanian movement that will extend from Constantinople to China, and will provide Germany with a weapon of even greater danger to the peace of the world than the control of the Baghdad Railway.

To secure these objects the first essential was "money to reorganise the Ukraine, to pay the Cossacks and Caucasian forces, and to subsidise the Persians." The memorandum suggested a division of responsibilities: if the French could finance the Ukraine and also send military missions and political agents to advise loyal forces there, the British would take charge of the other areas. Each power would appoint a general officer to supervise operations in the region for which it was responsible, and naturally, the closest liaison would be maintained between the two commands. And the memorandum added: "It is essential that this should be done as quickly as possible so as to avoid the imputation—as far as we can—that we are preparing to make war on the Bolsheviks."

The idea of leaving the Ukraine to the French was endorsed by the British Military Attaché in Jassy, who had reported that the French military mission in Rumania had entered into very close relations with the Rada. The French, he said, because they had distributed so many officers through the area, were in a much better position than the British to judge the course of Ukrainian events.[38]

Clemenceau and Pichon readily agreed to the terms of the British memorandum, and their agreement was formalised in a "Convention between France and England on the subject of activity in southern Russia," signed on the 23rd.[39] The area was divided into "zones of influence," the British being assigned "the Cossack territories, the territory of the Caucasus, Armenia, Georgia, Kurdistan." The French

[38] Gen. Ballard, Jassy, to C.I.G.S., transmitted in Barclay to Foreign Office, telegram 793A, 18 December 1917, 9:40 p.m.; Milner MSS, box D-2.

[39] The text of this convention is printed, in its French original, in *British Documents*, series I, vol. III, London, 1949, pp. 369-70, and in English translation in Louis Fischer, *The Soviets in World Affairs: a History of the Relations Between the Soviet Union and the Rest of the World, 1917-1929*, London, 1930 (Second Edition, Princeton, 1951), vol. I, p. 836.

zone was to be Bessarabia, the Ukraine, and the Crimea. Expenses were to be pooled and regulated by "a centralizing inter-Allied organ."

Soviet historians (and some of their Western colleagues who wrote during the early 1930's), prisoners of a conspiratorial view of history which never admits that decisions are often made haphazardly on the basis of immediate events and circumstances rather than as part of a grand and inclusive scheme, have always represented this convention as the height of capitalist villainy, whereby Russia was carved up for exploitation as China or Persia had been in the past. To these historians, it was logically necessary that the rest of Russia also be parcelled out at the same time, and they therefore state—without ever citing a source for their statements—that at the same time (even in the same convention) it was agreed that Japan and the United States should divide between them Siberia and the Far East.[40] There is no basis for this statement.

Actually, there is every reason to believe that the convention was simply a strategic document intended to set forth spheres for military action.[41] Besides setting forth the "zones of influence" it stated that the activities directed by the French were to be developed north of the Black Sea, against the Germans and Austrians, while the British

[40] Two recent Soviet histories, one Stalinist, the other a product of the thaw, have both viewed the convention not as a military arrangement but as a programme for the exploitation of Russia. The first is the only Russian study entirely devoted to Anglo-Soviet relations during this period: F. D. Volkov, *Krakh angliiskoi politiki interventsii i diplomaticheskoi izolyatsii sovetskogo gosudarstva (1917-1924 gg.)* (The Failure of English Interventionist Policy and the Diplomatic Isolation of the Soviet Union [1917-1924]), Moscow, 1954, p. 31. The second is the joint effort by a commission of historians headed by S. F. Naida, G. D. Obichkin, Y. P. Petrov, A. A. Struchkov, and N. I. Shatagin, *Istoriya grazhdanskoy voiny v SSSR* (History of the Civil War in the USSR), vol. III (1917-1922), Moscow, 1957, p. 175.

This latter work quotes from Chamberlin (*Russian Revolution*, vol. II, pp. 153-54), who implies that the convention was dictated by the patterns of French and British investment in Russia before the war. Both Soviet volumes simply state that the convention was accompanied by an agreement between Japan and the United States dividing up Siberia and the Far East. Volkov goes so far as to state that the same agreement assigned to Britain Central Asia and Northern Russia from Murmansk to the Urals. Louis Fischer, although he does not make any specific claims, states (also without citing any evidence) that "Apparently a parallel agreement disposed in similar fashion of other parts of Russia." (*Soviets in World Affairs*, vol. II, p. 836.)

[41] In December 1918, in a meeting of a committee of the War Cabinet which was meeting in order to determine upon a British policy for the Caucasus, the idea was specifically rejected that the convention of 23 December 1917 might serve to justify the extension of British authority into the Caucasus. It was authoritatively claimed that the convention related strictly to wartime military arrangements. This meeting will be treated in the first chapter of the second volume of the present work.

were to concentrate their efforts south of the Black Sea, against the Turks. In view of the distribution of French and British forces which prevailed at that time, and British concentration on the Mesopotamian front and on the protection of the frontiers of India, this was a very logical and natural arrangement. Finally, one article of the convention stated that because Alekseyev at Novocherkassk had begun the organisation of an army intended to operate against Germany, and because France had already allocated a credit of 100 million francs to assist him and had made provision for the organisation of inter-Allied control, the French would continue their supervision in the Don region until new arrangements were made with Britain.

On the same day that this convention was drafted, the Military Representatives of the Supreme War Council met at Versailles, at the request of the British government, to give their opinion as to whether Southern Russia and Rumania were "effectively able to resist the Bolshevik forces assisted and controlled by the Germans."[42] This was one of the earliest statements which identified Bolshevism with Germany, and therefore assumed that the Allies were fighting Bolsheviks as well as Germans.

The Military Representatives did not directly answer the question put to them, but they did make recommendations for policy in South Russia. If the Bolsheviks were left free to act, they said in their Joint Note No. 5 dated 24 December, the Germans could receive wheat through Odessa and oil through Batum. Therefore, even if the Allies lost control of South Russia, it was important that they kept possession of the Black Sea ports of Novorossisk and Batum for use as naval bases. For these purposes, and to preserve the Rumanian Army, "the Military Representatives are of opinion that all national groups who are determined to continue the war must be supported by all the means in our power." This resistance in South Russia could not be sustained unless it were possible to open "a more direct communication between the Allies and our friends in Russia either by way of Vladivostok and the Siberian Railway, or by operations in Turkey which might open a direct route to Tiflis, or lead to a separate peace and the opening of the Dardanelles."[43]

[42] Joint Note No. 5, Military Representatives, Supreme War Council, 24 December 1917; Supreme War Council records, Modern Army Branch, U.S. National Archives.
[43] *idem.* Parts of this Note are printed in Lloyd George, *War Memoirs*, vol. ii, pp. 1895-96.

Thus, by the end of 1917 Britain had become deeply involved in South Russia. The commitment which was formalised by the Anglo-French convention of 23 December was made against the advice of the British government's most expert advisers on the scene in Russia. It was to cost the British taxpayer many millions of pounds, and it was to last not simply until the end of the war with Germany, but well into the summer of 1920, when London finally told General Wrangel, the successor of Alekseyev and Kaledin, that he could expect no more British aid. From the beginning the contradictions implied in such a policy were apparent. As one of the senior officials of the Foreign Office asked in a memorandum written on 4 January 1918, could the British government support the anti-Bolshevik factions in South Russia without provoking a rupture with the government at Petrograd? And how could they be certain that even if they did support local governments in the provinces those governments would not be quickly swallowed up by Bolshevism? Lord Robert Cecil provided an answer of sorts when he wrote, as a minute to the same memorandum: "I think we must be prepared in the desperate position in South Russia to take risks."[44]

[44] Memorandum by Sir G. R. Clerk, 4 January 1918, Milner MSS, box B. Cecil's minute was dated 5 January.

CHAPTER III

THE BOLSHEVIKS MAKE PEACE

Internal affairs in Russia are no concern of ours. We only consider them in so far as they affect the war.—Balfour to Lockhart, 21 February 1918

JUST as the War Cabinet was finishing its meeting on 21 December 1917, there arrived at 10 Downing Street a small round-faced Scot who did not look even his thirty years of age. At the Cabinet session that day, it had been decided to send Milner and Cecil to Paris with a memorandum on Russian policy for the French government. The first sentence of that memorandum read: "At Petrograd we should at once get into relations with the Bolsheviks through unofficial agents, each country as seems best to it."[1] To the Prime Minister of Great Britain, the agent who seemed best was the young Scot who was first ushered into the Cabinet room on that gloomy December Friday. His name was R. H. Bruce Lockhart.[2]

Despite his youth, Lockhart was already an "old Russian hand." Since early 1912 he had been attached to the British Consulate-General in Moscow, first as a very junior vice-consul and then, from the summer of 1915, as acting Consul-General, a post which during wartime carried immense duties and responsibilities. Fluent in Russian, the young Consul-General had a wide circle of Russian friends, among them both premiers of the Provisional Government, Lvov and Kerensky. Six weeks before the Bolshevik Revolution, however, Sir George Buchanan had ordered Lockhart to return to Britain on the pretext that his health demanded it, but actually because he had formed an attachment to a Russian woman. The Ambassador feared that since Lockhart was already married, a scandal would wreck a promising career. Buchanan made this decision with

---

[1] Lloyd George, *War Memoirs*, vol. II, p. 1550.
[2] The following account of Lockhart's background is drawn from his own book, *Memoirs of a British Agent*, London, 1932, pp. 53-209.

great reluctance; Lockhart, he told the French Ambassador in August 1917, was his most able subordinate.[3]

In this manner, Lockhart found himself in London during the first days of the Soviet regime. His perceptive reports from Moscow had earned him a considerable reputation even in Cabinet circles and Milner had been greatly impressed with the young man during his Moscow visit. On 20 December, the morning after a dinner with Milner during which he had urged on the Minister the necessity of establishing contact with the Bolshevik authorities, Lockhart was summoned to Downing Street for two days of conference with Cabinet members, principally Milner, Smuts, Curzon, and Cecil. The conclusion of these conferences was the meeting with Lloyd George on the 21st. The Prime Minister fully endorsed Lockhart's views. After only a few minutes of discussion he turned to his Cabinet colleagues and announced that Lockhart obviously belonged in Petrograd, not London.[4]

The terms of Lockhart's mission were set forth in a note to the American government early in January. His function was simply "to keep unofficially in touch" with the Bolsheviks. At the same time, the note said, the British government would also keep in touch "by means of unofficial channels" with an agent that the Bolsheviks had just appointed to represent them in London, Maxim Litvinov. Some sort of relations with the Bolsheviks had to be maintained, the note continued, and the system of unofficial agents seemed to be the best that could be arranged, for it did "not entail the recognition of the Trotsky-Lenin government either by the British Government or the Governments of the Allies."[5]

Before Lockhart left for Russia he had several meetings with his Bolshevik counterpart, Litvinov. Surely, of all the figures who have taken part in Soviet diplomacy in the four decades since 1917, Litvinov was the most sympathetic. Although basically a moderate, scholarly type, his identification with revolutionary causes forced him to flee Russia in 1902. In 1908, after several years in France, he settled in London, where, under the pseudonym of Maxim Harrison, he worked in a succession of publishing houses. At the same time he

[3] Joseph Noulens, *Mon ambassade en Russie soviétique, 1917-1919*, Paris, 1933, vol.ii, p. 115.
[4] Lockhart, *British Agent*, pp. 199-200.
[5] Memorandum from the British Ambassador (Spring-Rice) to Secretary of State, 9 January 1918; *Foreign Relations, 1918, Russia*, vol. i, p. 337.

became the representative of the Bolshevik Party in the International Socialist Bureau in London—the party's first "ambassador" abroad. Litvinov soon made many friends, among them Reginald Leeper, of the Political Intelligence Department of the Foreign Office, who first came to him to learn Russian.[6] And he married Ivy Low, a novelist-journalist member of a Bloomsbury literary family. During the war, Litvinov worked for the purchasing commission of the Russian Delegation in London, but he also kept up his work in various émigré organisations.[7]

On 3 January 1918 *The Times* carried a report of a Soviet wireless message announcing that Litvinov had been appointed provisional Plenipotentiary in London. This message, signed by Trotsky, ordered all Russian officials in Britain to hand over to Litvinov all documents and funds. The new Plenipotentiary himself learned of his appointment from *The Times*. He immediately sat down and wrote a letter to the Foreign Office; it was returned unopened. Similarly rebuffed (as, of course, he expected to be) when he wrote to demand the immediate transfer to him of the Russian Embassy in Chesham House, he contented himself with opening a "People's Embassy" at 82 Victoria Street. Litvinov was not allowed to enter the Foreign Office. But as it happened (it was not a coincidence) his offices in Victoria Street were directly above those used by Reginald Leeper and some of his colleagues in the Foreign Office Political Intelligence Department. These arrangements were the "unofficial channels" of which the Americans had been told. Leeper, however, was the only British official allowed to see Litvinov.[8]

Sometimes their interviews occurred on "neutral ground," such as the Lyons Corner House in the Strand where Leeper introduced Litvinov to Lockhart in early January. Also present at this meeting was Feodor Rothstein, another Bolshevik who had lived for years in England (Rothstein, another old friend of Leeper, was then employed

[6] Sir Reginald Leeper has told the present author that he had been following the Russian press for the Foreign Office throughout the war, and that he came to Litvinov to improve his spoken Russian early in 1917. But instead of working on Leeper's Russian, the two men spent most of their sessions talking about Russian revolutionary politics; as a result, Leeper became the Foreign Office's expert on Bolshevism.

[7] Most of this information on Litvinov's past is drawn from Arthur Upham Pope's biography, *Maxim Litvinoff*, New York, 1943; the volume is filled with inaccuracies and must be used with extreme care.

[8] Interview with Sir Reginald Leeper.

as a translator in the War Office; he was later to be Soviet minister in Teheran). The four men discussed the status of Lockhart and Litvinov. Both were to be considered unofficial representatives, but each was to have certain diplomatic privileges, including the use of ciphers and the right to send couriers to their respective governments.[9] It is significant that at just this time the cipher privilege was taken away from the old Russian Embassy at Chesham House and the Embassy's funds, as well as those of all other institutions in Britain of former Russian governments, impounded.[10]

Litvinov wrote for Lockhart a letter of introduction to Trotsky, calling the British agent "a thoroughly honest man who understands our position and sympathises with us."[11] By then it was almost time for Lockhart's departure for Russia. The days before were filled with conferences in Whitehall and, especially, with almost daily meetings with Milner. It quickly became apparent to the young man that he had been selected for his mission by Milner and Lloyd George themselves, and not by the Foreign Secretary or the Foreign Office. Lord Robert Cecil, for instance, was convinced that Lenin and Trotsky were paid agents of Germany working for German ends, and he was therefore supremely sceptical of the usefulness of any mission which aimed at establishing relations with the Bolsheviks.[12] Lockhart's appointment, indeed, was typical of the way Lloyd George ran his wartime government; while the premier's methods sometimes led to spectacular results, they also aroused intense animosity within the permanent hierarchies of the administration. The British agent's position was epitomized by Joseph Noulens, the French Ambassador in Russia: "At once intelligent, energetic and clever, he was one of those whom the English Government employs, with rare felicity, for

[9] Lockhart, *British Agent*, p. 202.

[10] Nabokoff, *Ordeal*, p. 212. Britain was the only major power to impose these restrictions on the representatives of the former Russian government. In Rome, Tokyo and Washington, in the first five months following the Revolution, there was no perceptible change in attitude towards the Russian Ambassadors. The position of Maklakov, in Paris, was ambiguous, because he had not presented his credentials before the Revolution; he was, however, still accorded cipher privileges (*ibid.*, p. 188). The British attitude, however, was consistent with the fact that Britain was also the only power to send to the Bolsheviks a diplomatic agent in Lockhart's position.

[11] Lockhart, *British Agent*, p. 203.

[12] *ibid.*, p. 200. Sir Reginald Leeper has told me that throughout Lockhart's stay in Russia, Cecil remained convinced that his mission was useless and that any contact with the Bolsheviks was harmful.

confidential missions, and whom it reserves, should the occasion arise, for disavowal."[13]

✧

Lockhart left on a British cruiser for Bergen on 14 January. Not until three weeks later did he reach Petrograd. Meanwhile, the Bolsheviks continued their efforts to remove Russia from the war.[14] On 15 December they had signed an armistice providing for a month's cessation of hostilities and the commencement, as soon as possible, of formal peace negotiations.[15] The first plenary session of the peace conference was held at Brest-Litovsk on the afternoon of 22 December. At this session, Adolf Joffe, the head of the Soviet delegation, set forth his government's proposals. There should be no annexation of captured territory. Occupying troops should withdraw in the shortest possible time and political independence should be restored to nations deprived of it. National groups which did not enjoy political independence before the war should be given an opportunity to decide freely, by a referendum, whether to adhere to any already-constituted state or to be fully independent. The minority groups within territories should be protected by special laws guaranteeing them cultural, and as far as possible, administrative autonomy. "Colonial questions" should also be settled along these lines. Here were the points comprising the oft-stated Soviet aim of "no annexations." "No indemnities" was covered by the provision that none of the belligerent countries should pay "war costs" to any others, and that private individuals who had incurred losses owing to the war should be compensated from a special fund raised by proportional levies on all belligerent countries.[16]

These were sweeping terms, hardly the kind that a defeated country, with much of its territory occupied by enemy armies, proposes to a victor. Yet on 25 December the Central Powers informed the Bolshevik delegates that with a few exceptions these proposals

[13] Noulens, *Mon ambassade*, vol. II, p. 115.

[14] The course of the Brest-Litovsk negotiations has been so well charted by others that we shall confine ourselves here to a bare outline for background purposes. Wheeler-Bennett, *Brest-Litovsk, passim*, is the fullest account. Kennan, *Russia Leaves the War*, pp. 219-41, 458-517, adds many details.

[15] The armistice included a provision forbidding the transfer of troops, but as we have seen (above, Chapter 1, footnote 101) the Germans insisted upon construing this provision in a way so that it scarcely hampered them.

[16] The text of Joffe's declaration is printed in *Dokumenty vneshnei politiki*, vol. I, pp. 59-61. Excerpts are translated in Degras, *Soviet Documents*, vol. I, pp. 21-22.

formed a discussible basis for peace negotiations. To the Bolsheviks this implied that the Germans were willing to withdraw their forces from territories formerly part of the Russian Empire—primarily Poland and the Baltic provinces—which had been occupied during the war. Joffe immediately forwarded this happy news to Petrograd.[17]

The Germans quickly disabused Joffe of this impression however. On 27 December the German commander, General Hoffmann, pointed out that it was not forcible annexation if portions of the former Russian Empire elected to separate from Russia and assume either an independent existence or a protected status within the German Empire. Russian Poland, Lithuania, and Kurland, Hoffmann added, had already exercised this right; their future would be determined by direct conversations between their representatives and the Central Powers.[18]

This revelation produced complete deadlock in the negotiations, which were adjourned until 9 January. The Bolsheviks were faced with the disagreeable task of putting the truth about the German aims to a population already rejoicing at the earlier news that the Central Powers had accepted the Soviet proposals. This was not done until the first day of the new year, and even then the full meaning of the German position was not made clear.[19] On 2 January, Trotsky gave a defiant interview to the press, stating: "If the diplomats on the other side think that we regard the principle enunciated in our declaration as a hollow formality, they are profoundly mistaken."[20] But one fact of the situation was perfectly clear, no matter how boldly the Bolsheviks spoke. As Sir George Buchanan noted in his diary that night (five days, it will be remembered, before his departure from Russia), "Trotsky knows perfectly well that the Russian army is incapable of fighting."[21]

The negotiations at Brest were naturally followed with great interest in the Allied capitals. By a coincidence, the news of the German demands came just in time for Lloyd George to make it an important part of a long-awaited major address on war aims on 5 January. "No one who knows Prussia and her designs upon Russia

[17] Wheeler-Bennett, *Brest-Litovsk*, pp. 121-22; Kennan, *Russia Leaves the War*, p. 221.
[18] Wheeler-Bennett, *Brest-Litovsk*, p. 125.
[19] Kennan, *Russia Leaves the War*, pp. 223-27.
[20] Trotsky's statement is printed in Degras, *Soviet Documents*, vol. I, pp. 26-28.
[21] Sir George Buchanan, *Mission*, vol. II, p. 245.

can for a moment doubt her ultimate intention," the Prime Minister told a specially-called Trades Union Congress conference on man-power in the Central Hall, Westminster. And he continued:

Whatever phrases she may use to delude Russia, she does not mean to surrender one of the fair provinces or cities of Russia now occupied by her forces. Under one name or another—and the name hardly matters— these Russian provinces will henceforth be in reality part of the dominions of Prussia. They will be ruled by the Prussian sword in the interests of Prussian autocracy, and the rest of the people of Russia will be partly enticed by specious phrases and partly bullied by the threat of continued war against an impotent army into a condition of complete economic and ultimate political enslavement to Germany. We all deplore the prospect.

In the Prime Minister's view, the Russians had brought disaster upon themselves. "We shall be proud to fight to the end side by side with the new democracy of Russia," he affirmed. "But if the present rulers of Russia take action which is independent of their Allies we have no means of intervening to arrest the catastrophe which is assuredly befalling their country." Russia, he concluded, "can only be saved by her own people."[22]

But Russia was only a secondary theme in Lloyd George's address, called by *The Times* "the most important State document issued since the declaration of war."[23] And the statement of war aims it contained was not a response to the repeated Russian requests for such a state-ment. Rather, it was the result of a desperate decision by the govern-ment to institute a "comb-out" of industry to throw more men into the battlelines. This recruitment of men previously exempted was in violation of pledges previously made to the Trade Unions, and it came at a time—the winter of the fourth year of war—when discontent was mounting. Accordingly, Lloyd George decided to appear before the T.U.C. delegates to state the war aims for which the government was asking renewed sacrifice.[24] The Prime Minister's address was the

[22] Lloyd George, *War Memoirs*, vol. II, p. 1514 (the full address is printed on pp. 1510-17).
The Prime Minister engaged in no recriminations against Russia in this address. The preceding 20 December, however, in a general review of the military situation he made on the motion for the Christmas adjournment, he told the House of Commons: "It would be idle to pretend that the hope we had formed at the beginning of the year has been realised, and our disappointment has been attributable entirely, in my judgment, to the Russian collapse." (100 HC Deb. 5s cols. 2209-10.)
[23] *The Times*, 7 January 1918.
[24] For a complete account of the circumstances surrounding Lloyd George's address, see Mayer, *New Diplomacy*, pp. 313-28.

culmination of a great national debate that had run the course of the preceding two months, punctuated by Lord Lansdowne's famous letter to the *Daily Telegraph* on 29 November advocating an immediate compromise peace,[25] a reply by Winston Churchill, the Minister of Munitions, on 10 December,[26] a Labour declaration on war aims on 16 December, and numerous questions in the House of Commons.[27] All of these, of course, received some impetus from the events in Russia, but they were more directly the result of internal crises.

The specific terms of the Prime Minister's declaration do not concern us here. Drafted after consultation with Labour leaders, as well as with Asquith and Lord Grey, they differed relatively slightly from the terms contained in Labour's statement of 16 December, and in most important respects they corresponded with President Wilson's much more publicised Fourteen Points presented to Congress only three days later (and motivated to a much greater extent, as Wilson pointed out, by the events at Brest-Litovsk).[28] Lloyd George stated no "war-aims" concerning the territories of the former Russian Empire,

[25] See *ibid*, pp. 282-86.

[26] Churchill's speech, at Bedford, was printed in *The Times*, 11 December 1917. Britain had only one war aim, he said: that those who had committed such grave crimes would not emerge from the struggle stronger than when they began it, nor in a position ever to make war again. An important part of the speech was devoted to Russia. It was vintage Churchill: ". . . Russia has been thoroughly beaten by the Germans. Her great heart has been broken, not only by German might, but by German intrigue; not only by German steel, but by German gold. . . . It is this melancholy event which has prolonged the war, that has robbed the French and the British and the Italian armies of the prize that was, perhaps, almost within their reach this summer; it is this event, and this event alone, that has exposed us to perils and sorrows and sufferings which we have not deserved, which we cannot avoid, but under which we shall not bend."

[27] Labour's declaration was printed in *The Times*, 19 December 1917. Questions in the House of Commons were raised throughout the autumn and early winter. See particularly the outspoken attack on the government made on 19 December by Arthur Ponsonby (100 HC Deb. 5s cols. 2000-8).

[28] See Kennan, *Russia Leaves the War*, pp. 242-58, and Mayer, *New Diplomacy*, pp. 329-67. The Sixth of Wilson's Fourteen Points was entirely devoted to Russia: "VI. The evacuation of all Russian territory and such a settlement of all questions affecting Russia as will secure the best and freest cooperation of the other nations of the world in obtaining for her an unhampered and unembarrassed opportunity for the independent determination of her own political development and national policy and assure her of a sincere welcome into the society of free nations under institutions of her own choosing; and, more than a welcome, assistance also of every kind that she may need and may herself desire. The treatment accorded Russia by her sister nations in the months to come will be the acid test of their good will, of their comprehension of her needs as distinguished from their own interests, and of their intelligent and unselfish sympathy." The complete text of President Wilson's address to Congress on 8 January 1918 is printed in *Foreign Relations, 1918, The World War*, Supplement 1, vol. 1, Washington, 1933, pp. 12-17.

save that "an independent Poland, comprising all those genuinely Polish elements who desire to form part of it," was "an urgent necessity for the stability of Western Europe." He would say no more because events were moving so swiftly. Judgement must be suspended, he said, until the final terms of European peace came to be discussed.

It is doubtful whether the Prime Minister's address had any effect at all in Russia, either in Smolny or among the Russian masses.[29] Wilson's Fourteen Points, of which over half a million copies were printed and distributed at Petrograd and the front by the efficient American propaganda agents in Russia, made very little impression on Soviet officialdom save in arousing scorn and scepticism.[30] No such effort was made to publicise Lloyd George's declaration, and certainly it did nothing to disabuse Trotsky of the idea (which he expressed to two people on the day the Prime Minister spoke) that Lloyd George hoped that Russia would be compelled to make a disgraceful peace so that Germany, her desires satisfied in the east, would minimise her demands in the west.[31]

By a coincidence, the statements on war aims by the heads of the British and American governments were followed immediately by the renewal of negotiations at Brest-Litovsk.[32] Trotsky himself took charge of the Soviet delegation. His task was to spin out the negotia-

[29] At just this time, *The Times* Petrograd correspondent cabled to his paper that British propaganda in Russia, conducted at considerable government expense, had been utterly futile in influencing the Russian soldiers, who were absolutely indifferent to it. (*The Times*, 10 January 1917.)

[30] Kennan, *Russia Leaves the War*, pp. 258-64.

[31] As reported by Francis to Secretary of State, telegram 2204, Petrograd, 6 January 1918; *Foreign Relations, 1918, Russia*, vol. I, p. 425.

I have come across only two pieces of evidence which indicate that the idea of compensating Germany with Russian territory was ever given any consideration in British governmental circles. The first is the impression which C. P. Scott, the editor of the *Manchester Guardian*, carried away from an interview with Lloyd George on 28 December 1917 that the Prime Minister was thinking of "paying the Germans in the East in order to square them in the West" (diary entry quoted in J. L. Hammond, *C. P. Scott of the Manchester Guardian*, London, 1934, p. 232). The second is the report by Sir Henry Wilson's biographer (Callwell, *Henry Wilson*, vol. II, p. 49) of a meeting on 2 January 1918 between the C.I.G.S. and Bonar Law, then Chancellor of the Exchequer: "Wilson afterwards saw Bonar Law, who was thinking about peace terms and believed that Germany might be disposed to restore Alsace-Lorraine to France and to make other concessions if given a free hand on the Russian side, and he wrote in his diary: 'I don't believe a word of this, but, as I said to Bonar, if she is feeling like that she must be nearly beat, and if she is nearly beat let us beat her and have done with it. All this peace talk frightens me, for it creates a Boche atmosphere.'"

[32] This summary of the Brest negotiations is again drawn from the works of Wheeler-Bennett and Kennan, already cited.

tions as long as possible. If the Germans could be shown for the naked imperialists they were, the German people might begin the revolution which the Bolsheviks had so long awaited. Delay also gave the Russians time to reconstruct their army so they would not be totally helpless before German power. Trotsky was at least partially successful: despite himself, Kühlmann, the head of the German delegation, allowed the discussions to range for days over arguments of principle which had little bearing on the problems at hand.

At two points in the proceedings, Kühlmann forced the discussions from the level of abstract theorising to the more familiar plane of power politics. On 12 January General Hoffmann was allowed to state that the High Command would not tolerate any Bolshevik attempts to interfere in the affairs of the occupied territories, and that, at least for the time being, they refused to evacuate Kurland, Lithuania, Riga, and the Islands of the Gulf of Riga. And on the 18th, Hoffmann handed Trotsky a map on which a pencilled blue line, running north from Brest-Litvosk to the Baltic, indicated the new frontiers of Russia. The future of the occupied areas south of Brest, said Hoffmann, would be determined in direct negotiations with the Ukrainian Rada, which by then (as General Knox had predicted a month before) had become completely subservient to the Germans. In a fury, Trotsky took the map and boarded a waiting train to return to Petrograd and report to his colleagues.

Trotsky's return was followed by prolonged and agonising debate within the Soviet government. A bare majority, led by Bukharin and Radek, wanted to reject the German terms and wage "revolutionary war" against the Central Powers. The minority was divided into two factions. One, headed by Lenin, advocated the immediate conclusion of peace in order to obtain the respite which the shaky regime so badly needed for internal consolidation. Another was led by Trotsky, who put forth a policy of "no war—no peace" by which the Soviets would refuse to sign a treaty agreeing to Germany's conditions, but would nevertheless continue demobilising, declaring to the world that so far as Russia was concerned the war was over. This audacious policy would avoid the ignominy of agreeing to an "annexationist peace." Lenin resigned himself to Trotsky's formula as a compromise, but he feared that the German reaction would simply be to order a further advance into Russia.

When the Brest talks were resumed on 30 January the first days were occupied with the Ukrainian question. This time, Trotsky had brought with him a delegation of Bolshevik Ukrainians from the Kharkov Soviet, and as if to reinforce their claims against the rival Rada, Soviet troops were daily advancing further against Kiev. But the Central Powers were clearly calling the tune at Brest-Litovsk. On 8 February they signed a separate peace with the Rada. It did not matter that Kiev fell to Red forces the next day—German arms would soon enough restore the deposed Rada government. Trotsky refused to recognise the Ukrainian treaty, and on the 10th he announced his policy of "no war—no peace." Naturally it brought the conference to a standstill. Immediately the Bolshevik delegation again departed for Petrograd, congratulating themselves on a brilliant *coup de théâtre*, leaving behind the stunned Austrians and Germans, who could find no precedent for such an arrangement in their legal texts.

❖

During the course of these negotiations at Brest-Litovsk, the Soviet regime took two steps that, more than any others since the Bolshevik seizure of power, marked the gulf between them and the rest of the world. The first was their dissolution, in the early hours of 19 January, of the democratically elected Constituent Assembly.[33] By their ruthless intimidation and summary dismissal of this body (in which they themselves had only 175 seats out of 707, the majority being held by the Socialist-Revolutionaries with 410 seats) the Bolsheviks forcibly underlined what perceptive observers had long known: Lenin's government paid only the most cynical lip service to the principle of democracy, and had no right whatsoever to call themselves the chosen government of the people of Russia. The demonstration of this fact calmed the consciences of Western statesmen who felt uneasy in supporting dissident Russian groups against the central Soviet authority. Balfour made this explicit on 30 January in a cable to Colonel House:

. . . We have no desire to quarrel with the Bolshevics (sic). On the contrary, so long as they refuse to make a separate peace we look at them with a certain amount of favour. But they have no claim to be the Govern-

---

[33] For this episode, see Chamberlin, *Russian Revolution*, vol. 1, pp. 364-71 and Carr, *Bolshevik Revolution*, vol. 1, pp. 109-21; the most effectively written account of the dissolution is in Kennan, *Russia Leaves the War*, pp. 343-52.

ment of all the Russians either *de facto* or *de jure*. Especially since the dissolution of the Constituent Assembly they have no better claim to this position than the autonomous bodies in South East Russia which the Siberian scheme is intended to assist. . . .[34]

The dissolution of the Assembly turned moderate men implacably against the Soviet regime. Sir George Buchanan, as we have seen, favoured a policy of conciliation during the time he was in Russia. He heard the news of the dissolution after reaching England, and it caused him to change his views completely. From then on, he was a steadfast advocate of a complete break with the Bolsheviks, the withdrawal of the British Embassy, and all-out assistance to anti-Bolshevik groups loyal to the Allies.[35]

The other step taken by the Soviet regime during this period had international implications that were much more direct and permanent: long after the dissolution of the Constituent Assembly had been forgotten the world's statesmen fulminated over the decree published by the Central Executive Committee on 10 February, annulling all state debts, including the massive foreign loans.[36] In Britain's case these amounted to some £600 million.[37] Nearly all of this sum represented direct loans from the British to the Russian (first the Tsarist, then the Provisional) governments. In distinction from the case of France, where the overwhelming proportion of loans to Russia were in the form of Russian government bonds sold privately on the Paris Bourse, British private loans amounted only to the small figure of £17.5 million. They took the form of treasury bills issued on behalf of the Russian government by the Bank of England, with the approval and encouragement of the British government. Even this sum was largely transferred to the government, for on 17 January, possibly in expectation of the Soviet annulment decree, the Chancellor of the Exchequer announced in the House of Commons that the Treasury would take over these obligations at 82 percent of their value; "although we have no direct liability," he said, "in view of the circumstances of the issue, there is a certain amount of

[34] Balfour to House, relayed in telegram CXP 506 from Sir Eric Drummond to Wiseman, 30 January 1918; Wiseman MSS, also House MSS (drawer 2, no. 10).
[35] Sir George Buchanan, *Mission*, vol. II, p. 256.
[36] The text of this decree is printed in *Dokumenty vneshnei politiki*, vol. I, pp. 97-98, and is translated (and incorrectly dated 8 February) in *Foreign Relations, 1918, Russia*, vol. III, Washington, 1932, pp. 32-33.
[37] See above, pp. 4-5.

moral responsibility."[38] In other words, the government agreed to insure the bondholders against possible loss (the Bolsheviks had not yet annulled the debts, it must be remembered) for a premium of 18 percent. To *The Times*, this seemed "the only possible course that could have been followed."[39] Because of these factors, there never developed in Britain the powerful lobby of small bondholders which so plagued French relations with Russia in later years. The strongest pressure on the British government was to be exerted by the very large firms whose property in Russia was confiscated under the series of Soviet nationalisation decrees published throughout 1918.

The Allied governments, of course, vigorously protested against the repudiation of the debt. The entire Petrograd Diplomatic Corps (including all the neutrals) met on 12 February and collectively declared that they considered "the decrees regarding the repudiation of Russian state loans, the confiscating of property of all kinds and other analogous measures as without value as far as their nationals are concerned" and reserved the right to claim "at an opportune time" damages for all loss incurred under them.[40] And the Inter-Allied Council on War Purchases and Finance, meeting in Paris on the 14th, issued a ponderously-worded statement of the principles underlying international obligations, which could not be repudiated "without shaking the very foundations of the law of nations." These principles, the statement concluded, would be applied "in every negotiation relating to the recognition of the new state or new states that are eventually to be constituted in Russia."[41]

Meanwhile, during the first days of February, Lockhart had arrived in Petrograd. With him were three assistants he had selected before leaving England—Captain W. L. Hicks, who had been attached to the Military Mission in Russia and who knew the language and the

[38] 101 HC Deb. 5s cols. 502-4. All of the above information is taken from Bonar Law's statement.

[39] *The Times*, 18 January 1918. Reaction in the City, according to *The Times'* "City Notes" for 19 January, was luke-warm. Though a certain number of people felt that the holders were lucky to escape with a loss of only 18%, others (including the writer of "City Notes") felt this too hard a view, considering the pressure exerted by the government and the Bank of England to get people to take up the obligations when they were first put on the market.

[40] Reported by Francis to Secretary of State, telegram 2360, Petrograd, 12 February 1918. *Foreign Relations, 1918, Russia*, vol. III, p. 33.

[41] The text is printed in *ibid.*, p. 34.

country; Edward Birse, an Englishman who for years had been in business in Moscow; and Edward Phelan, a young official from the Ministry of Labour. To emphasise the fact that his little mission was separate from official British representation in the capital, Lockhart established them in a large and well-furnished flat a few hundred yards down the Palace Quay from the Embassy, directly across the Neva from the Fortress of Peter and Paul.[42]

Lockhart was well aware that his relations with the official British establishment would require delicate handling. Buchanan had left the Embassy in the charge of the Counsellor, Francis Oswald Lindley. The fourth son of a peer, Lindley had an easy-going appearance—he was a florid, pudgy, indifferently dressed product of Winchester and Magdalen, Oxford (where he read Law)—that belied his twenty-two years in the diplomatic service and somewhat disguised his considerable abilities. Although Lindley might well have resented the intrusion of a man sixteen years his junior and of much lower rank, Lockhart maintains that their relations were always extremely friendly.[43]

Because of his official status, Lindley was forbidden by London to have any dealings with the Bolsheviks. The Embassy staff, Lockhart found, was split between those who wanted to recognise the Soviet regime and those who would have nothing to do with it; Lindley, it seemed, was steering an indecisive course between the two groups.[44] Lockhart himself paid his first visit to Smolny, a courtesy call to introduce himself, the day after his arrival. Trotsky was still at Brest. In his absence the Soviet Foreign Office was in the charge of Chicherin, the only Bolshevik with experience in the old Tsarist Foreign Office. This curious figure, scarcely out of an English prison, so much a mixture of the old diplomacy and the new, welcomed Lockhart warmly.[45]

---

[42] Lockhart, *British Agent*, p. 224.

[43] *ibid.*, p. 223.

[44] *ibid.*, p. 220.

[45] *ibid.*, p. 221. Chicherin is alleged to have described his visitor, in a cable to Trotsky at Brest-Litovsk, in the following terms: "England and America are playing up to us separately. A few days ago there appeared a so-called head of a Commercial Mission, Lockhart, with a note from Litvinov stating that the bearer is an honest man who indeed fully sympathizes with us. Indeed he is a subtle and alert Englishman, expresses very liberal views, runs down his Government. He is a type of the diplomat of the new school. At present he is not an official representative but de facto he is an envoy, having been sent by the War Cabinet. After our recognition he will obtain an official position with us. He promises all kinds of favors from England."
The telegram is from Edgar Sisson, *One Hundred Red Days: A Personal Chronicle of the Bolshevik Revolution*, New Haven, Conn., 1931, p. 303. Sisson was in charge of American propaganda activities in Russia at this time and claims (p. 294) that the

For the Soviet regime, Lockhart's presence was a symbol that they were not totally cut off from the outside world; in the press the young British agent was described not only as a confidant of Lloyd George but as an influential politician who wholly sympathised with the Bolsheviks. This reception scarcely added to Lockhart's stature in the eyes of the other Allied representatives in Petrograd.[46]

On 15 February Lockhart had his first interview with Trotsky. The Commissar was just back from Brest-Litovsk, and for two hours he raged against the Germans. To Lockhart he seemed "the very incarnation of the revolutionary of the bourgeois caricatures . . . a man who would willingly die fighting for Russia provided there was a big enough audience to see him do it." But Lockhart was immediately and deeply impressed by Trotsky. In his diary he noted: "If the Bosche bought Trotsky, he bought a lemon."[47]

For his own part, Lockhart explained his government's willingness to reach a *modus vivendi* with the Bolshevik regime, but added that Bolshevik agitation within the United Kingdom could not be tolerated. Trotsky at once countered with a fierce condemnation of British support of anti-Bolshevik movements in Russia; he had documentary evidence, he said, of Allied financial aid to Kaledin and Alekseyev. The Allies had foolishly supported the Ukrainian Rada which had just dealt Russia and the Allies a most treacherous blow. Indeed, Trotsky continued, the Allies had openly sympathised with and secretly supported every anti-Bolshevik movement they could find, and despite their professions to the contrary they had not shown one sign of good will to the Bolsheviks.[48]

Although he hated British capitalism almost as much as German militarism, Trotsky maintained, he could not fight the whole world at once and knew that German militarism was the greater danger. Peaceful revolution was possible in England; in Germany it would come only by force. His one aim now was German revolution, not

texts of this and other telegrams between Smolny and Brest were given him by Commander E. T. Boyce, then head of British Intelligence in Russia, who, Sisson says, was disgusted with Lockhart. Boyce, in his turn, reportedly received the telegrams from Russian sources. This particular telegram, from its information about Lockhart and Litvinov, seems genuine enough.

[46] Lockhart, *British Agent*, pp. 221-22.

[47] *ibid.*, p. 226.

[48] All of these and the following details of Trotsky's conversation with Lockhart are taken from Lockhart's report to Balfour, transmitted in Lindley's telegram 480, Petrograd, 16 February 1918, 9 p.m.; Milner MSS, box B.

for love of the Entente but for the success of internationalism: it was necessary to crush German militarism to set free the German socialists, the best-organised in the world.

From this, Trotsky continued, followed the policy of "no war—no peace" which he had announced at Brest-Litovsk. There would be no renewal of peace negotiations and no question of trade relations with Germany. Therefore, the Commissar concluded, he was ready to co-operate with the Allies, but co-operation must be based on expedience, not love. He would willingly wage an active propaganda campaign in Germany. He was also anxious for trade with the Allies; Russia would provide flax and platinum in exchange for badly needed supplies. But all co-operation depended on the Allies ceasing their support of the counter-revolution; if that happened, the Bolsheviks would stop their agitation in Allied countries.

Lockhart came away from this first meeting convinced that Trotsky had offered a basis for a successful policy in Russia. He felt sure, he cabled the Foreign Office, that Trotsky, handled tactfully, would be a valuable asset against Germany. Although he himself had been back in Russia only a fortnight, Lockhart said, he had already found that the Bolsheviks were the party most opposed to Germany; the anti-Bolshevik parties would not hesitate to enlist German help to restore order. Co-operation on the lines Trotsky suggested, Lockhart said, was the only way the Allies could remain in Russia and continue, even slightly, to influence Soviet policy. He advocated acceptance of the trade proposals. Further, for the time being, the British government should ignore Soviet repudiation of debts and confiscation of property: the Bolsheviks would not remain in power forever. Finally, in view of the failure of the Rada and Alekseyev, an agreement to cease support of the counter-revolution in exchange for the end of Soviet propaganda would clearly be to the advantage of the Allies. And he added:

I would point out futility of attempting to justify our attitude or refute Trotsky's arguments. In view of complete divergence of our respective views such a course is mere waste of time. Policy I advocate is one of expediency. Trotsky will co-operate with us so long as it suits him. Our attitude should be the same.[49]

[49] *idem.*

Rejection of this policy, Lockhart concluded, must result in the complete failure of his mission. He therefore asked that his telegram be shown to Lloyd George and Milner.[50]

Balfour's reply was a rejection couched in the language of a vague acceptance.[51] The Foreign Secretary agreed that co-operation might be possible, and that it should be based on strict expediency:

In so far as Bolsheviki are opposing or embarrassing our enemies, their cause is our cause. In so far as they endeavour to foment revolution in this or in any other Allied country we shall thwart them to the best of our ability. In so far as they are dealing with internal politics in those parts of the country where they are *de facto* rulers we have no desire to interfere.

Balfour then set forth once more a formula which, with some modifications, was to be the basis of British policy towards Russia throughout the rest of the war. On the surface it seemed attractive and reasonable and undogmatic—qualities which made it appeal to Englishmen who prided themselves on their pragmatism. In conception it was all these things, but in application it quickly became a rigid maxim filled with inconsistencies.

"Internal affairs in Russia are no concern of ours," Balfour said. "We only consider them in so far as they affect the war." If large areas of the country had accepted the particular form of socialism favoured by the Bolsheviks, that was the concern of Russia, not of Britain. But, the Foreign Secretary said, the very principles which induced the government to cooperate with the Bolsheviks also led them to support any forces in Russia which seemed likely to oppose Britain's enemies or aid Britain's friends. On these grounds, because it was necessary to grasp at even the most shadowy chance for helping the Rumanian Army, "we did our best" for the Ukrainians and for the Cossacks. Now, since the Rada had thrown in its lot with the enemy and because the Cossacks had proved worthless, there was no likelihood that Britain would do anything more on their behalf to which Trotsky would object. Although the British government did

---

[50] Lockhart's views received implied endorsement from Lindley who, a day later, cabled the Foreign Office: "It is clear to me that if we are to be of any use here or even to stay here at all we shall have to give up all support of Don movement which seems in any case to have completely collapsed" (telegram 498, 17 February 1918, 3:26 p.m.; Milner MSS, box B).

[51] Balfour to Lindley (for Lockhart), telegram 287, 21 February 1918, 5:30 p.m., Milner MSS, box B. The text of this message was also sent to Wiseman in New York as telegram CXP 529, 22 February 1918, Wiseman MSS.

not have "the slightest intention of indulging in any anti-revolutionary propaganda," they could not pledge themselves to abstain from action in other parts of Russia which might, in their opinion, help to win the war. Trotsky's proposals, Balfour continued, "would require us to abandon our friends and Allies in those parts of Russia where Bolshevism cannot be regarded as the *de facto* Government"; Britain could never do that. As we shall see, Balfour here had in mind Siberia, North Russia, and the Caucasus. The Foreign Secretary was also convinced, he told Lockhart, that the Bolsheviks would never cease their propaganda in Allied territory, for such a step would require them "to abandon all their loudly advertised principles." On these fundamental questions, he said, Britain and the Bolsheviks could never come to terms.

When Balfour set forth this policy, it was indeed a reasonable one. Those who today criticise the initial Western response to the Soviet regime as short-sighted too often forget the fact that seemed paramount to the makers of Western policy: Bolshevism was an aberration, a transient phenomenon that would soon disappear when the "better elements" of Russia reasserted themselves. Any policy which based itself on co-operation with the Bolsheviks and rejected the hand of "our friends and Allies" in other parts of Russia seemed the height of folly, certain to make an enemy of the new Russia that would rise from the ashes of war.

By the time Balfour had telegraphed to Lockhart this statement of policy, the hiatus that followed the Soviet announcement of "no war—no peace" had ended. On 18 February the Germans began a new offensive. The evening before, General Hoffmann, the German commander, had noted in his diary: "The whole of Russia is no more than a vast heap of maggots—a squalid, swarming mass."[52] Unopposed, the Germans advanced as fast as their transport could carry them. Late on the evening of the 18th the Bolsheviks telegraphed their acceptance, under protest, of the enemy's conditions. The Germans responded with a new and harsher set of terms, in the nature of an ultimatum, delivered on the 23rd. Declaring that they were protecting civilisation from Bolshevism, they continued their advance.[53]

In Petrograd the offensive brought a burst of revolutionary ardour.

[52] Quoted from Hoffmann's memoirs by Wheeler-Bennett, *Brest-Litovsk*, p. 244.
[53] *ibid.*, pp. 244-46.

For a moment even Lenin favoured renewed war.[54] By this time Lockhart was seeing Trotsky every day; the Foreign Commissar told him that if the Allies would promise definite support, he would sway the decision of the Soviet government in favour of war. Several times Lockhart sent telegrams to London asking for an official assurance that would strengthen Trotsky's hand. He received no reply.[55] The French, however, did make a rather tenuous offer of both financial and military support and the provision of officers for the reconstruction of the Russian Army, if the Bolsheviks would give them a free hand and also call on the Japanese to help by sending troops across Siberia to the front.[56] A French overture to the Americans to join in supporting the Bolsheviks was rejected in Washington as out of the question.[57] Meanwhile, according to the American Ambassador, British and French engineer officers from the Military Missions were helping the Red Guard destroy the railroad in the path of the German advance.[58]

Although the Bolshevik Central Committee, meeting on 22 February, had approved Lenin's famous resolution to accept "potatoes and arms from the bandits of Anglo-French imperialism,"[59] when the German conditions arrived on the morning of the 23rd Lenin nevertheless insisted that they be accepted. Over the threat of his resignation he argued that acceptance would be the only way to save the Revolution. The next day, the Bolsheviks formally agreed to the German terms.[60]

That evening Lindley telegraphed London: "Practical result of Russian attempt to secure 'without annexations etc.' has been greatest single annexation which has taken place in Europe since break-up of Roman Empire."[61] For the Bolsheviks, the bitterest blows in the treaty signed at Brest-Litovsk on 3 March were the requirements that they

[54] Leon Trotsky, *My Life, The Rise and Fall of a Dictator*, London, 1930, p. 332.

[55] Lockhart, *British Agent*, pp. 228-32.

[56] Général Henri Niessel, *Le triomphe des Bolchéviks et la Paix de Brest-Litovsk: Souvenirs, 1917-1918*, Paris, 1940, pp. 279-80; Jacques Sadoul, *Notes sur la Révolution Bolchevique*, Paris, 1920, pp. 241-43.

[57] Kennan, *Russia Leaves the War*, pp. 432-33.

[58] Francis to Secretary of State, telegram 2402, Petrograd, 22 February 1918; *Foreign Relations, 1918, Russia*, vol. 1, p. 383.

[59] V. I. Lenin, *Sochineniya* (Complete Works), Third Edition, vol. xxii, Moscow-Leningrad, 1929, p. 607, n. 119.

[60] Wheeler-Bennett, *Brest-Litovsk*, pp. 255-62.

[61] Lindley to Balfour, telegram 579, Petrograd, 24 February 1918, 11 p.m.; Milner MSS, box B.

recognise the separate German-Ukrainian peace already signed, and, naturally enough, that they cease all anti-German propaganda.[62]

Meanwhile, because they knew that the German advance, even if it did not actually reach Petrograd, would bring the enemy close enough to be a source of danger, the Allied Chiefs of Mission decided on 25 February to evacuate the capital.[63] The bulk of the British and French Military Missions had already left the day before, bound for Murmansk. On the 26th, the personnel of the American, Japanese, Chinese, Siamese, and Brazilian embassies set out for Vologda, a provincial town located roughly at the intersection of lines due east from Petrograd and due north from Moscow. Finally, on 28 February, the French, British, Italian, Belgian, Portuguese, Greek, Rumanian, and Serbian missions left for the Finnish frontier on a train under the charge of French Ambassador Noulens. Included in the British party were about sixty members of the Petrograd British colony.

Their journey was not a happy one. In Finland they found themselves in the midst of a civil war between Red Finns and Whites, the latter supported by the Germans. What followed is not altogether clear. Although all of the missions had agreed in advance to stay together and face any obstacles as a unit, the British party was the only one that succeeded in getting through to safety. Noulens attributed this to the fact that many of the Red Finns could speak English, having lived in America or Canada, and that Lindley could therefore negotiate with them. The British Chargé succeeded, wrote Noulens, in arranging a safe-conduct for his own people, and then did not bother to tell his Allied colleagues of his *démarche*.[64] Stranded on the Red-Finn side of the battle-lines, the other missions lived for several weeks on their train and finally, on the instructions of their governments, retraced their steps and arrived at the end of

[62] The texts of the various treaties and agreements between Russia and the Central Powers, signed at Brest-Litovsk on 3 March, are printed in entirety in *Dokumenty vneshnei politiki*, vol. I, pp. 119-204. A map of the new western border of Russia, as provided in the treaties, is inserted between p. 124 and p. 125. Translations of the principal treaty between the Central Powers and Russia, and between the Central Powers and the Ukraine, appear (without subsequent protocols and appendices) in Wheeler-Bennett, *Brest-Litovsk*, pp. 392-408.

[63] Lindley to Balfour, telegram 601, Petrograd, 25 February 1918; Milner MSS, box B.

[64] Noulens, *Mon ambassade*, vol. II, pp. 20-22. It is difficult to believe that in so cosmopolitan a party, composed of the diplomatic personnel of eight nations, no English was spoken by anyone except the British.

March in Vologda, doubtless having whiled away their aimless journey cursing *perfide Albion*.[65] They then resigned themselves to another period of cramped living aboard their train, parked on a siding in the Vologda station (there was no accommodation for them in the town). Long before, Lindley had led his party to Helsingfors and safety.[66]

Behind them, in Petrograd, the official protection of British interests had been left in the charge of the Netherlands Legation. Over the vast Embassy building—deserted now except for Consul A. W. W. Woodhouse and an assistant—flew the flag of Holland, and on the door a large framed notice informed passers-by that the Dutch had taken over. The capital's diplomatic body was reduced to the neutrals: Holland, Switzerland, the Scandinavian countries, Spain, and Persia.[67]

Lockhart decided to remain in Russia. Entirely on his own, now, he girded himself for a final effort: to convince his government that if they committed themselves to the support of the Soviet regime, Russia could still resist Germany and, by guaranteeing this support, to persuade the Bolsheviks not to ratify the treaty their representatives had signed.

✧

Meanwhile, in London, Lockhart's counterpart, Litvinov, was having his troubles. On the very day that Lockhart left for Russia, 12 January, *The Herald*, George Lansbury's left-wing anti-war weekly, published a message from the "Plenipotentiary for Great Britain of the Russian People's Government" urging the workers of Britain to join their brothers in Russia in their efforts to make peace.[68] Litvinov was also the author of a number of pamphlets containing similar appeals. They were, as the Foreign Office told the State Department in a memorandum, flagrant violations of diplomatic privilege. Yet the government would take no action against Litvinov for fear of Soviet reprisals against Britons in Russia.[69]

Thus Litvinov's activities, such as they were, were allowed to continue unabated. Appearing as one of several foreign speakers at a

[65] Francis to Secretary of State, Vologda, 29 March 1918, *Foreign Relations, 1918, Russia,* vol. 1, p. 488. See also Francis' account in his book, *Russia from the American Embassy: April, 1916—November, 1918,* New York, 1921, p. 235.
[66] *The Times,* 7 March 1918 (from a Reuter report, Helsingfors, 6 March).
[67] William J. Oudendyk, *Ways and By-Ways in Diplomacy,* London, 1939, p. 264.
[68] *The Herald,* 12 January 1918.
[69] Memorandum, British Embassy, Washington, to Department of State, 16 January 1918; *Foreign Relations, 1918, Russia,* vol. 1, pp. 722-23.

Labour Party conference on war aims at Nottingham on 23 January, he made an obscure and harmless-enough reference to the possibilities of revolution in England which the *Daily Express* castigated as "the most menacing speech ever delivered by the Ambassador of a friendly country," a statement which begged at least several questions.[70] According to a Scotland Yard report upon him (filled, incidentally, with inaccuracies about his past) Litvinov was accused of inducing British, American, and Canadian servicemen of Jewish descent to circulate revolutionary matter in their regiments. The same report said that on 6 February he had incited to mutiny the crews of two Russian patrol boats which had been lying for months in the Mersey; the mutiny occurred, and was quickly put down, on the 11th.[71]

Litvinov's presence in England gave the Blimpish element in the House of Commons opportunity for almost unlimited indignation. Asked if the Soviet emissary had used six pseudonyms in his career, the Home Secretary replied that investigation had found only four so far, and that his real name was Finkelstein (actually it was Wallach). The questioner, Brigadier H. P. Croft, then asked whether the Home Secretary, "having regard to the fact that he is evidently a rolling stone, a dangerous character—seeing that he changes his name from day to day," would see that "he is sent back to Russia at the earliest moment?"[72] Despite (or perhaps because of) a plea by Ramsay MacDonald that pseudonyms were commonplace devices for escaping the old Tsarist secret police,[73] another member (N. P. Billing was moved to state: "There are some hon. Members who seem to think that this country should be not only the dumping ground for the rubbish of the commercial world, but also the dumping ground for the refuse in humanity in general."[74]

The government, nevertheless, refused to take any action in the case. The result was a rarity in British politics—a protest in the House of Commons by a Minister against the policy of the government. On 28 February, Sir George Cave, the Home Secretary (not a member of the War Cabinet), delivered himself of a long and acrid harangue:

[70] *Daily Express*, 23 January 1918. Litvinov's speech is reported in *The Times* of the same day.

[71] Undated report by Basil Thompson (head of Scotland Yard) to Sir George Cave (Home Secretary), circulated to the War Cabinet by Cave on 20 February 1918; Milner MSS, box B.

[72] 103 HC Deb. 5s cols. 1100-1 (25 February 1918).

[73] *ibid.*, col. 1604 (28 February 1918).

[74] *ibid.*, col. 1609.

There is no doubt that through the action of the Foreign Office there has been a kind of recognition of this envoy. That is the Foreign Office side of the question. But there is also a Home Office side. Litvinoff is not an Ambassador. He is not the representative of any recognised Government. to seize some of them and destroy them. He has interviewed many British soldiers and one can only conjecture what the object of the interviews . . . If he were in that position he would not be allowed to remain here for ten minutes, having regard to what he has done. Not holding that position, he feels free to work against order and against the Government of this country. He has issued manifestoes of such a nature that we have had were. It has been difficult for anyone in my position to refrain from taking the action which would have been taken weeks ago in the case of any other alien who indulged in conduct of this kind. It is a question of degree, I suppose, and as the sum of his revolutionary activities mounts up the Home Office considerations become more and more powerful, and, of course, the end must come. . . . We are all most anxious not to embarrass the Foreign Office, but there must be a limit. I say without hesitation that this must not continue.[75]

Of course, the Home Secretary assured his listeners, "I do not believe that the speeches of the Bolshevik envoys will mislead the working men of this country. . . . The bulk of our working men are much too sensible for that."[76]

Soon after this, Lockhart was instructed to protest against Litvinov's activities and to warn Smolny that more abuses would not be tolerated.[77] And the landlord who owned the Victoria Street premises of the "People's Embassy" was sufficiently emboldened to lock his controversial tenant out, although he had just signed a three-month lease. When Litvinov sought a legal injunction against the landlord, it was refused on the grounds that he had pledged himself not to use the premises for propaganda, and that the Court would not grant equitable relief to a litigant unless he came "with clean hands."[78] Thenceforth, the "rolling stone" had to operate from his tiny North London house. He was also deprived of a convenient place for his meetings with Reginald Leeper, and the two men were thenceforth forced to transact their business in St. James' Park. When it rained,

---

[75] *ibid.*, cols. 1623-24.
[76] *ibid.*, col. 1627.
[77] Lockhart, *British Agent*, p. 240.
[78] Chancery Division, High Court of Justice (Mr. Justice Neville): Litvinoff v. Kent; Law Reports, *The Times*, 2, 5, and 9 March 1918.

they withdrew to the shelter of a kiosk (since demolished) near the spot where the Guards Memorial now stands.[79]

Shortly before Litvinov was evicted from his offices, L. B. Kamenev, another Bolshevik emissary, arrived in London. Kamenev had been selected to go to France as Plenipotentiary, a capacity similar to Litvinov's in Britain. To get to Paris, however, he had first to travel by Norwegian ship to Scotland and then cross the Channel, and he had armed himself with a transit visa from the British Embassy, as well as a diplomatic visa from the French authorities in Petrograd.[80]

Despite his diplomatic visas and the agreement, made when Lockhart and Litvinov were appointed, providing for the immunity of diplomatic couriers, Kamenev was searched on his arrival in Aberdeen and deprived of most of his possessions, including his diplomatic bag and a cheque for £5,000. (Queried by Ramsay MacDonald in the House of Commons, Lord Robert Cecil said that the cheque seemed rather large merely for Kamenev's expenses in England.)[81] He was allowed to proceed to London, however, where, upon his arrival, he was informed that the French government had decided not to permit him to land in France. Since the original purpose of his mission no longer held, the Home Office insisted that he return to Russia without delay. But before he left he was interviewed in Litvinov's office by Leeper, who received his protests about the violation of his diplomatic bag and recorded his impressions of the proceedings at Brest-Litovsk.[82]

[79] Interview with Sir Reginald Leeper.

[80] That the decision to grant Kamenev his visas was made in London and Paris, and not by the British and French authorities in Petrograd, was affirmed by the American Ambassadors in the two capitals in telegrams to the State Department on 9 February 1918; *Foreign Relations, 1918, Russia,* vol. 1, pp. 370-71.

[81] 103 HC Deb. 5s. col. 1494 (27 February 1918).

[82] Interview with Sir Reginald Leeper. Wheeler-Bennett (*Brest-Litovsk,* p. 384) claims that before Kamenev left Russia, Lenin entrusted him with a message to the Allied governments urging that they give assistance to the Bolsheviks in resisting the Germans and in refusing to sign the peace, provided that such assistance were confined to western Russia and did not include Japanese participation. Leeper doubts very much if this was so, for during his conversation with Kamenev, the Bolshevik emissary did not mention the subject.

CHAPTER IV

RATIFICATION AND THE THREAT
OF INTERVENTION

Trotsky you tell me repudiates "friendly relations" with us but desires "a working agreement." I sympathise with his point of view. But why will he not also try a working agreement with the Japanese?—*Balfour to Lockhart, 6 March 1918*

WITH the coming of March, the drama of Brest-Litovsk entered its final phase, climaxed by the ratification of the treaty by the Special Congress of Soviets on the 15th. During this time Lockhart and other Western observers entertained high hopes that the Allied governments, by offers of support, could induce the Bolsheviks not to ratify the peace and to renew the struggle against Germany. For a brief period the Bolshevik leaders did nothing to disabuse them of these hopes, although there was never any real question that ratification would not take place. Soviet conduct in those few days and, as a matter of fact, during the two months following Brest-Litovsk, was to a great extent dictated by a marked fear of Japanese invasion in the Far East and of an Anglo-French occupation of the strategic ports of North Russia. These fears were far from groundless; only by first examining the course of events on Russia's periphery can we make sense of the final crisis at Petrograd and Moscow over ratification, and in particular, of the ambiguous attitude which the British government took towards it.

✤

Before we turn to this account, however, it is necessary to make some generalisations about the manner in which Britain's Russian policy was made at this time. So far as this policy was concerned, there were two wholly separate Russias. The first consisted roughly of the centres of Bolshevik power—Petrograd and Moscow. This was the Russia that was engaged in negotiations with Germany. The problems involved in dealing with it were diplomatic and the decisions to be made were those traditionally in the sphere of the diplomat: whether or not to recognise the Bolshevik authorities, what sort of contact to maintain with them, which (if any) opposition groups to encourage. These were Foreign Office problems. Moreover, because they were not technical (in the sense that military problems were technical), they could be discussed and debated by politicians. In a real sense, the guiding hand was that of the Cabinet.

The other Russia consisted of all the outlying areas: Siberia, North Russia, the Cossack territories, the Caucasus, Transcaspia. These were all looked upon as sectors where resistance could be organised—against the Bolshevik authorities in the centre, but, more important still, against the Central Powers. These areas, too, were formally the concern of the Foreign Office. But they were also the concern of the military and naval authorities and were viewed by the latter, in too many instances, solely as military problems. For the duration of the war, at least, most of the decisions concerning these areas were made by the military agencies. These decisions were—or rather, they were represented as being—technical decisions upon which the military authorities staked their reputations as trained technicians. Through such arguments the soldiers were usually able to impose their views upon the Cabinet. But sometimes—too seldom—the Foreign Office prevailed. The tension between these two different mentalities was at least partially responsible for the confusions and shifts in British policy toward Russia.

This sort of argument is difficult to document without full access to the minutes of the Cabinet and of the various departmental and inter-departmental committees which dealt with Russia, but it is the only way one can satisfactorily explain many facets of British policy.[1] Throughout this narrative instances of tension between the Foreign Office and the military authorities will be pointed out. There are, however, two examples which can usefully be adduced at once. In a letter to Balfour (who was on a brief holiday in the country) on 8 January 1918, Lord Robert Cecil wrote: "I have had to agree to a Committee called the Russia Committee, as the only means of unifying our action with that of the War Office." This Committee was concerned, in particular, with all of the outlying areas we have men-

---

[1] Sir Reginald Leeper has informed the author that his experience in the Foreign Office during 1918 corroborates the impression presented here.

tioned above. Cecil clearly regarded the Committee with great suspicion as a piece of military usurpation in the field of foreign policy. Although it met nearly every day, he declined, at this stage, to be a member of it, did not allow any high Foreign Office officials to attend its meetings, and, as he wrote to Balfour, insisted that "no urgent decisions" were "to await its consideration."[2] Ironically, a month later, Cecil himself was to take the chair of this committee.[3]

The second example is that of a Foreign Office *ad hoc* committee, which sat in early 1918 to consider the Caucasus and to determine ways in which the peoples of that region could be induced to oppose Turkish and German aggression. The line the Foreign Office took was that each of the two nationalities they were trying to support, the Georgians and the Armenians, should be approached and handled separately, because of the acute jealousy between them, and that each should be given equal support. Meanwhile, the tendency of British military authorities on the spot was to deal with the Armenians to the neglect of the Georgians. Before long the Director of Military Intelligence started to attend the committee's meetings; at one session, when he found that by cross-examination he could not shake the evidence of two Foreign Office experts who were arguing in favour of equal treatment, he strenuously urged the committee not to allow them to give any more information. In addition, he refused thenceforth to allow the committee to have access to War Office telegrams from the Caucasus, which gave the most complete political as well as military information about the area. In the Milner Papers there is a memorandum protesting against this action in the strongest possible terms, accusing the Director of Military Intelligence, because he disagreed with the committee's policy, of "trying to suppress information necessary to allow a Foreign Office Committee to come to a correct decision."[4]

❖

With this digression we can better understand the many changes in British policy concerning Siberia during early 1918. As we shall see, it was not unusual for a position taken one day to be directly

[2] Blanche E. C. (Mrs. Edgar) Dugdale, *Arthur James Balfour, First Earl of Balfour, K.G., O.M., F.R.S.*, London, 1936, vol. ii, pp. 254-55.

[3] "Minutes of the Proceedings of a Meeting of the Russia Committee held at the Foreign Office on the 9th February, 1918," Milner mss, box D-1 (this is the only meeting for which the Milner Papers contain the minutes).

[4] The memorandum, marked "Confidential" and dated 18 January 1918, was obviously written by a member of the committee. The signature, however, is totally illegible. Milner mss, box G-1.

reversed the next. There were two senses in which Siberia came to be discussed by Allied statesmen in the months following the Bolshevik Revolution. The first was as a channel of access through which the Allied Powers could make contact with and send supplies to the loyal forces in South Russia. Such a policy was recommended by the Military Representatives of the Supreme War Council in their policy note of late December 1917.[5] Second—and much more important— Siberia was envisioned as a conduit through which might pass the troops of the one major military power which had thus far scarcely committed its strength to the war: Japan.

Although Japan—Britain's ally since 1902—had been at war with Germany since late August 1914 and had adhered to the Declaration of London (in which the five major Allies had pledged themselves not to make a separate peace), her participation in the war had been limited by geography and national interest to seizing the Shantung Peninsula and Germany's other Pacific possessions, providing some naval support in the Indian Ocean and Mediterranean, and furnishing munitions and other implements of war, mostly to Russia. Japan's Russian policy was governed by the fear that if Russia collapsed and made a separate peace, a vengeful Germany would emerge as a power in the Far East. As Kennan aptly puts it: "To this danger, the Japanese responded, in the peculiarly dialectical fashion of the East, by a combination of military aid to Russia (for a serious price) and veiled threats of a military occupation of Russian territory in the Far East in case a German-Russian peace should become a reality."[6] For Japan, the best possible conclusion of the war would have seen Russia intact but so weakened as no longer to furnish a serious obstacle to the extension of Japanese interests in Manchuria.

The parochialism of the war in France had dulled Allied sensitivity to events in the Far East. When the Western Allies found that Russia could not answer their call for more pressure on Germany, London and Paris conjured up the mirage of a new Eastern Front manned by the Japanese. Viewed in any way but through the myopia of a wasteful war, the idea that a large army could have been transported, by poor and inefficient railroads, over the 7,000 miles from the Pacific to the Carpathians, would have been dismissed as madness. Yet, spurred by Russia's collapse, negotiations for just such an expedition took

[5] See above, Chapter II.
[6] Kennan, *Russia Leaves the War*, p. 276.

place in London and Paris in the early months of 1917. Balfour, at this time, had pressed Russia and Japan to enter into concrete negotiations, but the Japanese military attaché in London made it clear that Japan's price for sending troops out of Eastern Asia would be high, including the transfer to Japan of part of the Russian-owned Chinese Eastern Railway and the demilitarisation of Vladivostok. Balfour agreed with Nabokov, the Russian Chargé, that the price was too high.[7]

The plan was shelved but not forgotten. During the summer of 1917, the French, in particular, made repeated overtures for a Japanese expedition. In Japan, the Army resolved that the country would not be lured into a European war; such an involvement would divert energies and resources from Japan's major goal: the establishment of political and economic supremacy in China. They must use the war, the Army said, so to strengthen Japan's position in China that they could withstand Western competition after the war.[8]

The Allies knew something of Japan's reluctance to enter the European conflict,[9] and at the Paris discussions at the beginning of December, when Foch put forth a plan for using Japanese troops, it was not to involve them on an Eastern Front. Instead, Foch wanted Japanese and American forces to take possession of the Trans-Siberian Railway all the way from Vladivostok to European Russia, so that supplies could be shipped along it for the Rumanian Army, which would serve as a nucleus around which loyal Russian forces could gather. Foch envisioned simply a "security measure" to be accomplished by "police detachments."[10] On the instructions of their government, the Japanese representatives at the Paris meetings rejected Foch's proposal.[11]

At this time, however, the situation within Russia was growing increasingly chaotic, and the Allies began to look to Japan for action

[7] J. W. Morley, *The Japanese Thrust into Siberia, 1918*, New York, 1957, p. 29. Morley had access to the archives of the Japanese government in making his exceptionally thorough study.

[8] *ibid.*, p. 30.

[9] Colonel House, in Paris, noted in his diary on 30 November: "We discussed a more active participation in the war by the Japanese, but finally came to the conclusion that we would let Pichon see what he could do with them, without any of us believing he would be successful. It is hard for the Japanese to do anything, but they seem unwilling to do even the things they are able to do, such as sending two of their fast cruisers to join the British fleet, as they have been asked." (House diary, House MSS.)

[10] A copy, from the Japanese Archives, of Foch's memorandum, dated 4 December 1917, is printed as an appendix to Morley, *Japanese Thrust*, pp. 324-28.

[11] *ibid.*, p. 33.

much more limited in scope (and much more to the liking of the Japanese military clique) than an expedition to Europe: the protection of Allied interests in the Russian Far East, particularly the vast stores of war supplies in Vladivostok.

Throughout the war, the only means of sending supplies and equipment to the Russian armies had been through the ports on Russia's extremities—Murmansk and Archangel in the north, and Vladivostok in the east. Of the northern ports we shall hear more later. Vladivostok, the Pacific terminal of the Trans-Siberian and Chinese-Eastern Railways, had become a dumping ground for hundreds of thousands of tons of stranded goods. In a fashion perhaps typical of the ramshackle Tsarist regime, the Russians had asked their Allies for more supplies than the weak and poorly operated railways to the west could possibly handle, and from the spring of 1916 goods poured into Vladivostok in such quantities (some from Britain, but most, for geographical reasons, from America) that by the end of 1917, 648,000 tons of railway materials, shells and munitions, chemicals, metals, food, and the like were awaiting removal.[12] Long before this, all warehouse space had been filled, and these materials were piled, often rotting, in vacant lots throughout the city and in the fields and hill-sides which rimmed the Bay of the Golden Horn.[13]

Vladivostok was a garrison town, and by the end of 1917 Bolshevism had spread to the many soldiers and sailors of the port. Understandably, the Allied governments feared for the safety of the war stores and of their nationals. They were also afraid that the Bolsheviks might try to control the rail communications with the west. The situation was further complicated by the presence in Siberia, in camps located along the Trans-Siberian Railway, of large concentrations of enemy prisoners of war. The Allies feared (as we shall see, with little reason) that the Bolsheviks would re-arm these prisoners and use them to ship the war stores at Vladivostok to the Central Powers. In the midst of the chaos of Siberia, such an effort was scarcely possible; it would have taken years to ship the stores west. Even more improbable was the fear, first expressed early in January and reiterated again

---

[12] This figure was put forward in a telegram (CXP 73) from Lord Robert Cecil to the British Embassy in Washington, 1 January 1918; Wiseman MSS.

[13] Kennan, *Russia Leaves the War*, pp. 284-85. See also Gen. W. S. Graves, *America's Siberian Adventure, 1918-1920*, New York, 1931, p. 80.

and again in succeeding months, that the Germans would dismantle submarines in the Baltic, ship the parts all the way across Russia and Siberia by railroad, and then assemble them again at Vladivostok to menace shipping in the Sea of Japan.[14]

There were very serious arguments against any Allied intervention in Siberian affairs, even for so limited an aim as the preservation of order in one city. Principal among them was the fact that Japanese participation would be necessary in any sort of operation. The Russian population of Siberia had a fear of Japan that is reported to have taken on the quality of a general obsession as the war progressed and as Russia's position grew noticeably weaker.[15] In London, and particularly in Washington, it was thought that a Japanese invasion would drive Russia to seek assistance from the only power that could give it: Germany. This would open Russia for German exploitation, and would irrevocably widen the breach between Russia and her former allies.

Still, of all the Allies, Japan, with the most extensive commercial interests in Vladivostok, and with the additional worry that Bolshevik control of the great naval base would threaten her security in the Sea of Japan, had the most urgent reasons for intervention. Early in November the Japanese prepared to send ships to Vladivostok, but were restrained from doing so by the British Ambassador's statement that his government hoped that Japan would act only in concert with her Allies.[16] A month later, on 10 December, when Balfour suggested to Viscount Chinda, the Japanese Ambassador in London, that a purely American force be sent to Vladivostok to guard the stores (America, Balfour said, was "generally recognised" as having "no territorial ambitions"), Chinda answered that Japan could not accept such a plan. If the Allies were to send an expedition to Vladivostok, then, "in view of its position and natural right as well as its duty, Japan should conduct it."[17]

This attitude gave rise to a flurry of informal proposals, initiated by the British government, in London, Washington, and Tokyo.

[14] Genuine or simulated, this apprehension was voiced by the Japanese military authorities and reported by Sir C. Greene in telegram 13, 7 January 1918, 7:50 p.m. (Milner MSS, box E-1), to London, where it was soon adopted by the British military authorities as their own (see Memorandum of the Third Assistant Secretary of State, 10 January 1918, *Foreign Relations, 1918, Russia*, vol. II, p. 23).

[15] Kennan, *Russia Leaves the War*, p. 280.

[16] Morley, *Japanese Thrust*, p. 39.

[17] *ibid.*, p. 40. Morley cites the Japanese Archives for both of these references.

On 14 December, the British Ambassador in Tokyo, Sir Conyngham Greene, approached the Japanese Foreign Minister and discussed possible steps that might be taken to protect the stores and, in case of emergency, to control the Trans-Siberian Railway.[18] In Washington, when Sir Cecil Spring-Rice presented Secretary of State Lansing with a proposal for a joint U.S.-Japanese expedition to Vladivostok, Lansing replied that he was fully aware of the great danger of letting the Bolsheviks get control of Eastern Siberia and the stores, but that he feared the effect of any Japanese action. The State Department's attitude, Spring-Rice reported, was that since the United States occupied a special position in the minds of the Russian masses, this fund of good-will should be cherished. It was also probable, the Ambassador surmised, that the administration felt that an expedition to the Far East would be very unpopular domestically.[19]

On 26 December Balfour had another interview with the Japanese Ambassador. More from his manner than from anything that the Ambassador said, the Foreign Secretary got the impression that the Japanese were planning to land a force at Vladivostok. Balfour again told Chinda that independent action on the part of the Japanese would be most unfortunate, and urged upon him the necessity of consultation with the United States before any action was taken.[20] Although Balfour could not have known it, his fears were not justified. The next day, in a long and heated meeting of Japan's Advisory Council on Foreign Relations, it was decided that Japan should not intervene in Siberia, although the interventionist policy had the support of the Army, the Navy, and the Minister for Foreign Affairs. But the decision produced a grave split in the Japanese government.[21]

The attitude which then prevailed in London that something need be done about Siberia was intensified by another more-or-less false alarm. On 28 December the Foreign Office received from its Consul in the Manchurian city of Harbin the following disquieting telegram:

Irkutsk [a large town on the Trans-Siberian Railway west of Lake Baikal] has been under fire for seven days and is being bombarded by Bol-

---

[18] Reported by the U.S. Ambassador, Morris, in a summary despatch written 22 March 1918; *Foreign Relations, 1918, Russia*, vol. II, p. 84.

[19] Spring-Rice to Balfour, telegram 3991, Washington, 22 December 1917, Milner MSS, box E-1.

[20] Reported by Balfour to Spring-Rice, by Spring-Rice to U.S. Assistant Secretary of State William Phillips, and by Phillips to Lansing in a memorandum, 28 December 1917. U.S. National Archives, State Department file 861.00/912.

[21] Morley, *Japanese Thrust*, pp. 53-59 (again from Japanese Archives).

sheviks. French and British are being exterminated and their property destroyed. Help implored.[22]

This telegram was sent on the 26th. On the following two days, the Harbin Consul's sources at Irkutsk furnished him with further information—the Bolsheviks were murdering and plundering inhabitants and ravishing women, corpses of murdered children covered the streets, the French consular agent and two French officers had been murdered—and he duly forwarded the news on to London.[23]

These reports, it later developed, were hopelessly inaccurate. In the course of the quite severe fighting in Irkutsk, during which the local Soviet tried and failed to seize power from the moderate town administration (which was backed by Cossacks and military cadets), several western residents might have been accidentally wounded, but none were killed.[24]

The British War Cabinet, however, could not know this when it met on 1 January to consider the problem of the Vladivostok stores. Cecil, who was Acting Foreign Secretary, said he thought there were only two alternatives: either leave the stores alone or send in a really strong Japanese force. The C.I.G.S., General Sir William Robertson, thought that a force should be sent. He hoped it would not be wholly Japanese—the Russians would certainly object—but that (since the United States had already refused to take action) a few British troops should be sent to show the flag and convince the Russians that no sinister purpose lay behind the action. Robertson suggested sending two British infantry companies from Hong Kong.

The minutes of this meeting give no other individual views, but merely state that the War Cabinet were of the opinion that

. . . it was of the first importance that some action should be taken immediately, and that the plan open to least objection was to allow the Japanese to occupy Vladivostok. This, of course, raised a very large question of policy, involving the possible exploitation of Eastern Siberia by the Japanese, and probable resentment by the Russians.[25]

[22] Report from Henry E. Sly, Harbin, 26 December 1917, transmitted by Sir John Jordan, Minister in Peking, in his telegram 626, 27 December, 3:15 p.m.; Milner MSS, box E-1.

[23] Reported by U.S. Consul, Harbin, 29 December 1917, through U.S. Consul, Vladivostok; *Foreign Relations, 1918, Russia*, vol. II, p. 16.

[24] Kennan, *Russia Leaves the War*, pp. 308-9 (from State Department archives).

[25] War Cabinet paper 309A, "Draft Minutes of a Meeting at No. 10 Downing Street," 1 January 1918, 11:30 a.m.; Milner MSS, box AB-3.

The dangers, in other words, were all explicitly recognised. Several immediate actions were then decided upon: the cruiser *H.M.S. Suffolk* was to sail from Hong Kong to Vladivostok at once; two infantry companies at Hong Kong were to be held ready for departure; Cecil was to inform the Japanese Ambassador that Britain proposed joint action at Vladivostok to protect the stores, and he was also to telegraph Colonel House, explaining the situation and asking for American co-operation.[26]

Cecil saw the Japanese Ambassador on the afternoon of the same day. Chinda, in view of his government's decision not to intervene, did not receive the British proposal very favourably, and expressed the hope that everything would be done by peaceful means so as to avoid intervention. Cecil naturally agreed that it would be best if they could avoid taking action, but told Chinda that the War Cabinet felt that the stores were in too great a danger.

When Chinda's report of this interview reached Tokyo, it roused a reaction quite different from the calm with which the Ambassador had received Cecil's proposal. In ordering the *Suffolk* to Vladivostok, the British government was seen to be doing exactly what it had objected to Japan's doing: taking independent action. The Japanese government was not prepared to see Britain established in the Sea of Japan. Immediately, two warships, the *Iwami* and the *Asahi*, with a company of marines on board, were despatched to Vladivostok. The *Iwami* arrived on the morning of 12 January, two days before the *Suffolk*.[27]

On the evening of 11 January, as if to emphasise the tenuous nature of the link that often joins a general policy to a specific situation, the British Consul at Vladivostok, Robert MacLeod Hodgson, cabled that all was quiet in the town. Russian moderates, he said, were trying to eliminate Bolshevik influence by gradually demobilising the local garrison. In these circumstances, Hodgson said, the arrival of foreign warships—giving a pretext for the postponement of demobilisation—would be most inopportune.[28] He had not been informed what the morning would bring.

[26] *idem.* The Cabinet decision, as well as the afternoon's interview with the Japanese Ambassador, are described in Cecil's telegrams sent the same day to the British Ambassadors in Washington and Tokyo: CXP 73 to Washington (Wiseman MSS), and No. 4 to Tokyo (Milner MSS, box E-1). The former is printed in Kennan, *Russia Leaves the War*, pp. 316-17.

[27] Morley, *Japanese Thrust*, pp. 62-63.

[28] Hodgson's report was relayed to London by Sir C. Greene in Tokyo, telegram 27, 12 January 1918, 1:20 p.m.; Milner MSS, box E-1.

Thus, by 18 January, when the slower *Asahi* lumbered into port, there was a considerable display of foreign strength in Russia's Far Eastern gateway. For the moment, the warships lay peacefully at anchor, their companies of marines whiling away the time on shipboard. But when power is at hand, it presents a great temptation; as we shall see, it was not long before both the Japanese and the British authorities on the spot found the situation so dangerous that they had to use their forces, and thus added a further complexity to the confused relations that existed between the Allies and the Bolsheviks.

❖

Meanwhile, on 7 January, the French government made the first formal proposal for Allied intervention in Siberia. In view of the horrors which they assumed had been perpetrated against their nationals at Irkutsk, they proposed that a military expedition composed of French, British, American, Japanese, and Chinese contingents should proceed from Manchuria to cut the Trans-Siberian Railway between Vladivostok and the west. The expedition's object would be to prevent westward shipment of the war stores and to exact retribution for the "assassination" of the French consular officer at Irkutsk.[29] The impact of this proposal in London must have been somewhat weakened by the prior arrival, from the British Minister in Peking, of assurances that this gentleman was enjoying perfect health.[30]

From Tokyo the French overture drew a clear statement that the Japanese should be allowed to meet any emergency that might arise by themselves, without the co-operation (or interference) of the other governments.[31] The Japanese took pains to emphasise their position to the British and the Americans as well: if conditions should thereafter make necessary the occupation of Vladivostok and the various railways, ran their communication, this task should be left to Japan alone as evidence of Allied trust in her good faith.[32]

The American government, on the other hand, flatly rejected the

[29] Lord Bertie (British Ambassador in Paris) to Balfour, telegram 39, 7 January 1918, 9:40 p.m.; Milner MSS, box E-1. The appeal to the Americans, which does not refer to retribution for the "murdered" consul, dated 8 January, is in *Foreign Relations, 1918, Russia*, vol. II, pp. 20-21.

[30] Sir J. Jordan to Balfour, telegram 10, Peking, 4 January 1918, 8:45 p.m.; Milner MSS, box E-1.

[31] Sharp (U.S. Ambassador in Paris) to Secretary of State, telegram 3086, 23 January 1918; *Foreign Relations, 1918, Russia*, vol. II, p. 32.

[32] Morris (U.S. Ambassador in Tokyo) to Secretary of State, 17 January 1918; *ibid.*, p. 30.

French proposal. Their own reports indicated that the situation at Irkutsk was calm; an Allied military expedition, they said, would be likely only to drive the people of Siberia into opposing the Allies.[33] The exact terms of London's reply are not known, but Balfour informed the American Ambassador on 24 January that, for the moment, he agreed with the State Department's position, adding, however, that events could at any time produce a different situation.[34] Pichon, the French Foreign Minister, described the British reply as "rather evasive and not at all encouraging."[35]

Only four days after Balfour had told the American Ambassador that he agreed with the State Department that intervention in Siberia would only arouse opposition and result in a reaction favourable to Germany, the British Chargé d'Affaires in Washington handed the State Department a note urging that Japan, as mandatory for the Allies, be asked to occupy the entire Trans-Siberian Railway.[36] This was a complete reversal of British policy. The reason given for the proposal was the familiar one that the railway was the "one remaining line of communication" to the pro-Ally organisations in South Russia. Only a few weeks before, said the British memorandum,

. . . there appeared to be no political or military forces in Russia, outside the area ruled by the Bolsheviki, which could or would do anything to aid the cause for which the Allies are fighting. The whole country represented a spectacle of unredeemed chaos.

But this situation had changed. Now,

. . . local organisations appear to have sprung up in south and southeast Russia which, with encouragement and assistance, might do something to prevent Russia from falling immediately and completely under the control of Germany.

These were "the various Cossack organisations" north of the Caucasus and the Armenians to the south. The British General Staff, continued the note, were "strongly of opinion" that the railway ought to be used to bring support to them. Although at first sight the enormous

[33] Secretary of State to French Ambassador, 16 January 1918; *ibid.*, pp. 28-29.
[34] Page to Secretary of State, telegram 8388, London, 24 January 1918; *ibid.*, p. 33.
[35] Paris telegram 3086, cited above, footnote 31.
[36] Memorandum 112, British Embassy to Department of State, 28 January 1918; *Foreign Relations, 1918, Russia*, vol. II, pp. 35-36.

length of the line to be guarded (some 5,000 miles) might seem to prohibit the scheme, "the professional advisers of His Majesty's Government" took "a different view."

The basis for this shift in policy was the contention that the situation in South Russia had so improved that it was worth running the risks involved in Japanese intervention in order to supply the loyal southern forces. Was this contention justified? British reports from South Russia scarcely justify so encouraging a view. In a series of telegrams despatched in January and early February, General de Candolle, the British liaison officer sent to the Don from Jassy, reported that recruiting measures had largely failed, that desertion was rife, particularly in Caucasus units, that only passive resistance could be expected from the region, and that, in his opinion, the Cossack movement would ultimately fail. "People abroad," he said, "cannot be expected to form any idea of the universal chaos prevailing in Russia." Bolshevism was the only active political movement, and it permeated everything.[37]

Yet, despite these dismal conclusions, de Candolle ended nearly every one of his reports with the hope that massive Allied support might still avert total disaster. Such support, he said, could come only through Siberia. This wishful grasping at straws, then, was distilled into the forceful language of the appeal to the State Department; it was also responsible for the "conviction" which the American Ambassador found increasingly prevalent in London in late January that the Bolshevik regime would soon collapse and South Russia emerge as the "real" Russia.[38] And it was present in a note on the South Russian situation written earlier in the month by Lord Hardinge, the permanent under-secretary at the Foreign Office:

The elements we have to deal with are unsatisfactory and the position not quite but almost hopelessly impossible. But we must continue to do all we can whatever the cost and however great the difficulties. . . .[39]

[37] De Candolle to C.I.G.S., Rostov, 6, 22 and 28 January and 9 February 1918 (telegrams 17, 22, 24 and 27); Milner MSS, box D-2.

Kennan, citing American reports from South Russia at this time, takes an equally discouraging view; *Russia Leaves the War*, pp. 460-61.

[38] Reported in the telegram of 24 January, cited above, footnote 34.

[39] Minute by Lord Hardinge, 5 January 1918, on memorandum of 4 January cited above, Chapter II, footnote 44.

This attitude that something had to be done, whatever the cost, led the British government, in their note of 28 January to the State Department, to urge Japanese intervention.[40]

The British government were aware, this note continued, that objections could be raised on the grounds that occupation of the railway by the Japanese alone might drive the Russian people further towards Germany. This contention was rejected; instead, the note maintained:

All the information . . . which His Majesty's Government have been able to collect, appears to indicate that the Russians would welcome some form of foreign intervention in their affairs, and that it would be more welcome in the shape of the Japanese, engaged as mandatories of the Allies with no thought of annexation or future control, than in the shape of the Germans who would make Russia orderly only by making it German.[41]

Just two days later, however, in a private telegram to Colonel House, Balfour cut the ground from under this argument by admitting that it was quite possible that once the Japanese had occupied, say, the Maritime Provinces of Siberia, they would not leave. Indeed, the Foreign Secretary thought it most probable that Japan would take this action anyway on her own initiative whatever the wishes of the Allies. In any case—and here was a most curious argument—

As regards danger of Japanese aggrandisement the very fact that the Japanese will be forced into the open against the Germans, and their active interests brought into open conflict, should do much to lessen Japanese pressure in other directions.[42]

Here was another wildly exaggerated estimate of German ambitions and capabilities. There was no greater possibility of "open conflict" between the Japanese and the Germans than there was that Germany would ship dismantled submarines from the Baltic to Vladivostok. Germany was seeking a separate peace with the Bolsheviks to free valuable troops for the Western Front and to secure the

[40] Kennan (*Russia Leaves the War*, p. 461), who did not have access to British sources, speculates that the shift in British policy which resulted in this note was due simply to the cold calculation that Japan would act anyway. As we shall see, there was some truth in this, but to the present author the sheer desperation of the British government seems to have been the more persuasive factor.

[41] Memorandum 112 to State Department, cited above, footnote 36.

[42] Balfour to House, in telegram CXP 506 from Drummond to Wiseman, 30 January 1918; Wiseman mss (also House mss, drawer 2, no. 10).

grain and other resources of the Ukraine and the oil of the Caucasus. With her great concentration on the war in the west, there was scarcely any likelihood that she would make the enormous diversion of effort that would have been necessary to carry her forces into Siberia. Nor was there any likelihood that Japanese forces would penetrate into Europe; the Japanese, it will be remembered, wanted to establish themselves in Manchuria, possibly in the Siberian Far East, and did not contemplate more extensive operations.

The terms of Balfour's argument were almost exactly duplicated, although at greater length and in more vigorous language, in a General Staff paper to the French Ministry of War, written by Brigadier-General Edward Spears, the liaison officer between the British and French General Staffs, who had previously served for three years in Japan.[43] The time had come, he said, for "masculine and decided action" such as Japanese occupation of the railway from Vladivostok to the Urals. The Americans and "the more timorous among ourselves" who fear Japanese aggrandisement, Spears wrote, should realise that the Japanese "can, and will, seize Vladivostok and the Maritime Provinces when they like." Although German domination of Russia and Siberia would be a danger, the memorandum continued, "German-Japanese domination of the world" would be a greater one. Such an unpleasant possibility "could probably be avoided by bringing the Japanese out into the open. . . ." The Russians, Spears said, were crying for Japanese intervention. This he had been told by a Japanese officer just back from Petrograd. Finally, Spears' "close study of the Japanese character and history" had convinced him that if the Allies' own problems were "manfully and resolutely faced," no great danger was likely to come from Japan. The Japanese, he said, were "not psychologically constituted to dominate and administer alien populations or subject races," and Britain could contemplate their commercial rivalry with equanimity. This paper, although presented to the French on 15 February, was surely drafted some time earlier, and in any case it represented the considered opinion of the General Staff. The coincidence of its arguments with those used by Balfour with the Americans is so great that one cannot escape the conclusion that in this case it was the military view which lay at the root of policy. ✧

---

[43] A copy of Spears' paper, dated 14 February 1918, is in the Woodrow Wilson MSS, series II, box 135.

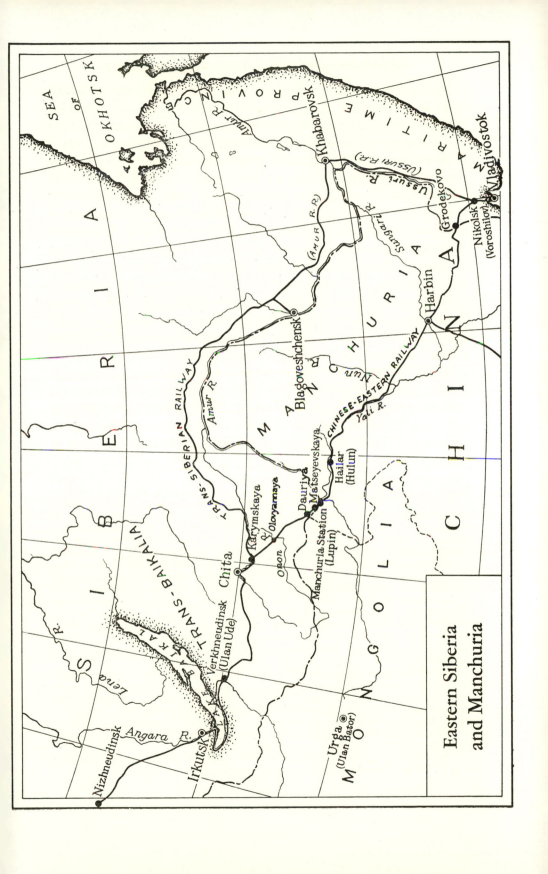

SEA OF OKHOTSK

AMUR PROVINCE

MARITIME PROVINCE

Khabarovsk

Vladivostok

Nikolsk (Voroshilov)

Grodekovo

Ussuri R.

Ussuri R.R.

(Amur R.R.)

Amur R.

Harbin

MANCHURIA

Sungari R.

Blagoveshchensk

CHINESE-EASTERN RAILWAY

Nun R.

Yali R.

TRANS-SIBERIAN RAILWAY

Amur R.

SIBERIA

Karymskaya

Olovyannaya

Dauriya

Matseyevskaya

Hailar (Hulun)

Manchuria Station (Lupin)

Onon R.

Chita

TRANS-BAIKALIA

LAKE BAIKAL

Verkhneudinsk (Ulan Ude)

CHINA

MONGOLIA

Urga (Ulan Bator)

Nizhneudinsk

Angara R.

Irkutsk

Lena R.

Eastern Siberia and Manchuria

Meanwhile, another solution, seemingly less dangerous, presented itself in the form of a 27-year-old Trans-Baikal Cossack, Gregorii Semenov, who had established himself at the head of some 750 men in the northern part of the Zone of the Chinese-Eastern Railway.[44] Semenov was one of the most extraordinary figures to emerge from the chaos of revolutionary Russia. Part Mongol himself, he had been sent in August 1917, after commanding a company of Cossacks on the Persian front, to southern Trans-Baikalia in order to raise a volunteer detachment of Buriat Mongols for service in Russia. An autocrat whose ambition was matched only by his ruthlessness, and something of a mystical dreamer, Semenov was determined, after the November Revolution, to drive the Bolsheviks out of Trans-Baikalia and to secure power in the region for himself.[45] Throughout December and January, from a headquarters in the railway zone just inside the Manchurian border, he circulated agents through the Cossack border villages seeking recruits and weapons.

At this point Semenov came to the notice of the British, who saw in him a Russian source of anti-Bolshevik activity in Siberia, and thus an opportunity to secure many of the objectives for which they had urged Japanese intervention while at the same time avoiding the obvious drawbacks of an alien occupation. In late January one of

[44] Running the direct route through Chinese territory from Vladivostok to Chita, the Chinese-Eastern Railway (and the strip of land through which the tracks ran—known as the railway zone) had been, before the Revolution, in large measure a protectorate of the Russian government. The Railway Company itself had been a virtual colonial administration whose head wielded an immense amount of power. In 1917 this post was occupied by General Dmitri L. Horvat, who, from his headquarters at Harbin, also commanded Russian forces in northern Manchuria. By December 1917, however, his authority had been so undermined by the spread of Bolshevism among his troops that he was forced to give the Harbin Soviet an equal share in the administration of the railway zone. This capitulation brought a quick response from the Chinese government: on Christmas day, at the request of the Allied ministers in Peking and with the support of the Japanese (who exerted great influence over the government of northern China), they sent in troops, drove the Bolsheviks out, and re-established Horvat's nominal authority. (See Peter S. H. Tang, *Russian and Soviet Policy in Manchuria and Outer Mongolia, 1911-1931*, Durham, North Carolina, 1959, pp. 35-117; see also Morley, *Japanese Thrust*, pp. 40-42, 45-48 and Kennan, *Russia Leaves the War*, pp. 303-6.)

It is interesting to note that at this stage the British, who were then trying to reach some sort of *modus vivendi* with the Bolsheviks in Petrograd, were much concerned about the possible effect upon the Bolsheviks of what they termed "such drastic action" by the Chinese, and they asked the U.S. government to join them in urging that the Chinese temper their blows. The State Department refused. See the exchange of memoranda, 28 and 29 December 1917, *Foreign Relations, 1918, Russia*, vol. II, pp. 14-16.

[45] Semenov's background is well covered in Morley, *Japanese Thrust*, pp. 42-45, and in J. A. White, *The Siberian Intervention*, Princeton, 1950, pp. 195-99.

Semenov's officers arrived in Peking to present his chief's plans and a plea for support to British (and presumably other Allied) representatives. Semenov's first goal, this officer said, was to occupy Karymskaya, the junction of the Chinese-Eastern and the Trans-Siberian railways, so as to control traffic and to prevent the entry into the Amur and Maritime territories of Bolshevik forces and supplies. From this position he would take Chita and then Verkhneudinsk, thus effectively securing the Trans-Baikal province against Bolshevism. Once this goal was accomplished and his forces strengthened, Semenov proposed to place himself under the orders of some well-known Russian military figure and take his whole force west to capture Irkutsk and Krasnoyarsk, with the eventual aim of joining Kaledin in the south.[46]

Semenov's forces, so his representative told Major D. S. Robertson, the British Military Attaché, then numbered only 750 men, including 300 Mongolians at Hailar in the railway zone, the remainder being officers, cadets, and Cossacks. They were armed only with rifles. From the Allies they asked for guns, shells, machine-guns, and even a couple of armoured cars; with this equipment they were confident of overcoming the more numerous but less organised Bolshevik forces—principally armed railway workers, but also some prisoners of war. Semenov also asked for funds to pay new Cossack recruits. He was, his representative said, strongly opposed to the use of foreign troops, especially Japanese, for they would further alienate the Cossack population, only half of which Semenov could claim as his sympathisers.

Robertson reported that he considered Semenov's plan "practical" and "almost entirely military in scope," attributes sure to appeal to the War Office. His assistant, moreover, had recently met Semenov, and was "most favourably impressed" by his soldierly qualities. With Allied support, said Robertson, Semenov's chances of success were good.[47]

These proposals found immediate favour in London. On 2 February (just five days after the memorandum to the State Department advocating Japanese occupation of the Trans-Siberian Railway) Balfour telegraphed privately to House to inform him that an official telegram would soon be sent to the State Department suggesting

---

[46] Robertson to Director Military Intelligence, transmitted in Sir J. Jordan's telegram 73, Peking, 28 January 1918, 8:35 p.m.; Milner MSS, box E-1.
[47] *idem.*

that "the precipitous question" of inviting the Japanese to occupy the Trans-Siberian Railway should be deferred until they knew how Semenov fared. In addition, Balfour said, he hoped to arrange for money, arms, and ammunition to be supplied to Semenov; while Britain would furnish money, arms would have to come from Japan, the only source available.[48]

When the promised official telegram was sent, only four days later, British policy on this "precipitous question" was reversed once again. After summarising much of the above information on Semenov's plans and including details of some additional successes (e.g. on 30 January he had occupied Olovyannaya, half-way between Chita and the Manchurian border), the memorandum to the State Department said that for a force of 3,000 men, Semenov would require £10,000 of assistance per month. The Consul at Harbin had therefore been instructed to inform Semenov that Britain intended to support him with money, and such arms and munitions as might be available. The memorandum asked the United States to join in this assistance, for the British government felt that it was "of the greatest importance to support any purely Russian movement in Siberia" whose leaders were ready, as Semenov appeared to be, "to act with energy." Yet— and here was the change in policy—

It should be added that, while Captain Semenov has hitherto been successful, it is of course not certain that his success will necessarily continue. The British Government would suggest therefore that his movement should not be allowed to defer urgent consideration of the scheme already suggested under which Japanese occupation of the Trans-Siberian Railway would be sought.[49]

This return to the original policy of Japanese intervention was hardly explained by another private telegram from Balfour to House, two days later, attributing the shift to the fact that the situation had changed since his first telegram. It seemed, Balfour said, that Semenov at his most successful could occupy only a small part of the Trans-Siberian Railway; in any case, if "the German peril" seemed immi-

[48] Balfour to House, through Wiseman, telegram CXP 513, 2 February 1918, Wiseman mss; also House mss, drawer 2, folder 10 and a copy in U.S. National Archives, State Department file 861.00/1049½.

[49] Colville Barclay (British Chargé d'Affaires) to Secretary of State, 6 February 1918; *Foreign Relations, 1918, Russia,* vol. ii, pp. 38-41.

nent or if the Vladivostok stores seemed threatened, Japan would take independent action at once.[50]

These observations did not mean that the situation had changed. There had scarcely been time to see how Semenov would fare; besides, in the intervening week he had met only with success. Here again one can only speculate as to the reasons for shifts in policy, and again military pressure seems the most satisfactory explanation. Balfour later told House that he himself had been opposed to Japanese intervention until after the Bolsheviks had accepted the German peace terms (on 24 February).[51] The Foreign Secretary was the kind of man who found it congenial to defer action until he knew how Semenov fared. But there were others in London—particularly the General Staff—who were not so patient.

The American response to all of these overtures for Japanese intervention was simply a firm refusal. The basic American position was put concisely by Colonel House in a note to the President after receiving the first British memorandum: Japanese intervention could produce no military advantage that would offset its harm. Leaving aside the ill-feeling it would create among the Bolshevik leaders, "it would arouse the Slavs throughout Europe because of the race question."[52] This attitude was embodied in a note to the British government on 8 February. Information at the disposal of the American government, the note said, did not lead it to share the British opinion that the Russians would welcome any sort of foreign intervention—on the contrary, intervention at the present time would be most inopportune. The State Department had not yet given up hope that a change for the better would be possible without intervention; however, if in the future any military expedition to Siberia or occupation of the Trans-Siberian Railway became necessary, it should be undertaken by international co-operation and not by one power acting as the mandatory of the others. Semenov was not even mentioned in the American note.[53]

Thus far, the Japanese had taken no position, but on this same

[50] Balfour to House, through Wiseman, telegram CXP 519, 8 February 1918; Wiseman MSS, also House MSS, drawer 2, folder 10.

[51] Telegram, Balfour to House, 6 March 1918; Seymour, *Intimate Papers*, vol. III, pp. 409-10.

[52] House to Wilson, 2 February 1918; Kennan, *Russia Leaves the War*, p. 463.

[53] Memorandum, State Department to British Embassy, 8 February 1918; *Foreign Relations, 1918, Russia*, vol. II, pp. 41-42.

day—8 February—the Foreign Minister, Viscount Motono, summoned separately the British and American Ambassadors and informed them of his "personal" opinion that the time had come for the Allies to agree upon action to prevent the spread of German influence in Siberia. Control of the railways up to Karymskaya would, he thought, keep German influence out of the Far East—an indirect indication that Japan was thinking in terms of action only in this eastern area, not of occupying the whole railroad. Finally, Motono pointed out that America, who was not a signatory of the 1914 agreement not to make a separate peace, could not be expected to take the same attitude as did the rest of the Allies regarding Russia's exit from the war.[54] This was, perhaps, the most delicate of hints that if Britain and France approved, Japan would proceed with intervention regardless of America's attitude.

Whether or not it was a hint it was taken as such in Washington.[55] This *démarche*, combined with indications that the French were willing to accede to the Japanese request for a free hand,[56] led to a more vigorous assertion of the American refusal. On 13 February the Secretary of State instructed the U.S. ambassadors in London, Paris, Tokyo, and Peking to tell their governments that the Japanese request, if acceded to, "might prove embarrassing to the cause of the powers at war with Germany." Washington's position was that intervention would antagonise the Russian people; there was no immediate need for it; if the need arose action should be joint and not unilateral; and if the Chinese-Eastern Railway were to be occupied, the United States might find it necessary to insist that occupation be by Chinese, rather than by Japanese troops.[57] In laying down these conditions—as Kennan points out—the Americans were doing precisely what the Japanese least wanted: retaining the freedom to use their own forces in Siberia if and when they chose.[58] To emphasise this point the cruiser *Brooklyn* was ordered to Vladivostok from Yokohama. For the following seven months the problem of intervention in Siberia became one of Anglo-American and Japanese-American relations.

[54] Morris to Secretary of State, Tokyo, 8 February 1918, 6 p.m.; *ibid.*, pp. 42-43.
[55] See Kennan, *Russia Leaves the War*, p. 466.
[56] Morris to Secretary of State, Tokyo, 8 February 1918, 10 p.m.; *Foreign Relations, 1918, Russia*, vol. II, p. 44.
[57] Secretary of State to Page, London (repeated to Paris, Tokyo, Peking), 13 February 1918, 7 p.m.; *ibid.*, pp. 45-46.
[58] Kennan, *Russia Leaves the War*, p. 468.

Ambassador Page did not have a chance to put the State Department's position to Balfour until 18 February (the day on which the Germans renewed their offensive against the Russians), and when he did so he found that the Foreign Secretary had shifted his ground again. Balfour stated flatly that the British government had made no approaches to the Japanese government on the subject. The only act that could possibly be regarded as contrary to this assertion, he said, was a request by "a British military commander" (presumably the Military Attaché at Peking) that the Japanese Army should supply arms to Semenov, and this was certainly not an inter-governmental request. All that the British government had done had been to make "preliminary inquiries" at Washington and Tokyo. Although the plan of asking Japan to occupy the Siberian railways had once been discussed, the request had never been made, and had now been abandoned.

Balfour told Page that he was now trying to get the government to formulate some sort of Siberian policy for discussion with the United States and the Allies, but that the Cabinet had not yet taken the matter up. He recalled that the French Ambassador had recently asked him if he would raise the subject with France without raising it with America, and he had answered "No." And the Foreign Secretary told Page: "You may be assured that I will not recede from that position."[59]

This was a most disingenuous statement; the forcefully-worded British memoranda to the State Department were scarcely preliminary inquiries, nor could it fairly be said that Britain had abandoned the idea of Japanese intervention. While Balfour himself, never very much attached to such a policy, might have momentarily dismissed it, the General Staff certainly had not. A few days later General Bliss, the American Military Representative to the Supreme War Council, wrote to Washington that the British Military Section at Versailles unanimously thought that intervention in Siberia was an urgent military necessity. Their French and Italian colleagues agreed that the entire length of the Trans-Siberian Railway should be occupied. "I found," Bliss wrote, "the general conviction that the situation was desperate and warranted taking a desperate chance."[60]

[59] Page to Secretary of State, telegram 8723, London, 18 February 1918, 11 p.m.; *Foreign Relations, 1918, Russia*, vol. II, pp. 48-49.
[60] Letter, Bliss to Baker (Secretary for War), Versailles, 25 February 1918; U.S. National Archives, Modern Army Branch, Supreme War Council folder 323.

Meanwhile, in Tokyo, where there had once been reluctance there now seemed to be impatience. The British Military Attaché reported his impression that the Japanese might take independent action in the Maritime Provinces at any moment; the General Staff, he said, feared that delay would give the Bolsheviks time to destroy tunnels and bridges along the railroads.[61] When the news reached Tokyo that the Bolsheviks had agreed to the German peace terms, Foreign Minister Motono told the House of Representatives: "Should peace be actually concluded, it goes without saying that Japan will take steps of the most decided and most adequate character to meet the occasion."[62] And to the French Ambassador, he indicated that the day might come when Japan would no longer be able to wait, and said that despite the American attitude, the Japanese might go ahead if only Britain and France agreed. But they were prepared, he said, to go only as far as Irkutsk; further progress would have to be discussed among the Allies.[63] Irkutsk was a long way from any German forces.

Undoubtedly, the Soviet capitulation and the resultant quickening of the pace by Japan led the British government once more to take up the policy which Balfour had so recently declared "abandoned." On 26 February the Foreign Secretary telegraphed Lord Reading, in Washington, that recent events in Russia, "in the considered opinion of the British Cabinet," had rendered the adoption of this previous policy "a matter of great urgency."[64] The most important Allied interests in Siberia, said the telegram, were to preserve the Vladivostok stores and to deny to the enemy the vast agricultural resources west of Lake Baikal. The government did not doubt, Balfour said, that Japan would take care of the stores with or without Allied consent, and he added: "It would neither be difficult nor dangerous nor costly for her to occupy the junction of the Amur and Siberian

[61] Reported by Sir C. Greene to Balfour, telegram 157, Tokyo, 21 February 1918, 2:20 p.m.; Milner MSS, box E-1.

[62] Reported by Reuters, 24 February 1918, in *The Times*, 28 February. Motono's declaration received due attention in London. "It seems probable," Balfour telegraphed Wiseman, "that Japanese Government is preparing public opinion for definite action in Siberia." (Balfour to Wiseman, no. 57, in Drummond to Wiseman, telegram CXP 537, 1 March 1918; Wiseman MSS.)

[63] Morris to Secretary of State, Tokyo, 24 February 1918, 11 p.m.; *Foreign Relations, 1918, Russia*, vol. II, p. 56.

[64] Balfour to Reading, Washington, telegram 1080, 26 February 1918; Wiseman MSS (paraphrases sent to Lansing and President Wilson on 27th; Woodrow Wilson MSS, series II).

Railways, as she is both anxious and ready to do." This action would provide Japan with security, and also satisfy her ambitions in Siberia—once entrenched there, the Japanese might stay. But it would do nothing to hinder German exploitation of the wheat fields of Western Siberia, which in the existing conditions were the most important source of food in Russia.

The only way the Japanese could be induced to penetrate further west than Irkutsk, Balfour said, would be to offer them an Allied mandate and financial assistance. Moreover, the Foreign Secretary was absolutely certain that the Japanese would not tolerate a joint intervention; "in their view, the presence of small Allied forces, such as those which are accompanying General Allenby in Palestine, not only give no assistance, but imply distrust." The Japanese should be urged to issue a declaration that they were acting as the mandatory of the Allies, not intending to occupy the country. This, Balfour said, would do much to calm Russian opinion and counter the argument that Japanese intervention would throw Russia into the arms of the Germans. In any case, national feeling in Russia seemed at the moment non-existent. It would be incredible that intervention should produce support for the "bankrupt Bolshevik foreign policy."

The final decision, said the telegram, was up to America. Since the "complete surrender" of the Bolsheviks, the British government believed that there was "no other alternative open." The French, as well as the Italians, concurred. Without U.S. agreement common action would be impossible. In that case Japan would act alone, and her action would not be extensive enough, nor would it be carried out under the safeguards of an Allied mandate.[65]

This powerful appeal, combined with a message that Motono had told the French Ambassador in Tokyo that "he was ready to pledge his country to act so far as the Ural Mountains,"[66] made a deep impression upon Secretary of State Lansing, who had previously agreed with House and President Wilson that intervention would be disastrous. During the next few days (27 February and 1 and 2 March) Lansing managed to sway the opinions of the other two men.[67] On 1 March the President himself drafted a note saying that

[65] *idem.*
[66] French Ambassador to State Department, 27 February 1918; Woodrow Wilson MSS, series II (quoted in Kennan, *Russia Leaves the War*, p. 475).
[67] Kennan, *Russia Leaves the War*, pp. 475-78.

the American government (not being a member of the Entente) had throughout the war sought to retain its diplomatic freedom and for that reason, not from any distrust of Japan, had not thought it wise to join the Entente governments in inviting Japanese action in Siberia. However, the note said, the American government

has no objection to that request being made, and it wishes to assure the Japanese Government that it has entire confidence that in putting an armed force into Siberia it is doing so as an ally of Russia, with no purpose but to save Siberia from the invasion of the armies and intrigues of Germany. . . .[68]

This note, intended for the Japanese government, was never sent. Almost immediately, House had misgivings that by acquiescing in Japanese intervention, the President would lose his position of moral leadership. By Tuesday, 5 March, he managed to persuade Wilson to withdraw the original message and to substitute a new one, which expressed the same faith in Japan's motives, but added that even if these intentions were set forth in a declaration to the Russian people, they would be discredited by German propaganda to the extent that "a hot resentment would be generated in Russia itself." Intervention, therefore, would

play into the hands of the enemies of Russia, particularly of the enemies of the Russian Revolution, for which the Government of the United States entertains the greatest sympathy, in spite of all the unhappiness and misfortune which has for the time being sprung out of it.[69]

Thus the initial American acquiescence was reversed. The original message, however, although never despatched, was shown on 1 March by the State Department's Counsellor to the British Chargé d'Affaires (Colville Barclay) and to the French Ambassador, and to the Italian Ambassador on the following day. Because the Department wanted British and French approval first, the Japanese Chargé was stalled off with a statement that no decision had been reached.[70]

Barclay (and Wiseman) immediately telegraphed the good news

[68] *ibid.*, p. 478 (quoted from *Foreign Relations, The Lansing Papers*, vol. II, Washington, 1940, p. 355).

[69] The text of the 5 March message, telegraphed to Tokyo for presentation by Ambassador Morris, is in *Foreign Relations, 1918, Russia*, vol. II, pp. 67-68. See Kennan, *Russia Leaves the War*, pp. 478-82, for an account of this episode.

[70] See Polk's memorandum to Lansing, 15 March 1918; *Foreign Relations, 1918, Russia*, vol. II, pp. 68-69.

to London.[71] Balfour reacted by cabling Greene, in Tokyo, that the
United States government had no objection to Japanese intervention;
he also set forth a vague set of conditions under which, if the Japanese agreed, Britain would join with France and Italy in formally
extending a mandate to Japan. The basic condition was simply that
the Japanese should issue a declaration making clear that while
Germany sought to destroy Russia and to impose upon her certain
forms of government, the Allies desired only to assist her, had no
wish to interfere in her internal affairs, would leave her territory
intact, and would not attempt to exploit her economically. Further,
the telegram stated that in order to keep the foodstuffs of Siberia
out of German hands, it was necessary to occupy the railway at least
as far as Omsk, if not Chelyabinsk; this was an implied condition.[72]
Balfour was sure Japan would accept these terms. In a telegram of
the same day, 4 March, to Lockhart in Petrograd, he said that the
day of Japanese intervention seemed near at hand.[73]

For some unexplained reason, Sir Conyngham Greene in Tokyo
did not communicate Balfour's telegram to the Japanese government
until Monday, 11 March, although the Foreign Secretary revealed its
substance to Viscount Chinda in London on the 6th.[74] During the
intervening five days, the situation changed considerably. Primarily,
London learned that the Americans had not, after all, acquiesced in
Japanese intervention.[75] And the American fears of action by Japan
received strong endorsement from the British Consul at Vladivostok,
who reported his opinion that the introduction there of Japanese
forces would be disastrous. "Distrust of Japan ... exists in all classes,"
he telegraphed, "and has to be reckoned as fact of primary importance
in handling political situation in Eastern Siberia."[76] Finally, it also

[71] Wiseman's telegram CXP 549 to Sir Eric Drummond, 2 March 1918, is in the
Wiseman MSS. It says that the Embassy had already sent the news.
[72] Balfour to Sir C. Greene, Tokyo, telegram 198, 4 March 1918; Wiseman MSS. A
paraphrase was given on 5 March to the State Department (U.S. National Archives,
State Department file 861.00/1246).
[73] Balfour to Lockhart, 4 March 1918 (paraphrase given to the State Department
on 13 August); *Foreign Relations, 1918, Russia*, vol. I, pp. 390-91.
[74] Morley, *Japanese Thrust*, pp. 131-32 (from Japanese archives).
[75] House saw Reading on 6 March and wrote that day to the President: "I think I
talked Reading out of his position into ours. He tried to argue but could not maintain
his position, and agreed to send a cable to his government this afternoon advising
them to conform with your ideas in the matter." (Woodrow Wilson MSS, series II.)
[76] Hodgson to Balfour, telegram 11, Vladivostok, 4 March 1918 (in Tokyo telegram
192, 4:40 p.m.); Milner MSS, box E-1.

became apparent that the Japanese were by no means so anxious to take action as had been generally thought.

Although the Western chancelleries did not know it, Foreign Minister Motono was almost alone in the Japanese government in urging a policy so precipitous as intervention without the approval (and financial assistance) of the United States, the other major Pacific Power. Most members—including Prime Minister Terauchi and Baron Goto, Motono's successor—of the Advisory Council on Foreign Affairs, where the final decision lay, felt that intervention with America uncommitted, and hence liable to oppose Japanese action, would be disastrous. But it was Motono who had conducted the negotiations with the Allies, and he had obviously contrived to give the appearance that independent Japanese action was imminent. Probably he felt that by generating pressure for intervention in London and Paris he could use it to force the hand of his colleagues in Tokyo.

As we have seen, by early March Motono had nursed the negotiations along to the point where a definite Japanese decision was necessary; on 2 March he informed the Council members of the progress he had made, and though he did not face the Council as a body until the 9th,[77] he must have known long before that he would meet strenuous opposition, for he proceeded on his own account to take the pot off the boil. On the 7th he told the British Ambassador that the situation in Siberia was not so critical that it was worth a rift among the Allies to save it, and that if the American attitude made it impossible for the Japanese to obtain both financial and material aid from the United States, it would be very difficult for them to act on the Allied invitation. Ambassador Greene surmised correctly that Motono's former eagerness had been reduced by his more cautious colleagues in the Cabinet.[78] Chinda, in his interview with Balfour the previous day, had also expressed his "personal opinion" that his government was likely to move cautiously.[79] Greene closed his telegram, however, by noting that the General Staff was continuing to prepare for action at very short notice; simultaneously, his American

[77] Morley, *Japanese Thrust*, pp. 136-37.
[78] Greene, Tokyo, to Balfour, telegram 204, 7 March 1918; Wiseman MSS. Considerable parts of a paraphrase of this message, in the Woodrow Wilson MSS, series II, are quoted in the second volume of Kennan's history: *Soviet American Relations, 1917-1920*; Volume II: *The Decision to Intervene*, Princeton, 1958, p. 85.
[79] Telegram, Balfour to Greene, 6 March 1918 (paraphrase given to the State Department, 7 March, filed as 861.00/2676 in U.S. National Archives).

colleague reported that troops were being concentrated at ports on the Sea of Japan, that reserves had been notified, and that two divisions had already been despatched to Korea.[80] The Japanese Empire spoke with more than one tongue. Is it any wonder that the Bolshevik leaders felt that a blow from the east was imminent?

✦

Before we can return to what we have called the Foreign Office's Russia—Petrograd and the British government's efforts to prevent Bolshevik ratification of the peace of Brest-Litovsk—we must turn to another military problem on another part of Russia's periphery. On 6 March a company of British marines landed at the North Russian port of Murmansk. Because their presence formed part of the background against which the Soviets viewed their relations with the Allies and with the Germans during these critical first weeks of March, it is necessary at this point to give a brief account of the events which brought them there.

Archangel and Murmansk were the other two ports, besides Vladivostok, which served during the war years as funnels through which military supplies flowed into Russia. Murmansk did not even exist when the war began. Archangel, although ice-clogged for more than half each year, had been left by the German blockade of the Baltic and Black Seas as Russia's only accessible European port. Relative proximity to England made it the chief landing place for British supplies. During the summer of 1916, over 600 steamers—roughly four per day—had deposited at Archangel a million tons of coal and a million and a half tons of food and munitions.[81] But as at Vladivostok, the railways were not capable of handling all the supplies that the ships landed; by the end of 1917, 12,000 tons of explosives and 200,000 tons of other valuable military supplies and metals, desperately needed in Britain and France, had accumulated in the discharging areas around Archangel.[82]

The need for a port open the year round led the Russians, under British instigation and with massive British assistance, to begin in September 1915 the construction of a port on the Kola Inlet, which

---

[80] Morris, Tokyo, to Secretary of State, 7 March 1918, 1 a.m.; *Foreign Relations, 1918, Russia*, vol. ii, pp. 71-72.

[81] Henry Newbolt, *History of the Great War Based on Official Documents, Naval Operations*, London, 1931, vol. v, p. 301.

[82] *ibid.*, p. 312.

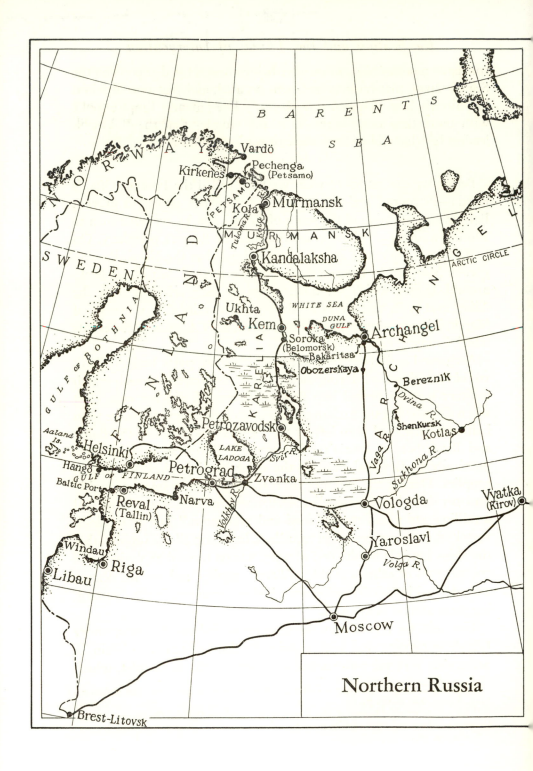

Northern Russia

was kept ice-free by a branch of the Gulf Stream. From the ramshackle town of Murmansk which rose some 40 miles up the inlet from the open sea on the site of the tiny fishing village of Romanov, a flimsy single track railroad was built with immense effort, to span the 600 miles of marshland and dense forest to Petrograd. Port and railroad were completed only at the end of 1916. They had just begun to prove their worth when the shipment of supplies was cut off by the Bolshevik Revolution.[83]

Throughout the war, the task of protecting the northern sea lanes against German submarines and mines had been, largely through Russian default, in the hands of a small British squadron under Rear Admiral Thomas W. Kemp. In November 1917, as in previous winters at the close of navigation in the White Sea, the squadron retired to the Kola Inlet. In past years, Kemp and the British transportation staff had remained at Archangel, frozen in. But after the Revolution the Admiralty feared for their safety, and in mid-December ordered them and all other British naval personnel at Archangel, and as many of the British commercial community that would go, to break through the thickening ice to the comparative safety of Murmansk.[84]

An excitable and impetuous officer, Kemp carried out the departure in a hasty manner that scarcely endeared the British to the local community, who received the impression, not unreasonably, that Britain had abandoned them to the Germans, the Bolsheviks, or whomever else the unpredictable winter might bring.[85] Actually, there was no need for haste. Bolshevism came slowly to the north. The elections to

[83] *ibid.*, pp. 301-2. General Knox, *Russian Army*, vol. II, pp. 509-11, tells of the difficulties of building the railroad. The best description of Murmansk at this time is in Kennan, *Decision to Intervene*, pp. 21-26.

[84] Newbolt, *Naval Operations*, vol. v, p. 304. See also Admiral Kemp's report to the Admiralty, dated 29 April 1920, in *The London Gazette*, 6 July 1920 (Fifth Supplement, 8 July, No. 31970), henceforth called "Kemp Report."

[85] The American Consul at Archangel, Felix Cole, reported to Ambassador Francis that Admiral Kemp combed the town, urging all British subjects to leave on less than 36 hours notice. He tried to include the wife of the British Consul, who strenuously objected because of the bad impression that would have been made. Cole said that this precipitous action did the Allied cause no good. (Letter of 7 March 1918; U.S. National Archives, Petrograd Embassy 800 file.)

Apparently, Kemp was often inclined to act in this manner. On 1 December 1917 he sent an officer from Archangel to the Embassy at Petrograd to warn Sir George Buchanan and the British community to flee a massacre that Kemp thought would take place when the "northern armies" descended on the capital to loot and murder (diary entry, Knox, *Russian Army*, vol. II, p. 728).

the Constituent Assembly, in late November, showed that the Bolsheviks could claim less than 20 percent of the votes in the Archangel district, where the overwhelming majority were Socialist-Revolutionaries.[86] The war and the breakdown of communications in its wake accentuated the sense of remoteness from the centres of Petrograd and Moscow felt by the people of Archangel. To a considerable extent they had become dependent on a food supply imported by the British, Scandinavian, and American ships which had filled their harbour; they also had come to regard the Allies, whose representatives necessarily played a prominent part in the life of the town, as friends.

For several months following the Bolshevik Revolution the Kerensky-appointed Governor-General of Archangel remained in office, but real power in the area was wielded by a so-called Revolutionary Committee, composed of representatives of all the anti-Bolshevik socialist factions, whose principal aim was to prevent the transfer of power to the Bolsheviks.[87] Early in January there assembled in Archangel a conference of delegates from similar committees from the eight north-eastern provinces—some as far away as Perm and Yaroslavl. At first it seemed that the conference held the germs of a separate pro-Ally federation, an idea naturally appealing to the Foreign Office, which instructed the British Consul at Archangel, Douglas Young, to keep in close touch with the conference and to let it be known that the British government sympathised with its aims and might, if approached, be prepared to give financial support to the movement.[88]

Young soon found that the idea of a separate federation had little support except from the Archangel delegates; the others were afraid of provoking civil war. The majority of the delegates, he reported,

... took narrow view of war-weary and hungry men ready to accept indifferently any connection which will give them peace and satisfy their immediate needs at reasonable cost. This is undoubtedly psychological condition of vast majority of population and should be taken into account very seriously by His Majesty's Government in framing any policy.

[86] See the figures in O. H. Radkey, *The Election to the Russian Constituent Assembly of 1917*, Cambridge, Massachusetts, 1950, p. 78. Also the summary of the U.S. Consul's reports in telegram 2228, Francis to Secretary of State, Petrograd, 13 January 1918, *Foreign Relations, 1918, Russia*, vol. II, pp. 468-69.

[87] *idem.* See also telegram 6 (part 3) from Young to Balfour, Archangel, 15 January 1918, 6:34 p.m.; Milner MSS, box D-1.

[88] Foreign Office to Young, Archangel, telegram 2, 8 January 1918, 11 p.m.; Milner MSS, box D-1.

The Archangel leaders, however, struck Young as intelligent socialists mostly convinced of the necessity of finishing the war in connection with the Allies in order to get the food the population so desperately needed. The Consul advised the Foreign Office that Britain should carefully consider its objectives in the region—the most that could be hoped for would be to keep the war stores and the resources of the area out of enemy or Bolshevik hands. That could be accomplished, he thought, by offering to guarantee that even in the event of a separate peace an adequate supply of food and manufactured goods (such as fishing implements) would reach the White Sea in 1918, on condition that the war stores and the surplus products of the region should be available for export only by the Allies. These considerations, Young thought, were vital for the future. The vast undeveloped territory was ready for a commercial agreement, which would be extremely profitable after the war, with any Allied, enemy, or neutral government that would supply its immediate needs. As an earnest of Allied intentions, Young recommended that a relief ship be despatched to Archangel as soon as possible.[89]

Young admitted in his report that if the central Bolshevik authorities decided to appropriate the war stores at Archangel, the local population would not be able to resist them. Probably sooner than he had expected he was proved correct. In late January, a Bolshevik "Extraordinary Commission" arrived to take control of the town and its region and to ship the stores off into the interior. Through a combination of agitation and threats the Bolsheviks rapidly gained a majority on the Archangel Soviet; from this position they dissolved the governing Revolutionary Committee and began to control the town in the name of the Soviet. On 10 February Young reported that Archangel "must be pronounced definitely Bolshevik."[90] Within little over a month war stores were moving inland to a storage site near Vologda at the rate of about 3,000 tons per week.[91] To the Allies, who badly needed the supplies and who, after all, still owned them (they had never been paid for), this was a bitter blow.

Meanwhile, in early January, Sir George Buchanan telegraphed London from Petrograd that the British evacuation of Archangel

---

[89] Young to Foreign Office, Archangel, parts 1 and 2 of telegram 6, 15 January 1918, 1:16 and 1:35 p.m.; Milner MSS, box D-1.

[90] Young to Foreign Office, telegram 12, Archangel, 10 February 1918; 4:24 p.m.; Milner MSS, box D-1. See Kennan, *Decision to Intervene*, pp. 17-21.

[91] *ibid.*, p. 20.

had caused dismay among the Allied missions and among Britain's Russian friends. "I trust," he added, "that there is no intention of withdrawing from Murmansk." A new Northern State was in the process of formation, with Archangel as its capital, and it was most important, Buchanan said, "that we should have the moral influence afforded by our being at Murmansk."[92] The government's response to this message was an assurance that they considered the continued occupation of the Kola Inlet most desirable, and that they had no intention of withdrawing the naval forces at Murmansk.[93]

In the Murmansk harbour, the only remaining vessels of Admiral Kemp's squadron were the battleship *Glory* and eight trawler mine-sweepers. Along side them lay the Russian battleship *Chesma*, the cruiser *Askold*, four destroyers, and several yachts and mine-sweepers. The Russian Navy had long been a hot-bed of revolution, and of all the elements in Murmansk at that time (some 1,800 of the town's population of 5,000 were sailors) the sailors were perhaps the most extreme. They had taken over their ships from their officers. Kemp wrote afterwards that at times he could not overlook the possibility of an attack from the fully manned and armed *Chesma* and *Askold*.[94]

Whether or not there was a real danger from unruly elements in the fleet, both the inhabitants of the town and the British naval personnel were growing continually more afraid that the Germans would attempt to seize the region.[95] Accordingly, on 12 February, spurred by the assassination by unknown gunmen of the former Russian commander of the port, Admiral Kemp and the British Consul (T. Harper Hall) met secretly with two Russian officers who had the confidence of the Murmansk Soviet—Lt. Commander Georgi M. Vesselago, the assassinated commander's assistant, and Major-General Nikolai I. Zvegintsev, a former Guards officer who had somehow been assigned by the Bolsheviks to command land forces at Murmansk. The four men met to consider how there could be estab-

[92] Buchanan to Balfour, telegram 53, Petrograd, 7 January 1918, 3:25 p.m.; Milner MSS, box D-1.

[93] Balfour to Lindley, Petrograd, telegram 156, 29 January 1918, 10:15 p.m.; Milner MSS, box D-1.

[94] Kemp Report, *loc.cit.*

[95] Until more British official material is available, it would be impossible to improve upon the account of the events at Murmansk in Kennan, *Decision to Intervene*, pp. 31-57. Unless otherwise cited, all information in the following few pages is taken from this source or from Leonid I. Strakhovsky, *The Origins of American Intervention in North Russia (1918)*, Princeton, 1937, pp. 24-53.

lished some orderly governmental authority which could co-operate with the British naval forces in the defence of the area.

They decided that the three principal Murmansk political bodies—the town Soviet (elected by the port and railway workers), the Railway Workers' Union, and the local fleet Soviet—should join in forming a People's Collegium to function as the chief civil authority in the region. Not long after 16 February, when this new body was established (with Vesselago as its executive secretary), the news was received that the Germans, in response to the Bolshevik refusal to sign a peace, had renewed their offensive. The Murmansk naval base was naturally a probable objective, and with the occupation of Petrograd expected at any moment, the little garrison grimly awaited the arrival of Germans—or the White Finns who were thought to be in league with them[96]—along the railway from the south.

During these last days of February Kemp telegraphed London that only a British expeditionary force of at least 6,000 men could assure that the valuable base would not fall into enemy hands. The Russian garrison, Kemp said, would only support a winning side: if the British seemed stronger the Russians would resist the Germans; if the Germans came in greater force, the Russians would eject the British.[97] Since all available Allied troops were being sent to the Western Front, Kemp's request was refused. But the Admiralty immediately despatched the cruiser *Cochrane* and asked the Americans and the French to send similar ships.[98] The French responded by immediately ordering to Murmansk the heavy cruiser *Amiral Aube*; the Ameri-

---

[96] In mid-January, Finnish communists had moved to seize power throughout Finland, causing the outbreak of civil war. Anti-communist "White Guard" forces began military operations from a nucleus in north-central Finland. The cadres of the White forces had been trained in Germany as part of a Jäger battalion whose role was to liberate Finland from Russian rule. The German equipment of these forces, and the fact that a few German officers occupied higher command posts in them, gave rise to the misleading impression that the Germans were deeply involved in the Finnish White movement, which was in fact entirely devoted to the cause of Finnish nationalism. (For the Finnish civil war, see C. Jay Smith, Jr., *Finland and the Russian Revolution, 1917-1922,* Athens, Georgia, 1958, pp. 8-91; G. Mannerheim, *The Memoirs of Marshall Mannerheim,* London, 1953, pp. 151-57; Kennan, *Decision to Intervene,* pp. 39-43.) As we shall see, British troops were eventually to be involved in combat with the White Finns.

[97] Newbolt, *Naval Operations,* vol. v, p. 312.

[98] *ibid.,* p. 313. The request to the Americans, memorandum 232 from the British Embassy, Washington, to the Department of State, 4 March 1918, is printed in *Foreign Relations, 1918, Russia,* vol. ii, p. 469.

cans, on the other hand, did not despatch their cruiser *Olympia* until early April.[99]

Before the arrival of even the *Cochrane* there occurred one of the most notorious and (by the Soviets) most misrepresented events of the Allied intervention: the agreement with the Murmansk Soviet. We have seen that every element in Murmansk—Allied and Russian —momently expected an attack by Germans or White Finns. These fears led the head of the local Soviet, A. M. Yuryev, formerly a fire-man on various Russian and Allied naval vessels, a long-time revolu-tionary but not a Bolshevik, to telegraph on 1 March to Petrograd that the Soviet was setting up a local armed defence force and that the Allied representatives at Murmansk continued "to show themselves inalterably well-inclined toward us and prepared to render us assist-ance, running all the way from food supply to armed aid." The Mur-mansk Soviet hesitated, Yuryev said, to make independent decisions as to how the region ought to be defended, and accordingly he requested "instructions from the central Soviet authority, particularly with regard to the forms in which aid in men and material may be accepted from the friendly powers."[100]

Kennan has shown that this message arrived in Petrograd at just the time when, because of a misleading telegram from Brest-Litovsk, the Bolshevik leaders were under the impression that the talks with the Germans had been broken off, the treaty left un-signed, and war renewed.[101] In a desperate mood, Trotsky thereupon telegraphed the Murmansk Soviet that Petrograd was menaced and that it was their duty to defend the Murmansk railway. Trotsky continued:

Resistance is possible and obligatory. Abandon nothing to the enemy. . . . *You must accept any and all assistance from the Allied missions* and use every means to obstruct the advance of the plunderers. . . . We have done everything possible for peace. The bandits are now attacking us. We must save the country and the Revolution. . . .[102]

---

[99] Newbolt, *Naval Operations*, vol. v, p. 313.

[100] Yuryev's telegram is printed in M. S. Kedrov, *Bez bolshevistkogo rukovodstva* (Without Bolshevik Leadership), Leningrad, 1930, p. 27 (quoted in Kennan, *Decision to Intervene*, p. 45).

[101] See Kennan, *Russia Leaves the War*, pp. 490-91, for this incident.

[102] Kennan, *Decision to Intervene*, p. 46, quoting Kedrov, *Bez . . .*, p. 28. The emphasis is Kedrov's. Confirmation of the quotation is given by Strakhovsky, *Origins*, p. 29, who cites a Murmansk newspaper dated 2 March, and also a manu-script by Vesselago as his sources.
This telegram, which was the basis for the subsequent close co-operation between

This message arrived late on the evening of 1 March. The following day, Vesselago called a meeting of the People's Collegium with Admiral Kemp, the British Consul, and a French military representative, Captain Charpentier. After several sessions they came to a so-called "oral agreement" by which the Murmansk Soviet was to be considered the supreme power in the region; executive command in defence matters was to be in the hands of a Military Council of three persons, one appointed by the Soviet and one each by the British and French representatives; the latter two would not interfere in internal affairs, but would do all in their power to assure the supply of the region with food and military matériel.[103]

It is unclear whether or not this agreement ever received formal approval from the British government. The Navy's historian says that when Kemp reported it, the Admiralty replied that the Allies must not undertake the military defence of Murmansk, nor should they support operations beyond the range of the guns of the Allied warships. But the Admiralty would permit Kemp to take any steps compatible with the resources on the spot. If the Russians would defend themselves, Kemp might land British sailors to stiffen resistance against the Germans, but he was not himself to share in the executive command of the Russian forces and must not forget that his

---

the Allies and the Murmansk Soviet, has been one of the keystones in the Stalinist indictment of Trotsky. Kennan (*Decision to Intervene*, pp. 46-48) shows how Kedrov's treatment of it changed from reasoned criticism in 1930 to violent condemnation in 1935. More recent works have continued, and even intensified, this abuse. Volkov, *Krakh angliiskoi politiki*, published in 1954, says that the Murmansk Soviet was influenced in its counter-revolutionary activities by the order of "the enemy of the people, Trotsky" and that "the Trotskyist, Yuryev" was an agent of the British secret police (pp. 33-34). The post-Stalinist *Istoriya grazhdanskoy voiny*, vol. III, takes the same approach, calling Yuryev "one of Trotsky's henchmen" (p. 176).

[103] Kennan, *Decision to Intervene*, p. 49, from Kedrov, *Bez* . . . ; Strakhovsky, *Origins*, pp. 29-30, from Vesselago's manuscript account; Newbolt, *Naval Operations*, vol. v, p. 313, probably from Admiralty records.

Kennan (p. 53, n. 36) cites, with considerable scepticism, an alleged direct-wire conversation between Stalin and Yuryev, undated but obviously immediately after this agreement (and quoted by Kedrov in a *Pravda* article in 1935), in which Stalin is reputed sagely to have warned Yuryev that he had got in over his head, and that the British would exploit the situation by occupying the region; Yuryev was told to get a written guarantee that the Allies would not proceed with an occupation. Since Kennan wrote, this conversation has been elevated to "party-line" status by inclusion (again undated) in the new collection of documents on foreign policy, *Dokumenty vneshnei politiki*, vol. I, pp. 220-21. Curiously enough, Volkov, *Krakh angliiskoi politiki*, although a fiercely Stalinist tract, does not mention this conversation, but only says that the Soviet government knew that the object of the British descent at Murmansk was not to aid in the struggle against Germany, but to occupy the region as the first blow in intervention against Bolshevism (p. 34).

main interests were the preservation of the Allied stores at Archangel, the safety of the Russian warships in Murmansk harbour, and the repatriation of Allied refugees.[104]

The three-man Military Council was immediately formed, consisting of British and French army captains and the executive officer of the Russian cruiser *Askold*, with the addition of three Russian commissioners, one representing each element in the People's Collegium, as observers. The Council proclaimed a state of siege for the region, and began supplying the few hundred local troops with hand grenades, machine guns, and Allied officers as instructors.[105]

This process was carried a step further on 6 March, when a company of Royal Marines, about 130 men, were landed from the battleship *Glory* and sent into barracks on shore.[106] The reason for their landing is unclear. Strakhovsky, who was Vesselago's secretary, claims it was in response to a new appeal by the Military Council for active assistance, occasioned by rumours that White Finns, with German support, had crossed the frontier into Russian territory.[107] Newbolt, drawing, presumably, on the Navy's records, says that the Murmansk Soviet wrote to Kemp urging that he promise armed forces for the prevention of disturbance and anarchy; Kemp's orders, says Newbolt, gave him discretion to employ his forces "to prevent disturbance or anarchy locally if Allied interests were involved or threatened."[108] While both of these explanations may well contain some truth, neither seems really adequate: the force was too small to resist serious opposition, and it seems to have taken no part in the administration or preservation of order in the community. Major Thomas D. Thacher, of the American Red Cross, the observer who has given us the most detailed

---

[104] Newbolt, *Naval Operations*, vol. v, pp. 313-14. The "refugees" were several hundred Allied citizens, former residents of Russia, who had made their way by one means or another to Murmansk and were awaiting repatriation. (See Kennan, *Decision to Intervene*, pp. 36-37.) Along with the *Cochrane*, the Admiralty despatched two ships to collect some of the refugees.

[105] Strakhovsky, *Origins*, p. 30.

[106] Report of Major Thomas D. Thacher of the U.S. Red Cross, 6 April 1918; U.S. National Archives, Naval Records, file WA-6, box 609. Thacher arrived in Murmansk on 4 March and remained until the 26th, when he left on a British ship. His report on the landing is the most detailed I have been able to find, and his figures as to the number of men taking part are to be accepted in place of the 200 estimated by Strakhovsky (p. 31) and Kennan (p. 50). Despite rumours to the contrary, Thacher said, no additional troops were landed from the cruiser *Cochrane*, which arrived at Murmansk on the 7th.

[107] Strakhovsky, *Origins*, pp. 30-31.

[108] Newbolt, *Naval Operations*, vol. v, p. 314.

description of this first landing since the Revolution of Allied troops on Russian territory, says that the Royal Marines marched into barracks, mounted several guns on them, and (at least for the next three weeks) remained there, not even helping to organise and drill the local Red Guard. The landing did, of course, take place with the consent of the Soviet; shortly afterwards the *Glory* fired a salute to the Red Flag—the only Russian flag visible at Murmansk—and it was answered by the guns of the *Chesma*.[109]

Thacher had just come from Petrograd. On the morning of 6 March, immediately before the British landing, he called on Admiral Kemp and tried tactfully to suggest that a landing at Murmansk might have serious repercussions on Lockhart's work in the capital. Thacher reported that Kemp, in his conversation, demonstrated that he knew nothing of Lockhart's dealings with the Bolshevik leaders nor of the objects of British policy in Petrograd. The Admiral had ordered the marines ashore as a strictly local measure, apparently without specific instructions from London and without regard to the larger fabric of Anglo-Soviet relations.[110]

❖

During these same first days of March, while British marines were landing at Murmansk and while the British government was pressing the Japanese to take action in Siberia, Lockhart was working desperately in Petrograd on the slim hope that the Bolsheviks could be persuaded not to ratify the Brest treaty. It was here, in Lockhart's efforts, that the "two Russias" of British policy came together. In London there could seem to be many different Russian problems, some political, some military, at widely scattered points of the former Empire. But in Petrograd, in the eyes of the Bolshevik leaders, such distinctions were not so apparent. There was only one "Allied problem": how to keep them from taking advantage of Russia's weakness and encroaching on Russian territory. The Japanese were expected to descend upon the Maritime Provinces of Siberia at any moment. In North Russia, British marines were at Murmansk. They had come, it could be argued, by Bolshevik invitation. But perhaps they would soon land in greater force, not only at Murmansk but at Archangel as well? Against these critical and puzzling uncertainties

[109] Thacher Report.
[110] *idem.*

the Bolsheviks could place the fact that ratification of the peace with Germany would bring at least temporary relief from one grave anxiety. Thus Lockhart's efforts were virtually doomed from the start. Working against him were not only the Germans, but his own government's policy towards the "other Russia" on the fringes of Bolshevik power.

With the departure of Lindley and the rest of the Embassy, Lockhart had been left entirely on his own. Two members of his little mission, Phelan and Birse, had left with the British party; in the prevailing circumstances there had seemed to be little need for commercial or labour experts. Captain Hicks stayed, and from the Military Mission Lockhart borrowed a young cavalry captain, Denis Garstin. Emphasising the unofficial nature of the contact between Lockhart and Smolny, Lindley had refused to allow any members of the Diplomatic Service to remain.[111]

Lockhart was not discouraged by the Soviet decision to make peace. "Peace between two so widely different parties can never be real peace," he cabled on 23 February, the day before the Bolsheviks formally accepted the German terms, "and I am not sure that a Bolshevik peace is not perhaps the best way out of a very hopeless position as far as we are concerned." The Bolsheviks still seemed to him the party most likely to oppose German interests in Russia. True, they were not likely to promote Allied interests, but more than any other party, he felt, they would delay and hamper German economic penetration.[112] His views were reinforced a few days later, on 1 March, by his first interview with Lenin. Germany, Lenin told him, had long before withdrawn all of her best troops from the Eastern Front. As a result of "this robber peace" the Germans would have to maintain larger, not fewer, forces in the east. Nor would they be able to obtain large quantities of supplies from Russia. "Passive resistance," Lenin said, "is a more potent weapon than an army that cannot fight."[113]

The Bolshevik leader wanted assistance from the Allies, but he doubted that it would be coming, and he told his caller:

We can afford to compromise temporarily with capital. It is even necessary, for, if capital were to unite, we should be crushed at this stage of our development. Fortunately for us, it is in the nature of capital that it cannot

[111] Lockhart, *British Agent*, p. 237.
[112] Lockhart to Balfour, in Lindley telegram 563, Petrograd, 23 February 1918, 11:10 p.m.; Milner MSS, box B.
[113] Lockhart, *British Agent,* p. 240.

unite. So long, therefore, as the German danger exists, I am prepared to risk a co-operation with the Allies, which should be temporarily advantageous to both of us. In the event of German aggression, I am even willing to accept military support. At the same time I am quite convinced that your Government will never see things in this light. It is a reactionary Government. It will co-operate with the Russian reactionaries.[114]

Lockhart threw himself into an effort to provide the assistance the Bolsheviks wanted. "There are still considerable possibilities of organising resistance to Germany," he telegraphed the next day, "and I shall remain in the country as long as there is the slightest hope."[115]

From this day forward the separated (and often isolated) events in Petrograd, Siberia, and North Russia became closely connected. In a long conversation on the afternoon of 2 March Trotsky told Lockhart that he was very disturbed at reports of a probable occupation of Vladivostok by the Japanese. Such an action, Trotsky said, would throw all Russia into the hands of Germany and make further resistance useless. Reporting this interview to the Foreign Office, Lockhart implored that Japan be restrained until it was conclusively proved that the Bolsheviks were incapable of organising opposition to Germany. No class of Russian society, he said, would forgive Britain for giving Japan a pretext for aggrandisement in Siberia; on Britain, as head of the Alliance, would fall the chief blame. He concluded:

> War between Bolsheviks and Germany is inevitable and it is still too early to assume Soviet power in Russia will be destroyed by the fact of Germans taking Petrograd or Moscow.[116]

This telegram arrived in London on the morning of 4 March. Balfour's reply, that same day, was to tell Lockhart that Japanese action seemed imminent.[117] The British government, the Foreign Secretary said, would gladly do everything in their power to help the Bolsheviks resist the Germans; as a "practical" demonstration of this willingness he cited the steps that had been taken at Murmansk. At the same time, he said, the Soviet regime had itself done nothing but issue manifestoes which had neither caused the Germans to withdraw nor inspired the Russians to fight. Perhaps Lockhart was justi-

---

[114] *ibid.*, p. 239.

[115] Lockhart to Balfour, telegram 2, Petrograd, 2 March 1918, 5:15 p.m.; Milner MSS, box B.

[116] Lockhart to Balfour, telegram 3, Petrograd, 2 March 1918, 10:30 p.m.; Milner MSS, box B.

[117] Balfour's telegram of 4 March is cited above, footnote 73.

fied, the telegram continued, in hoping that the Bolsheviks might have the power and the will to reconstruct the forces which they had purposely destroyed; Balfour certainly hoped that Russia's paralysis was temporary. But meanwhile, he asked, what were the Allies to do? Even if Britain were prepared to await the outcome of the present crisis, the Japanese were not: it seemed certain that they would be compelled to take action in their own interests—to prevent the extension of German power to the Pacific—and the British government felt that they would be justified in doing so.

Lockhart had not yet received Balfour's message when, after another long conversation with Trotsky on 5 March, he sent off an even more impassioned appeal. The Special Congress of Soviets was to meet in Moscow on the 12th to consider the ratification of the Brest treaty. If at least some support from the Allies were apparent, so Lockhart reported Trotsky as saying, the Bolsheviks would either declare a Holy War against Germany, or take some other action which would make a declaration of war by Germany inevitable. But if Japan were allowed to enter Siberia, or if the rumours were true that Britain intended immediately to occupy Archangel (an action Lockhart should have known was impossible: Archangel was frozen solid and the thaw would not come before late May or early June) the Bolsheviks would be driven towards Germany.

Again Lockhart asserted that in his opinion the situation was by no means hopeless. If tact were used it might be possible for the British and the Americans to secure an invitation from the Soviet government to cooperate in the defence of Archangel and Vladivostok. The harshness of the German terms gave the Allies a magnificent opportunity, yet they proposed to ruin it by allowing the Japanese to act. Asking that his telegram be shown to Lloyd George and Milner, he concluded:

If His Majesty's Government consider suppression of Bolsheviks is more important than complete domination of Russia by Germany, I should be grateful to be informed.

Congress meets on 12th. Empower me to inform Lenin that question of Japanese intervention is shelved ... that we will support him so long as he will fight Germany and that we invite suggestions as to help required. In return for this I feel sure that war will be declared, that it will meet with considerable enthusiasm and that Russian Government will refrain from Revolutionary propaganda in England for the present. This is our last chance. In taking it we have everything to gain and nothing to lose which we have not lost already.[118]

Balfour's reply to what he called this "earnest appeal" once more showed how little London comprehended the nature of the internal struggle then going on in Russia and how it could be influenced by external power. "Your observation about the 'suppression of Bolshevism' is not understood," he telegraphed. "I have repeatedly and clearly explained that H.M.G. have no desire to interfere with internal affairs of Russia but are only concerned in rigorous prosecution of the war." If the Japanese consented to intervene they would come as friends and allies, not—like the Germans—as enemies and conquerors. Both puzzled and indignant, the Foreign Secretary continued:

Trotsky you tell me repudiates "friendly relations" with us but desires "a working agreement." I sympathise with his point of view. But why will he not also try a working agreement with the Japanese?[119]

Neither in his despatches nor in his book does Lockhart indicate that he knew that at just the time when he was pleading most strongly with London for sympathetic Allied action to prevent ratification of the treaty, the emergency (and highly secret) Seventh Congress of the Bolshevik Party was meeting in Petrograd to decide whether or not to recommend ratification to the forthcoming Congress of Soviets. Had Lockhart known of it, he would not have been so optimistic. Throughout its sessions (on 6, 7, and 8 March), Lenin took a line implacably opposed to renewing the war and in favour, instead, of immediate ratification. Russia, he maintained, was desperately in need of a breathing space before the Japanese invasion which he believed inevitable, and before Germany continued the penetration which Brest-Litovsk had only delayed.[120] At one session he is reported to

[118] Lockhart to Balfour, telegram 10, Petrograd, 5 March 1918, 10:10 p.m.; Milner MSS, box B. A rather inadequate paraphrase of this message is printed in Cumming and Pettit, *Russian American Relations*, pp. 82-84.

The Soviet treatment of this interview between Lockhart and Trotsky is interesting. Volkov, in his recent work on Anglo-Soviet relations (*Krakh angliiskoi politiki*, p. 33), says simply: "The traitor Trotsky did everything in his power to bring about the intervention of Anglo-American Imperialism. To this end, the Jew Trotsky had a meeting with Lockhart on 5 March 1918."

[119] Balfour to Lockhart, telegram 4, 6 March 1918; Wiseman MSS (as no. 1288 to Lord Reading in Washington). A paraphrase, handed to the State Department on 13 August, is printed in *Foreign Relations, 1918, Russia*, vol. I, p. 393.

[120] Lenin's long and important speech on 7 March is printed in his *Sochineniya*, vol. XXII, pp. 313-36. Excerpts are translated in Degras, *Soviet Documents*, vol. I, pp. 57-61. See Wheeler-Bennett, *Brest-Litovsk*, pp. 275-83, and Kennan, *Russia Leaves the War*, pp. 500-4.

have said that because German imperialism would bog down in the Ukraine, in Finland, and in France, Japanese imperialism was still more to be feared. Hence it might be necessary to conclude "a series of the most shameful agreements with Anglo-French imperialism," with America and even Japan, simply to buy time.[121] Trotsky took a prominent part in the Congress, which resolved by a vote of 30 to 12 to recommend ratification; though he was sick at heart, he could not support non-ratification.[122] That he evidently did not tell Lockhart of even the existence of the Congress indicates that the relationship between the two was less open than the British agent believed.

After the secret Party congress the Soviet government was transferred to Moscow as a safeguard in the event of renewed hostilities, and the Congress of Soviets that would formally ratify the treaty was postponed from 12 to 14 March. Of the important members of the Council of People's Commissars, only Trotsky remained in Petrograd to organise the defence of the city. After the decision to sign the treaty, he had given over the conduct of foreign affairs to Chicherin and would soon assume the post of Commissar for War. He invited Lockhart to remain with him in Petrograd; "preferring the virile action of Trotsky to the vacillation of Chicherin," Lockhart accepted.[123]

As a result of this contact with Trotsky, Lockhart's telegrams continued to reflect a bellicosity not characteristic of the majority of the Bolshevik leaders. Again and again Lockhart maintained that the peace would be ratified to gain only a fortnight or so of time, that the Bolsheviks were in fact pledged to war, and that the whole population would be armed as soon as possible.[124] It is no wonder that a high Foreign Office official could remark that Lockhart treated Trotsky "as if he were a Bismarck or a Talleyrand."[125] Balfour, too, was critical of the young agent. After receiving a warning, cabled by Lockhart on 10 March, which said:

By sheer logic of events the working classes are the only force in Russia which does not welcome German intervention. . . . If by permitting

[121] Lenin, *Sochineniya*, vol. xxii, p. 614, n. 148 (quoted in Kennan, *Russia Leaves the War*, p. 502).
[122] Deutscher, *Prophet Armed*, pp. 395-98.
[123] Lockhart, *British Agent*, p. 243.
[124] Lockhart to Balfour, Petrograd, telegrams 9 (5 March 1918, 8:10 p.m.), 14 (10 March, 7:57 p.m.) and 17 (12 March, 7:5 p.m.); Milner MSS, box B.
[125] Dugdale, *Balfour*, vol. ii, p. 258.

Japanese intervention at the present moment we destroy the only force in Russia which will oppose Germany, we must take the consequences.[126]

Balfour commented in a marginal minute:

I have constantly impressed on Mr. Lockhart that it is *not* our desire to interfere in Russian affairs. He appears to be very unsuccessful in conveying this view to the Bolshevik Government.[127]

Yet the Foreign Secretary was also loyal to his subordinate. When a high Foreign Office official annotated one of Lockhart's despatches with the marginal advice: "Let us recall this impudent young man," Balfour at once added: "Certainly not."[128] In his last telegram to Lockhart before the ratification of the Brest treaty, Balfour said: ". . . even when I have reason to doubt the conclusions you draw, I wish to know exactly what you think and your reasons for thinking it."

This statement, however, was the preface to a lecture-like set of observations delivered with Balfour's heavy sarcasm in order to clarify certain of Lockhart's "misunderstandings," so that the government could "make full use" of his "unbiassed judgement." It began:

To suppose that Lenin and Trotsky are German agents is, you say, the most fundamental mistake in our policy, and I am prepared on this point to accept the word of those who know the leaders of the Bolsheviki personally—which I do not. I accept without reserve the statement that Trotsky and Lenin are not traitors but only fanatics, if those who know them say so. But if this be the case I should have thought that by careful search it would have been possible to detect in Russian policy some aspect that did not favour the Germans and did favour the Allies. There is none that I can find. [129]

On the contrary, continued Balfour:

They hinder us in every way from helping them and have done nothing to help themselves. It is only on the North and the East that the Allies can reach Russia with assistance. As to the Northern approach we have not been asked to use it, while it seems to be looked on as an unbearable wrong that we should so much as suggest that Japan should use the Eastern, whatever safeguards may be given for the security and integrity of Russia.

---

[126] *ibid.*

[127] *ibid.*, p. 259.

[128] Wheeler-Bennett, *Brest-Litovsk*, p. 296, n. 3 (derived from Wheeler-Bennett's personal sources).

[129] Balfour to Lockhart, telegram 12, 13 March 1918, 12:30 p.m.; Wiseman MSS (as no. 1458 to Lord Reading in Washington).

It was only at Russia's request that Britain would hope or wish to do anything in Russia, the telegram concluded. Its last words were:

The greatest service you could render to Russia and the Allies of Russia would be to persuade those who control her fate to see things in this light and wholeheartedly to work with those Powers who alone wish that she should be secure and independent.

Two days before, however, the newspapers reported a statement made at the Foreign Office by Lord Robert Cecil. It was considerably more to the point:

I should be glad if Japan will take what action she may see fit, both in her own interest and in that of the Alliance as a whole, to prevent the Germanization of Russia. . . .

I do not think it is sufficiently realized how dangerous the penetration of Russia by Germany really is. . . .

We have always found Japan scrupulously loyal in the performance of her obligations. If she accepted the duty of preventing German penetration of the East she would carry it out with loyalty and with great efficiency.[130]

The Special Congress of Soviets opened in the Kremlin, which had just become the seat of government, on 14 March. It was the first of a long series of similar conventions which would be summoned to approve the decisions of the Party élite. Of the foreign governments so concerned with the events occurring in Russia, only the American took any notice of the Congress. President Wilson despatched a message to the "people of Russia through the Soviet Congress" expressing the sympathy of the American people with their struggle for freedom, and stating that although the government of the United States was "unhappily not now in a position to render the direct and effective aid it would wish to render," it would do everything in its power in the future to restore to Russia complete sovereignty and independence.[131] For the Bolsheviks, who wanted aid, not sympathy, this message contained little comfort.

Lockhart, it will be remembered, did not even come to Moscow for the Congress. Ratification of the treaty was little more than a formality after Lenin had given the Party's decision in a long and cogently reasoned address.[132] Raymond Robins, the head of the

[130] *The Times*, 11 March 1918.
[131] Kennan, *Russia Leaves the War*, pp. 510-11.
[132] Lenin's 14 March address is printed in his *Sochineniya*, vol. XXII, pp. 388-402.

American Red Cross mission in Russia and a figure who had worked desperately for Allied cooperation with the Bolsheviks,[133] related afterwards that just before rising to speak Lenin asked whether he or Lockhart had heard anything from their governments promising military aid. After his negative reply, Robins stated, Lenin moved ratification, which was passed by 784 votes to 261, with 115 abstentions.[134]

Robins—and Lockhart, too—were surely misguided in thinking that any Allied action could have altered Lenin's course. Of the 14 days (from 3 March) which the Germans had given the Russians in which to ratify the treaty, only *one* was left. Allied aid, had it been promised at this stage, would have been months making its effect felt. And Hoffmann's armies, poised and ready, would long before have liquidated the Soviet regime. Even the possibility of removing the dreaded threat of Japanese invasion could not have prevented the Bolsheviks from acting when they did to confirm the peace with Germany, and thus to save the Revolution.

[133] Much of Kennan's two volumes is devoted to Robins' often-bizarre activities on behalf of a U.S.-Soviet understanding; there is no point in elaborating them here. Robins' greatest success, in his own estimation, came on 5 March 1918, when he secured from Trotsky a series of written questions asking what aid America and Britain would give the Soviet regime if they renewed hostilities with Germany. Robins always put this document forward as proof that the Bolsheviks were willing to collaborate with the Allies; as Kennan points out (*Russia Leaves the War*, pp. 497-98), it was, in fact, a set of exploratory questions which committed the Bolsheviks to nothing.

As head of the Red Cross mission, Robins had no direct contact with the American government, and he had to work largely through Ambassador Francis, on whom he occasionally exerted considerable influence. Lockhart was particularly impressed with this spectacular and wealthy American, and the two worked closely together.

Just as energetic as Robins, but no more effective, was Captain Jacques Sadoul, a socialist lawyer and old friend of Trotsky who was attached to the French Military Mission. Sadoul, like Robins, was untiring in his optimism; he even believed that the Bolsheviks might be induced to cede certain Far Eastern territories to the Japanese in exchange for Allied military help in European Russia (Sadoul, *Notes*, p. 254). But Sadoul, too, had no contact with his own country's government; he could only work on General Niessel, his military superior in Russia (who was largely unconvinced) and on any of the Allied diplomats with whom he could gain a hearing.

Thus, of Sadoul, Robins and Lockhart—the three Allied agents in touch with the Bolshevik leaders—only Lockhart was an official representative with direct access to the highest circles of his nation's government.

[134] Kennan, *Russia Leaves the War*, pp. 515-16; Wheeler-Bennett, *Brest-Litovsk*, pp. 302-4.

CHAPTER V

SEMENOV, VLADIVOSTOK, AND THE
MYTH OF CO-OPERATION

*... in my view situation is entirely altered by apparent willingness
of Trotsky to invite Allied assistance against German aggression.*
—*Balfour to Colonel House, 24 April 1918*

AT 4:30 on the morning of Thursday, 21 March 1918, 6,000 German guns commenced a five-hour bombardment of the entire front held by the British Fifth Army, from Vimy to La Fère. The massive offensive which began on that cold, foggy morning, called by Ludendorff "the greatest military task ever imposed upon an army," fell entirely upon the British. In a week's time the German armies, reinforced, as Curzon noted bitterly in the House of Lords, by 35 divisions transferred from the Eastern Front since the first of the year,[1] had driven the Fifth Army back 30 miles, and had inflicted upon it 120,000 casualties.[2] "For the next four months after March 21st, 1918" an historian of the war has written, "the enemy imposed his will by battle,"[3] winning more than ten times as much territory as the Entente had so dearly purchased in all of 1917, advancing his lines to within 40 miles of Paris, and costing the Allies nearly 1,000,000 casualties. Unless the immense scope of the Allied defeat in the west—particularly the defeat suffered by Great Britain—is at all times kept in mind, it is impossible to make sense of the desperate, confused, and often contradictory policy which led to intervention in Russia.

In the face of destruction and despair in the west, the Allied military planners never gave up hope in the panacea of a restored Eastern Front. So great was this despair and so wild were these hopes that a

[1] 29 HL Deb. 5s. 618 (9 April 1918).
[2] Special telegram, Lloyd George to Lord Reading, Washington, 29 March 1918; Wiseman MSS.
[3] Cruttwell, *Great War*, p. 503.

British War Office policy memorandum written in late June could open with the simple declaration: "Unless Allied intervention is undertaken in Siberia forthwith *we have no chance of being ultimately victorious*, and shall incur serious risk of defeat in the meantime."[4] The key to intervention was massive use of the armies of Japan, the only power with forces to spare, and the key to Japanese participation was American approval. Yet President Wilson and Colonel House remained convinced that intervention could have no military advantages that would counterbalance the harm of the racial antagonisms that would be generated in Russia by a Japanese invasion. American approval was not forthcoming and without it the Japanese would not act. In the crucial session of Japan's Advisory Council on Foreign Relations held on 17 March it was decided to reply to the British *démarche* of the 11th that for Japan to undertake military action in Siberia, the moral and material support of the United States would be essential.[5]

For the next four months British diplomacy set itself the task of obtaining this American support. At the same time, Lockhart, in Moscow, was encouraged to woo the Bolshevik leaders in the hopes that they would accept Allied assistance in a renewed war against Germany, while in Siberia and North Russia, British agents worked to build up local Russian centers of resistance. As we shall see, these policies proved incompatible.

They were also based upon an assumption that was wholly unrealistic and unwarranted: that Japan would engage in operations as far west as the Urals. From the beginning the Japanese made it quite clear that they would not. In an interview with the British Ambassador on 19 March, Foreign Minister Motono said he had the impression that a *sine qua non* of the British proposals was Japanese penetration as far as Chelyabinsk, or at least as far as Omsk. Japan, he said, did not intend to have her action dictated or limited beforehand; she must be permitted to decide for herself as she considered best.[6] This position is reported to have been set forth still more explicitly in a note delivered by Chinda in London. Even with

[4] Undated War Office memorandum transmitted by Balfour to Lord Reading in Washington on 20 June 1918, telegram 82 (sent secretly through Wiseman as CXP 658); Wiseman MSS (italics added).

[5] Sir C. Greene, Tokyo, to Balfour, telegrams 260 and 261, 19 March 1918 (sent to Lord Reading on 26 March); Wiseman MSS.

[6] *idem.*

American support, it said, Japan could not consider operating beyond the Amur River basin. Acceptance of that fact was "an indispensable condition" of any Japanese expedition.[7]

As we shall see, so strong was the wish for a new Eastern Front that those responsible for Britain's policy persistently refused to recognise the purport of these Japanese statements, which were continually reiterated over the next few months. The assumption that Japan *would* fight 5,000 miles from the sphere of her own interests rested upon another equally unrealistic assumption: that Japanese troops *could* get to western Siberia in force. The Trans-Siberian Railway was in chaotic condition; east of Karymskaya it was only single-tracked (as was the Chinese Eastern Railway, which joined it there). Yet in June another British General Staff paper could blithely assume that these ways would be made double-tracked and the general efficiency of the system improved, presumably within the next year, to the point where it could handle 60 trains a day each way, enough to maintain 30 divisions at full combat-strength on the mythical Eastern Front in the Urals.[8] Of such stuff, during the desperate months of the German offensive, was Britain's Russian policy made.

❖

For the four months between Brest-Litovsk and the American decision to intervene, British policy consisted of an effort, first, to bring about Allied intervention by the invitation or at least by the consent of the Bolsheviks and, second, from about the middle of May, to achieve it regardless of the Bolsheviks. To an amazing degree this policy followed the recommendations and appeals of Bruce Lockhart—amazing because among the circles most responsible for British policy Lockhart himself was discredited.

We have noted that within the Foreign Office there was more than a little alarm at the apparent extent to which Lockhart was influ-

---

[7] Morley, *Japanese Thrust*, p. 142, quotes this note from the Japanese Archives. I have been able to find no British copy of it.

Also on 19 March, the Japanese government told Washington that they would take no decision regarding intervention until complete accord on the subject had been reached between America and the Entente Powers. (Telegram, Morris to Secretary of State, Tokyo, 19 March 1918; *Foreign Relations, 1918, Russia*, vol. II, p. 81.)

[8] "Paper on Intervention in Russia, Drawn up for the Chief of the Imperial General Staff by the British Section, Supreme War Council, Versailles," undated and unsigned, copied by General Bliss, the American representative, on 17 June 1918; U.S. National Archives, Modern Army Branch, Supreme War Council Papers.

enced by Trotsky and to which he in turn believed that he could influence Soviet policy. He had remained in Petrograd with Trotsky; the two did not set out for Moscow until 15 March, by which time ratification of the treaty was virtually certain. Lockhart's final telegram from the former capital clearly showed his state of mind and the boundless confidence he had in himself as a prescient, flexible, articulate young man in the midst of a chaotic, unique, and (he felt) pliable situation. "If you can prevent Japanese intervention," he pleaded to Balfour,

there is almost nothing here that we cannot do. If Japanese intervention is permitted, everything is lost. . . .

I can only repeat Bolsheviks must fight Germany and . . . it [is] with you to decide whether they are to fight Japan as well.

If Britain could hold off the Japanese, he said, he could surely reach an agreement with Trotsky for co-operation. And he concluded:

I have achieved far more than I thought possible. Why will you not give me a chance to prove my conclusions when you risk nothing by deferring an action which is at present totally unnecessary?[9]

It is not surprising that messages of this sort found a cool reception in London.

Particularly in military circles, there was powerful opposition to Lockhart, and, as we have seen, the soldiers played a major rôle in the determination of policy towards Russia. The most influential soldier and Lockhart's bitterest enemy was Major-General Alfred Knox, the former Military Attaché. In the interval between Knox's return from Russia in January and his departure for Siberia in August, he was the War Office's chief advisor on Russian matters, and his opinions always received a sympathetic hearing in the Cabinet.[10]

On 18 March, therefore, just after Lockhart's arrival in Moscow, General Sir Henry Wilson (who had replaced General Sir William Robertson as Chief of the Imperial General Staff) circulated to the War Cabinet a paper by Knox headed "The Delay in the East."[11] In a covering note Wilson commented: "Mr. Lockhart's military

[9] Lockhart to Balfour, telegram 22, Petrograd, 15 March 1918 (sent 16 March, 8:20 p.m.); Milner MSS, box B.
[10] It will always remain somewhat of a mystery why Knox concluded his memoirs (*Russian Army*) with his return from Russia in January 1918, and did not attempt to deal with his extremely important rôle in the intervention.
[11] Milner MSS, box B.

advice is so bad that I hope he will be told not to give a military opinion in future *or* be recalled."

Knox's paper, however, did not confine itself to Lockhart's military opinions. He began by stating that the delay in Japanese intervention was inexcusable and that two individuals were responsible for it: Lockhart and the American, Raymond Robins.[12] The latter Knox described as

... a fanatic with the temperament of a hero-worshipping schoolgirl, and while without the mental equipment or the experience to enable him to advise on policy, ... a dangerous companion for anyone as impressionable as Lockhart.

He then turned his attack upon Lockhart, whom, he said, he had known for five years during the young man's consular days. After quoting a series of extracts from Lockhart's telegrams to show that their contents were "in a political sense unsound" and "in a military sense criminally misleading" Knox asked:

Why is he retained in Russia? There is no evidence from his telegrams that he puts the moderately worded reasoning of our telegrams adequately before his friends [the Bolshevik leaders]. I am convinced that our cause in Russia is being more damaged by keeping a British official in communication with the Bolsheviks than it could possibly be by Japanese intervention, no matter how stupidly arranged. The policy of flirtation with the Bolsheviks is both wrong as a policy and immoral.

Britain's aims in Russia, he concluded, were to win the war and safeguard her position in the east; hence he urged action by Japan, adding:

If we merely desire the happiness of Russians of all classes, we had better withdraw and allow Germany to absorb the whole country and stamp out Bolshevism once and for all.

It is worth noting the sort of reception given to this memorandum. Balfour, who, it will be remembered, firmly refused to recall Lockhart,[13] telegraphed a detailed summary of Knox's views to Lord Reading in Washington "for your information and ... such use as you may consider desirable."[14] This was an incredible procedure.

[12] For Robins, see above, Chapter IV, footnote 133.
[13] See above, p. 125.
[14] Balfour to Reading, telegram 1599, 20 March 1918; Wiseman MSS.

Reading (on Balfour's instructions) had been supplying the State Department with a steady stream of paraphrases of Lockhart's telegrams, and continued to do so throughout the latter's tenure in Russia, in an effort to influence U.S. policy. Now Balfour went to the trouble of sending to Washington (without any comment of his own, but the mere fact of sending implied endorsement) an attack upon Lockhart which, if its allegations were correct, could only discredit the British agent and the government which retained him in Moscow.

What was Reading supposed to do with the information? Balfour explicitly left the decision to the Ambassador. Perhaps he was to give it to the American government in order to throw doubt upon Lockhart's anti-interventionist opinions and hence to further British efforts to achieve intervention? In that case, never in the future would he have been able to cite Lockhart's advice in support of a given policy. There is nothing in the State Department Archives or the papers of President Wilson, Secretary Lansing, or Colonel House to show that Reading did anything with Knox's attack but keep it to himself and, one cannot help but think, wonder at the complexity of mind and purpose of a Foreign Secretary who retained in a crucial position an agent he did not fully trust and whose labours he allowed to be undermined.

Lockhart, it is also worth noting, sensed Knox's influence, and was just as hostile to the General as the latter was to him. "Who is responsible for the General Staff's opinion on policy?" he queried in late March,

I sincerely trust it is not General Knox. Much as I like him I must point out that since Revolution his complete misunderstanding of situation has been one of the chief reasons for our failure in this country. Our expert military advice on Russia has been so notoriously wrong throughout the whole war that it is hardly worthy of consideration and I should be more than sorry if at this critical hour a man of General Knox's hasty and changeable judgement should be considered as a more reliable authority than myself. . . .[15]

Well might Lockhart comment, as he did later in his memoirs, that "the man in London has a thousand advantages over the man on the spot."[16]

[15] Lockhart to Balfour, telegram 59, Moscow, 31 March 1918, 7:20 p.m.; Milner MSS, box B.   [16] Lockhart, *British Agent*, p. 198.

Lockhart was not, as it happened, the only man on the spot. Oliver Wardrop, as Consul-General in Moscow, headed an establishment which included a consul, three vice-consuls, and two passport officers. But, following the dicta previously laid down for Lindley and all other British representatives officially accredited to the former Russian governments, they had no relations with the Bolsheviks. Their duties were exclusively consular and they concerned themselves only with the interests of the many British citizens still in Russia.

Before Lockhart moved to Moscow, he appealed to Balfour that he should be allowed to remain independent and not be placed under the Consul-General (who was considerably his senior).[17] The friction he anticipated never developed, however. Wardrop reported in early April that their relations were of the most cordial and confidential character. But there were others of whom he did complain—a Lieutenant Reid "and at least four colleagues," who referred to themselves simply as the "Mission," to whom he had to give office space in the Consulate-General. Wardrop had no control over them and only the slightest knowledge of what they were doing. "They all seem to have independent policy and overlapping spheres," he telegraphed.[18] Lockhart, too, was concerned about them, and others like them. "I was completely in the dark," he later wrote, "regarding the work of a whole group of British officers and officials for whose presence in Russia and for whose protection my position with the Bolsheviks was the only guarantee."[19]

These were intelligence agents of various sorts. Probably they carried on relations with various counter-revolutionary groups (though, as we shall see, Lockhart was to handle important aspects of this work). Certainly they had a major share in obtaining the notorious Sisson documents, purporting to prove that the Bolshevik leaders were in German pay.[20] "Without knowing what I was doing," Lockhart wrote, they "intrigued against me."[21] In addition, there were

[17] Lockhart to Balfour, telegram 16, Petrograd, 10 March 1918; Milner MSS, box B.
[18] Wardrop to Balfour, telegram 149, Moscow, 2 April 1918, 6:5 p.m.; Milner MSS, box B.
[19] Lockhart, *British Agent*, p. 263.
[20] British agents helped Sisson obtain the documents from bourgeois sources; Sisson, *One Hundred Red Days*, pp. 357-59. For a complete account of their subsequent history, see Kennan, *Russia Leaves the War*, pp. 412-21, 441-57.
[21] Lockhart, *British Agent*, p. 263. On 18 March Lockhart cabled Balfour: "With very few exceptions your agents here have only one policy—to prove that Bolsheviks are pro-German." (Telegram 23, Moscow, 6:25 p.m.; Milner MSS, box B.)

other British agents who operated wholly underground. To judge from their own highly sensational accounts, they did nothing more useful than avoid arrest.[22] In none of the many documents the author has seen is there even a hint that British information about Russia was derived from these sources. They did not—it may safely be stated—influence British policy.

✧

Lockhart, in his reports from Petrograd shortly before the ratification of the Brest treaty, had accurately described the Soviet attitude when he telegraphed that the peace would be only a temporary truce and that the Bolsheviks might soon again find themselves at war with Germany. Trotsky, who had brought his enormous energies and skills to the Commissariat of War, earnestly set about reorganising the anarchical Red Guard into a disciplined army capable of defending the Soviet Republic against further invasion. His task was not easy: revolutionary fervour, although a powerful force, can never wholly take the place of prolonged training and experienced leadership. These circumstances, together with the presence in Moscow of a group of Allied representatives favourably disposed towards the Bolsheviks, gave rise to the illusion, shared by nearly all of these representatives, that military collaboration with the Bolsheviks would be possible.

The Allied Embassies, it will be remembered, had either retired from Russia entirely (like the British) or had retreated to the temporary haven of Vologda (where the American, Japanese, and Chinese ambassadors were joined on 29 March by their French, Italian, and Serbian colleagues). When Lockhart reached Moscow in mid-March he found there a group of Allied officers who, like himself, were charged with maintaining unofficial contact with the Soviet authorities. They were General Lavergne, head of the large French military mission (who used Sadoul as his contact with the Kremlin); General Romei, the Italian Military Attaché; and Captain E. F. Riggs, the American Assistant Military Attaché. Daily, these four (often with the addition of Raymond Robins, sometimes with Sadoul) met in

---

[22] See, for example, Sir Paul Dukes, *Red Dusk and the Morrow: Adventures and Investigations in Red Russia*, London, 1922, and *The Story of "ST 25": Adventure and Romance in the Secret Intelligence Service in Red Russia*, London, 1938; and Dorian Blair and C. H. Dand, *Russian Hazard: the Adventures of a British Secret Service Agent in Russia*, London, 1937.

Lockhart's rooms in the Hotel Élite. From the outset, they found themselves unanimous in thinking, first, that the Bolsheviks would accept Allied military assistance, and, later, that they could be induced to invite or at least consent to intervention.

Trotsky at this stage was both frank and conciliatory towards these Allied representatives, probably because he genuinely felt that their governments could, in the event of more German pressure, help him organise his army, but also because he thought that the prospect of collaboration might induce the Allies to prevent the Japanese invasion he so much feared. He made no single or comprehensive request for assistance. Rather, he seems to have more or less thought out loud about the possibilities of co-operation; so eager were his listeners—particularly Sadoul—for such a course that they amplified and elaborated Trotsky's vague conjectures into concrete proposals.

After an interview which he and Riggs had with Trotsky on 20 March, for instance, Sadoul carried away the impression that the Soviet government would formally request U.S. and French officers for both instruction and staff duty. The Bolsheviks were not interested, Sadoul noted, in British or Italian assistance.[23] The next day, however, Lockhart reported that Trotsky had asked for British and American instructors, but might be forced to turn to the French because they were the only power with enough officers already on the spot (the large French military mission to Rumania—several hundred officers—was then in Moscow in the process of evacuation).[24] To the Americans, on the other hand, went a written request for help only in the restoration of Russia's railways.[25] A few days later Riggs reported that thirty-eight officers (presumably French) had already been assigned to the Bolsheviks, and that the Italians had ordered ten to be sent out from Italy.[26] This development Sadoul saw as the beginning of an Allied influence in Russia equal to that of Germany before the war.[27]

Lockhart, meanwhile, was exploring the other side of the question of co-operation: intervention by invitation. On 27 March, according

[23] Sadoul, *Notes*, pp. 275-76.
[24] Lockhart to Balfour, telegram 32, Moscow, 21 March 1918, 5:20 p.m.; Milner MSS, box B.
[25] Its text is given in Kennan, *Decision to Intervene*, pp. 114-15, n. 4.
[26] Francis to Secretary of State, Vologda, 26 March 1918; *Foreign Relations, 1918, Russia*, vol. I, p. 487.
[27] Sadoul, *Notes*, p. 278.

to Lockhart, Trotsky told him that Russia was engaged in a "life struggle" and would welcome Allied help even if this would entail a socialist army's fighting side by side with an imperialist army. Trotsky said he saw no objection to Japanese troops taking part provided that there were other Allied forces with them and that the Allies gave certain guarantees. Lockhart described this statement as a complete change in the Bolshevik attitude, brought about by the German danger, and emphasised that London should realise it. He felt sure that an agreement would be possible if the Allies proceeded cautiously. And he added:

Difficult as task of Trotsky must be in creating even a small fighting force, I feel most strongly that we should support him in every way towards the realisation of this task. Once war begins again, once a Russian force of any kind is fighting the Germans, it will not be long before Military situation dominates completely the Political situation.[28]

Lockhart was indeed correct: if war had broken out again, the military situation *would* have been dominant. Almost surely it would have meant the downfall of the Soviet regime. For that reason the Bolsheviks had no intention of provoking German attack. Allied intervention would have provided such a provocation. Nor did the Germans want a new war in the east. One of their most important objectives in hastily concluding the Brest peace was to free troops for service in the west. Although the Germans continued throughout April to push into the Ukraine in search of grain, their move was made on the careful calculation that Bolshevik resistance there would not extend to repudiation of the treaty and a declaration of war.[29] Here was Lockhart's greatest error: the assumption that renewed war was inevitable. It was an assumption that went unchallenged by London, so desperate was the government for the restoration of an Eastern Front.

Lockhart concluded this important telegram by stating that the greatest danger to the Allied cause would be counter-revolution; the Bolsheviks were still the element most opposed to Germany. For that reason, he said, he had always been very anxious about the danger of Japanese intervention and of supporting isolated anti-

[28] Lockhart to Balfour, telegram 51, Moscow, 28 March 1918, 4:10 p.m. (transmitted to Lord Reading in Washington as no. 1842, 30 March); Wiseman mss.
[29] Wheeler-Bennett, *Brest-Litovsk*, p. 312.

Bolshevik movements, such as Semenov's, in the Far East. Lockhart's telegram was important because the policy he advocated became in broad outline, British policy for the following two months, particularly regarding his final point—restraint of both the Japanese and anti-Bolshevik movements like Semenov's in order to secure a Bolshevik invitation for intervention. Events in the Far East, however, were moving with a momentum of their own. We must turn to them before we continue our account of the situation in Moscow.

❖

Action by Semenov's tiny band of Mongols and Cossack adventurers, it will be remembered from the preceding chapter, had been briefly put forward by the British government in early February as a possible alternative to Japanese intervention. This policy had been quickly reversed, probably because of military pressure for the much more decisive effects anticipated from large-scale Japanese action. Nevertheless, Semenov had been informed that Britain would assist him with money, arms, and munitions. It was estimated that he would require £10,000 per month, and on 23 February Balfour instructed Sir John Jordan, the British Minister in Peking, to give him an advance of £20,000.[30] Jordan telegraphed on 4 March that Semenov urgently needed arms, and asked permission to give him two five-inch howitzers, with ammunition, from the Legation guard.[31] His request was granted.[32]

Unknown to the Western Allies, however, the Japanese had already reached an agreement with Semenov to supply him with considerably larger quantities of weapons, including 10 guns, 50 machine guns, and some 10 million rounds of machine-gun and rifle ammunition.[33] Rapidly, and to a degree not wholly sensed by London or Paris, Semenov became a tool for the execution of Japan's rather devious purposes in Manchuria and Eastern Siberia. These were, principally, to prevent the establishment of any strong and united Russian author-

[30] Balfour to Jordan, Peking, telegram 102, 23 February 1918 (taken from "Diary of Events in Russia and Siberia, December, 1917, to December, 1918," appended to the paper by the General Staff, War Office, *Short History of Events in Russia from November, 1917 – February, 1918* [hereafter cited as "Diary, Short History of Events"], Milner MSS, box J).

[31] Jordan to Balfour, telegram 207, Peking, 4 March 1918, 11:50 p.m.; Milner MSS, box E-1.

[32] U.S. Chargé, Peking, to Secretary of State, 8 March 1918; *Foreign Relations, 1918, Russia*, vol. II, p. 73.

[33] Morley, *Japanese Thrust*, pp. 97-98 (from Japanese Archives).

ity that would block Japanese exploitation of the region's temporary state of near anarchy. Obviously, the Japanese had to declare their sympathy for any anti-Bolshevik and pro-Ally movement in Siberia, and hence they gave lukewarm support to an attempt by Horvat (whom they thought they could manage) to establish a government at Harbin.[34] But Semenov was a much better instrument for Japanese policy: at heart he was a bandit and, despite any professions to the contrary, he aimed at a bandit's hegemony rather than civil authority. Although fiercely anti-Bolshevik, he was also unmanageable by Horvat and by the Siberian "governments" which followed Horvat's.

The Japanese sent Semenov not only weapons but men. With the first consignment of field and machine guns, in mid-March, came 22 Japanese gunners.[35] More important, the British Assistant Military Attaché at Peking, Captain Porter, who inspected Semenov's force in early April, reported that a Japanese General Staff captain named Kuroki was acting virtually as the Cossack leader's executive officer, and seemed to look upon Semenov as a "smokescreen" for Japanese operations.[36]

Porter's report also shows how slowly the British became aware that Semenov was more like a cruel oriental war-lord than a conventional military leader. Porter described him as an "unassuming officer of calm temperament and of considerable strength of character," who seemed "exceptionally patriotic and disinterested and thoroughly deserving of support." Semenov's force, however, was "not altogether satisfactory"; it was a Cossack organisation and therefore not only strongly anti-Bolshevik but anti-socialist as well. Many Russians regarded it with suspicion "as a force of bandits and as an instrument for imposing a reactionary regime." There was, Porter admitted, some ground for these suspicions. "Requisitions" of food and supplies and summary executions of all captured Bolsheviks had not endeared Semenov to Russians living on either side of the Manchurian border, and his consequent failure to attract Russian recruits had forced him to enlist Chinese "ex-bandits" and to employ prisoners

[34] *ibid.*, pp. 171-80. The Japanese did not, however, give any support or encouragement to the socialist "Provisional Government of Autonomous Siberia" established by Peter Derber, a Socialist-Revolutionary, in Vladivostok; it was considered much too left-wing (*ibid.*, pp. 167-71).

[35] Henry E. Sly (Consul at Harbin) to Balfour, 18 March 1918 (transmitted as telegram 260 from Jordan, Peking, 19 March, 3:20 p.m.); Milner MSS, box E-1.

[36] Porter's report was transmitted by Jordan to Balfour as telegram 307, Peking, 4 April 1918, 5:20 p.m.; Milner MSS, box E-1.

of war from the Siberian camps for non-combatant duties. Even so, his force came to barely over 1,000. From these facts, Porter might have concluded that Britain should steer clear of so risky a commitment. On the contrary, he recommended that Semenov's position be clearly defined and openly recognised by the Allies without delay. In order to allay the fears of the largely Socialist-Revolutionary Russian population of the region, he thought, the Allies should announce their support of Semenov, provided that he used his force for putting down disorder and fighting armed prisoners of war, not for political purposes.[37]

Meanwhile the Bolsheviks, who by then controlled most of Siberia's cities, had become thoroughly aroused by Semenov's forays among their Trans-Baikal garrisons, and they brought up superior forces which drove him to seek the safety of the Chinese side of the Manchurian border. But he still straddled the Chinese-Eastern Railway, forcing the Bolsheviks to depend on the much longer Amur line for traffic between Chita and Vladivostok. His raids also caused trouble between the Chinese and the Soviet forces; the latter threatened to pursue his troops back across the frontier unless the Chinese took steps to restrain him. The situation then eased for a few weeks—Semenov in any case needed a breathing spell to re-build his little force—but in early April, Porter reported that the Japanese were once again urging him to attack the Bolsheviks. Captain Kuroki even threatened to take back the Japanese weapons if an advance were not soon undertaken.[38] Semenov agreed, and told Porter of his plans to sweep through Dauriya, take Karymskaya, and then, if the Japanese would support him and garrison the rail junction themselves, continue on to attack Chita.[39]

By this time, however, London began to have second thoughts: support of Semenov's marauding but, after all, small-scale activities might jeopardise much more important goals. Bolshevik resentment, Lockhart reported, fell not so much on the Chinese for failing to restrain Semenov as on the Allies and Japan for goading him on.[40] Accordingly, on 7 April Balfour telegraphed to Jordan in Peking

[37] *idem.*
[38] *idem.*
[39] Porter telegram no. 2, transmitted by Sly, Harbin, as no. 117, 6 April 1918; Milner MSS, box E-1.
[40] Lockhart to Balfour, telegram 66, Moscow, 3 April 1918 (despatched 4 April, 1:25 p.m.); Milner MSS, box E-1.

that the British government was endeavouring, with some appearances of success, to induce the Soviet government not only to renew the war against the Germans but even to accept Allied, including Japanese, co-operation and assistance. "It is evident," Balfour said, "that an advance by Semenov at this moment, encouraged by the Allies, must seriously indispose the Bolshevik Authorities and may prove fatal to our policy." Besides, he added, Semenov's unit was so small that it did not seem likely to achieve much in the way of military results. If and when Allied or purely Japanese intervention in Siberia materialised, his troops would become a useful adjunct to the occupying forces both from a military and political point of view. (Here, again, was the mistaken idea that Semenov's force was Russian, and would provide a *Russian* nucleus for resistance.) In the meantime, the telegram concluded, he should be restrained from new operations, and told to confine his efforts to training and recruiting for the future.[41]

Jordan fully agreed with this policy, and ordered Porter to halt Semenov's attack. But the British Minister warned that it might be too late—things had been allowed to drift too long. Britain had originally looked upon Semenov as an alternative to Japanese occupation; now the Japanese had taken him over and Kuroki had promised him funds if the British and French payments ceased. Jordan's advice was that, in effect, Britain should pay Semenov *not* to advance by giving him what he would have taken as spoils from his conquests in order to sustain his troops.[42]

Porter, who was still with Semenov, and had, it seems, fallen victim to the myopia which too frequently prevents the man on the spot from viewing a situation from any but the local angle, thought little of his government's policy. Whatever the Russian political situation might be, he telegraphed on 13 April, "the facts here" were that armed prisoners of war, in conjunction with the Soviet forces, were blocking Semenov's advance, and he would appear justified in attacking them not as Bolsheviks but as enemies. A British *démarche* to restrain Semenov, Porter said, would only result in his taking inde-

[41] Balfour to Jordan, Peking, telegram 194, 7 April 1918, 9:30 p.m.; Milner MSS, box E-1. A paraphrase, given to the State Department on 8 April, is printed in *Foreign Relations, 1918, Russia*, vol. II, p. 109.

[42] Jordan to Balfour, telegram 323, Peking, 9 April 1918, 8:45 p.m.; Milner MSS, box E-1.

pendent action in conjunction with the Japanese.[43] Nevertheless, Porter followed his orders and made the suggested *démarche*; one can only wonder what terms he used.

On 23 April, Jordan reported from Peking that the Japanese and White Russian legations there were gravely suspicious of Britain's leanings towards the Bolsheviks, and were urging Semenov to advance in order to produce a rupture between Moscow and London.[44] The following day, Porter cabled that Semenov's attack had begun, adding: "In view of the attitude taken by the British Government, I have protested against making an advance which however could not be avoided."[45] On 1 May, reporting that Semenov was continuing to advance into Trans-Baikalia with a force now enlarged to 2,000 and heavily armed, Porter again stated his opinion that the advance was Semenov's only course under the existing military conditions, and that he was therefore loath to interfere. Moreover, Semenov's chances of success were good.[46] Sly, the Consul at Harbin, telegraphed that Semenov was receiving strong encouragement from the French attaché as well as the Japanese Captain Kuroki; both were fluent in Russian, whereas the British officer did not know the language.[47]

Semenov's advance was clearly embarrassing to the British government in relation to the main stream of their Russian policy. Balfour cabled to his ambassadors in Paris and Tokyo that Britain had taken steps to restrain Semenov, and asked them to urge the French and Japanese to do the same. "So long as we are negotiating with Trotsky," he said, "we feel it is important to give him no pretext for charging us with attempts to bring about counter-revolutionary movements." Lockhart had been instructed to tell the Bolsheviks that if Semenov continued to advance, he would be doing so on his own responsibility.[48]

---

[43] Porter telegram no. 4, in Jordan to Balfour, no. 337, Peking, 13 April 1918, 5:30 p.m.; Milner MSS, box E-1.

[44] Jordan to Balfour, telegram 362, Peking, 23 April 1918, 8:15 p.m.; Milner MSS, box E-1.

[45] Reported in Jordan to Balfour, telegram 378, Peking, 27 April 1918, 11:30 a.m.; Milner MSS, box E-1.

[46] Reported in Jordan to Balfour, telegram 388, Peking, 1 May 1918; 8:25 p.m.; Milner MSS, box E-1.

[47] Reported in Jordan to Balfour, telegram 379, Peking, 28 April 1918, 1:20 p.m.; Milner MSS, box E-1.

[48] Balfour to Lord Bertie, Paris (telegram 900) and to Greene, Tokyo (telegram 408), 2 May 1918, 11 p.m.; Milner MSS, box E-1.

Balfour's statement was little more than wishful thinking: unfortunately, Britain had long since ceased to have any real responsibility for Semenov. The monthly payments were not discontinued because Japan was only too willing to take complete control and would gladly have done so. As a result, the British were left in the position of silent partners—silent to Semenov, silent to the Japanese, but not silent to the Bolsheviks. In Moscow, Britain's dealings with the Siberian movement, reluctant though they may have been, had the sound of counter-revolution.

❖

A month earlier, on 9 April, two days after he first asked Jordan in Peking to restrain Semenov, Balfour sent another telegram to Greene, his Ambassador in Tokyo, in another attempt to curb a Japanese policy which seemed seriously to endanger Britain's effort to secure intervention by Bolshevik invitation. The action he protested against then caused far greater alarm in Moscow than Semenov's advance; again it was one in which Britain played the rôle of silent partner—the landing on 5 April of Japanese and British marines at Vladivostok.

The landing was the result of a decision made on the spot by the Admiral commanding the Japanese ships in the city's harbour in response to a particular local situation. In no way did it reflect the inter-Allied negotiations which continued in a desultory manner throughout March.

These negotiations were so inconclusive they are hardly worth summarising. They amounted to a British effort to surmount the obstacles, first, of President Wilson's refusal in early March to agree to Japanese intervention of any sort,[49] and, second, of the Japanese government's statement on 19 March expressing unwillingness to proceed without American support, but requesting a free hand, with no obligations to extend operations outside Eastern Siberia, in the event that U.S. support were forthcoming.[50]

To the Americans, Britain proposed an additional reason for intervention: that the restoration of an Eastern Front would go far to counteract "an impression of enemy might and invincibility" very damaging to Allied morale.[51] After the start of the German offensive,

---

[49] See above, p. 106.
[50] See above, p. 130, n. 7.
[51] This particular approach to the Americans was first suggested in a telegram from Balfour to Reading on 11 March 1918 (no. 1364; Wiseman MSS). When Reading

Colonel House admitted to Lord Reading that intervention might become necessary for the sake of Allied morale, but he was still doubtful as to whether its practical effects would be worth the great risks it entailed.[52] President Wilson's attitude was best expressed in a note to his Secretary of State commenting on all the many British and French appeals for intervention, among them a solemnly-worded declaration drawn up by Balfour after an Anglo-French-Italian conference in London on 15 March.[53] The President wrote:

> They still do not answer the question I have put to Lord Reading and to all the others who argue in favor of intervention by Japan, namely, What is it to effect and how will it be efficacious in effecting it?[54]

Reading reported that both Wilson and House always reverted to making Russian assent indispensable to American agreement. House, he said, wondered whether Lockhart could not secure this assent.[55] Obviously, this American attitude gave additional impetus to British efforts to secure a Bolshevik invitation.

In the midst of these exchanges, the landings at Vladivostok were a first *fait accompli*. By March, Vladivostok was the only Siberian city not entirely under communist control; the presence of the Allied warships in the harbour had prevented the usual coup. But the non-Bolshevik local administration continued to exist only on the sufferance of the city Soviet, and Bolshevism had undermined the military and naval garrisons and the municipal police. During March the Bolsheviks began increasingly to assert themselves; they especially harassed the large commercial community, which included many foreign firms.[56] A crisis was reached on 24 March when the Soviet took control of the telegraph office; the resulting strike of post and telegraph workers left the city without communications. The Allied

---

indicated that the approach might be fruitful, Balfour sent him another message, dated 29 March, which the Ambassador handed in paraphrase to Secretary of State Lansing on 2 April (U.S. National Archives, State Department file 861.00/1436½).

[52] Reading to Balfour, New York, 27 March 1918 (transmitted through Wiseman to Drummond as CXP 576); Wiseman MSS.

[53] The text of this statement, which contained nothing new but was sent on the urgings of the French, is printed in Lloyd George, *War Memoirs*, vol. II, pp. 1898-99.

[54] Wilson to Lansing, 22 March 1918; *Foreign Relations, The Lansing Papers*, vol. II, p. 357.

[55] Reading to Balfour, 27 March 1918; cited above, footnote 52. In reply to House's query, Reading says that he "expressed strong doubt as to Lockhart's suitability for such a mission." Perhaps this was one of the results of Balfour's transmission of Knox's attack upon Lockhart.

[56] Kennan, *Decision to Intervene*, pp. 59-61.

consuls met immediately, and except for their American colleague (who was supported by the American naval commander[57]) found themselves unanimous in agreeing that their governments should consider intervention. By the 28th, with the Bolsheviks shipping 40 carloads of Allied war stores out of Vladivostok each day and openly boasting of their strength, even the Americans agreed.[58]

A day later, the British Consul, Hodgson, and Captain Payne, commanding *H.M.S. Suffolk*, described the situation to London in a long joint telegram. It was obvious, they said, that the Bolsheviks were relying on the continued inactivity of the Allies to allow them to take over piecemeal all local institutions. The Ussuri Cossacks,[59] whom British representatives had been counting upon (and encouraging) as a potential nucleus of anti-Bolshevism in Far-Eastern Siberia, were no longer a factor: their organisation had been broken in a premature rising at Blagoveschensk. Neither were the secret White Guard organisations which had been formed at Vladivostok adequate to resist. Only active opposition by the Allies, said Hodgson and Payne, would prevent the Soviet from gaining complete control. The Bolsheviks realised that the warships in the harbour would not protect the town unless so ordered by their governments, and they believed that the political situation was such that the Allies would take action only to protect their consulates. If Britain had adopted a policy favourable to Japanese intervention, the joint telegram concluded, the critical moment when action should be taken had come. If the Bolsheviks took power, all possibilities of guarding the war stores would vanish.[60]

[57] This officer, Admiral A. N. Knight, Commander of the United States Asiatic Fleet, had telegraphed his opinion (received in Washington on 18 March) that there was "absolutely no danger" that the munitions at Vladivostok would reach the Germans (Woodrow Wilson MSS, series II). Knight's message was cabled by Wiseman to London, where it was circulated to the War Cabinet (Milner MSS, box E-I).

[58] Kennan, *Decision to Intervene*, pp. 95-97.

[59] In early March Sir John Jordan at Peking relayed to London his military attaché's opinion that the Cossacks of the Ussuri Province seemed ready to act against the Bolsheviks if immediately provided with funds, arms and ammunition (telegram 202, 3 March, 11:25 a.m.; Milner MSS, box E-I). Very little else is known about Britain's relations with this group. Japanese sources indicate that a British Major Dunlop did give them some money, and that on 11 March Greene in Tokyo presented the Japanese Foreign Minister with a memorandum indicating Britain's willingness "to consider" supplying the Ussuri Cossacks, but desiring first to know Japanese opinion (Morley, *Japanese Thrust*, pp. 96-97).

[60] Hodgson to Balfour (telegram 18) and Captain Payne to Admiralty (telegram 35), Vladivostok, 29 March 1918 (transmitted by Sir C. Greene, Tokyo, as telegrams 298 and 301, 11:45 p.m.); Wiseman MSS.

The British government's reaction to this telegram was to send Captain Payne a set of instructions that, in view of the complex situation prevailing in Vladivostok and the grave implications that would flow from an Allied landing and occupation, were remarkably vague: he was simply to act in concert with his Japanese and American colleagues to prevent removal of the military stores if such an event seemed likely.[61] The Japanese commander, Admiral Kato, had similarly vague orders: he was to occupy the city only in self-defence, or to prevent an exclusive Anglo-American occupation. Moreover, Kato was empowered to effect a landing without prior approval from Tokyo.[62] Only the American commander, Admiral Knight, had anything like specific orders: he was to take no part in any action unless instructed to do so by the Navy Department. American force would be used only to protect Americans.[63]

Tension mounted rapidly in the first days of April. Admiral Knight reported that the Red Guards numbered 3,000; there was talk of plots to blow up the munition stores and fire on the Allied ships.[64] Then, at mid-morning on the 4th, several armed men (their identity has never been determined) entered a Japanese shop, demanded money, and upon being refused shot three Japanese clerks, at least one of whom died.[65] Admiral Kato immediately conferred with the Japanese Consul-General and an army representative and decided that "self-defence" required a landing of marines. At 4 a.m. the next morning Kato notified the British and American commanders of his decision, and an hour later the first of six companies of Japanese marines (about 500 men) landed. Their mission, Kato informed the city's Russian officials, was simply to protect the lives and property of Japanese citizens in the city.[66]

Captain Payne at once offered to take similar action and, after conferring with Consul Hodgson, landed 50 men to guard the vicinity of the British consulate.[67] Thus, British involvement came as a result of a decision taken independently by the Japanese com-

[61] As reported by Balfour to Lockhart, Moscow, telegram 32, 30 March 1918 (to Lord Reading as no. 1851); Wiseman MSS.
[62] Morley, *Japanese Thrust*, p. 145.
[63] Kennan, *Decision to Intervene*, p. 98.
[64] *ibid.*
[65] Morley, *Japanese Thrust*, p. 146.
[66] *ibid.*, pp. 147-48.
[67] Hodgson to Balfour, telegram 26, Vladivostok, 6 April 1918, 3:5 a.m.; Milner MSS, box E-1.

mander on the spot, without any consultation between the two governments. Nor, it seems, had there been consultation between either commander and his own government before troops were landed. The landing parties met no resistance as they took up positions in the city; the Bolsheviks, apparently, were taken completely by surprise.[68]

No American troops were landed: Admiral Knight did not feel that American lives or property were endangered.[69] Washington held to this position and refused to take any part despite a strongly-worded appeal from Balfour emphasising "the essential importance of our acting together in this question."[70] The French, since they had no ships in the harbour, were absolved from the necessity of deciding what to do. The French Consul, however, publicly welcomed the Japanese marines;[71] there is no question that had French forces been available, they would have participated.

The landings precipitated a crisis which laid bare all the many complex and diverging strands of British policy towards the Soviet government.

In Moscow, naturally enough, it seemed as if the long-expected intervention from the east had come. Immediately upon receipt of the news, Chicherin summoned Lockhart. Much perturbed, the Commissar for Foreign Affairs told the British agent that he found it difficult to believe that the Allies could be guilty of supporting such an action at just the time when the Bolsheviks were preparing to conclude an alliance with them.[72] Trotsky, the only Bolshevik leader who was by nature even more volatile than Chicherin, was furious. By participating along with the Japanese, he told Lockhart, the British had betrayed *him*. The policy of agreement with the Allies, of which he was the chief architect, had been dashed to the ground on the very eve of fruition.[73]

Reporting these interviews to London, Lockhart emphasised the seriousness with which he viewed the situation: the Bolsheviks had

[68] Kennan, *Decision to Intervene*, pp. 99-100.
[69] *ibid*., p. 100.
[70] Paraphrase of a telegram from Balfour to Reading, 7 April 1918, handed by Reading to Secretary of State Lansing on 8 April; *Foreign Relations, 1918, Russia*, vol. II, p. 108.
[71] Morley, *Japanese Thrust*, p. 147.
[72] Lockhart to Balfour, telegram 72, Moscow, 5 April 1918 (sent 6 April 12:55 p.m.) Milner MSS, box B.
[73] Lockhart to Balfour, telegram 73, Moscow, 5 April 1918, 7:30 p.m.; Milner MSS, box B.

given orders for the mobilisation of all their forces in Siberia; local Soviets had been instructed to resist Japan and destroy the railway if necessary. If the incident were not settled within the next few days Russia would declare war upon Japan, and that would mean the collapse of all Allied efforts in Russia. Intervention could be effective, Lockhart said, only if it had the consent of the Russian government.[74]

Meanwhile, the Soviet government released a public statement on the landings. For months, it said, the Japanese had been seeking an appropriate pretext for invading Russia. They were responsible for the "monstrous statements" about the German menace in Siberia and the rumours about the arming of German prisoners of war which had made the rounds of the world's press. Now they had used the incident of the murder in Vladivostok for such a pretext, and had landed troops without even investigating its circumstances.

All this was to be expected of Japan, the statement said. But what was the policy of the other Allied governments towards her predatory intentions? America, it seemed, was opposed to the invasion, but it appeared that Britain intended "to act hand in hand with Japan in working Russia's ruin."[75] A note to each of the Allied representatives in Moscow demanded an explanation of his government's attitude and an immediate withdrawal of the troops.[76] And Lenin telegraphed to the Vladivostok Soviet that a further Japanese invasion was inevitable, and ordered them to give their attention to "the best way out, the best retreat, the carrying off of stores and railroad material."[77]

In London, on 7 April, Balfour's first reaction to the landings (before he had heard from Lockhart, whose telegrams did not arrive until the 8th) was both to reassure and to berate the Bolsheviks. After telling Lockhart the circumstances in which the landings had taken place, the Foreign Secretary instructed him to assure Trotsky that their sole object had been to protect the lives and property of Vladivostok's foreign residents. At the same time, Lockhart was to point

[74] *idem.*

[75] The text of the Soviet statement, dated 5 April, from *Izvestiya*, 6 April, is printed in *Dokumenty vneshnei politiki*, vol. 1, pp. 224-26. Most of it is translated in Degras, *Soviet Documents*, vol. 1, pp. 67-68.

[76] Chicherin to Lockhart, 6 April 1918 (identical notes to Robins and to French Consul-General Grenard); *Dokumenty vneshnei politiki*, vol. 1, pp. 230-31. Degras, *Soviet Documents*, vol. 1, pp. 68-69.

[77] Lenin to Vladivostok Soviet, 7 April 1918; *Dokumenty vneshnei politiki*, vol. 1, pp. 233-34.

out to Trotsky "how unfortunate" it was "that there should be dis-
orders in Vladivostok at a moment when the Allied Governments
[were] most anxious to do all in their power to give him assistance
and support."[78] Balfour virtually implied that the Bolsheviks, and not
the Japanese, were to blame for the landings.

Into this air of rather detached reproach, Lockhart's telegrams
brought a first realisation of how grave a view of the situation the
Bolsheviks had taken. To Captain Payne, in reply to his account of
the incident and its causes, careful instructions were sent. "The
declared objects of the landings referred to in your telegram are so far
as we are concerned the real objects," the message began. Therefore,
Payne was to "discourage any larger schemes" that might be entertained by the Japanese, and in any case not associate himself with
them. It would be a great advantage to British policy "if the troubles
which necessitated the landing could be amicably settled with the
local authorities and the incident brought to a close."[79]

To Greene, in Tokyo, Balfour sent the texts of his telegrams to
Lockhart and Captain Payne, asking the Ambassador to urge the
views they contained on the Japanese government and to express
London's hope that they would send similar instructions to Admiral
Kato. "There is," he concluded, "a real prospect that Trotski may
assent or even invite Allied intervention if present incident is treated
as purely local and amicable settlement reached."[80] This was only four
days after the Foreign Secretary had asked that Semenov be restrained
for the same reasons.

To Lockhart, simultaneously with the telegrams to the *Suffolk* and
to Greene, Balfour sent a message again stating that the incident had
no relation to the larger question of intervention in Siberia, and telling him of Payne's instructions. The Soviet attitude, Balfour said,
"must be due either to imperfect information, or to a desire to pick a

---

[78] Balfour to Lockhart, Moscow, telegram 55, 7 April 1918, 1:30 p.m.; Milner MSS,
box E-1. A paraphrase, to the State Department on 8 April, appears in *Foreign Relations, 1918, Russia*, vol. II, p. 109.

[79] Admiralty to *H.M.S. Suffolk*, 9 April 1918 (repeated to Paris, Tokyo, and
Washington Embassies, 10 p.m.); Milner MSS, box E-1.

[80] Balfour to Sir C. Greene, Tokyo, telegram 311, 9 April 1918, 10 p.m.; Milner MSS,
box B.

Replying to a question in the House of Commons on 11 April, Lord Robert Cecil
stated that the action at Vladivostok was of purely local significance, and had been
undertaken "with the sole object of protecting life and property." (104 HC Deb. 5s
cols. 1612-13).

quarrel with us." If the former, Lockhart would undoubtedly be able to set the matter right; if the latter, then the outlook was indeed gloomy.[81]

Lockhart did not, it seems, choose to inject this argumentative tone into his dealings with the Soviet government, which had already stated that it would believe the Allied assurances, "irreproachably friendly in their outward form," when the troops were withdrawn.[82] His note of explanation to Chicherin contained none of Balfour's remonstrances, stated that the incident was only local, and ended with assurances of the British government's support "to the Russian Government in its struggle against Germany"—a phrase that was optimistic, if not strictly accurate.[83]

Unknown to all of the other parties in this complex episode, the Japanese were just as anxious as anyone else to avoid an entanglement at Vladivostok. Before the landing, on 30 March, Admiral Kato had been warned that provocative action in the port would "invite a misunderstanding in foreign relations" that would seriously endanger Japan's position "should operations be necessary later in Siberia."[84] He had taken the decision to land entirely on his own initiative; faced with a *fait accompli*, the Japanese government could only order him not to go beyond measures necessary to protect Japanese citizens, and warned him "not to be drawn into so-called positive action by intriguers."[85] When the British Ambassador was told, in reply to his *démarche*, that the Japanese fully agreed with Balfour's position and had already sent orders to restrain their Admiral, the statement was completely sincere.[86] In Tokyo the incident caused a governmental crisis that ended with the resignation of the bellicose Foreign Minister, Motono, and his replacement by Baron Shimpei Goto, who also favoured intervention in Siberia, but urged a much slower and more careful involvement on Japan's own terms.[87] Accordingly, on 25 April the Japanese marines were withdrawn (the fifty British had previ-

---

[81] Balfour to Lockhart, Moscow, telegram 62, 9 April 1918, 10 p.m.; Milner MSS, box B.

[82] Degras, *Soviet Documents*, vol. I, p. 69 (from *Izvestiya*, 9 April, 1918).

[83] Lockhart to Chicherin, 10 April 1918; *Dokumenty vneshnei politiki*, vol. I, p. 231.

[84] Morley, *Japanese Thrust*, p. 144.

[85] *ibid.*, p. 153 (from the navy vice-minister's orders to Kato on 6 April).

[86] Greene's telegram to Balfour, 12 April 1918, was summarised in a memorandum to the State Department from the British Embassy on 15 April; U.S. National Archives, State Department file 861.00/1627.

[87] Morley, *Japanese Thrust*, pp. 155-56.

ously retired to the *Suffolk*) and by 2 May the Vladivostok Soviet, without any opposition, took control of the city. The Japanese explicitly made them responsible for maintaining order and protecting foreigners.[88] Thus, if only for a brief interval, the Bolsheviks controlled all of Siberia. But in the few days between the Japanese departure and the consolidation of Soviet power, a new and vastly more complicating element entered the turbulent city in the form of 6,000 Czechoslovak soldiers.[89]

❖

During the early part of the war there had been incorporated into the Russian army a detachment composed of Czechs and Slovaks who were then living on Russian soil. This force, although small, fought with distinction. Perhaps because its members were aiming at a specific goal—the constitution of an independent Czecho-Slovak state —it was not subject to the disintegration and loss of discipline which destroyed the bulk of the Russian army. Quickly it became one of the major bargaining counters used by the Czechoslovak National Council, established in Paris in 1916, in their efforts to gain Allied recognition for their national status.

Under the Provisional Government, at the instigation of the Czech Council, the force in Russia was expanded by the addition of Czech and Slovak prisoners of war until it reached the size of an army corps. With the Russian collapse in the summer of 1917 it became clear that the Czechs could accomplish little by remaining in the east, and the Council opened negotiations with the Allies for their transport to the Western Front. So desperate was the need for manpower in the west that this idea became almost an obsession with the French. On 16 December 1917, the French recognised the Czechs as an autonomous army placed under the general direction of the French Supreme Command, with the understanding that they would be evacuated to France as rapidly as possible.[90]

[88] *ibid.*, pp. 159-60. All Morley's information is from Japanese Archives.

[89] U.S. Consul, Vladivostok, to Secretary of State, 30 April 1918; *Foreign Relations, 1918, Russia*, vol. II, p. 148.

[90] The text of the French decree, signed by Poincaré, Clemenceau, and Pichon on 16 December 1917, is in the Milner MSS, unfiled folder 33. Unless otherwise cited, the background information in the foregoing paragraphs is drawn from Kennan, *Decision to Intervene*, pp. 136-65, and James Bunyan, *Intervention, Civil War, and Communism in Russia, April-December 1918: Documents and Materials*, Baltimore, 1936, pp. 75-101.

In early 1918, Thomas Masaryk came to Petrograd to negotiate with the Bolsheviks for the evacuation of the Czech Corps. He had to leave Russia before any definite agreement was reached, but on his departure, just after the signing of the Brest treaty, he firmly laid down the principle that the Corps was to take no part in internal Russian dissensions; only those parties which sided openly with the Central Powers were to be opposed as enemies.[91] The Corps was at this time in the neighbourhood of Kiev. Their evacuation was cut off by an advancing German column; at the rail junction of Bakhmach, during the second week of March, fighting side by side with Ukrainian Bolshevik forces, they broke through the enemy encirclement and began a long trek eastwards.[92] Meanwhile, on 15 March the Sovnarkom, under Lenin's prodding, formally decided to allow the Czechs to cross Siberia and leave Russia via Vladivostok (Archangel, the alternative port, being frozen).[93] By this time the force numbered 42,000 men;[94] it was constantly growing with the addition of more Czech and Slovak prisoners of war.

From this point, relations between the Czechs and the Bolsheviks became increasingly embittered. The Bolsheviks immediately began to doubt the wisdom of allowing a highly disciplined and well-armed force to enter into the explosive Siberian situation,[95] and individual Siberian Soviets expressed considerable alarm.[96] Accordingly, on 26 March Moscow issued new conditions: the non-communist Russian officers who still led the Corps were to be removed, and the Czechs were to proceed to Vladivostok "not as fighting units but as a group of free citizens," disarmed except for a few rifles and a machine gun on each train.[97] At Penza, which their foremost trains had now reached, the Czechs agreed to a modified version of these terms under which they retained certain of their Russian officers. Moreover, they managed to conceal additional quantities of arms

[91] Thomas G. Masaryk, *Making of a State*, p. 259.
[92] Gustav Bečvar, *The Lost Legion: A Czechoslovakian Epic*, London, 1939, pp. 67-70.
[93] Bunyan, *Intervention*, p. 77; Kennan, *Decision to Intervene*, p. 139.
[94] General Staff Paper: "Precis of Intelligence regarding Czech Troops" (no date); Milner MSS, unfiled folder 33.
[95] By 18 March, Eduard Beneš has written, "the situation in Moscow had changed, and the military authorities began to make difficulties about the departure of our troops, their explanation being that the Czechoslovak Army might join Semyonov or the Japanese." (*My War Memoirs*, London, 1928, p. 355.)
[96] Bunyan, *Intervention*, pp. 80-81.
[97] This order, signed by Stalin, is printed in *ibid.*, pp. 81-82.

over and above the small quantities allowed them.[98] A few days later, because of the Japanese landing at Vladivostok, the Bolsheviks again temporarily halted their progress.

This further antagonism, combined with Bolshevik efforts to spread revolutionary propaganda among the Corps, caused the Czechs to fear that the Soviet government was acting under German pressure. On 14 April, meeting secretly at Kirsanov, the battalion and company commanders of the First Division decided that they could not rely upon agreements with the Bolsheviks, and that they had to be prepared to force their way eastwards.[99] This decision, soon adopted by the whole Corps, was to have the most serious consequences.

Meanwhile, the Czechs had begun to figure prominently in inter-Allied discussions of Russian policy. The British had never contracted, to the degree that the French had done, the Western Front mentality which viewed every other theatre as subordinate, and no nation's contribution as really significant unless made in the west.[100] This attitude made the French insist, throughout the spring and early summer of 1918, that the Czech Corps be brought to France; on the other hand, almost from the outset the British War Office began to doubt the worth of the enormous effort and diversion of resources necessary to bring the Czechs to the west, through either Vladivostok or Archangel. Once brought, moreover, they would be only a relatively small addition to the massive Allied armies, whereas in the midst of the Siberian chaos the disciplined, efficient Czechs would be of enormous military significance. And the bitter pill of Japanese intervention would be much more palatable for the Russian people if it had a Czech (and hence Slavic) coating. Left in Russia the Czechs could control Siberia from a base at Omsk, or else they could proceed to Archangel, whence communications with Siberia could be maintained by way of Perm. Finally, they might go beyond Lake Baikal and join Semenov, thus creating a nucleus around which a reorganised Russian army could form. These views were put forward in a memorandum from the War Office to Beneš, communicated to him

---

[98] Kennan, *Decision to Intervene*, p. 142.

[99] The text of the Kirsanov Resolution is printed in Bunyan, *Intervention*, pp. 83-85.

[100] This French attitude did not make them any the less zealous in seeking a new Eastern Front. Victory, they insisted, could come only in the west; new pressure from the east would, however, make the western task easier. But they envisioned the use in the east *only* of forces which could not by any means be made available for service in the west: the Japanese.

through the French government on 1 April. The last solution, Beneš says, particularly appealed to the British.[101]

This British *démarche* initiated a series of conversations, between the French and the British and between each of them and the Czech Council, that were extremely ambiguous; the misunderstandings they engendered produced a minor crisis in Anglo-French relations when the matter came to a head in mid-May. Beneš, who saw that the Corps would have much greater political value if it could share in Allied victory in the west, began the confusion with his reply to the British. Drafted with the aid of the French General Staff, it opposed any action which might delay the passage of the troops to France.[102]

On 8 April, however, the Permanent Military Representatives to the Supreme War Council (with French assent, but with U.S. General Bliss abstaining) approved a British Staff paper which implied that the Czechs would form part of a future Allied force in Siberia.[103] On 16 April the French General Staff proposed to the British that the Czechs be removed by way of Archangel and Murmansk, whence transport to France would be much quicker than from the Far East. While awaiting shipment the Czechs might protect the ports.[104] Somehow, either wilfully or by accident, the British War Office construed this French offer as an indication that the Czechs might, after all, stay in Russia. Beneš' assent was obtained on 22 April to a British proposal that the Czechs west of the Urals be moved to Archangel while those east continued on to the Pacific.[105] This plan was incorporated into a British memorandum[106] which subsequently became the basis of another Joint Note by the Permanent Military

---

[101] Beneš, *War Memoirs*, p. 357, and p. 506, n. 50. Many of these suggestions were made almost parenthetically in a memorandum dated 25 March 1918, by Brig. Gen. H. W. Studd, "A" Branch, British Section, Supreme War Council, entitled "Allied Intervention in Siberia, its Importance from a Military Point of View"; copy in U.S. National Archives, Modern Army Branch, Supreme War Council Records.

[102] Beneš, *War Memoirs*, pp. 357-58.

[103] Minutes, Military Representatives, 25th Meeting, Versailles, 8 April 1918, 10:30 a.m., and text of Joint Note 20; U.S. National Archives, Modern Army Branch, Supreme War Council Records.

[104] General Spears, Paris, to War Office, telegram 2506, 16 April 1918; summarised in "Precis of Intelligence regarding Czech Troops," *op.cit.*, Milner MSS, unfiled folder 33.

[105] Memorandum "Notes on conversation with Representatives of the Bohemian National Council at Versailles on 22nd April 1918," by Lt. Col. Stanhope, British Section, Supreme War Council (circulated to War Cabinet); Milner MSS, unfiled folder 33.

[106] General Staff memorandum, "Proposed Movement of Czech Troops in Russia to Archangel and Murmansk," 23 April 1918; Milner MSS, unfiled folder 33.

Representatives. After stating that "there is everything to be gained" by bringing the Czechs to France as rapidly as possible, the note went on to confirm the policy of splitting the Corps into two groups, one part to go to the Pacific and the other to North Russia. And it further stated that while the troops were awaiting shipment, they could profitably be employed to guard the Murmansk Railway and "to co-operate with the Allies in Siberia" on the lines laid down in Joint Note 20.[107]

These two conflicting policies—to pull the Czechs out or to allow them to become embroiled in the Russian conflict—were not reconciled by the Supreme War Council when it met at Abbeville on 2 May. Sir Henry Wilson suggested that Britain take responsibility for shipping the Corps, but then voiced pessimism about the prospects of finding sufficient tonnage. And Milner suggested that since it might be some time until the tonnage were found, it would be better if the Czechs were stopped on their way to Vladivostok, to avoid concentration in the port, and were stationed at Omsk or Chelyabinsk along the railway. Reluctantly, the French agreed, and the following resolution was adopted:

(a) The British Government undertake to do their best to arrange the transportation of those Czech troops who are at Vladivostok or on their way to that port.

(b) The French Government undertake the responsibility for those troops until they are embarked.

(c) The British Government undertake to approach M. Trotski with a view to the concentration at Murmansk and Archangel of those Czech troops not belonging to the Army Corps which has left Omsk for Vladivostok.[108]

The Abbeville Resolution, as it came to be called, settled nothing. The French went away from the historic Chambre des Notaires convinced that the Czech Corps was shortly bound for the Western Front; the British, on the other hand, were grateful that they had managed to salvage the freedom of action by which the Czechs could be used according to the dictates of the rapidly changing Russian

[107] Minutes, Military Representatives, 27th Meeting, Versailles, 27 April 1918, 10 a.m., and text of Joint Note 25; U.S. National Archives, Modern Army Branch, Supreme War Council Records.

[108] Minutes, Supreme War Council, 5th session, 2nd and 3rd meetings, Abbeville, 2 May 1918, 11:35 a.m. and 2:45 p.m.; U.S. National Archives, Modern Army Branch, Supreme War Council Records.

scene. Meanwhile, strung out from Penza, west of the Volga, all the way to Vladivostok, the Czech trains crawled eastward along the railway. For the legionaries themselves, now numbering over 60,000, the explosive situation about them was infinitely more vital than any decisions concerning them which might be made in France.

✧

One of the most troubling aspects of the Siberian situation, both for the Czechs on the scene and for the Allied statesmen faced with making a Russian policy, was the presence east of the Urals at the time of the Revolution of as many as 800,000 enemy prisoners of war.[109] Technically placed at liberty by the treaty of Brest-Litovsk, many of them were left, in the general chaos that prevailed, fairly much to their own devices. It was only natural for the Allied governments to fear that these prisoners would find arms and serve the purposes of the Central Powers, perhaps in collaboration with the Bolsheviks.

A very small proportion of the prisoners—less than a tenth—were German. The majority were from the non-Austrian portions of the Austro-Hungarian Empire. Kennan has well described the conditions in which they lived and the assiduous efforts made by the Bolsheviks to spread propaganda among them, including attempts (that went a great deal beyond propaganda) to recruit them into the Red Army. He has also told of the vigorous measures taken by the enemy officers to combat this disaffection among their soldiers, how Soviet proselytizing ceased due to strenuous protest from the German and Austrian governments, and how the communist formations were almost entirely broken up with the arrival of German and Austrian repatriation and welfare commissions at the end of May.[110] Finally, Kennan cites Swedish Red Cross reports placing the number of prisoners in the whole of Russia who were actually armed by the Bolsheviks as 15,000, of whom 5,000 were in Turkestan alone. Most of these were Hungarians; the very few Germans, however, usually assumed positions of leadership, a fact which Kennan suggests might have helped to mislead Allied observers about the extent of German participation.[111]

These were, as well as can be determined, the facts. But the situa-

[109] Kennan (*Decision to Intervene*, p. 71) discusses the various estimates of the number of prisoners, and selects 800,000 as a reasonable figure.
[110] *ibid.*, pp. 71-73.
[111] *ibid.*, pp. 73-74.

tion was dominated not by fact but by rumour, such as the report on 9 June by the British Consul at Vladivostok that, according to the "best information," there were some 275,000 prisoners still in Siberia, and of these:

Accounts vary as to the proportion which is armed but it is certainly considerable. Many have joined the Red Army and individuals have acquired dominating influence in local Soviets.[112]

This information was incorporated, without comment on its nature or its origins, into the War Office's intelligence summary for the week, which added: "Whilst many of these may have joined the Bolsheviks in accordance with their political convictions, the fact that this wholesale recruiting may be part of the enemy plans must not be lost sight of."[113]

Some explanation of the origins of many of these rumours was put forward in a report written in late April by Lockhart's assistant, Captain W. L. Hicks, and Captain W. B. Webster, of the American Red Cross Mission, who were sent from Moscow by Lockhart and Raymond Robins, with the warm approval and support of Trotsky, to investigate the arming of prisoners. Their conclusions, they wrote, "differed materially from those set forth by Allied consular reports and other sources of information in Siberia." For this difference they listed three reasons:

We found, first, that the Allied consuls in Irkutsk [the seat of the All-Siberian Soviet] were unanimously anti-Bolshevik in sympathy, had had nothing to do with the Soviet authorities personally, and had not even met . . . the President of the All-Siberian Soviet. . . .

Second, their sources of information were, in all cases, pre-revolutionary —as coming from property-holders, officers, Cadets, White Guards, who were strong enemies of the present regime and were naturally desirous of strengthening their own position and damning those now in power; while

Third, the Consuls seemed to have no time to make proper investigation on account of their staffs being so small that, as one consul said to us, he was so busy coding the information he received that he did not have time to confirm it. If they heard a story concerning great intrigues or secret movements of (sic) unseen German activities, especially in regard to armed

[112] Hodgson to Balfour, telegram 59, Vladivostok, 9 June 1918, 1:40 p.m. (from Balfour to Reading on June 12 as no. 3625); Wiseman MSS.
[113] General Staff (M.I.O.), War Office, "Summary of Intelligence No. 10, relative to Affairs in Siberia, for the period ending June 14th, 1918" (transmitted to the U.S. Ambassador); U.S. National Archives, State Department file 861.00/2178.

prisoners, they did not get to the bottom of the particular rumour but reported the statements as they had received them. Even those things which were at hand and which could have been checked easily by proper care on their part did not receive the attention necessary to draw out the real truth.[114]

Another source of considerably inflated estimates of the number of armed prisoners was the Japanese General Staff. Like their Western allies, the Japanese tended hopelessly to exaggerate German capabilities in the east; perhaps because their interests were more immediately threatened, they tended to exaggerate them even more.[115] One cannot but suspect that the Japanese often passed on to their allies figures which they knew to be based on the slightest of evidence, in order to increase the pressure for intervention and thus to gain the freedom of action they sought.

Hicks and Webster, on the other hand, who conducted the most thorough investigation for the Western Allies, erred on the side of under-estimation.[116] They found only 931 armed prisoners, and reported that Soviet officials at Irkutsk (the military centre of Siberia) were prepared to guarantee that no more than 1,500 would be armed. And at Omsk, where a Hungarian Red Guard had been formed from prisoners who had opted for Soviet citizenship, the authorities set a maximum of 1,000. The prisoners were being armed, Hicks and Webster were told, to combat Semenov; if the Allies would cease supporting him, his movement would fail and then, it was implied, there would be no more incentive to arm the prisoners.[117] As Kennan points out, the situation was more complex than these two officers realised, and their figures were too low, although much more nearly correct than the swollen estimates of other sources. But their basic conclusion—that there was no appreciable danger to Allied war interests from the Siberian prisoners—was sound.[118]

In the climate of opinion that prevailed in London in the spring of 1918, at the flood-tide of German success, the Hicks-Webster report

[114] Hicks' and Webster's complete final report, Moscow, 26 April 1918, is printed in Cumming and Pettit, *Russian-American Relations*, pp. 177-84. This quotation is from pp. 180-81.

[115] In early February, for instance, the Japanese General Staff reported that the Germans were "making use of Russia," and might soon release more than 100,000 prisoners against the Far East (Morley, *Japanese Thrust*, p. 114).

[116] The best account of their mission is in Kennan, *Decision to Intervene*, pp. 75-81.

[117] Cumming and Pettit, *Russian-American Relations*, pp. 179-83.

[118] Kennan, *Decision to Intervene*, p. 81.

was dismissed out of hand; their findings never seem to have been referred to in the many British policy memoranda drafted during this period. The War Office even went so far as to ask for Hicks' recall immediately after it had received his final despatch. It was over-ruled only after a vigorous protest by Lockhart, who affirmed his complete confidence in Hicks and stated that if his assistant were recalled he would have no choice but to resign himself.[119]

❖

Lockhart, during all of these complex developments in Siberia, was continuing his efforts to reach an agreement with the Bolsheviks. On 11 April—when Balfour, in London, was working to secure Japanese evacuation of Vladivostok and to prevent further action by Semenov —Lockhart summarised the situation as he saw it from Moscow.

The Bolsheviks, he maintained, were the only real power existing in Russia. They were not popular but they were well organised. They ruled by force and were not afraid to use it. (This statement was forcibly underlined barely eight hours after the telegram was despatched, at 3 a.m. on the 12th, when the Cheka descended simultaneously on 26 anarchist centres in Moscow, killing over 100 and arresting 500.)[120] The Bolsheviks were not pro-German, but they were opportunists who would treat with anyone who would support them. If the Allies drove them to it, they would not hesitate to bargain with Germany.

Allied intervention, Lockhart said, was opposed by every class. The universal outcry over the Japanese landings, from bourgeois as well as proletarian parties, proved this. If intervention had to take place, Lockhart insisted, the consent of the Bolsheviks was vitally necessary. Their consent might still be obtainable, but the events at Vladivostok had made it much less likely. Only immediate withdrawal of the landing forces could allay Bolshevik suspicions.

The Allies had made another great mistake, Lockhart continued, in

[119] Lockhart, *British Agent*, p. 252.

[120] Both Lockhart and Oliver Wardrop were tremendously impressed by the vigour and utter ruthlessness with which the Bolsheviks acted against the anarchists. Both testified to their complete victory, Lockhart adding (not, it seems, wholly correctly) that a source of counter-revolution and German influence had been crushed, and that it "affords a significant lesson to Allies in their estimate of power of Bolsheviks." (Lockhart to Balfour, telegram 90, 12 April 1918, 8:5 p.m.; Wardrop to Balfour, telegram 192, 6:35 p.m.; Milner MSS, box B.) See also the account in Lockhart, *British Agent*, pp. 258-59.

supporting Semenov—this also had rendered intervention by agreement less likely. Further, they had greatly exaggerated the danger from armed prisoners of war, although in the event of forced intervention by Japan the Bolsheviks would certainly arm those willing to fight. Intervention by Japan alone, Lockhart concluded, would afford no guarantee that the Japanese would ever reach European Russia. Without such a guarantee, it was difficult to see what military or political advantage could come from Japanese occupation of Siberia.[121]

Two days later, Lockhart discussed intervention with Trotsky. The Commissar realised, Lockhart reported, that the Bolsheviks were faced with a choice between agreement with the Allies or forced intervention which would either destroy their regime or drive them into the arms of the Germans. He was impressed by the British agent's assurances that the Allies would give the most solemn guarantees of Russia's territorial integrity and of their non-interference in internal politics. Trotsky said that since he did not yet know the exact form of intervention the Allies proposed, he could not give a definite acceptance, but he made the following statement, which he authorised Lockhart to transmit to London:

> Realising that Russia must sooner or later fight Germany in order to rid herself of the yoke of an unfair peace and that in these circumstances Allied help would be most desirable, he invites the Allied Governments to submit to him at the earliest opportunity full and proper statement of help which they could furnish and of guarantees they are prepared to give. If conditions are (? satisfactory) he considers conclusion of an agreement both necessary and desirable.[122]

This statement, it should be noted, committed the Bolsheviks to absolutely nothing; instead, it threw responsibility for reaching an agreement upon the Allies who, Trotsky well knew, were themselves divided as to what policy should be pursued. It was a skilful move, probably designed only to increase the desperately-needed breathing space and room for manoeuvre.

If this was its purpose it succeeded. Before Lockhart's message arrived in London, Balfour telegraphed his opinion that the Allies could not suggest a detailed scheme of military aid to Russia until

[121] Lockhart to Balfour, telegram 87, Moscow, 11 April 1918, 6:52 p.m.; Milner MSS, box B.

[122] Lockhart to Balfour, telegram 94, Moscow, 13 April 1918, 8:45 p.m. (received in London 18 April, 7:15 p.m.); Milner MSS, box B.

there was some agreement on "general principles"—by which the Foreign Secretary meant simply agreement to oppose the Central Powers in every possible way.[123] In a further telegram to Moscow, he stated that time was of such essential value that if Trotsky did not agree to fight, say by the end of April, the government would reluctantly be compelled to reconsider their whole policy towards the Soviet regime.[124] And in a message to the State Department, he said pessimistically:

Our military advisers are unanimous in thinking that we cannot hope to set up at the present moment any military force in Russia which would be really effective, at any rate by Russian effort alone, and unless such a force exists it is impossible to carry out any of the main purposes of our policy. Even assuming that the Soviet Government could, by their own efforts, call a new army into being, it is most uncertain that this army would be employed to fight or impede the enemy. The object of the Soviet Government is to produce a world wide social revolution, not to gain a military victory, and they might very well consider that their main object would be more easily obtained by encouraging peaceful penetration by the Germans than by resisting the German army.[125]

Balfour's tone changed completely, however, following the receipt of Trotsky's statement. His optimism was now unbounded.[126] On 24 April he cabled to Reading in Washington:

Please explain to Colonel House that in my view situation is entirely altered by apparent willingness of Trotsky to invite Allied assistance against German aggression. Allied troops would be able to traverse Siberia at a great speed provided Russians are friendly, and if joined by Bolsheviki and other Russian contingents would certainly constitute such a menace to

---

[123] Balfour to Lockhart, telegram 65, 13 April 1918, 11:30 p.m.; Milner MSS, box B.

[124] Balfour to Lockhart, telegram 68, 15 April 1918, 7:30 p.m.; Milner MSS, box B.

[125] Balfour to Reading, Washington, telegram 2204, 15 April 1918, 10 p.m.; Milner MSS, box B (paraphrase, to State Department on 19 April; in Woodrow Wilson MSS, series 11, box 138).

[126] So, it seems, was that of his colleagues. After a session of the War Cabinet on 22 April, General Sir Henry Wilson cryptically entered into his diary: "It was decided that Smuts should go to Kola to see Trotsky." (Callwell, *Henry Wilson*, vol. 11, p. 93.) This is the only piece of evidence I have come across that indicates that a meeting between a member of the British government and the Soviet leadership was even considered, but Wilson was present at the Cabinet meeting, and could hardly have misunderstood so important a decision. And it must be remembered that Smuts had, since December 1917, already made two secret missions to Switzerland to talk with Austro-Hungarian leaders.

the Germans in the East that latter could hardly withdraw further divisions and might even be compelled to strengthen the forces already there.[127]

Reading was told to see House first because House was (in his own words) "responsible for the President's refusal to consent to the Japanese going into Russia without an invitation from Russian sources,"[128] a reference to the American decision at the beginning of March. This time, the Foreign Secretary's enthusiasm spread to the Colonel. "Balfour has sent an entirely new proposal regarding Russia," House wrote to the President when Reading had left him, "one that I think you will approve."[129]

The proposal, prefaced with the remark that the War Cabinet had decided that it was essential to treat Europe and Asia for purposes of strategy as a single front, arrived in Washington the following day. Its stated object, "a national revival of Russia, such as ... in the time of Napoleon," was cast in terms which showed how naïve and misguided it was:

Russia has an immense supply of soldiers trained to arms, and with experience of modern warfare, including capable generals, and if the necessary spirit could be aroused, an effective army could in a short time be produced, and supplied from the stores now at Russian ports. The Germans would then be compelled either to withdraw or strengthen their forces in Russia.[130]

In other words, the same soldiers who had fled before, using the same weapons that were available to them then, were now to be called upon to expel the German invader—this was the real meaning of the British proposal. The incentive (directed not at the soldiers but at their government) was to be recognition of a sort: "if the Bolshevist government will cooperate in resisting Germany, it seems necessary to act with them as the *de facto* Russian Government." Balfour asked the Americans to join Britain in proposing intervention to the Bolsheviks, with guarantees that all Russian territory would be evacuated at the end of hostilities, and he also asked that America should send to Siberia, for co-operation with larger Japanese forces, a complete

[127] Balfour to Reading, private telegram sent through Wiseman, 24 April 1918; Wiseman MSS.
[128] Diary entry, 24 April 1918; House MSS.
[129] House to Wilson, 24 April; Woodrow Wilson MSS, series II, box 139.
[130] Balfour to Reading, Washington, 25 April 1918 (paraphrase sent same day to State Department); *Foreign Relations, 1918, Russia*, vol. II, p. 135.

division and various technical experts. American participation would be a primary factor in making intervention acceptable to the Russians.[131]

The hint at *de facto* recognition was the most novel feature of this British *démarche*—previously the Bolsheviks had been looked upon as one among many Russian authorities. Here again the guiding influence seems to have been Lockhart's. On the morning of the day Balfour sent the above telegram to Washington, he received a message from Lockhart saying that Chicherin and Trotsky agreed with most of the British ideas and that the only real difficulty was Japanese participation. Would the government, Lockhart asked, be prepared, if necessary, to "play the card of recognition?"[132]

At this point, however, the three to six days which were then required for cable messages between Moscow and London (as opposed to the overnight transmission which had been the case until a few weeks before) began seriously to impede Lockhart's usefulness as an intermediary. By the time Balfour had proposed to his American partners that they play the card of recognition, Lockhart had begun to have second thoughts. On 21 April he cabled that he was wrong in saying that Japanese intervention was the only part of Balfour's general scheme which the Bolsheviks would have difficulty in accepting; in fact there would be difficulties about all of it.

The Bolsheviks, he said, realised that if they declared war they would be crushed by the Germans long before Allied aid could arrive from Vladivostok. They thought that given a few months more to prepare they might be able to offer real resistance; this, Lockhart said, was doubtful. The Allies, therefore, should give the Bolsheviks a short period more and then lay down an ultimatum that intervention would come even if they did not agree to it. Lockhart's new position was this: while every effort should be made to gain Soviet consent, intervention was necessary in any case.

Lockhart did not explain his rather sudden change of opinion, but one of the major influences was the relationship he had now begun to have with anti-Bolshevik organisations. During the preceding fortnight, he indicated, he had been in direct or indirect contact with all of the various groups of any importance in Moscow, from

[131] *ibid.*, pp. 136-37.
[132] Lockhart to Balfour, un-numbered telegram, 19 April 1918, 7 p.m. (received 25 April, 8 a.m.); Milner MSS, box B.

supporters of the old monarchy, who based their hopes on Germany, through Cadets, Right SR's, and Mensheviks. All of them except the most extreme reactionaries would welcome Allied intervention provided it did not consist simply of an occupation of Siberia. Any intervening forces, he suggested, should be accompanied by a really efficient political mission, headed by some popular Allied representative such as Sir George Buchanan.[133]

Lockhart had not completely abandoned the Bolsheviks, however. On 25 April he telegraphed:

> It is useless . . . to pretend that we can intervene without first making an honest attempt to gain Bolshevik assent. This is absolutely essential to put us straight with all parties in the event of a refusal and to leave a door open for other Socialist parties whose influence may still count amongst working classes.

But his attempts to reach an agreement with the Soviet regime were made much more difficult by the fact that Britain was the only Allied power which had ever thought such an agreement necessary. And although all of the military representatives in Moscow shared his views (Generals Lavergne and Romei, he said, were even more confident than he was), their efforts were undermined by the diplomats at Vologda, particularly Noulens.[134]

Indeed, from the moment Noulens had arrived at Vologda at the end of March, he had worked against any collaboration with the Soviets. He had first contrived to have the chiefs of mission at Vologda agree that before any military help would be given to the Bolsheviks, the latter should first consent to Japanese intervention.[135] Thus, even the few French officers assigned to helping Trotsky were withdrawn. And on 23 April the day on which the first German ambassador to the Soviet government, Count Mirbach, arrived in Moscow, one of the few remaining non-Bolshevik newspapers in Moscow published an interview with Noulens in which he stated that the Soviet regime was too weak to be truly independent (thereby

[133] Lockhart to Balfour, telegram 115, Moscow, 21 April 1918 (despatched 22 April, 12:20 p.m., received 25 April, 12:5 p.m.); Milner MSS, box B.

[134] Lockhart to Balfour, telegram 126, Moscow, 25 April 1918, 8 p.m. (received 1 May, 9 p.m.); Milner MSS, box B.

[135] The text of the agreement reached at Vologda on 3 April, presented to the State Department by the French Ambassador on 8 April, is printed in *Foreign Relations, 1918, Russia*, vol. II, p. 111.

implying German influence), and plainly threatened that the Allies would "resort to military operations" through Siberia. The French government then quietly ignored the ensuing Soviet request that the Ambassador be recalled.[136]

Noulens' remarks, Lockhart bitterly reported on 4 May, had caused the Bolsheviks to lose all faith in the sincerity of Allied intentions. And other factions had lost faith because Noulens and some of his colleagues had spoken of intervention and had done nothing. Thanks to Noulens' loquacity, the Allies risked being evicted from Russia before they were ready to act. Their position, said Lockhart, was tragic in its feebleness. He then put forward five recommendations:

(1) The Allied governments should agree on a policy of intervention by Bolshevik invitation if possible, but without invitation if one were not forthcoming.

(2) They should take action at Vladivostok and at Archangel and Murmansk simultaneously and as soon as possible. Intervention in the north would be much more popular than in the east and was equally important.

(3) The Allied representatives should hold on by hook or by crook in Russia, concealing their intentions until intervention was ready. To depart before then would only give Germany warning.

(4) The Bolsheviks would accept intervention only if they saw that all the Allies were united and determined upon it.

(5) Whatever the Allies did, any further delay would be fatal. His own position, Lockhart concluded, grew more difficult each day. "I am in touch with practically everyone here," he said, "and it becomes exceedingly dangerous for me to continue on these lines."[137]

In London, meanwhile, the British government found itself in just the position Lockhart feared most—without a definite policy. It will be remembered that Balfour had stated to Washington on 25 April that Trotsky was on the verge of agreement to Japanese intervention. The next day, after receiving Lockhart's telegram of the 21st, which said that the Bolsheviks were by no means so near to consenting as he had thought, the Foreign Secretary again cabled Washington. This

[136] The text of Noulens' interview and of the Soviet protest (on 28 April) are printed in *Dokumenty vneshnei politiki*, vol. 1, pp. 271-73; a translation appears in *Foreign Relations, 1918, Russia*, vol. 1, p. 509, n. 2.

[137] Lockhart to Balfour, un-numbered telegram, 4 May 1918 (no time of despatch or reception); Milner MSS, box B.

time he implied that the *only* reason Trotsky would not invite intervention was fear of instant German retaliation—not by any means all that Lockhart had meant.[138] The Americans did not reply to either of these communications, but it was clear that without an invitation from Trotsky, the prospects for which had made Colonel House momentarily so optimistic, American policy would be unchanged; and without U.S. consent the Japanese would not act. The situation had returned, in other words, to the point where it had begun.

Balfour was clearly in a quandary. As the chances for a Bolshevik invitation seemed more and more remote, he vented his disappointment by sending to Lockhart on 6 May another tirade against Trotsky, whose

. . . methods only seem effective when directed against his political opponents. Against the enemy they evaporate in words: while the only words that would really do something—namely, those appealing for Allied assistance—he refuses to pronounce. Would a German agent do differently? Please urge Trotsky to immediate action. . . .[139]

Lockhart had heard all this before. Three days later, to the French government, always mistrustful of British dealings with the Soviet regime, the Foreign Secretary sent a justification of a policy which was virtually dead—working with the Bolsheviks. It was a classic exposition of empiricism:

No one is concerned to defend their methods or to sympathise with their policy; but they are there and must be counted with. Nobody else is there, and no one else *need* be counted with. . . . His Majesty's Government, though they have refused to recognise the Government of Messrs. Lenin and Trotsky, desire to work with them while they are in power. We are well aware that they may not be in power long, and that their fall may be as rapid as their rise. [Until] the Russian people decide on replacing them, we should endeavour to work with the Bolsheviks, as before the days of the Bolsheviks we tried to work with Kerensky, and as before the days of Kerensky we tried to work with the Government of the Czar.

The key to the whole Russian situation, Balfour told the French, was American consent to Japanese intervention; so far, without a Russian

---

[138] Balfour to Reading, Washington, 26 April 1918 (paraphrase to State Department on 27 April); *Foreign Relations, 1918, Russia*, vol. II, p. 140.

[139] Balfour to Lockhart, Moscow, telegram 121, 6 May 1918, 7:30 p.m.; Milner MSS, box B.

invitation, Washington was reluctant. However, he cryptically added, "The march of events may induce President Wilson to modify his attitude, even if through fear, or some less reputable motive."[140]

Less than a week later, the hoped-for march of events had begun.

[140] Balfour to Lord Derby, Paris, telegram 941, 9 May 1918, 11:30 a.m.; Milner MSS, unfiled folder 32.

CHAPTER VI

~~~~~~

EMBROILMENT

That is the great foundation stone of our policy. We have no other wish at all; we only desire to see Russia a great and powerful non-German nation.—*Lord Robert Cecil in the House of Commons, 16 May 1918*

If the English continue their robber policy, we will fight them.
                                        —*Lenin, 26 June 1918*

~~~~~~

ON 14 May, in the dreary railway station of Chelyabinsk, just east of the Urals, there were drawn up two trains of soldiers bent on leaving Russia. One was filled with Hungarians, freed from Siberian captivity, bound for their native land. Alongside it lay one of the many trainloads of Czechs who had barely begun the long journey from the Ukraine to Vladivostok, and from there across the Pacific, North America, and the Atlantic to the battlefields of France. The unfortunate juxtaposition on neutral soil of these two trainloads of enemies created an atmosphere ready for ignition. The spark came when one of the Hungarians picked up a piece of scrap iron and hurled it into the neighbouring train, mortally wounding a Czech soldier; enraged, the comrades of the dying man seized the guilty Hungarian and lynched him on the spot.[1] This was the incident which began the chain of events resulting in American agreement to intervention in Russia. Although the British Foreign Secretary heard of it only months later, it led to the situation for which he had been hoping.

His Russian policy, in that first fortnight of May, sorely needed an "incident." Collaboration with the Bolsheviks had proved only a chimera, and his pursuit of it had mystified and worried his conti-

---

[1] Margarete Klante, *Von der Wolga zum Amur: Die tschechische Legion und der russische Bürgerkrieg*, Berlin, 1931, pp. 145-46; Bečvar, *Lost Legion*, pp. 87-88. See also Kennan, *Decision to Intervene*, p. 150, who draws his account from the official report of the Chelyabinsk Soviet's military commissar, printed in J. Kratochvíl, *Cesta Revoluce*, Prague, 1928, pp. 550-51.

nental allies. As the Italian Ambassador told the American Assistant Secretary of State, British efforts to secure Soviet consent for Allied intervention might result in an agreement between Britain and the Bolsheviks, an eventuality which to Paris and Rome seemed filled with danger.[2] The War Cabinet had been spurred in their course by dire prophecies, such as a General Staff memorandum on 16 May, that if the war continued until 1919, the Germans would be able to dragoon two million men from the Russian provinces under their control. A million of these would be fit for combat on the Western Front; the other million would swell the German home labour force, reproducing "the conditions of the ancient Roman Empire, with legionaries fighting on her frontiers and slaves working at home, both recruited from subject races." In following such a policy, said the memorandum,

Germany is not hampered, like the Western Powers, by any standards of Christianity. . . . The Germans are frankly pagan and opportunist, and will not hesitate to employ any methods that may be necessary for their purpose. Starvation and flogging, backed by machine-guns, soon produce the required effect in a community of illiterates with centuries of serfdom behind them.[3]

It was with forebodings of this sort, and without knowledge of the Chelyabinsk chunk of iron, the repercussions of which we shall examine in a moment, that the Cabinet seized on the Czechs as a means of bringing about intervention. At the direction of his colleagues, on 18 May, Lord Robert Cecil despatched a long letter to Clemenceau in Paris. The problem, he said, was simply that the Americans, for reasons such as "tenderness towards Revolutionary Russia" and suspicion of Japan, would not approve of Japanese intervention. In the resulting deadlock the situation became daily more grave. "I ask myself," wrote Cecil,

can nothing be done to impede the German progress and prevent our enemies, while over-running Russia with third-rate troops, from continuing to send their better divisions to fight us on the West? Is there no way of

[2] Memorandum by Assistant Secretary W. Phillips of a conversation with Count Cellere, the Italian Ambassador, 7 May 1918; U.S. National Archives, State Department file 861.00/1827.

[3] Memorandum by "E" Branch, British Section, Supreme War Council, Versailles, "Manpower from the Conquered Russian Provinces," 16 May 1918 (to War Cabinet); Milner MSS, box AD-1.

creating a diversion in the East if the Japanese and Americans combine to delay matters?

He then answered himself: there was "one possible plan"—utilisation of the Czech troops now reaching Vladivostok. He was satisfied, he wrote, "that they could be used to start operations in Siberia." Once started, there could be "little doubt that the Japanese would move and the Americans would find it impossible to hold back." After all, the Japanese and American governments could "scarcely expect us who are bearing the whole brunt of the offensive on the West to wait indefinitely till they can reconcile one another to intervention."[4]

Cecil went on to point out that shipping the Czechs from Vladivostok through North America to France would involve long delays and would tie up tonnage badly needed to carry American troops to Europe.[5] Further, he said that Beneš had approved his plan, on condition that the Powers issued a declaration recognising the Czechs as Allies and affirming the justice of their claims for independence, and also on condition that at least 20,000 of the 70,000 Czech troops then in Russia should be sent from Archangel to France.[6]

It would be most important, Cecil said, properly to represent in Moscow the Allied retention of the Czechs in Siberia. He did not think it necessary to insist upon Bolshevik approval, but the Allies should take every possible step to secure at least the acquiescence of the Soviet regime and should make it clear that they were acting against Germany, and not simply interfering in Russian domestic affairs. "I am sure you will agree," he concluded his message to the French premier, "that in a policy really designed for the assistance

[4] Letter, Lord Robert Cecil to Clemenceau, 18 May 1918; Milner MSS, unfiled folder 33.

[5] This point was made in a letter from the Ministry of Shipping to Lt. Col. L. S. Amery, of the War Office, on 9 May, also stating that if the Czechs were taken not by America, but around India and through Suez, the operation would tie up troop-ships already insufficient to meet the needs of India and Mesopotamia. (Milner MSS, unfiled folder 33).

[6] It seems that Cecil was on rather shaky ground here. Beneš told Amery on 14 May that the Czechs could be used in connection with an Allied intervention provided that the intervention were a real one that extended right through to the Western frontiers of Russia and involved actual operations against the Germans. They would not allow themselves to be dragged back into Russia merely to participate in Russian internal disturbances. And Beneš was anxious that *at least half* of the troops should be sent back to Europe, not the 20 out of 70 thousand Cecil indicated. (Memorandum by L. S. Amery, "Note of a Conversation with Dr. Beneš," 14 May 1918; Milner MSS, unfiled folder 33.)

and support of Russia we should not find ourselves obliged to shoot down Red Guards if that can by any means be avoided."

The Cabinet was hardly prepared for Clemenceau's indignant reply.[7] The British proposal, said the French premier, was "a formal contradiction" of all that the two powers had agreed concerning the Czechs at Abbeville.[8] "This is not the hour," he maintained,

when English effectives are diminishing, when France has imposed upon herself the last sacrifices to maintain the numerical superiority of our armies, for you to think of depriving us of soldiers who are courageous, well-trained, and profoundly devoted to our cause.

To keep the Czechs in Russia would be to deprive them of their "ideal, their unique goal," fighting for their independence in France. The British had evidently misunderstood Beneš, who had assured Clemenceau that he had never supposed that the Czechs could be used as the "point of departure" for Allied intervention. "For my part," wrote Clemenceau, "I could never admit that. I insist absolutely upon the execution pure and simple of the engagements taken at Abbeville," by which the British would transport the troops to the Western Front—an operation he had assumed was already under way.[9]

These two letters—the British proposal and the French response— were typical of the different approaches of the two governments to the problem of Russia and the war. Each regarded Japanese intervention as urgently necessary to relieve the German pressure in the west. Yet when it was suggested that one way of bringing about intervention would be to leave the Czechs in Siberia, the French took refuge—indeed, ostrich-like they buried themselves, as they did so often when dealing with Russia—in an appeal to the absolute sanctity of formal agreements (and as we have seen, the Abbeville agreement was no model of lucidity). The British, on the other hand, consistently probed for a solution; the one they chose—forcing President Wilson's hand by seeing to it that the Czechs became embroiled in Siberia—had the defect of being devious, but at least it was a means of securing the end that both they and the French desired.

[7] Cecil telegraphed Lord Derby in Paris, referring to Clemenceau's letter: "I will not comment on its form beyond saying that it would have made him very angry if he had received it." (Telegram 1040, 25 May 1918; Milner MSS, unfiled folder 33.)

[8] For the Abbeville agreement, see above, Chapter v.

[9] Clemenceau to Cecil, 22 May 1918; Milner MSS, unfiled folder 33.

By the time that Clemenceau had written his angry letter, however, events at Chelyabinsk had gone far towards creating the situation that Cecil had outlined. Following the lynching of the Hungarian soldier on 14 May, the local Soviet authorities imprisoned several Czechs whose presence was desired as witnesses to the disturbances. A delegation sent to secure their release was also arrested. Enraged, the Czechs took armed action on 17 May, releasing the prisoners, disarming the local Red Guards, and seizing their arsenal. Within a few days the incident was amicably settled by the disputants on the spot. But when the news reached Moscow the Bolsheviks responded by issuing an order that the Czechs should be stopped from going further east and should either be organised into labour battalions or drafted into the Red Army. Two members of the Czech National Council in Moscow were arrested and required to sign an order for the Corps to surrender unconditionally all its arms.[10]

Meanwhile, during the whole affair there had been meeting at Chelyabinsk a "Congress of the Czechoslovak Revolutionary Army," composed of delegates from all the Czech detachments. Even before they learned of the Moscow directives, and despite the outraged protests of French military representatives present, they had unanimously decided that the whole Corps should go to Vladivostok, in disregard of the orders from Paris that half should proceed to Archangel. Then, on 23 May, they voted to defy the Bolsheviks and shoot their way through to the Pacific if necessary. Trotsky responded by telegraphing all Siberian Soviets that "every armed Czechoslovak found on the railway is to be shot on the spot," and the breach between the Czechs and the Bolsheviks was complete.[11] By 26 May combat had begun at many points along the railway from Penza to Irkutsk. Within a fortnight, the Czechs had ousted the Bolsheviks from authority in nearly all the railway towns from a point west of Samara, on the Volga, to one somewhat west of Irkutsk.[12]

❖

In London, meanwhile, on the very day that the Czech Congress decided to defy the Bolsheviks, the War Cabinet ordered the

---

[10] Bunyan, *Intervention*, p. 86. The texts of these orders and decrees are on pp. 87-89. See also Klante, *Wolga zum Amur*, pp. 145-46, and Kennan, *Decision to Intervene*, pp. 150-51.

[11] Klante, *Wolga zum Amur*, pp. 146-57. The texts of these resolutions by the Czech Congress and Trotsky's order are in Bunyan, *Intervention*, pp. 89-91.

[12] *ibid.*, p. 87; Kennan, *Decision to Intervene*, pp. 153 and 277.

despatch to North Russia of a military training mission and a small expeditionary force. The expeditionary force, composed of an infantry company, a machine-gun company, and a company of engineers, was to aid in defending the Murmansk region against expected attacks from White Finns and Germans. The training mission, comprising some 560 officers and other ranks drawn from all arms and services, was to accompany the expeditionary force and proceed as soon as the ice melted to Archangel in order to train and equip the Czech troops supposedly on their way there and also local Russians who, it was anticipated, would volunteer. Both British contingents were to be under the command of Major-General F. C. Poole, while the actual operations of the Murmansk force were to be led by Major-General C. C. M. Maynard.[13]

These forces were sent out as a result of a unilateral British decision brought about by a growing concern for the safety of Allied interests in North Russia. Although little could be done about it, the removal by the Bolsheviks of the military supplies at Archangel continued seriously to concern the British government. In mid-March, the Foreign Office told Consul Douglas Young that two ships containing food and supplies were about to be despatched to relieve the town's population. He was to announce that if the inhabitants wanted the food (which they sorely needed) they must hand the military stores back to the British, rather than allow them to be packed off by the Bolsheviks.[14] Accompanied by an armed icebreaker, the ships arrived a month later. The Soviet "Extraordinary Evacuation Commission" was adamant, however; the war stores would continue to be moved even if the population starved. So the ships anchored down the channel from the city and waited. One returned to England in June, its cargo intact; the other finally discharged its supplies in mid-summer, by which time all the military stores had been removed.[15]

Lockhart, in Moscow, also protested against the evacuation of the stores. On one occasion, 1 April, Balfour even instructed him to ask

[13] The Cabinet decision is noted as 23 May 1918 in the General Staff's "Diary, Short History of Events," cited above, Chapter v, footnote 30. See the memorandum by Col. R. Steel, General Staff, "The Direction of Allied Operations in the North of Russia," 24 May 1918; Milner MSS, box C-1. See also Major-General Sir C. Maynard, *The Murmansk Venture,* London, n.d. (circa 1928), pp. 12-14.

[14] Balfour to Young, Archangel, telegram 16, 18 March 1918, 7 p.m.; Milner MSS, box D-1.

[15] Kennan, *Decision to Intervene,* pp. 248-50.

Trotsky whether the Bolsheviks would accept badly needed goods, such as boots, in exchange for an agreement to prevent the stores at Archangel and Vladivostok, the grain of the Ukraine, and the factory plant equipment in Petrograd, from falling to the Germans.[16] Trotsky assured Lockhart that the stores were not going to the Germans, but were being shipped to the Urals, where the Bolsheviks hoped to re-establish industry along war lines.[17] It is hardly surprising that as the Archangel depots visibly melted away, less and less faith was placed in these assurances.

More serious in the eyes of London were the developments around Murmansk. Almost immediately after Admiral Kemp had ordered ashore 130 Royal Marines to help in the defence of the naval base,[18] he had asked the Admiralty for reinforcements. On 23 March the whole North Russian situation was taken up at a joint meeting of the Military Representatives of the Supreme War Council and the Allied Naval Council at Versailles. This was just two days after the start of the German spring offensive, and the meeting reluctantly decided that there were no Allied troops available either for an effort to safeguard the Archangel stores or for bolstering the defences of Murmansk. In any case, the naval leaders were extremely reluctant to divert the necessary escort vessels from Atlantic convoy duty. It was decided that the only thing that could be done was to hold Murmansk as long as possible, using only the forces already there.[19]

German landings in the south of Finland during the first week in April, although aimed at helping the White Finns against the communists and never reaching within hundreds of miles of Murmansk, caused the British to reconsider this decision. On 5 April the Russia Committee approved and sent to the War Cabinet a paper by General Poole, then a member of the Committee, urging that reinforcements should be sent to Murmansk and predicting that Trotsky would give them "whole-hearted support" because they would only "preserve the port intact for Russia against any outside force."[20]

The Cabinet apparently took no positive action on Poole's paper,

[16] Balfour to Lockhart, Moscow, telegram 37, 1 April 1918, 7 p.m.; Milner MSS, box B.
[17] Lockhart to Balfour, telegram 70, Moscow, 3 April 1918; Milner MSS, box B.
[18] See above, Chapter IV.
[19] The minutes of this meeting are in the Milner MSS, box B.
[20] Poole's paper, dated 5 April and sent to the War Cabinet with a covering note by Lord Robert Cecil on 10 April, is in the Milner MSS, box B.

but his sanguine views on Trotsky's probable "support" characterized British thinking about North Russia until well into May. It was not a groundless optimism—Trotsky had, after all, in a moment of panic in early March, ordered the Murmansk Soviet to accept military support from the Allies. On 12 April Lockhart reported that Chicherin was quite willing that the Allies should do anything they could to help defend the port and the railroad, asking only that they act in concert with the local authorities and keep him informed of their actions.[21]

Around this time, at the request of the Murmansk Soviet, British forces along the railway began to help Finnish Red troops to fight off attacks by German-equipped Finnish Whites.[22] In mid-April, an armoured train manned by British marines and some members of the French Military Mission to Rumania (which had finally made its way to Murmansk) went 80 miles down the line to protect a detachment of Red Finns near the town of Kandalaksha.[23] But the first real fighting involving the British came in early May at Pechenga, a tiny fishing village at the head of a fjord 50 miles west of the Kola Inlet. This was another harbour which the Allies feared the Germans would capture for a submarine base (a use for which it was, actually, quite unsuitable).[24] On 3 May the Murmansk Soviet reported that some White Finns had reached Pechenga, and asked the Allies to drive them out. Admiral Kemp immediately despatched

[21] Lockhart to Balfour, telegram 91, Moscow, 12 April 1918, 2:35 p.m.; Milner mss, box B.

[22] On 8 April the Moscow representative of the so-called Finnish Socialist Government called on Lockhart to request aid for the Red Finn forces from the British at Murmansk. Lockhart endorsed his plan as a useful means of securing additional troops to defend the railroad. (Lockhart to Balfour, telegram 78, Moscow, 8 April 1918, 1:10 p.m.; Milner mss, box B.)

[23] See Kennan, *Decision to Intervene*, pp. 250-51. The importance of this very minor action seems to have been vastly over-estimated in London. Balfour telegraphed Lockhart on 24 April that the White Finns had been led by Germans. This was incorrect. He also said that relations between the Allies and the Soviet were of the best. This was true, but applied only to the Murmansk Soviet, not, as Balfour seems to have thought, to the Petrograd Soviet as well. Obviously, the Foreign Secretary regarded the incident as the beginning of the co-operation with the Bolsheviks for which he had been working. (Balfour to Lockhart, Moscow, telegram 99, 24 April 1918, 11:30 p.m.; Milner mss, box B.)

[24] General Maynard reached this conclusion, with relief, when he inspected Pechenga in July. He found it absolutely cut off from land communication with the interior, lacking in any base facilities, and too shallow near the shore, and concluded that it could be used only as a temporary place of refuge, and then only during the summer months. (Maynard, *Murmansk*, pp. 66-69.)

[175]

the cruiser *Cochrane*, with a detachment of Royal Marines and some Russian Red Guards. When an advance party of marines first engaged the Finns on the 10th, they found that their enemy was on skis, and they were forced to retreat, floundering through deep snow, though miraculously suffering no casualties. Subsequent Finnish attacks were beaten off. A few weeks later, the coming of the thaw, which turned the tundra throughout the north into a quagmire, effectively ended any serious danger to the British positions until after the summer.[25]

The presence of Allied forces in North Russia—a breach of the Treaty of Brest-Litovsk—was as much a source of concern to the Germans as the threat of a German attack was to the Allies. For a while, the Bolsheviks met German protests with evasive statements like Chicherin's note of 2 May, stating that "in reality there was no landing of troops in Murmansk at all," but simply an evacuation of various Allied military missions from the interior of Russia. The Murmansk Soviet had been attacked, he said, by bands of Finnish White irregulars, for whom the German government had explicitly denied responsibility. Thus, Chicherin said, it was not surprising that under the circumstances, "the local Soviet has turned to the British and French who had not yet left Murmansk in order to obtain their help." The Bolsheviks did not protest, Chicherin concluded, against "this temporary help extended for purposes of self-defence," but now they were "protesting against the prolonged stay of the British in Murmansk."[26]

Lockhart later wrote that "for form's sake" the Narkomindel sent him several notes on the subject, which they duly published so that the Germans could also see them. On their receipt, says Lockhart,

. . . I took the notes to Chicherin. "What am I to do with them?" I asked. He replied that it would help if we would take the local Soviet into greater consideration. "Otherwise," he said cynically, "you can put them in your waste-paper basket."[27]

During one of these interviews in which Chicherin passed on to Lockhart the German complaints and warnings (7 May) the Commissar drew the British agent aside and, always a realist, gave him

[25] Newbolt, *Naval Operations*, vol. v, p. 315.
[26] Quoted by Strakhovsky, *Origins*, p. 22, from *Izvestiya*, 3 May 1918.
[27] Lockhart, *British Agent*, p. 253.

his personal opinion that the Allies ought either to withdraw from Murmansk completely or else greatly increase their forces there.[28] In any case, as Lockhart had already told London the day before, the Germans were not likely to accept the Bolshevik evasions much longer. Soon they would act.[29] Within ten days of this warning a German submarine operating near Pechenga had sunk five Russian steamers and five Norwegian fishing boats, with considerable loss of life.[30] When Chicherin protested, Mirbach told him that Germany would respect the rights of the Soviet government if the Bolsheviks would protect those rights themselves—especially with regard to Murmansk.[31]

Before this, on 14 May, Lenin had told a joint session of the All-Russian Central Executive Committee and the Moscow Soviet that Murmansk was one of the issues upon which hung the entire question of maintaining the peace with Germany. He left his listeners with no doubts that the Soviet regime would do everything it could "to preserve that brief and precarious respite" which it had won at Brest-Litovsk. That meant denying to both the warring coalitions any pretext for attacking Russia. Murmansk was such a pretext. But he also pointed out that in their present state of weakness, there was little the Bolsheviks could do to prevent the British from doing what they liked at Murmansk.[32]

On the same day that Lenin spoke, Admiral Kemp in Murmansk telegraphed London that he expected Moscow at any moment to replace the local Soviet with more militant Bolsheviks and issue an ultimatum demanding Allied withdrawal. Kemp asked the government immediately to tell him what their policy for Murmansk was. He himself saw only two possible courses: the Cabinet should either withdraw all of his forces or, preferably, reinforce them with at least a brigade and give definite promises of continued food and supplies for the local population.[33]

---

[28] Lockhart to Balfour, telegram 163, Moscow, 7 May 1918, 9:30 p.m.; Milner MSS, box B.

[29] Lockhart to Balfour, telegram 153, Moscow, 6 May 1918, 2:25 p.m.; Milner MSS, box B.

[30] Newbolt, *Naval Operations*, vol. v, p. 316.

[31] U.S. Consul, Moscow, to Secretary of State, 24 May 1918; *Foreign Relations, 1918, Russia*, vol. i, p. 541.

[32] Lenin, *Sochineniya*, vol. XXIII, Moscow-Leningrad, 1930, p. 15.

[33] Kemp to Admiralty, telegram 387, Murmansk, 14 May 1918, 9:30 a.m.; Milner MSS, box D-4.

London's reply gave the Admiral little comfort. The German pressure on Moscow had been expected, it said, but Lockhart had definitely stated that the Allies should not take Chicherin's protests seriously. In any case, Allied policy was to stay in North Russia. Kemp's difficulties, said the message, were fully appreciated, but the war in France made it impossible to send the reinforcements for which he had asked. It was his duty to carry on, with the forces at his disposal, to defend the port, the coast, and as much of the railway as possible.[34]

To take charge of operations on land, the government sent out General Poole as "British Military Representative in Russia" to command all British troops who might come there. But Poole's main function, for the defence of North Russia, was to direct the organisation, training, and operations of locally-recruited Russians, and especially of the Czechs, who were expected at Archangel at any moment. He would be under the control of a "co-ordinating diplomatic official" who would shortly be appointed; in the meantime he was to co-operate with Lockhart and was not to interfere with his activities. Attached to Poole's orders was a memorandum on financial arrangements. One section of it was to be the source, subsequently, of serious trouble:

Russian Personnel   Pay and allowances will be issued at the rates applicable for their ranks in the Russian Army before the revolution at the pre-war rate of exchange. It should be clearly understood that they are to be administered as nearly as possible on Russian and not English lines and no departure from this should be made without reference to the War Office.[35]

Poole arrived in Murmansk on 24 May aboard the U.S. cruiser *Olympia*, which had come to join the growing list of Allied warships in the Kola Inlet. The British Military Representative was an officer who had spent twenty-nine of his forty-nine years in the Army and who had distinguished himself as a gunner in France. More important, he had been chief of the British Artillery Mission with the Russian Army and had a special knowledge of the port of Archangel (where British guns had been landed) and of the general conditions of the Russian winter. An active man and an optimist with a marked distaste for official red tape, he was apparently a good

[34] Admiralty to Kemp, telegram 292, 18 May 1918, 8:30 p.m.; Milner MSS, box D-4.
[35] "Instructions for General Poole," 18 May 1918, signed by C.I.G.S.; Milner MSS, box D-4.

soldier, but he was stepping into a situation which called for consummate political ability as well. This he lacked. Like other British professional soldiers with such long service, most of his experience had been in the Colonies, and his dealings had been to a great extent with primitive and backward peoples. Naturally, he brought with him to North Russia the attitudes he had acquired elsewhere. As we shall see, they were to be his undoing. General Maynard, who arrived at the head of the three-company expeditionary force a month later, made the following observation about Poole's treatment of the commander of the local Russian forces and the executive secretary of the Murmansk Soviet (both officers with considerable experience in the Tsar's service).[36] It was an observation which said as much about Maynard as it did about Poole:

> Poole's attitude towards Zvegintzoff and Vaselago caused us new arrivals considerable amusement. To him they were his pals Sviggens and Vessels, and as such he addressed them. Taking Vaselago by the arm, he would say, "Now, Vessels, when are you going to fix up that agreement with us?" or to Zvegintzoff, "Hullo, Sviggens, what do those old Red Guards of yours intend doing?" He treated them rather as a house-master might treat a couple of his prefects; giving them to understand that they must realize their responsibilities, and act for the good of the house, yet determined none the less that no action taken by them should run contrary to his own preconcerted plans.[37]

Just a day after Poole reached Murmansk there arrived there one S. P. Natsarenus, a Lithuanian communist sent from Moscow with Yuryev, the President of the Murmansk Soviet. The latter had gone to the capital in early May to sort out the differences between the local and the central authorities. Natsarenus had been sent back with him as a "special commissar" to take charge of the Murmansk situation and to attempt the impossible task of reaching a balance whereby the local Soviet could avoid a rupture with the Allies and yet so curtail their activities that the Germans would no longer complain. Even before Natsarenus' arrival, Chicherin had telegraphed instructions to the Murmansk Soviet that thenceforth no local Soviet should seek aid from one of the "imperialist coalitions" against the other. "In view of the general political situation," said the message, "any appeal to the English for help is quite impermissible." Although the

[36] See above, p. 114.
[37] Maynard, *Murmansk*, pp. 38-39.

British might themselves fight the advancing White Finns, "we must not join them as allies, and we shall protest against their actions on our territory." Vesselago showed this message to Kemp and assured him that the Murmansk Soviet would continue as before to look to the Allies for help.[38]

Natsarenus remained in Murmansk only a week, during which time he actually tempered some of Moscow's harsher instructions to the local Soviet.[39] On 1 June he had a long talk with General Poole and Admiral Kemp. Apparently they got on well. (Poole later described the Commissar to Maynard as "quite a good old bird.")[40] According to Poole's report to the War Office, Natsarenus refused to speak officially so long as the Allies did not recognise the Moscow government. But unofficially he maintained that the Bolsheviks really did intend to fight the Germans; indeed, they were in the process of sending two divisions up to Murmansk, and the Czechs were also on their way.[41]

Poole and Kemp, also speaking "unofficially," replied that the Bolsheviks were much more likely to obtain recognition if they gave clear proof that they were in earnest and threw in their lot with the Allies against Germany. Poole guaranteed to equip and feed the Czechs as soon as they arrived, and also to help train any other troops the Bolsheviks might produce. They parted, Poole said, on excellent terms and with a mutual understanding regarding unofficial co-operation; the Commissar appeared pleased to have British help and seemed likely to assist the Allies as far as possible. The two British commanders scarcely imagined that Natsarenus would soon be back in the Murmansk region—at the head of attacking columns of Red troops sent up from Petrograd.

Poole closed his account of the interview with a recommendation: for Britain to reach any real arrangement with the Bolsheviks, "we shall be obliged to recognise them as the *de facto* government, which policy I have always advocated." Similar advice was sent at the same time by Admiral Kemp; Allied intervention for the defence of Murmansk or any other Russian port, he said, would be possible

---

[38] Kennan, *Decision to Intervene*, pp. 272-73. Kennan quotes Chicherin's telegram, dated 23 May, from a manuscript by Vesselago in the U.S. National Archives.

[39] *ibid.*, p. 274.

[40] Maynard, *Murmansk*, p. 26.

[41] Natsarenus had evidently not yet learned of the final break between the Bolsheviks and the Czechs, which had occurred just a few days previously.

only as a hostile act unless recognition were accorded the "present Russian *de facto* government." If the Allies maintained their existing attitude towards the Moscow regime, Kemp said, they would only play into the hands of Germany.[42]

This was, surely, the last time for at least two years in which a responsible British official would recommend recognition of the Bolshevik regime. For by this time, Moscow had felt the full impact of the Czechoslovak rising in Siberia; the month of June was to be characterised by a rapid deterioration in the relations between the Allies and the Soviet government. This fact, combined with the growing German concern about the Allied presence in North Russia, resulted in increasing pressure upon the Murmansk Soviet by the central authorities. Moscow's anxieties were expressed quite clearly in a telegram from Chicherin to the Murmansk Soviet on 15 June. There was, Chicherin said, a possibility that the British and their allies would take belligerent action in support of the Czechoslovak uprising. Further, the Germans had guaranteed to respect the freedom of Russian shipping if the Allies left. Therefore, the Soviet government demanded the immediate departure of British, French, and American warships from Russian ports.[43]

At Archangel, where authority was firmly in the hands of a local Soviet loyal to Moscow, these directives resulted in a request for the immediate withdrawal of the British armed ice-breaker *Alexander*, which had escorted the two freighters carrying food for the town.[44]

[42] Poole's message to Director of Military Intelligence, telegram E. 16, 1 June, 1918 (despatched 4:14 p.m. 2 June), is in Milner MSS, box D-4. A copy of it, along with Kemp's message, was given to the commander of the *U.S.S. Olympia*, who relayed them to U.S. Naval Headquarters; they are in U.S. National Archives, Naval Records Branch, file WA-6, box 607.

[43] Telegram, Chicherin to Yuryev, Murmansk, 15 June 1918; *Dokumenty vneshnei politiki*, vol. 1, p. 367.
According to Louis Fischer (*Soviets in World Affairs*, vol. 1, p. 126), however, Chicherin told him that in June (Fischer does not specify when) he sent one of his subordinates, a Left S-R named Vosnisensky, to tell the Allied diplomats at Vologda (among them Lindley, who had gone there from Murmansk) that the Bolsheviks would not resist landings of foreign troops in North Russia provided they moved inland toward Finland, to oppose the German forces there. But if they moved toward Petrograd or Moscow, the Bolsheviks would be forced to fight.
This reminiscence of Chicherin may well have been accurate—we have seen how he told Lockhart he could put the Soviet protests about Murmansk in the wastebasket—but I have found no other evidence that such, in fact, was Soviet policy at the time.

[44] Consul Young, Archangel, to Balfour, telegram 84, 22 June 1918, 11:48 p.m.; Milner MSS, box D-4. A similar request was made to the American consul (though there were no U.S. ships at Archangel); *Foreign Relations, 1918, Russia*, vol. II, p. 487.

After "an ugly demonstration" by Russian ships in the port and field guns ashore, Admiral Kemp ordered her departure.[45] At Murmansk, however, the Soviet continued to co-operate with the Allies. In his reply to Chicherin's order for the departure of Allied ships, Yuryev, the President of the Soviet, said that the Allies enjoyed the sympathy of the local population, whom they were protecting from the Finns and Germans and were supplying with food; in any case, Yuryev said, the vastly superior power of the Allies made it impossible to compel their departure.[46] This situation was described in blunter terms by F. O. Lindley, who had just come back to Russia as the "co-ordinating diplomatic authority" referred to in Poole's orders, when he reported to London that the Murmansk Soviet was "being used as a façade" through which the Allies could control the region.[47]

The arrival of Maynard's 600-man force on 23 June precipitated the final acrimonious exchange that ended with a complete break between the Murmansk Soviet and Moscow. As soon as he heard of the landings, Chicherin wrote to Trotsky (as Commissar for War) that the "English invasion" at Murmansk meant the start of a struggle between Allied and German imperialism on Russian soil. The North Russian situation was even more critical than the German front around Pskov or Vitebsk, he said, and asked that if Soviet forces in the north were insufficient to repel the British, troops should be diverted from the west and sent up the railway.[48] To Yuryev, with another order for the Soviet to protest against the landings, he sent the news that Natsarenus was returning to take charge. And over the direct-wire telegraph, Lenin told Yuryev on the 26th:

If you still refuse to understand Soviet policy—equally hostile to the English and the Germans—you have only yourself to blame. If the English continue their robber policy, we will fight them.[49]

Meanwhile, on 30 June, a joint public meeting of the Murmansk Regional Soviet, the Fleet Soviet, and the railway union passed a resolution, opposed only by the sailors from the *Askold*, to defy

[45] Newbolt, *Naval Operations*, vol. v, p. 321.
[46] Strakhovsky, *Origins*, pp. 57-58 (Strakhovsky, then a young midshipman, was Vesselago's private secretary).
[47] Lindley to Balfour, telegram 2, Murmansk, 21 June 1918, 3:55 p.m.; Milner MSS, box D-4.
[48] Letter, Chicherin to Commissar for War, 24 June 1918; *Dokumenty vneshnei politiki*, vol. I, p. 375. (Here, again, the Soviet volume omits Trotsky's name.)
[49] Lenin to Yuryev, Murmansk, 26 June 1918; *ibid.*, p. 376.

Moscow's demands, to continue the existing co-operation with the Allies and to formalise it with a written agreement.[50] The resolution also stated that the Regional Soviet would remain the supreme authority, that the Allies would not interfere with internal affairs, and, finally, that every effort would be made to end the conflict with Moscow. This was the vainest of gestures in Moscow's direction. The situation was more accurately described by General Poole, who reported that the deputies of the Murmansk Soviet "have put the rope around their own necks and if they show signs of faltering I shall be there to stiffen them." Telling how the resolution had come about, Poole said:

I have talked very kindly and firmly to them and last night Vesselago came to Kemp and me and told us that they had at last decided to come in with us to fight for a free Russia against the Hun and denounce Moscow as pro-German.

Martial law, he said, would shortly be proclaimed, and then he would arrange for a general mobilisation.[51] But in a further telegram, he admitted that the inhabitants showed no great enthusiasm for fighting; that, he said, might be fostered later.[52] Lindley, for his part, accurately delineated in the following terms the problem the British faced in North Russia:

General Poole is fully alive to the necessity of avoiding if possible any fighting with Bolshevists as we do not want to be maneuvered into position of Czechs who are wasting their forces on Russians instead of on Germans. At the same time we cannot allow armed forces to penetrate into our zone. I hope that Bolshevists themselves will avoid actual encounter though they must of necessity take up hostile attitude to formation and existence of any force not completely under their control.[53]

---

[50] The text of the resolution, sent to Washington by the captain of the *U.S.S. Olympia*, is printed in *Foreign Relations, 1918, Russia*, vol. II, pp. 492-93.
It should be noted, incidentally, that by this time the Russian sailors from the *Askold* had been removed and replaced with a British crew, and the *Askold* had been renamed *H.M.S. Glory IV*. But *Glory IV* saw virtually no action under British colours: it was soon discovered that ammunition for her Russian-bore guns was impossible to obtain.

[51] Poole to War Office, telegram E.91, Murmansk, 30 June 1918, 5:9 p.m.; Milner MSS, box D-4.

[52] Poole to D.M.I., telegram E.104, Murmansk, 1 July 1918 (sent 11:40 a.m. 2 July); Milner MSS, box D-4.

[53] Lindley to Balfour, telegram 9, Murmansk, 1 July 1918, 10:22 p.m.; Wiseman MSS (Balfour to Reading, no. 4114, 3 July).

At this very time, deep in the interior near Kandalaksha, General Maynard and a small portion of his tiny force, aided by part of a battalion of Serbs who had also made their way to the Murmansk area, were in the process, largely through bluff, of disarming a detachment of over 1,000 Red Guards who had been sent out from Petrograd by Natsarenus. Maynard gave them some rations and packed them off south again.[54] Neither side suffered any casualties, but on 5 July, when Maynard ordered his men to search Kandalaksha, Kem, and neighbouring villages for concealed weapons, the Kem Soviet refused to co-operate and it was disbanded by British troops, who arrested seven Bolshevik leaders and killed three who tried to resist.[55] Natsarenus, on orders from Moscow the same day, cut the telegraph wires between Murmansk and Petrograd and blew up a number of bridges between Kem and Soroka, thus completely isolating the region from the interior.[56] Before the wires were cut, there was a last bitter exchange between Yuryev and Chicherin, who passed on Lenin's denunciation of the Murmansk leaders as traitors. Yuryev himself was declared an enemy of the people.[57]

On 6 July General Poole and the captains of the French and American cruisers in the port joined the Presidium of the Regional Soviet in signing the agreement called for in the resolution of 30 June. It bound the Allies to the fulfilment of far-reaching obligations. Principally, they agreed to supply, as far as possible, food, textiles, fishing equipment, and many other goods, as well as military supplies, for the whole population of the region (which included Kem, Kandalaksha, Alexandrovsk, and other neighbouring towns). Food was to be provided "on the basis equivalent in nourishment to the scale used in the Allied military forces in Murmansk." The Soviet was to remain supreme in internal matters and was to have charge of all Russian military units, except at the front. The purpose of the agreement was "the defence of the Murmansk Region against the powers of the German coalition"; the Allied representatives again disclaimed any territorial ambitions on the part of their governments and stated that "the sole reason of concluding this Agree-

[54] Maynard, *Murmansk*, pp. 42-53.
[55] Poole to D.M.I., telegram E.120, Murmansk, 5 July 1918, 10:25 p.m.; Milner MSS, box D-4.
[56] Strakhovsky, *Origins*, p. 68.
[57] The texts of the various messages are in Bunyan, *Intervention*, pp. 133-35.

ment is to save the Murmansk Region in its integrity for the great Undivided Russia."[58]

In signing this agreement the Murmansk leaders had conclusively demonstrated their defiance of Moscow and had linked their destinies with the foreign military establishment which had now appeared in their midst. Just before the agreement was signed, General Poole, the commander of the foreign troops, sent to the War Office a message which, had its contents been known, would have somewhat dimmed the optimism of Yuryev, Vesselago, and their colleagues. Poole said: "Now that they have broken with Moscow they realize their dependence on us for everything so they will become more and more pliable."[59]

❖

We have thus seen how two widely separated Allied forces—the Czechs in Siberia and Maynard's troops in North Russia—became embroiled in combat with the Bolsheviks. Their involvement came as a result of their particular responses to local situations, and the decisions which involved them were taken by their own leaders on the spot; the Czechs actually acted against the wishes of their National Council in Paris, while the general directives which bound Poole and Maynard certainly did not explicitly discuss action *against* the Bolsheviks.

These involvements in Siberia and North Russia changed the whole fabric of relations between the Allies and the Soviet government. Soviet historians have maintained that from the very first days of the October Revolution the Allies planned to intervene with armed force to overthrow the young Soviet republic.[60] That this is not true should be evident from all that has been said so far. Lord Robert Cecil was being wholly honest when he answered a Labour M.P.'s criticism in mid-May with the statement:

I think the hon. Member opposite has a kind of idea that we have, as it were, some personal or political quarrel with the Bolsheviks, arising, not, I think, from the direction of their foreign policy, but from some disapproval

[58] The text of the agreement, sent to Washington by Captain Bierer, its American signatory, is printed in *Foreign Relations, 1918, Russia*, vol. II, pp. 493-95. A slightly different translation, transmitted by Moscow wireless, appeared in *The Times*, 24 July 1918.

[59] From Poole's telegram E.120, 5 July, cited above, footnote 55.

[60] See, for example, Volkov, *Krakh angliiskoi politiki*, pp. 20-21, and *Istoriya grazhdanskoy voiny*, vol. III, p. 173.

of their domestic policy. I assure the hon. Member he is entirely mistaken. In our view the domestic policy of Russia is a matter for Russia alone. Whatever Government the Russians desire to have, the Russians ought to have, and it is not for us to interfere in any way in that matter ... but we wish to see Russia preserved as an Allied country, or, if that is impossible, as a non-German one. That is the great foundation stone of our policy. We have no other wish at all; we only desire to see Russia a great and powerful non-German nation.[61]

As we have seen, it was this "foundation stone"—keeping Russia non-German—that in the context of events in the early summer of 1918 caused the British government to feel that it was increasingly urgent that they should interfere.

Certainly it seemed that Russia was rapidly falling under German influence. A German ambassador was well established in Moscow. German armies continued, in April and May, to press into the Ukraine, Georgia, the Crimea, and the Baltic provinces in fulfilment of Ludendorff's directive that "it is of decisive importance for us to secure a place for ourselves in Russia's economic life and to monopolize her exports." All Russian grain, without regard to Russia's own needs, was to go to Germany; Russia was to be bled until she was "forced to bind herself to Germany." Any other policy, Ludendorff concluded, "would seriously undermine our war and post-war economic interests."[62] This was the military side of German policy. The political side, as directed by Kühlmann, Hintze, and Hertling, was diametrically opposed to this, and aimed at establishing friendly relations with the Bolshevik regime; any other Russian government, it was considered, would move closer to the Entente.[63] Thus a rather uneasy balance was achieved. Its result was that Ludendorff was restrained from pushing his predatory programme to the brink of renewed hostilities.

The implications of this German policy were accurately perceived by Lockhart in Moscow. On 23 May (the very day of the Czech resolution to force their way to Vladivostok and of the War Cabinet's decision to send Maynard's force to Murmansk), in one of his most

[61] 106 HC Deb. 5s. cols. 624-25 (16 May 1918).
[62] Gerald Freund, *Unholy Alliance: Russian-German Relations from the Treaty of Brest-Litovsk to the Treaty of Berlin*, London, 1957, p. 13.
[63] *ibid.*, pp. 13-14. This was, it should be noted, precisely the reverse of the view, long held by Lockhart and others, that the Bolsheviks were more strongly opposed to Germany than any other Russian party.

important telegrams,[64] Lockhart told Balfour that during the preceding ten days the situation had undergone a marked change,
owing to a sudden alteration in German policy. The Germans had
informed the Bolsheviks that their military operations in Russia
were completed, that they had no intention of occupying Petrograd
or Moscow, and that they were anxious to enter into economic
cooperation with the Soviet government.[65] They had reached this
decision, Lockhart surmised, because their offensive on the Western
Front left them too few troops for the occupation of Central Russia.
Accordingly they would concentrate their operations in regions like
the Caucasus and the Ukraine, where they had more to gain materially and where, because these areas were not under Moscow's rule,
they would not risk war with the Bolsheviks.

With this change in German policy, said Lockhart, the Allies had
lost their last chance of securing either an invitation to intervene or
even the consent of the Bolsheviks for intervention. Now that they
felt secure from German attack, the Bolsheviks would never permit
any Allied action likely to provoke Germany. The Moscow leaders
would do everything they could to prolong the *status quo*, a situation wholly favourable to the Germans, who could simply sit back
and exploit the rich grain and mineral resources of the lands they
occupied.

In these circumstances, Lockhart felt, the only policy left to the
Allies was to prepare, quickly and secretly, to intervene on the
largest possible scale. But until the last moment they should continue
to take a conciliatory line with the Bolsheviks, in the hope that some
German action would bring them Bolshevik consent. Once the
Allies were fully prepared, they should seize the first favourable
moment in the Russian political situation to proclaim their purposes
to the Russian people, appealing to their patriotism and guaranteeing
Russia's territorial integrity, and then follow within twenty-four hours
with landings at Vladivostok, Archangel, and Murmansk.

This action, Lockhart said, must be as imposing as possible. He
begged the Cabinet to have no illusions, such as those entertained by
the French in particular, of substantial help being available at the

[64] Lockhart to Balfour, telegram 210, Moscow, 23 May 1918, 8:10 p.m.; Milner MSS,
box C-1.
[65] See the long despatch from Joffe, the Soviet Ambassador in Berlin, to Chicherin,
20 May 1918; *Dokumenty vneshnei politiki*, vol. 1, pp. 311-13.

outset from anti-Bolshevik elements in Russia. If intervention were obviously successful the Russians would support it, but they were in too great a state of demoralisation to risk supporting an effort that did not seem likely to succeed.

Lockhart reiterated these points in another telegram three days later.[66] Without massive Allied intervention, he said, a pro-Ally counter-revolution would have no chance of success, and if it failed the Allied position in Russia would be irretrievably damaged. The same would happen unless they acted rapidly, for they were fast losing the little prestige they had left. Most of the prevailing discontent was due to famine; if the Allies wished to take advantage of it, they must intervene long before the harvest. Lockhart put forward 20 June as the latest suitable date. Finally, he again emphasised the need for secrecy. Should the Soviet leaders learn that an anti-Bolshevik intervention was coming, they were fully capable of turning to the Germans for help.

Thus Lockhart became an advocate of intervention regardless of whether or not the Bolsheviks consented. In March he had hoped for a Soviet invitation; in April he conceded that an invitation was unobtainable and that the best that could be hoped for was consent; now, in May, he held that even consent was impossible, but that intervention was all the same an urgent necessity. It is difficult to know what to make of these changes in Lockhart's attitude.[67] Assuming that the danger from Germany was as great as he assumed, then his advice was sound enough. In particular, as events were to show, he was right in insisting that if there were an intervention it should be both massive and decisively executed.

In his own relations with the Bolshevik authorities, Lockhart had always taken pains to be conciliatory. But he found himself, at the beginning of June, treading an extremely fine line. On 1 June he cabled to Balfour:

[66] Lockhart to Balfour, telegram 222, Moscow, 26 May 1918, 8:50 p.m.; Milner MSS, box C-1.

[67] It is interesting to note that Lockhart's telegrams show that his change in attitude took place under quite different circumstances from those that he indicates in his *British Agent*. There (pp. 281-89) he states that he came to advocate intervention without Bolshevik consent rather against his better judgement, after a long conversation with Noulens, the French Ambassador, at Vologda on 29 May. But, as we have seen, he first stated the case for action regardless of the Soviet attitude on 23 May, before his Vologda visit. His telegrams of the ten days preceding 23 May, in the Milner MSS, boxes B and C-1, show that his shift of position was not abrupt but gradual.

I feel and hope now that my work here is coming to an end. My position, as I am sure you will realize, has been very difficult one and recent march of events has not made it any easier. There is still much work to be done here in preparing our way with other parties and in allaying suspicions of Bolsheviks. With your approval I propose to see this show through trusting however that Allies will act with least possible delay.[68]

His first real conflict with the Bolsheviks came only three days later, when he accompanied the American, French, and Italian Consul-Generals in Moscow to the Narkomindel to protest against the Soviet attempts to disarm the Czechs; any such action, they said, would be considered as inspired by Germany and hostile to the Allies. Chicherin, so Lockhart reported afterwards, seemed seriously frightened, and asked if the Allied demands, which he considered an ultimatum, were a prelude to a declaration of war. The Commissar promised to do his best to help the Czechs leave Russia as rapidly as possible, but pointed out that after all that had happened, it was impossible to allow them to retain their arms.[69]

Lockhart later wrote that he himself had delivered the strongest of the Allied protests. Months afterwards, when he was in prison, he learned that Chicherin and Karakhan, the Assistant Commissar, had been completely surprised by the vehemence of his language, and that their first suspicions of him had dated from that day.[70]

The Bolsheviks' suspicions were well-founded. By April, as we have seen, Lockhart was in contact, either direct or through intermediaries, with most of the important anti-Bolshevik organisations. In May, as he lost hope that the Bolsheviks would ever invite or consent to intervention, these contacts increased. He was particularly impressed by a highly conspiratorial organisation, composed mostly of former officers, called the "Union for the Defence of Fatherland and Freedom." Based on the Volga and led by Boris Savinkov, the terrorist and adventurer who had briefly been Kerensky's Minister for War, it had links with most of the left-wing and centre groups working against the Soviet regime (the right-wing groups, including one led by Milyukov, tended to be pro-German).

[68] Lockhart to Balfour, telegram 248, Moscow, 1 June 1918, 8:10 p.m.; Wiseman MSS (as no. 3607 to Reading, 11 June).

[69] Lockhart to Balfour, telegram 254, Moscow, 5 June 1918, 4:40 p.m.; Milner MSS, box C-1.

[70] Lockhart, *British Agent*, pp. 286-87.

In mid-May Lockhart reported to Balfour on his talks with Savinkov's representatives. They admitted, he said, that their organisation was as yet too weak to act unless supported by Allied intervention; the French, however, had been in close touch with them and had told them that intervention had already been decided upon and would occur shortly. Lockhart himself thought that until the Allies had more definite plans they should not associate themselves too closely with opposition groups. But he asked Balfour to allow him to continue to maintain informal contacts with Savinkov through third parties.[71] Balfour's reply, despatched on 3 June, was curt and mystifying: "You should have nothing whatever to do with Savinkoff's plans, and avoid enquiring further into them."[72]

This was hardly the sort of advice Lockhart wanted to hear, coming as it did after he had severely strained his relations with the Bolsheviks. He was further exasperated by the news that Lindley was returning to Russia to take charge of British diplomatic affairs,[73] and that Lindley had been accompanied, incredibly enough, by a four-man mission from the Department of Overseas Trade sent out to investigate the possibilities of trading with the Soviet regime.[74] All this, combined with a message from General Poole at Murmansk telling him just how far the Allies were from actual intervention, profoundly depressed Lockhart. Bitterly, he telegraphed Balfour that all Russians, including the Bolsheviks, expected intervention at any moment. The Czech uprising had created just the right situation for decisive action; unless the Allies took advantage of it, the firm line he and his colleagues had adopted would only risk Czech lives. The anti-Bolshevik groups were rapidly losing hope; soon they would look to see what the Germans could offer them. Never, Lockhart concluded, would the Allies have another opportunity so favourable, and added: "I feel it is my duty to state that I must be freed from my responsibility in the event of any further delay."[75]

[71] Lockhart to Balfour, un-numbered telegram, Moscow, 17 May 1918, 8:10 p.m., and telegram 224, 26 May, 6:7 p.m.; Milner MSS, unfiled folder 23 and box C-1, respectively.
[72] Balfour to Lockhart, Moscow, telegram 186, 3 June 1918, 10:30 p.m.; Milner MSS, unfiled folder 23.
[73] As we have seen, Lindley arrived in Murmansk in mid-June as "co-ordinating diplomatic representative."
[74] For an account of the experiences of this economic mission in Russia, see below, Chapter VIII.
[75] Lockhart to Balfour, telegrams 255 and 261, Moscow, 6 June 1918, 5:15 and 7:40 p.m.; Milner MSS, box C-1.

CHAPTER VII

LONDON—TOKYO—WASHINGTON:
THE CRUCIAL NEGOTIATIONS

I feel that the President is now committed to intervention on a
small scale and that this will eventually lead to what we want. We
must now work to [the] end that he shall commit himself finally
and irrevocably, when I think we will find the whole matter will
go through in entire accordance with our wishes.

— *Sir William Wiseman to Sir Arthur Murray, 10 July 1918*

LOCKHART's fervent appeal for immediate intervention drew from
Balfour one of his most school-masterish lectures, but it was one
which the younger man fully deserved. Because it was in the nature
of a lecture, it carefully outlined the problems which beset Britain's
Russian policy in early June 1918, and therefore much of it is worth
quoting here.

Balfour began by considering Lockhart's own situation. "You
need not fear," said the Foreign Secretary,

that your work is unappreciated here or that you have in any way lost the
confidence of His Majesty's Government. I fully understand the difficulties
of your situation.

And he continued, with perhaps a shade of sarcasm:

Your telegrams during the last five months have faithfully reflected the
variations in opinion produced and no doubt justified by the constantly
changing aspects of the present transitional period of Russian History.[1]

These variations in Lockhart's opinions, the Foreign Secretary continued, clearly reflected the difficulties of the situation as seen from
the Russian side; no-one, indeed, knew them better than Lockhart.
"But I am not sure," Balfour said,

[1] Balfour to Lockhart, Moscow, telegram 191, 11 June 1918, 6:30 p.m.; Milner MSS,
box C-1.

that you equally comprehend the difficulties as seen from the side of the Allies. You constantly complain of indecision, as if all that was required was that His Majesty's Government should make up their minds. But there has been no indecision on the part of the particular members of the Alliance. They have severally determined their policy as quickly as could reasonably be expected in the face of the varying opinions expressed by their agents, the contradictory reports which poured into them from Russia, and the novelty of the problems presented to them for solution.

Delays, he admitted, had arisen—not, however, because the governments concerned had failed to make decisions, but because they did not all decide the same way. And he elaborated:

Britain, France, and Italy have thought the dangers of intervention less than its advantages; America has thought the advantages less than the dangers; Japan will do nothing on a grand scale until she receives an invitation from her co-belligerents. The only thing on which everybody agrees is that without the active participation of America nothing effective can be accomplished through Siberia; and the active participation of America has been so far refused.

In these circumstances, Balfour concluded,

. . . there is little use in crying out for "decision" since what is wanted is not decision but agreement. It is unfortunately true that, when this agreement (for which we are earnestly striving) is reached, it may be too late. . . . We can therefore do no more at the moment than press our views on the Administration at Washington and hope that by the time the necessity for intervention is universally admitted and common action becomes for the first time possible it may not prove too late.

By the time Balfour had sent this telegram the American Administration had already begun to modify its attitude. In the following month, primarily owing to British pressure, President Wilson was to change his position even more.[2] Yet, despite the Foreign Secretary's didactic emphasis on the difference between "decision" and "agreement," the British government themselves lost sight of it in the crucial June and July negotiations with America and Japan. So desperately did they wish for intervention that they convinced themselves that if once they could secure a decision on the necessity of

---

[2] There are two excellent accounts, written from the American side, of the way in which the American government made its decision to act in Russia: Kennan, *Decision to Intervene,* and Betty Miller Unterberger, *America's Siberian Adventure, 1918-1920: A Study of National Policy,* Durham, North Carolina, 1956, pp. 39-89.

taking action of some sort, an agreement on the aims, scope, and method of the action would follow. As a result, intervention was launched before any agreement was reached; it therefore completely failed to achieve the goals the British government had set for it.

The decision on Siberia was preceded by one on North Russia. On 11 May, in an interview with Lord Reading, Secretary of State Lansing had put forward the American government's view that there was a sharp distinction to be drawn between intervention in North Russia to protect the ports and the military supplies and intervention in Siberia: the former involved no racial difficulties. Moreover, the Americans could understand the military advantage of safeguarding the northern ports, which seemed to be directly threatened by the Germans. The success of action there did not depend on factors so problematical as a trek of 5,000 miles across Siberia. In other words, Washington regarded the two spheres as wholly separate problems.[3]

As it happened, these views were directly contrary to those which were being developed at the same time in Britain. With the collapse of the various schemes for collaboration with the Bolsheviks, it was felt that intervention would almost certainly have to be carried out in opposition to them, and with the co-operation of White (or "loyal") factions. From these premises there was developed a grandiose project for a two-part intervention, with one force coming down from Archangel, joining with anti-Bolshevik elements in the Vologda area, and eventually being met there by the other forces crossing Siberia from Vladivostok.

So far as can be seen, this plan was first suggested on 10 May by Captain Denis Garstin, Lockhart's second assistant, as a result of his secret contacts with organisations of former army officers and of his calculations that without some supporting operations in Central Russia the Japanese could never work their way across Siberia to a new Eastern Front. But Garstin emphasised—and this was most important—that the expedition to North Russia would require at least two Allied divisions. This figure, so he stated, as well as his plan as a whole, had been approved by Generals Lavergne and

---

[3] Reading to Balfour, telegram 2137, Washington, 12 May 1918; Milner MSS, unfiled folder 32. Lansing's version of the conversation, set down in a letter to the President, 11 May, appears in *Foreign Relations, 1918, Russia*, vol. II, p. 160.

Romei, his French and Italian colleagues in Moscow.[4] Garstin had put forward this project before the Czech revolt; by the time the plan began to appear in British General Staff papers, it was modified to include the Czechs as one of its most important elements. Their arrival on the upper Volga, it was hoped, would provide a nucleus around which could rally all elements loyal to the Allied cause.

This plan for a combined Northern and Siberian intervention came to be the basis of British military policy for Russia.[5] But in May 1918, because of American opposition to the Siberian part of it, the government decided that *some* action was better than none, and pressed for a decision on the North Russian phase at least. Accordingly, on 28 May Balfour instructed Reading to impress upon the President that American assistance on the Murman coast was essential. The situation there was daily becoming more critical, he said, and emphasised that only by retaining Murmansk could the Allies retain any possibility at all of sending their troops directly into European Russia. He told Reading of the decision to send out Maynard's small force. That was an insufficient measure; no more British or French troops could be spared, however, because every available man was needed either on the Western Front or to serve as cadres for the training of the American troops now on their way. But it was not necessary that the troops for Murmansk be fully trained. Therefore, Balfour requested that America should send a brigade, with some artillery, to North Russia.

In concluding his appeal, the Foreign Secretary put forward another reason for American assistance: the enemy had already gained much from the divergence of views between America and her allies regarding Russia. It was of the greatest importance that America should demonstrate her agreement by helping to keep open "the only door" through which assistance could be given "to Russia in her hour of need."[6]

As we have seen, the naval base at Murmansk was not in nearly so much danger as the British government assumed. With the nearest

[4] Garstin's message was sent by Lockhart as his telegram 175, Moscow, 10 May 1918, 1:30 p.m.; Milner MSS, box C-1.

[5] It was incorporated, for example, in the memorandum, "The Direction of Allied Military Operations in the North of Russia," 24 May 1918 (cited above, Chapter VI, footnote 13), and, as we shall see, in many subsequent papers.

[6] Balfour to Reading, Washington, 28 May 1918; paraphrase sent to Secretary of State printed in *Foreign Relations, 1918, Russia*, vol. II, p. 476.

German troops hundreds of miles away in the south of Finland and in the Baltic provinces, the port was menaced by only a few small detachments of White Finns who had come into the area not to drive out the British but apparently to hunt down the Red Finns who had sought refuge there. The Americans, however, had also been receiving highly exaggerated reports of German pressure in the region. The President and the Secretary of State, therefore, agreed on 1 June that, provided General Foch approved the diversion of troops and shipping from the Western Front, American troops could be sent to Murmansk.[7]

Two days later, General Bliss joined the British, French, and Italian Permanent Military Representatives at Versailles in signing Joint Note 31, embodying their decisions regarding North Russia and, incidentally, showing just how erroneous was their information about the region. In view of the greatly increased German threat to the ports, said the note, the Allies should make a military effort to retain control of Murmansk and, if possible, of Archangel (thus wrongly equating the existing military and political situations at the two ports). The Allied effort should be strictly limited: since the Czechs were still assumed to be coming to Archangel, some of them could be retained there, and in order to train the Czechs it would be necessary to send out only four to six battalions of Allied troops. Finally—and this was a point which the French, who wanted a share in the command, at first disputed—there would be a single commander who would have charge of both the land and the naval defence of the Russian Arctic ports as well as of important points on the railways which terminated at the ports. That command would be exercised by a British officer until the Supreme War Council directed otherwise.[8] Poole, already on the spot, was the natural choice for this post.

This plan was quickly approved by the Supreme Council; soon afterwards Milner saw Foch and obtained the Generalissimo's approval for the diversion to North Russia of American troops originally scheduled for France. Milner then sent a message to the President asking for three battalions of infantry, two batteries of

[7] Memorandum by the Secretary of State, 3 June 1918; *ibid.*, pp. 484-85.
[8] The minutes of the meeting and the text of Joint Note 31 are found in the U.S. National Archives, Modern Army Branch, Supreme War Council Records.

artillery, and three companies of engineers.[9] This request, although modest, was much greater than either the American Secretary of War or Chief of Staff had expected, and they complained to the President that the venture would be an unprofitable diversion of resources from the Western Front. Nor did they want American troops under British command.[10] Throughout the latter part of June the number of American troops to be sent was debated between London and Washington, but the fundamental decision had been made. Eventually, in early July, against the wishes of his military advisers, President Wilson agreed to the full total that Milner had requested. Although still convinced that the action was in itself unwise, the President was decisively swayed by the final reason set forth by Balfour in his appeal of 28 May. He told the Secretary of War that he felt obliged to agree because the British and French were pressing him so hard, and because he had refused so many of their requests that they were beginning to feel that he was not a good associate, much less a good ally.[11]

Thus American consent to North Russian intervention was secured. It was agreement to a project which seemed to be both limited in scope and straightforward in purpose—keeping the Germans or their allies from taking over the area themselves.

Siberia, however, was an altogether different matter. President Wilson clung steadfastly to his position that military action by the Japanese would only make matters worse by driving the Russians to seek German support. But, as in the North Russian question, he felt that *something* ought to be done simply to placate his allies. So on 30 May, in a long interview with Sir William Wiseman, he suggested that the United States, Britain, and France send out a high-powered civilian commission to help re-organise the railways and food supplies and to set up a system of barter trade. Thus Russia would be helped back onto her own feet without the great risk that would be inherent in Japanese intervention.[12]

---

[9] Milner's request was sent as Balfour's telegram 3590 to Reading, 11 June 1918, 11 p.m.; Wiseman MSS.

[10] General Peyton C. March, *The Nation at War*, New York, 1932, p. 134.

[11] Kennan, *Decision to Intervene*, pp. 367-69, 376-78.

[12] Wiseman to Sir Eric Drummond, telegram 97 (CXP 627-9), Washington, 30 May 1918; Wiseman MSS.

The news that the Americans were considering a civil commission, and also that they might take part in North Russian intervention, reached London during the first days of June. By this time the tremendous attack which the Germans had unleashed on 27 May had carried them to within 37 miles of Paris, and the French had begun to evacuate their capital.[13] There is little wonder that the War Office, whose principal concern in Russian policy was to re-build an Eastern Front, looked on these American projects with contempt and sought to prevent them from gaining acceptance in Britain. Thus, on 9 June, the Army's spokesman on Russian matters, General Knox, addressed a long and rather ill-tempered memorandum to the Cabinet.[14]

There was a tendency in some circles, Knox wrote, to push the idea of economic assistance to the exclusion of military intervention. It was an idea which naturally appealed to commercial circles who hoped to extend British markets after the war, but its advocates had apparently forgotten all about the war. They surely knew, Knox said,

. . . that the Russian people will not be induced to fight even if we sacrifice our labour and tonnage and the wants of our own people in order to provide each man of the 160 millions of our former allies with a calico shirt and a pair of boots. Such a policy will sacrifice the cause of freedom for which we are fighting in the interests of a few capitalists.

Knox was equally scornful of attempts to make North Russian intervention a substitute for action through Siberia. An invasion through Archangel would require men, tonnage, food, and supplies vitally needed in France; it would deprive Russia of no necessary resources (all of the important war stores at Archangel had already been evacuated by the Bolsheviks); the north's population was too sparse to provide the Allies with Russian manpower; and, finally, action there would only provoke enemy occupation of Petrograd and Moscow, which could be accomplished without diverting a man from France.

Knox then recited the familiar arguments in favour of Siberian intervention—that the Japanese troops and shipping would not otherwise be used in France, that the Allies would get control of a populous and food-producing region, that only through the Far East

[13] Cruttwell, *Great War*, pp. 526-27.
[14] "Policy in the Eastern Theatre," Milner MSS, box AD-1.

could intervention bring to bear sufficient numbers so that the Germans would be forced to detach troops from France. But for the preceding four and a half months, the Allies had been wasting their opportunities in Siberia because of President Wilson's reluctance to act. Knox's solution to the Siberian problem was, he felt, simple and straightforward: the heads of the British, French, and Italian governments should approach Wilson and point out that the unanimous opinion of their military advisers was that without the reconstruction of an Eastern Front of some kind the Allies could not win the war, and that his delay in agreeing to intervention had already cost the Allies thousands of lives. Then, Knox said, once assured of the President's support,

... we should ascertain the minimum terms on which Japan will consent to undertake the main burden of intervention, and we should agree to those terms, recognising that we have no other possibility of saving the situation, and that Japan has national interests as well as other Powers and is unlikely to risk the lives of her soldiers for purely Allied interests or to save a situation brought about by Allied miscalculation.[15]

For Knox, the situation resolved itself into a simple matter of ascertaining the extent of Japan's demands and satisfying them. The Foreign Office, however, could not take quite so sanguine a view. It was no easy task to ascertain the "minimum terms" of the Japanese, because any terms they stated would really be short-hand expressions (commercial privileges, mineral rights, and the like) for their territorial ambitions both in Manchuria and in the Russian Far East. Although the Foreign Office might allow itself to be talked into believing that the Russian people would welcome Japanese intervention to save them from Germany or Bolshevism, not even the most ardent optimist could doubt how they would react if it seemed that the Japanese were staying. On 15 May, from the Embassy at Tokyo, Sir Conyngham Greene neatly put the British government's dilemma: if Japan were invited to intervene, Britain must be careful not to be "made a catspaw" of Japanese efforts to gain control of China and eastern Siberia. But on the other hand, he said,

There remains a possibility that if we do nothing Japan will think her "opportunity of a 1,000 years" has come and, either by supporting Semenov or otherwise, advance to Irkutsk and stay there. Such a policy would not

[15] *idem.*

be inconsistent with ideas of Japanese pro-German party who believe Germany cannot be defeated and should be conciliated.[16]

Thus, at the end of May and in early June, there began a new round of Anglo-Japanese negotiations over the delicate problem of Siberia. Much had happened since the combination of Japanese and American reluctance had put an inconclusive end to the conversations in early March. The Germans had begun their great offensive. Japan and Britain had embarked together on the temporary occupation of Vladivostok. Semenov, against British urgings but supported by Japan, had advanced into Siberia from his Manchurian sanctuary. The Czechs had just become a factor—still a very uncertain one—in the Siberian situation. And Britain had earnestly pursued a policy which caused the Japanese government great discomfort—the attempt to secure a Bolshevik invitation for intervention.[17]

It was this discomfort which, on 18 May, moved Baron Goto, the newly-appointed Japanese Foreign Minister, to request that his ambassador in London should seek to re-open discussions with the Foreign Office. Chinda was first to inquire about the prospects for success of Lockhart's efforts in Moscow and then go on tactfully to suggest that an invitation to intervene, if it were forthcoming, would necessitate collaboration with the Bolsheviks, serving only to strengthen the Soviet regime and to help it extend its writ throughout Siberia. Obviously this was the last thing the Japanese desired. Chinda was also to point out that so long as the German invasion of Russia did not extend to Siberia, Moscow was hardly likely to invite a Siberian expedition.

Finally, the ambassador was to ask what the British thought should be done about Semenov. Previously, continued Goto's telegram of instructions, London had requested that the Japanese should join in restraining Semenov for fear that his offensive might hinder Lockhart's work in Moscow. Nevertheless, it had been impossible to dissuade him from his advance, and according to the Japanese officer attached to him, he was growing stronger every day owing to the continuous enlistment of more Cossacks. Now numbering some

[16] Greene to Balfour, telegram 516, Tokyo, 15 May 1918, 8:45 p.m.; Milner MSS, unfiled folder 32.
[17] The French government, also, was acutely troubled by the British efforts to come to terms with the Bolsheviks, and made quite clear that they considered it a wholly futile policy which, because of Bolshevik duplicity, could lead only to harm. See Lord Derby's telegram 648 to Balfour from Paris, 17 May 1918; Milner MSS, box C-1.

5,000, his force was menacing Karymskaya. Semenov originally set out on his offensive, said Goto, relying completely upon the moral and material support of Britain, France, and Japan. Not unreasonably, he counted on it to continue. If the Powers suddenly left him in the lurch, Goto asked in concluding, would they not lose prestige in the eyes of the Russian people, who would decide that the Allies were unreliable and hence move even further into the arms of Germany?

When he called at the Foreign Office on 22 May Chinda handed Lord Robert Cecil a translation of Goto's telegram.[18] In reply the Under Secretary told the Ambassador that he could not speak authoritatively at such short notice, but was quite prepared to express his private opinions. Cecil did not tell Chinda that the government had given up its efforts to secure a Bolshevik invitation (although, as we have seen, this was virtually the case) but he did pass on Lockhart's opinion that the Allies should take action whether invited or not. He indicated that he himself was quite willing that Semenov should be supported if that were the wish of the Japanese military authorities. In the same way, he said, the British government was anxious to make use of the Czechs then collecting at Vladivostok. He recognised that Semenov and the Czechs could be effective only if strongly supported by Japan; and if that happened, he was quite willing that the Japanese should take direction of the whole Siberian intervention, provided they made clear they were not acting for territorial advantage but to assist Russia and the Allied cause generally, and provided they were prepared to push their expedition as far west as Chelyabinsk.

At this, Ambassador Chinda drew back. An expedition to Chelyabinsk was an entirely new idea, he said. His government had so far considered only the necessity of intervening to prevent German penetration to the Pacific coast. Thus, the old game of cat and mouse had started again. As we have seen, Foreign Minister Motono had assured the French Ambassador early in March that he was willing to pledge his country to intervention as far as the Urals.[19] But later that same month Motono had made it very clear to the British Ambassador that Japan wanted a free hand and would make no such pledge.[20] And now, as Chinda sat across from Lord Robert Cecil and protested that

[18] A copy of this translation is in the Milner MSS, box C-1.
[19] See above, p. 105.   [20] See above, p. 129.

an expedition to Chelyabinsk was a new idea, he was not aware that Cecil had on his desk a telegram from Greene, in Tokyo, reporting a private visit from Baron Goto the previous day, during which the Japanese Foreign Minister had stated that when he spoke of intervention he certainly meant an expedition as far as the Urals, assuming that the military details could be arranged among the Allies.[21] Cecil said nothing to his caller about the telegram from Tokyo, nor about the differing Japanese statements. (Later he was to learn that the conversation between Greene and Goto had been strictly secret— the Foreign Minister had not informed his Foreign Office of its substance.)[22] He ended the interview by urging on Chinda the view that Siberian intervention might affect the outcome of the whole war, and by earnestly appealing to the Japanese as allies to come to Britain's assistance.[23]

A week later, on 30 May, Chinda heard a similar appeal from Balfour. The Foreign Secretary told the ambassador that he was sure that the Siberian question would arise at the Supreme War Council at Versailles during the following few days, and he wanted to be able to assure his Allied colleagues that Japan would agree to go as far as the Urals. It would be most unfortunate, he said, to secure American agreement and then find Japan unwilling. Chinda promised to seek his government's views at once.

Balfour then went on to tell the ambassador that Britain had given up all hope of a Bolshevik invitation, but that he was certain that the Allied armies would be welcomed even by those who did not dare to invite them—a sanguine hope indeed. Finally, turning to the question of Semenov, Balfour suggested that the Japanese had mis-stated the issues: the Allies had not asked Semenov to advance, and therefore he could not claim any right to their support. Britain would help him so long as he furthered British policy, not when he hindered it.[24]

[21] Greene to Balfour, telegram 535, Tokyo, 21 May 1918, 1 p.m. (received in London 8 a.m. 22 May); Milner MSS, box C-1.

[22] Greene to Balfour, telegram 612, Tokyo, 9 June 1918; Wiseman MSS (as Balfour to Reading, no. 3606, 11 June). Greene's surmise that the talk was not reported by Goto to his staff is borne out by the fact that it is not mentioned in Morley, *Japanese Thrust*, although the author had full access to Japanese archives.

[23] Cecil described this entire conversation with Chinda in a paper headed "Note of a conversation between Lord R. Cecil and the Japanese Ambassador in the form of a draft telegram to Sir C. Greene, Tokio," 22 May 1918; Milner MSS, box C-1.

[24] Balfour's interview with Chinda was described in telegram 527 from Cecil to Greene in Tokyo, 30 May 1918, 3:50 p.m.; Milner MSS, unfiled folder 32. See Morley,

Meeting at Paris on the morning of 3 June the British, French, and Italian Foreign Ministers decided to ask the Japanese whether, provided America consented, they would be prepared to intervene on condition that Japan should (a) promise to respect the territorial integrity of Russia, (b) take no side in Russian internal politics, and (c) advance as far west as possible, "for the purpose of encountering the Germans."[25] When the subject was taken up by the full Supreme Council at Versailles that afternoon, Balfour expressed some doubt as to whether the Japanese would agree to these conditions.[26]

The Council itself never formally approved the proposal, because the Americans objected to the consideration of political affairs in a body which they felt should confine itself solely to military matters. Thus, the note which Balfour handed to Chinda on 7 June was on behalf of the governments of Britain, France, and Italy, and not of the Supreme War Council. On receiving the note, Chinda asked how far west the Powers wanted Japan to go. Balfour replied at least to Omsk, and preferably to Chelyabinsk.[27]

At this point it is worth noting, however, that even so great an advance would have accomplished relatively little: the nearest places where the Japanese could have encountered German troops would have been on the Don or in the Caucasus (where a few German units were assisting the Turkish advance)—places 1,000 miles from Chelyabinsk and 1,500 miles from Omsk. The occupation of western Siberia would have kept the region's cereals out of the hands of the Central Powers, but its military value would have been negligible. Unless the Germans had chosen to advance deeper into Russia to meet the Japanese they would not have had to withdraw a single man from the Western Front. As we have seen, and as the Allies knew, German policy in Russia from May onwards was to stand still, not to advance.

When the Allied proposal reached Tokyo it precipitated another great debate in the Advisory Council on Foreign Relations. The representatives of the Army General Staff, considerably closer to the

---

Japanese Thrust, pp. 222-24, for short summaries of Chinda's telegrams describing to the Japanese government this interview and the one with Cecil on the 22nd.

[25] Minutes of the third meeting of the sixth session of the Supreme War Council, Versailles, 3 June 1918, 3 p.m.; U.S. National Archives, Modern Army Branch, Supreme War Council Records.

[26] *ibid.*

[27] Morley, *Japanese Thrust*, p. 226.

immense logistical problems of a Siberian expedition than were their counterparts in London, argued that a venture on the scale envisioned by the Allies[28] would involve all of Japan's permanent divisions and some reserve ones as well, and that in the existing condition of the Chinese-Eastern and Trans-Siberian railways, three years might be required to get all the troops as far as Chelyabinsk. The Army strenuously objected, not because such an effort (subsidised by the Allies, of course) would be impossible, but because it would leave Japan no forces with which to further her interests in East Asia. Much more to the Army's liking was an occupation of Trans-Baikalia, whence they "could protect the Russian Far East, insure China's northwestern borders, and indirectly be able to suppress disturbances within India."[29] The General Staff thought that Japan should agree to an expedition, but should make clear to the Allies that its sphere must be limited to Eastern Siberia and that the command of all troops must be Japanese. After several days of prolonged debate, and under the urging of Foreign Minister Goto, the Council accepted this view.[30]

The official Japanese reply to the Allied proposal was handed to Balfour by Ambassador Chinda on 24 June.[31] Although addressed to the British government, it was circulated in Paris, Rome, and Washington as well. At the outset, it reaffirmed the position originally declared in the Japanese note of 19 March to the United States government:[32] that the Japanese government did not feel at liberty to make any decision regarding intervention until complete accord

[28] Actually, the Allies had made no definite proposals to Japan as to the size of the force required for the Siberian intervention, but it was generally assumed, in British War Office memoranda and other papers, that it would require at least several hundred thousand men. And on 1 June Lloyd George told General Bliss that in his opinion it would be necessary for Japan to "come in with every man that they could put in the field, even up to the extent of 2,500,000 men, because they must be strong enough to overcome any possible resistance and reach the Germans in the West as rapidly as possible; and after they reach the Germans they must be amply strong enough to fight them." (as reported by Bliss to Secretary of War Baker in a letter of 8 June 1918; U.S. National Archives, Modern Army Branch, Supreme War Council folder 355, item 1.)

[29] Quoted by Morley, *Japanese Thrust*, p. 227, from a Japanese General Staff report. Morley leaves unexplained this most extraordinary reference to the suppression of disturbances within India. Perhaps the Japanese expected to be called upon to help the British in the event of the Turks or Germans pressing their attacks from the Caucasus, through Transcaspia, into India.

[30] *ibid.*, pp. 227-28.

[31] The text of the Japanese note, handed to Balfour on 24 June, was telegraphed to Reading in Washington, no. 3988, 28 June 1918; Wiseman MSS.

[32] See above, Chapter V, footnote 7.

on the subject had been reached between America and the Western Allies.

Apparently, only this much of the Japanese note was communicated to the American government.[33] The note, as communicated to the other governments, then went on to examine the details of the new Allied proposals. Of the three conditions which the British, French, and Italian Foreign Ministers put forward, the Japanese found themselves in entire accord with the first two (respect for the territorial integrity of Russia and non-interference in Russian internal politics). But—and here was the crux of the note—while they were in full sympathy with the object of the third condition (the requirement that Japanese forces advance until they encountered the Germans),

They regret that they should find it impossible for them to engage to extend Westward their military activities beyond the limits of Eastern Siberia in view of the grave difficulties with which such operations will be practically confronted.

Finally, the note expressed the hope that because of Japan's geographical position and the strength of the forces she was being called upon to provide, she should be given supreme command of all forces, Japanese and other, that might take part.

Since the Allies had already recognised (among themselves at least) the Japanese claims to supreme command and were fully aware that Japan would not act if American opposition seemed probable, the only important part of this note was the statement about a westward advance. Over the next fortnight, the combination of the British government's desperation and the Japanese government's tact and desire not to offend led to an elaborate exegesis which wholly lost sight of the intended meaning of the passage quoted above. From the moment he received the note Balfour interpreted it as stating that the Japanese would do their best to push as far west as possible, but did not want to assume a binding obligation because of the embarrassment that might accompany failure to fulfil it. When Balfour asked if this were, in fact, the case, and Chinda said that it was, the Foreign Secretary replied that the British government fully understood the Japanese attitude. After placing the note before

[33] The Japanese Ambassador in Washington gave Secretary of State Lansing only this first part of the note (*Foreign Relations, The Lansing Papers*, vol. II, p. 365).

Balfour on 24 June Chinda added his personal opinion that the "somewhat ambiguous formula" was chosen to mollify "a not un-important section of the Japanese public" who considered that Japan's obligations to the Entente Powers were based on the Anglo-Japanese Treaty of 1902, limiting Japanese military obligations to the eastern theatre of war.[34] Balfour should have been warned by this remark, but his own interpretation was supported by Greene in Tokyo, who telegraphed on 30 June that he felt that the hesitation of the Japanese to commit themselves was perfectly comprehensible, particularly when America's uncertain attitude was taken into account.[35]

Foreign Minister Goto, however, did not intend that the Japanese attitude should be ambiguous at all, and he was plainly disturbed by Chinda's failure to make the position clear. On 1 July he sent the ambassador a telegram (a translation of which Chinda gave to the Foreign Office) which should have left no shred of doubt. It was quite true, Goto said, that a certain section of Japanese opinion objected to the extension of military activities beyond Eastern Siberia as a matter of principle. "But in this matter," he continued, "the Imperial Government were guided in their reply to [the] British memorandum by considerations of practical feasibility, and their inability to engage to the effect suggested is categorical and final." Not only would Japanese troops almost certainly meet great obstacles if they tried to extend operations beyond Eastern Siberia, but the efficiency of the expeditionary army as a fighting force would drop so much as its lines of operations grew longer that it would meet failure against the enemy. "In these circumstances," Goto said,

the Imperial Government find it incompatible with their sense of responsibility vis-à-vis their Allies to pledge themselves to undertake such an operation which is, in their judgment, a task of extreme difficulty.[36]

Because Balfour was in Paris at a session of the Supreme War Council, Ambassador Chinda gave this telegram to Lord Robert Cecil; now it was the Under Secretary's turn so to misconstrue a frank and straightforward refusal that it became an acceptance. We

[34] Balfour described his interview with Chinda in a telegram to Reading in Washington, no. 3989, 28 June 1918; Wiseman mss.

[35] Greene to Balfour, telegram 699, Tokyo, 30 June 1918; Wiseman mss (as Balfour to Reading, no. 4128, 3 July).

[36] The text of Goto's telegram, handed to Cecil on 3 July, was despatched to Balfour that day as telegram 1343 to Paris, noon; Milner mss, unfiled folder 32.

shall let Cecil tell the story in his own words, the ones he used in telegraphing an account of the interview to Balfour:

I took the opportunity of pointing out to the Japanese Ambassador that the so-called condition that Japanese Forces should proceed as far as Urals was more properly an indication of what was regarded as the most valuable form that Japanese assistance to Allied Intervention could take, but that the British Government would, as far as they were concerned, gladly accept Japanese co-operation on the terms indicated in Baron Goto's telegram feeling sure that Japanese Government would desire to assist their Allies to the utmost of their power and would therefore be ready if they found it possible to extend their operations beyond Irkutsk.

The Ambassador quite accepted this way of looking at things and seemed to have no doubt that Japanese willingness to help was limited only by their power and if they found their advance to Irkutsk militarily simple and especially if, as he hoped, Russian opinion rallied to the Allies, there would be no difficulty in pushing further forward.[37]

Cecil's assurances to Chinda, one is tempted to conclude, provided Goto with exactly what he was seeking—Britain's agreement that Japanese participation would be entirely on Japan's own terms. Of the conditions (and they were originally put forward, for all practical purposes, as conditions) which the Allied foreign ministers set for Japan, the only one of any substance was the demand for an advance westward. "Territorial integrity" and "non-interference in domestic politics" are, after all, capable of concealing a multitude of sins, but the extent of an army's progress through a foreign country is less ambiguous.

Now that Goto could be sure that Japan was not bound by this condition and, therefore, would have a virtually free hand in Siberia, he could again afford to take a more conciliatory line. In general, he told Ambassador Greene on 5 July, it was best not to talk so soon of the later phases of intervention (i.e. those west of Lake Baikal) but to leave them to be dealt with according to future eventualities. If American approval were forthcoming, he added, the Japanese government would not be disposed to be exigent as to the course of future policy.[38]

✧

[37] Cecil to Balfour, Paris, telegram 1345, 3 July 1918, 3:45 p.m.; Wiseman MSS (as telegram 4147, Cecil to Reading, 4 July).

[38] Greene to Balfour, telegram 708, Tokyo, 5 July 1918, 11 a.m.; Milner MSS, unfiled folder 32.

Thus, once again, the problem became one of obtaining the consent of the United States government. While the Anglo-Japanese negotiations were proceeding, President Wilson was coming around to a position much more satisfactory to London and Tokyo. At the end of May, it will be remembered, he had been thinking in terms of a civilian economic commission for the relief of Siberia. During the first fortnight of June suggestions for such a commission came to the White House from many different American sources, both governmental and private. In the circles close to Wilson the name of Herbert Hoover, who had so successfully led the Commission for the Relief of Belgium, came to be mentioned as the logical man to head a Siberian mission.[39] Both Lord Reading and Sir William Wiseman enthusiastically approved such an appointment. Wiseman, because of his intimacy with Colonel House, knew the President's mind better than any other foreigner; on 14 June he sent a long telegram to London describing and endorsing the American plans.[40]

Hoover would go at once to Vladivostok, Wiseman said, as head of an Allied commission which would give the Russians food and other supplies and help them to re-organise their economic life. A military force would be sent to protect the commission and reinforcements would be held ready in case Hoover advised their use. Once the commission was on the scene, Wiseman predicted, the President would necessarily be guided by Hoover's advice, and if the latter should advise large-scale intervention, even primarily by the Japanese, his advice would almost certainly be accepted.

The British government might naturally object, Wiseman continued, that such a plan would mean a long delay between the despatch of the civil commission and the desired military action. "My reply," he said, "is that at any rate we should be on the right road, and I do not believe it is possible to persuade the President to agree to armed intervention without some such preliminary movement."

During the following two months Wiseman's attitude came to be shared by many people in Britain who were faced with the problem of Russia. Simply stated, it was this: any American commitment, even to a course of action that London felt to be wholly inadequate, was better than none. Once a commitment was made, then "the march of events" (as Balfour had called it) would transform it into the

[39] Kennan, *Decision to Intervene*, pp. 385-86.
[40] Wiseman to Sir Eric Drummond, telegram CXP 644, 14 June 1918; Wiseman MSS.

major involvement necessary to divert German troops from the Western Front.

Despite the enthusiasm which the idea had generated, President Wilson did not appoint Hoover to lead a Siberian mission, perhaps because the latter's services as Food Commissioner were more vitally needed at home, but more probably, as Kennan suggests, because the President was not yet ready to see the Russian problem lifted from his hands and placed in those of the man on the spot.[41] Still, Washington did not give up the idea of a civil commission, and the State Department and other branches of the government continued to devote much time to plans for one. The President, however, was pursuing a different line of thought. On 18 June he told a French special emissary that he was "considering anew the entire situation" and would express his conclusions within ten days.[42]

While Wilson was thus occupied, there arrived in London a Russian visitor who, of all his countrymen, was perhaps least qualified to offer advice to the Allied governments: Kerensky. He had travelled incognito on a Serbian passport which (because Kerensky was fleeing for his life) Lockhart had viséd on his own authority, without approval from London.[43] As soon as the British government learned of Kerensky's presence in London, they took steps to keep all references to him out of the press, and asked the American government to do the same. "It is most important," Balfour telegraphed Reading on 20 June, "to avoid if possible the fact of Kerensky's presence in England being twisted into proof that there is an ill-will to the Bolshevik Government." He had only been allowed to enter Britain because he was a fugitive, and the government was anxious for him to proceed as soon as possible to America, where he would be "much less embarrassing to the Allied cause" and more useful in enlightening American opinion.[44]

Despite the government's precautions, Kerensky soon made known his presence in London and was promptly invited by the Labour Party to address its annual conference on 27 June. When he appeared on the platform he received a tremendous ovation; with Litvinov and his wife sitting stonily in the gallery, he passionately appealed for

[41] Kennan, *Decision to Intervene*, p. 387.
[42] *ibid.*, p. 388.
[43] Lockhart, *British Agent*, p. 278.
[44] Balfour to Reading, Washington, telegram 3805, 20 June 1918; Wiseman MSS.

Allied intervention. When he asked the Labour Party whether it could remain "a calm spectator of that unheard-of tragedy" then taking place in Russia, the assembled delegates answered him with tumultuous cheering.[45] Their cheers had no echo in Russia. A week later, on a visit to Archangel, F. O. Lindley telegraphed that the reception given Kerensky in Britain had produced "the worst impression" among Russians, and urged that if it were impossible to prevent his public speeches, no mention should be made of them in the news telegrams to Russia. The former premier, Lindley concluded, had "not a single friend in this country among any party," and was "universally blamed as the person principally responsible for the existing state of things."[46]

Kerensky met Lloyd George in a secret interview on 24 June.[47] Declaring that he had come to England "for the special purpose of clearing up relations between Russia and the Allies," the former premier claimed to speak "for the whole of Russia except the reactionaries and the Bolsheviks." Intervention through Siberia, he said, would be welcome if it were an Allied and not solely a Japanese venture. Lloyd George surmised that Kerensky's primary object was to secure recognition for himself and his exiled friends as the legitimate government of Russia. Yet he was not unimpressed by his visitor.[48] That afternoon in the House of Commons, making his first statement dealing with Russia at any length since the November Revolution, the Prime Minister maintained that he had it "on expert authority" that Russia was more ready than ever before to expel the Germans, and then ruminated that Japan was the only country with access to Russia on a great scale. But he would say no more about these specific aspects of the situation as yet.[49]

He did, however, reveal to the House some of his thoughts on the difficulties of coping with the Russian problem. He was most

[45] *The Times*, 28 June 1918. For Kerensky's address, see *Labour Party, Report of Annual Conference, June 1918*, pp. 60-61.

[46] Lindley to Balfour, telegram 12, Archangel, 6 July 1918, 5:40 p.m.; Wiseman MSS (as no. 4382, Balfour to Reading, 14 July).

[47] "Note of an Interview between the Prime Minister and M. Kerensky, at 10, Downing Street, S. W., on June 24th, 1918"; Milner MSS, box AD-1. Some excerpts from this document are printed in Lloyd George, *War Memoirs*, vol. II, pp. 1904-6.

[48] Sir George Riddell entered in his diary on 29 June: "L. G. has met Kerensky. He says he has the most piercing eyes he has ever seen. K. is an attractive personality, but L. G. does not regard him as a man of action." (Lord Riddell, *War Diary*, p. 335.)

[49] 107 HC Deb. 5s. cols. 783-84 (24 June 1918).

troubled—and this was an attitude which would appear in his speeches again and again in the following year—by the fact that there was no established authority with which Britain could deal. "How many Governments are there in Russia?" he asked a critical Labour member. When the reply came "Only one," Lloyd George heatedly asserted:

> That is exactly where he is wrong. What is the Government of the Ukraine? What is the Government in Georgia? . . . He will hardly find the same Government in any two villages [in Siberia]. It is of no use talking about "the Russian Government" as if there were one Government for the whole country. That is one of the difficulties with which you are dealing there. You are not dealing with anyone who is responsible for Russia as a whole.[50]

Yet so far as intervention was concerned, Lloyd George seems to have regarded the Bolsheviks as the only authority with which the Allies could deal. To Kerensky's appeal during their interview for immediate Allied action, the Prime Minister replied that so long as the *de facto* Russian government (i.e. the Bolshevik regime) maintained its present position, the situation was extraordinarily difficult. If there were a government in Russia willing to stretch out its hand to the Allies (and here Lloyd George, in hinting again at the need for an invitation, was taking a line that the British government had finally rejected a month before), the Allies would help it in every way. But what could they do, he asked, so long as the only government appeared as friendly to the Germans as to the Allies?[51]

The only other evidence we have as to how Lloyd George personally regarded the Russian problem at this time indicates that in this interview he was not simply holding back so as to conceal Allied intentions from his visitor. Five days previously, General Sir Henry Wilson noted in his diary, after a conference with the Prime Minister and Milner: "Milner and I pressed for Japanese intervention in Siberia, but Lloyd George hangs back for some unaccountable reason."[52] This reason, surely, was reluctance to intervene without the assurance of Bolshevik support. Yet the Prime Minister's reluctance apparently had no real effect on British policy: the formal

[50] *ibid.*, cols. 781-82.
[51] Kerensky interview, *loc.cit.*
[52] Diary entry, 19 June 1918; Callwell, *Henry Wilson*, vol. II, p. 109.

proposal to the Japanese had been made a fortnight before, and it could hardly have been issued against the wishes of the premier.

In any case, the War Office kept up its resolute pressure for intervention. At about this time it circulated yet another memorandum stating with absolute certainty: "Unless Allied intervention is undertaken in Siberia forthwith we have no chance of being ultimately victorious and shall incur serious risk of defeat in the meantime."[53] And at a War Cabinet session on 19 June, the C.I.G.S. stipulated that if the Japanese did not come in, Poole and all his force in North Russia should be withdrawn, else they would be lost.[54]

During the last week of June, therefore, the British government set about preparing a final appeal to the President. Since the appeal was to be in the name of the Allies, it would first have to be approved by the Supreme War Council when it met early in July. In the meantime, however, Balfour was worried that the product of Woodrow Wilson's "considering anew" of the Russian situation would be a decision to take no action. And if *any* American commitment would have been better in British eyes than none, continued indecision was preferable to a definite and positively stated refusal to act. Thus, Balfour telegraphed Lord Reading on 28 June that "it would be a serious blow" if the President were to "commit himself publicly" against intervention at the present moment. The Ambassador was instructed to beg the Administration to wait until after the Supreme Council had met.[55]

When the Council met at Versailles on 2 July the British text of the appeal was approved virtually unchanged. Lloyd George himself moved that the sentence "The Japanese have now agreed to send an expedition into Siberia as far as Irkutsk . . ." be amended by the addition of ". . . and though they have not engaged themselves to go

[53] The text of the memorandum was sent from Balfour to Reading (through Wiseman as telegram 82, CXP 658), 20 June 1918; Wiseman MSS. Neither the British Ambassador nor Colonel House (at whose Massachusetts estate Reading was staying) was much impressed by the War Office's arguments. "It is a panicy document in the main," House wrote to the President on 21 June, "and neither Reading nor I agree to the statement that a decision is not possible on the Western Front without an Eastern Front as well." (Woodrow Wilson MSS, series II, box 141.)

[54] Henry Wilson's diary entry for 19 June 1918; Callwell, *Henry Wilson*, vol. II, p. 109. The same view was also put in a memorandum from the Director of Military Operations to Milner on 24 June (Milner MSS, box D-4).

[55] Balfour to Reading, Washington, telegram 3983, 28 June 1918; Wiseman MSS. Reading immediately passed the message on to the President (Woodrow Wilson MSS, series II, box 142).

beyond Irkutsk there is no ground for thinking that this necessarily represents the limits of their effort," an amendment for which, as we have seen, there was very little justification. The bulk of the document was simply a lengthier and more ponderous recasting of all the old arguments, underlined with statements like: ". . . the Supreme War Council feel bound to point out that in their judgment failure to intervene immediately must inevitably cause effects which can only be described as disastrous to the Allied cause."[56]

But the Council did put forward one new argument that somewhat justified its opening assertion that "since its last meeting a complete change has come over the situation in Russia and Siberia, which makes Allied intervention in these countries an urgent and imperative necessity." This argument was that unless the Allies acted immediately, great harm would come to the Czech troops in Siberia.

The Czechs were, indeed, in a precarious situation. After their decision at the end of May to force their way to Vladivostok, they had seized virtually the entire railway between Penza, west of the Urals, and Irkutsk. This latter town, the seat of the all-Siberian Soviet and the principal Bolshevik military centre in Siberia, was denied them because of the well-intentioned but disastrous mediation of the American Consul-General there.[57] The Corps was thus split in two; between the two parts was the formidable strategic barrier of Lake Baikal and large concentrations of Bolshevik troops, aided by most of the prisoners of war who had been enlisted under the Soviet banner. These defectors, it will be remembered, numbered only a few thousand, but inaccurate accounts from Irkutsk[58] so swelled their ranks that the Supreme Council's appeal declared that the Czechs were "in grave danger of being cut off by the organization of German and Austro-Hungarian prisoners of war. . . ."

At Vladivostok, where some 15,000 of the total Czech force of 60,000 had gathered, representatives of the Czecho-Slovak National Council met with the Allied consuls and naval commanders on

[56] Minutes, first meeting of seventh session of Supreme War Council, Versailles, 2 July 1918, 4 p.m.; U.S. National Archives, Modern Army Branch, Supreme War Council Records. The text of the appeal to President Wilson, as approved by the Council, is in *Foreign Relations, 1918, Russia*, vol. II, pp. 241-46.

[57] For an account of this mediation, see Kennan, *Decision to Intervene*, pp. 279-91.

[58] Among them one from the British Consul at Irkutsk, who reported that the town was completely in the hands of the prisoners of war (cited by Hodgson at Vladivostok in telegram 71 to Balfour, 25 June 1918; in Wiseman MSS as no. 4047, Balfour to Reading, 29 June).

25 June. The Czech leaders stated that they would have to turn their forces west again to rescue their compatriots, and urgently requested that the Allies should send to their aid an expeditionary force of 100,000 men and large quantities of arms.[59] And on 29 June, after weeks of mounting tension between themselves and the Vladivostok Soviet, the Czechs seized control of the city. This action was heartily approved by the British, Japanese, and American naval commanders, and each of them landed small contingents of marines to help the Czechs keep order. On 6 July, in a proclamation signed by the representatives of Britain, France, Japan, the United States, China, and the Czech Army, the whole Vladivostok area was "taken under the temporary protection of the Allied powers" who would take all necessary measures "for its defense against dangers both external and internal."[60] This was, by a coincidence, the same day on which Murmansk formally came under Allied protection.

It was the plight of the Czechs, rather than the Supreme Council's note or a strongly-worded appeal from General Foch delivered on 27 June,[61] that finally led to the American decision to intervene. Sir William Wiseman predicted as much on 4 July, when he wrote to Sir Arthur Murray, his colleague in British Intelligence and the one who passed his telegrams on to Balfour, that the Czechs might yet prove to be the decisive factor. Wiseman commented that to President Wilson the Russian question was not simply a passing political situation, but a matter of principle. And he added:

I am not saying he is right, but I think we should realise that we are up against a new conception of foreign policy which no amount of argument will reconcile with, for instance, traditional British policy.[62]

On the very next day, Secretary of State Lansing wrote in a memorandum to the President that the seizure of Vladivostok and the

[59] Captain Payne (commanding *HMS Suffolk*) to Admiralty, telegram 60, 26 June 1918; Hodgson, Vladivostok, to Balfour, telegram 74, 27 June (both in Wiseman MSS as nos. 4097 and 4101, Balfour to Reading, 2 July). See also the report of the U.S. Consul to Secretary of State, 25 June; *Foreign Relations, 1918, Russia*, vol. II, p. 226.

[60] The text of the Allied proclamation is in *ibid.*, p. 271. Consul Hodgson's report of the Czech take-over of Vladivostok, sent from Tokyo as telegram 730, 6 July, is in the Wiseman MSS as no. 4336, Balfour to Reading, 11 July.

[61] Foch's message is printed in Ray Stannard Baker, *Woodrow Wilson, Life and Letters*, vol. VIII, Garden City, New York, 1939, p. 237.

[62] Letter, Wiseman to Murray, New York, 4 July 1918; printed in Lt. Col. Hon. Arthur C. Murray, *At Close Quarters: A Sidelight on Anglo-American Diplomatic Relations*, London, 1946, p. 26. Murray was a close friend of Balfour, and served as the London end of Wiseman's unofficial chain of liaison. See pp. 1-11 of his book.

Czech involvement in Western Siberia had "materially changed the situation by introducing a sentimental element into the question of our duty." America, he said, had a responsibility to aid the Czechs.[63] The President had arrived at a similar conclusion. On Saturday, 6 July, he summoned to the White House his Secretaries of State, War, and Navy, and the Chief of Staff and the Chief of Naval Operations, and read to them a memorandum he had written. The text was approved by the meeting with no substantial changes, and formed the basis for America's Russian policy in the months to come.[64]

Its basic premise was that even if it were considered wise to employ a large Japanese force in Siberia (and the memorandum passed no judgement on this point), the establishment of a new Eastern Front, even one east of the Urals, would be physically impossible. Under existing conditions, any advance west of Irkutsk seemed impossible, and therefore would not be considered. In other words, the purpose for which the British had urged Allied intervention was expressly dismissed at the outset.

Nevertheless, the memorandum continued, the situation of the Czech forces made it mandatory for the American government and other governments "to make an effort to aid those at Vladivostok in forming a junction with their compatriots in western Siberia." Therefore, "in view of the inability of the United States to furnish any considerable force within a short time" to go to the aid of the Czechs, the President and his advisers proposed that a force of approximately 7,000 Americans and 7,000 Japanese be landed at Vladivostok "to guard the line of communication of the Czecho-Slovaks proceeding toward Irkutsk." Both governments would publicly declare that they had landed troops only to aid the Czechs "against German and Austrian prisoners" and that they had no intention of interfering with Russian internal affairs or of infringing upon Russia's territorial sovereignty. The only use foreseen for the forces of other Powers was that small contingents from Allied naval vessels would co-operate with the Czechs in policing Vladivostok. Finally, no further steps, beyond supplying the Czechs with weapons, would be taken until it was seen whether these measures were effective.

[63] Kennan, *Decision to Intervene*, p. 395.
[64] The text of this memorandum is printed in *Foreign Relations, 1918, Russia,* vol. II, pp. 262-63, and also in Kennan, *Decision to Intervene*, pp. 396-97.

President Wilson could limit the size of the intervening forces to 14,000 because he clearly expected that they would be used only to guard Vladivostok and the railways and thus free Czech troops for front-line service. The figure of 14,000 was evidently derived from the fact that the Americans could spare only 7,000 men themselves and were afraid of the consequences of their being outnumbered by the Japanese. It should be noted, moreover, that while the American memorandum ran directly counter to British policy in denying the possibility of the re-establishment of an Eastern Front, its confinement of military operations to territory east of Irkutsk was exactly what the Japanese wanted; as we have seen, one of the major problems facing British diplomacy was getting Japan to agree to move further west. Finally, the memorandum reduced the Siberian situation to a simple conflict between Czechs and armed German, Austrian, and Hungarian prisoners. "In this dramatic image," Kennan has pointed out, "there was no room either for the Bolsheviki, who were the real opponents of the Czechs in Siberia, nor the Russian Whites, who were their real allies."[65]

Not only were the Allies conspicuously denied a major part in the proposed American policy, but they were not even informed of it until a day after the Japanese—a "flagrant discourtesy," as Kennan says, in view of the appeal just made by the Supreme War Council.[66] This was, incredibly, an oversight: no-one had thought to inform them.[67] On the morning of 9 July Secretary Lansing saw the British, French, and Italian ambassadors individually. Immediately afterward, the three met at the British Embassy and found that the accounts of American policy that Lansing had given them did not correspond in all respects. In order to remove any misunderstanding, Reading brought his colleagues back to the State Department that afternoon.[68] Acting as spokesman (although the French Ambassador was *doyen* of the Diplomatic Corps), Reading demanded to know whether the Americans did in fact intend to confine the Siberian operations to their own and Japanese troops.

Lansing replied testily that Reading's question seemed to be based on national pride and sentiment, that he could not understand why

[65] Kennan, *Decision to Intervene*, p. 401.
[66] *ibid.*, p. 405.
[67] *ibid.*, pp. 405-6.
[68] Reading to Balfour, telegram 3112, Washington, 9 July 1918, 9:10 p.m.; Wiseman MSS.

it had been raised, and that it simply demonstrated the wisdom of the American course in not consulting the Allied governments "as apparently there would have been delay in discussing the details which would have been very unfortunate in view of the necessity of prompt action." This was, it should be noted, after weeks of Allied pleading for just the speed Lansing now demanded. The Secretary of State went on curtly to state that "details" such as the inclusion in the force of troops from other Powers would be discussed after the Japanese had agreed to the American plan; prior discussion would be useless.[69]

The full explanation for this extraordinary conduct on the part of the American government will probably never become clear. Kennan is obviously correct in stating that much may be attributed to the asperities bred by wartime strain and weariness, and that the President and the Secretary of State "had both now worked themselves into a high state of suspicion of British motives and resentment of British pressures in the Siberian problem."[70] Perhaps the best comment on the whole affair was made by that most diplomatic of gentlemen, Colonel House:

I know exactly what the President has in mind. He knows what the French and English want, therefore he thinks it essential to work out a plan with the Japanese. When he does this he will undoubtedly advise the other Powers, but until then, he considers it unnecessary. In this he is mistaken. The better way—the diplomatic way, and the way to keep from offending sensibilities, would be to have them all cognizant of everything that is going on.[71]

If one of the functions of an ambassador is to ease the friction between his own government and that to which he is accredited, Lord Reading earned full marks for trying to do this on 9 July. The telegram he sent that evening reflected none of the bitterness he had encountered during the day, but simply summarised the American decision and suggested that despite its obvious failings it still represented "a distinct advance in the direction of the policy advocated by the Supreme War Council."[72]

---

[69] Lansing described the interview in a letter to the President written immediately afterward: it is printed in *Foreign Relations, 1918, Russia*, vol. II, pp. 269-70.

[70] Kennan, *Decision to Intervene*, pp. 406-7.

[71] Diary entry, 9 July 1918; House MSS.

[72] Reading's telegram 3112, 9 July, cited above, footnote 68. With no little justice the Washington correspondent of *The Times*, Arthur Willert, could cable his editor,

Reading's efforts, however, did nothing to calm the Prime Minister. As soon as he received the Ambassador's report, Lloyd George sent a long telegram, marked "Private and Secret," in reply.[73] The American proposal to send an expedition limited arbitrarily to 14,000 without reference to military necessities, he said, was "really preposterous." The only analogy the Prime Minister could find was the "fatal error" of the Khartoum expedition to relieve Gordon; unless it were modified, the President's Siberian expedition might have exactly the same tragic results.[74] It was daily becoming clearer, he said, that the Bolsheviks were going over to the side of the Germans; it was "now really a race between the Germans and ourselves" for the control of Siberia. Indeed, if the Allies were to act at all, what mattered was "that we should send a force which can make sure that the Czecho-Slovaks will not have their throats cut by German and Austrian prisoners" and would "definitely secure Siberia to the Urals against German-Bolshevist attack."

The Prime Minister was also "very anxious" as to the possible effect of the American proposal on the Japanese who, "after months of hesitation and doubt" on the part of the United States, were now told that the Allies would agree to their entry into Siberia only if "an American Police Force" of equivalent numbers was sent with them. His telegram continued:

Seeing that Far East is Japan's special sphere of interest, to insist on conditions now proposed may have effect of deeply injuring their national pride and driving them into a resentful neutrality which would inevitably produce disastrous results on the whole Far Eastern situation. I am sure that the proper way to deal with Japanese is to ask them to undertake same obligations towards Russia as rest of Allies and to make expedition part and parcel of Allied plan of campaign against Germany and in future to agree to trust them completely.

Surely, Lloyd George concluded, the presence of the large numbers of Czechs would counter-balance the effects of a large Japanese force.

Geoffrey Dawson: "I am convinced that but for [Reading's] diplomacy and the success of his personal contact with the President the Russian issue, the delicacy of which cannot be exaggerated, would never have been pushed to a successful conclusion." (Telegram sent through Wiseman as CXP 683, 30 July 1918; Wiseman MSS.)

[73] Lloyd George to Reading, unnumbered telegram, 10 July 1918; Wiseman MSS.

[74] On 26 January 1885, the forces of the Mahdi Mohammed Ahmed took Khartoum, massacring General Charles Gordon and the British garrison there. A relief force sent out from Wadi Halfa the previous August reached Khartoum just too late.

And for that reason, he also insisted upon the participation of British, French, and Italian contingents. The Prime Minister closed with the hope that "this private expression of my views" might help the ambassador to prove to the President the "total inadequacy of his present proposals" and "induce him to amend them" along the lines of the Supreme Council's resolution. "Of course," he added,

if we can get this expedition and cannot get more we must accept it and press on with it as fast as we can for essential thing is that we should get movement started without delay. We have only a few months before Russian harbours freeze and if we are to save Russia from becoming a German province we must have firmly established ourselves before the winter arrives.

Balfour sent Reading a similar telegram, welcoming the American decision finally to do something, but doubting the efficacy of the President's proposal. It might be good policy from the point of view of American public opinion, he said, but he added: "from a military point of view it is indefensible and plainly cannot stand."[75]

There was another less pessimistic reaction to the news from Washington, however, more akin to the attitude Sir William Wiseman had been taking[76]—that any American commitment was better than none, and that, inevitably, a small involvement would become a large one. Lord Milner put this view to Sir Arthur Murray in their club on the evening of 8 July. London had not yet learned of the American decision, and Milner allowed himself to muse over the whole subject of intervention. "He felt," reported Murray,

that if some sort of start could be made, if only in a small way, matters could then develop as changing circumstances showed to be necessary. In other words, it was in his opinion much better to go slow to begin with rather than to suggest that no start could be made unless very large force was to be employed from the commencement.[77]

Wiseman learned of Milner's views just after he had heard from Reading of President Wilson's proposal. "I take a more cheerful view than Lord Reading," he reported to Murray,

Speaking personally, I agree with Lord Milner's ideas and feel it is along these lines that I have been working. I feel that *the President is now*

[75] Balfour to Reading, Washington, telegram 4313, 10 July 1918; Wiseman MSS.
[76] See above, pp. 207-08.
[77] Murray to Wiseman, telegram CXP 682, 9 July 1918; Wiseman MSS.

committed to intervention on a small scale and that this will eventually lead to what we want. *We must now work to end that he shall commit himself finally and irrevocably*, when I think we will find the whole matter will go through in entire accordance with our wishes.[78]

That this view differed from that taken by Lloyd George was pointed out by Milner himself. "I have this morning had a confidential talk with Lord Milner and showed him your telegram," Murray telegraphed Wiseman on 13 July:

He was very pleased with it and said it entirely coincided with his views. He said that frankly speaking he was not in entire harmony with the views of the Prime Minister. What he was principally concerned about was that a start should be made, and the rest would follow as you suggest.[79]

Milner took this approach not because of any desire to deceive the American government. Rather, as he told Murray in their talk on the 8th, he had always felt that it was extremely difficult to convey adequately through the medium of Supreme War Council resolutions and transatlantic telegrams the reasons why intervention was so urgently necessary. It was an attitude epitomised by Arthur Murray when he wrote to Wiseman, on 16 July, his personal prediction "that once American troops were landed at Vladivostok, matters would probably develop in a way which would be satisfactory to all concerned."[80] It was an eminently "British" attitude. But it was also a terribly dangerous one, for it meant that there was never a common understanding between London and Washington on the aim or scope of intervention in Russia.

The State Department had not yet cast its informal announcement to the Allied ambassadors into a formal written statement of the American plan for Siberia. Before it could do so, the British War Cabinet made two independent decisions. One, on 10 July, was to order the despatch from Hong Kong to Vladivostok of the 25th Battalion of the Middlesex Regiment, a garrison battalion of troops unfit for service on the Western Front. Lord Reading was instructed to tell the American government that the despatch of the battalion

[78] Wiseman to Murray, telegram CXP 667, 10 July 1918; Wiseman MSS (italics added).

[79] Murray to Wiseman, telegram CXP 692, 13 July 1918; Wiseman MSS. All three of these telegrams were marked "Personal and Secret."

[80] Personal letter, Murray to Wiseman, 16 July 1918; Murray, *Close Quarters*, pp. 28-29.

was in no sense the start of intervention. Rather, it was the Cabinet's reaction to the urgent plight of the Czechs: the British troops were to help maintain order in Vladivostok and thus enable additional Czechs to go to the rescue of their compatriots west of Irkutsk.[81]

The other Cabinet decision was that General Knox should go to Vladivostok "to examine the situation on the spot and to take counsel with the pro-Ally Russians."[82] When Lord Reading learned of Knox's mission, he sent Lloyd George a "personal and most secret" telegram of warning.[83] According to the Ambassador, the American government felt that Knox had always been against even the March Revolution, and that he would be likely to gather round him a circle of former Tsarist officers, thereby giving a reactionary appearance to the British part of a Siberian expedition. The Americans, indeed, were afraid that any interventionist movement would be controlled by friends of the old regime. Reading suggested that, in addition to military men, the British government should send a socialist delegation led by some prominent labour leader. Such a delegation, he thought, would have a good effect in Russia; in any case, he was "quite certain it would have a most excellent effect" in America and be in itself "an answer to much of the present doubt and criticism." The President's suspicions would have to be stilled if he were ever to be in a frame of mind to allow American action on a sufficient scale. The President, concluded Reading,

. . . is still opposed to intervention and somewhat apprehensive lest the step he is now willing to take should lead him into a much more extended policy. It is for this reason I think it is important to give a liberal turn to our assistance to Russia.

Reading's objections were put before the War Cabinet by Balfour on 16 July. Sir Henry Wilson was furious that the Americans presumed to comment upon a British military appointment, and he was supported by the Prime Minister and Lord Robert Cecil.[84] It was decided that Knox would go regardless, but that he would be

---

[81] Balfour to Reading, Washington, telegram 4311, 10 July 1918; Wiseman MSS.

[82] Lloyd George, *War Memoirs*, vol. II, p. 1906. Since Knox would have to pass through North America on his way to Vladivostok, Balfour asked Reading to arrange conversations for the General with State Department and U.S. Army officials (Balfour to Reading, Washington, telegram 4287, 9 July 1918; Wiseman MSS).

[83] Reading to Lloyd George, telegram 669 through Wiseman and Murray, 12 July 1918; Wiseman MSS.

[84] Henry Wilson's diary entry, 16 July 1918; Callwell, *Henry Wilson*, vol. II, p. 116.

instructed to avoid Washington and pass through the United States as unobtrusively as possible.[85] He started immediately. The following day, Lloyd George vented his own anger in a very long personal telegram to Reading (which he did not even show to Balfour).[86] He began with a defence of Knox—a defence important not only for what it said about the former Military Attaché who was then, as we have seen, the architect of the War Office's Russian policy, but for what it implied about Knox's influence at the very highest levels. The Prime Minister said:

> There is no man in the British Army who knows Russia as Knox does. He knows Russian perfectly; he is not a politician, his whole interest lies in soldiering. . . . It is an absolute mistake to think he was identified with the old regime. He was the only man who consistently pointed out the corruption and inefficiency of the old military system. He alone in the Czar's day among the military attachés of the Allies refused to be bamboozled with the optimistic information which was issued to them. In consequence of his pessimistic reports he was so unpopular with the old Russian General Staff that Kitchener sent out to Russia a court soldier, Hanbury Williams, who was more acceptable. . . . After considering your representations most carefully we decided to confirm decision to send him to Siberia because he is much the best man for dealing with the military aspect of the Russian problem. . . . In going out he will not be concerned with politics but solely with the conduct of efficient military operations. . . .

The Prime Minister then turned to what Reading had said about the American fear that British policy was sympathetic to Russian reactionaries. The "last thing I would stand for," he said, "would be the encouragement of any kind of repressive regime under whatever guise." He would consider that his government had failed in their war purposes "unless by the end of the war Russia is settled on liberal, progressive and democratic lines." He wanted such a solution not only from the point of view of the Russian people, but from that "of the peace of the world and of the peace and security of the Indian frontier." A reactionary Russia was "certain to be aggressive and to be in close alliance with Germany." He should have thought, he said, that the relations which Britain had maintained with the

---

[85] Balfour to Reading, Washington, telegram 4565, 23 July 1918, 6:30 p.m.; Milner MSS, unfiled folder 33.

[86] Lloyd George to Reading, telegram CXP 697 through Murray and Wiseman, 17 July 1918; Wiseman MSS. In the telegram cited in the preceding footnote Balfour said that he did not see Lloyd George's message.

Bolsheviks since the beginning of the year "ought to be sufficient proof that we have no desire to encourage reaction in that country and that it is the basis of our policy to leave [the] Russian people perfectly free to determine for themselves the form of government under which they are to live."

Lloyd George then came to the crux of his complaint against the American attitude:

As to the future the real security against President Wilson's fear lies in the President himself. . . . So far as I am concerned I am prepared to back policy of President through thick and thin, always provided it is an effective policy and not a policy of drift. You can tell President that provided he will really act in Siberia and make it primary object of his policy to establish effective Russian and Allied control over whole Siberian railway to the Urals before winter sets in, I will give him all the support of which I am capable whether it be with the Japanese or with other allies. What I am frightened of, however, is that we shall drift along until it is too late to save Russia from falling under German domination. I do not believe that the Russian people, suffering as they are from the effect both of autocracy and Bolshevism, can liberate themselves from Germanic penetration and domination unless the Allies can bring effective assistance to bear at once. . . . If we once do that we create rallying point close at hand for all liberal and democratic forces in Russia, and we shall be able to bring economic assistance and propaganda effectively to bear in Russia itself.

"I am interventionist," the Prime Minister declared, "just as much because I am a democrat as because I want to win the war. But we can do nothing without the United States. . . ."

Finally, Lloyd George considered Lord Reading's idea of sending a socialist delegation with the British military leaders. His telegram concluded:

I am much attracted by your suggestion about sending labour representative. There are two difficulties: one, that we have practically no labour leaders who have had experience in this kind of work. They are competent trade's union leaders but commission Henderson headed to Russia shows they are not likely to make a success of this job. Second, I am not quite clear what they are to do. They could not presumably make speeches to a population which understands no English, and it would be difficult to give them any position of real influence or authority. If, however, the President proposes to send powerful political delegation . . . we would certainly send liberal or labour representative to accompany it.[87]

In his anger with the Americans, the Prime Minister did not squarely face the issues raised by President Wilson's fear that intervention would aid the forces of reaction in Russia. Balfour, however, did. In a memorandum written the day before Lloyd George despatched his telegram, the Foreign Secretary also predicted that a restored Russian autocracy would inevitably find itself in league with Germany against the democracies. But he took a more realistic view of the effects of intervention on Russian internal politics, and aptly stated, as follows, the dilemma of the interventionists:

It is of course true that, however strong and genuine be our desire to keep out of Russian politics, it will probably be in practice almost impossible to prevent intervention having some (perhaps a great) effect on Russian Parties. The intervening Force must necessarily work with those who are prepared to work with it. Indirectly it will strengthen the Parties who are prepared to fight the Germans. It will directly injure the Parties which turn to Germany for assistance. We can do no more than attempt to the best of our ability to keep aloof from these internal divisions, and to give full opportunity to the Russian people to determine the future of their country.[88]

Yet Balfour did not reduce this argument to its simplest form, which was that Allied intervention would assist *any* Russian party or faction which offered its help and friendship to the intervening forces. Since the Bolsheviks were opposed to intervention, they would hardly benefit from it. On the other hand, because it was opposed by the Bolsheviks, intervention would benefit anti-Bolshevik elements, many of which were reactionary.

On 17 July, the same day on which Lloyd George sent his telegram, the United States government finally presented the Allied ambassadors with an *aide-mémoire* formally setting forth the American proposals for Russia in the form of a reply to the request of the Supreme War Council. Drafted by the President himself, without

[87] From this statement, incidentally, one may infer that the 25th Middlesex Battalion was not selected to go to Vladivostok because its commanding officer was Lt.-Col. John Ward, a trade union leader and Labour M.P. Ward says nothing in his book (*With the "Die-Hards" in Siberia*, London, 1920) about his selection; almost certainly it was simply a matter of chance.

[88] Lloyd George, *War Memoirs*, vol. II, p. 1907.

consultation, this document was essentially a restatement of the conclusions reached by him and his advisers on 6 July.[89] After stating that the whole of America's war effort was directed toward action on the Western Front and that its forces should not be dissipated in attempting important operations elsewhere, the *aide-mémoire* made its principal point: that it was "the clear and fixed judgment of the Government of the United States," reached after searching consideration of the whole Russian situation, "that military intervention . . . would add to the present sad confusion in Russia rather than cure it, injure her rather than help her," and be of no use in the war against Germany. Therefore, the United States could not "take part in such intervention or sanction it in principle."

Moreover, even if by some chance intervention *should* achieve its goal of re-opening an Eastern Front against Germany, it would "be merely a method of making use of Russia, not a method of serving her." For it would not help the Russian people in their "present distresses," and it would only saddle them with the burden of foreign armies. In short, the U.S. government felt that military action in Russia was admissible

. . . only to help the Czecho-Slovaks consolidate their forces and get into successful cooperation with their Slavic kinsmen and to steady any efforts at self-government or self-defense in which the Russians themselves may be willing to accept assistance. Whether from Vladivostok or from Murmansk and Archangel, the only legitimate object for which American or Allied troops can be employed . . . is to guard military stores which may subsequently be needed by Russian forces and to render such aid as may be acceptable to the Russians in the organization of their own self-defense.

The American government could "go no further than these modest and experimental plans." It was in no position, and had "no intention of being in a position, to take part in organized intervention in adequate force from either Vladivostok or Murmansk and Archangel." If it later saw that intervention was developing in a direction inconsistent with this policy it would feel at liberty to withdraw its forces and use them instead on the Western Front.

These general directives, said the memorandum, applied only to American forces, and they were not "meant to wear the least color of

[89] The text of the *aide-mémoire* is printed in *Foreign Relations, 1918, Russia*, vol. ii, pp. 287-90, and in Kennan, *Decision to Intervene*, pp. 482-85.

criticism of what the other governments associated against Germany may think it wise to undertake." The United States government wished "in no way to embarrass their choices of policy" and did "not wish it to be understood that in so restricting its own activities it [was] seeking, even by implication, to set limits to the action or to define the policies of its associates."

The memorandum touched only briefly on the matter which had made the British Prime Minister so angry—the allocation of forces for Siberia. The American government, said the document, hoped "to carry out the plans for safeguarding the rear of the Czecho-Slovaks operating from Vladivostok in a way that [would] place it and keep it in close cooperation with a small military force like its own from Japan, and if necessary from the other Allies. . . ."

Finally, the United States government hoped

. . . to take advantage of the earliest opportunity to send to Siberia a commission of merchants, agricultural experts, labor advisers, Red Cross representatives, and agents of the Young Men's Christian Association accustomed to organizing the best methods of spreading useful information and rendering educational help of a modest sort, in order in some systematic manner to relieve the immediate economic necessities of the people. . . . The execution of this plan [would] follow and not be permitted to embarrass the military assistance rendered in the rear of the westward-moving forces of the Czecho-Slovaks.

Here, then, were the meagre fruits of two months of the most intense diplomatic effort on the part of the British government. The *aide-mémoire* of 17 July was a wholly unsatisfactory statement of policy, not only from the British point of view but also from the American. Although it set the United States government squarely against intervention, it was studded with ambiguities.[90] What, for instance, were the Czechs to do once their position in Siberia was secure? What would the American attitude be when it was found that the Czechs were fighting not only prisoners of war but Russian Bolshevik forces as well? Did the memorandum really give the Allies a free hand, without "the least color of criticism" from the Americans even if the Japanese were to use much larger forces than the Americans contemplated?

[90] See Kennan, *Decision to Intervene*, pp. 399-404, for a detailed analysis of the *aide-mémoire*.

The reaction of the British government to this American *démarche* followed what we might call the Milner-Wiseman line that has been set forth above. This attitude was strongly endorsed by the British Military Representative in Washington, who telegraphed on 20 July that it seemed probable that the President's hand would be forced by events and that meanwhile, Britain "should accept the situation and make no further representations" until the troops were "on the spot."[91] On the same day Balfour instructed Greene in Tokyo to use all of his influence in urging the Japanese government, which had thus far made no reply to the American proposals, to accept them. If necessary the British Ambassador was even to appeal to the spirit of the Anglo-Japanese Alliance. And the Foreign Secretary added:

At the same time have clearly present in your mind the fact that in our opinion the proposed numbers will prove wholly insufficient; and that events will almost certainly compel the Allies either to increase their Armies or to withdraw them. On this point however the Japanese General Staff are as capable of judging as we are; and in the meantime main thing is to get proposed expedition prepared and conveyed straight to destination with all possible speed.[92]

The actual British note of reply to the Americans was drafted over the weekend of 20 and 21 July by Philip Kerr, the Prime Minister's private secretary, with constant reference to Lloyd George and Balfour.[93] On Monday, 22 July, it was approved (evidently to give it additional stature) by the Imperial War Cabinet, which happened to be in one of its infrequent sessions, and despatched to Washington. Along with it Balfour telegraphed a private message to Lord Reading. "For obvious reasons," the message began, "it is not very easy to devise a satisfactory answer to [the] President." On the one hand the government gladly welcomed the fact that Wilson had decided to commit American troops, "a policy which we know he regards with much misgiving." But on the other hand

. . . we cannot pretend for ourselves, nor ought we to convey to him, that we regard size of American Japanese force as in any way adequate to necessities of case. To us it seems almost certain that either Allied expedi-

[91] British Military Representative, Washington, to C.I.G.S., telegram BS 32, 20 July 1918, 11:20 a.m.; Milner MSS, unfiled folder 32.
[92] Balfour to Greene, Tokyo, telegram 692, 20 July 1918; Wiseman MSS (as no. 4521 to Reading in Washington).
[93] Diary entry, 21 July 1918; Riddell, *War Diary*, pp. 339-40.

tion will fail or it will have to be largely reinforced; we hope the latter. But these are hopes which you can hardly convey to President.[94]

The memorandum that *was* conveyed to the President scarcely touched upon the sensitive point of the size of the intervening force.[95] It simply stated that the British government welcomed the American decision to come to the aid of the Czechs, although they had "serious misgivings" that the proposed force might prove "inadequate for its purpose." The bulk of the paper was concerned with refuting the American arguments that intervention in Russia could give the Allies no help in their war against Germany, and that the Allies wished to make use of Russia merely for their own purposes. The first argument was countered with a recitation of the familiar assertions about intervention being the only way the armies of Japan could be brought against the Germans; the second was met with the contention that if the Allies did nothing, Germany would make use of Russia in the most brutal ways and that, far from themselves wanting to make use of Russia, the Allies wished only to save her. The British reply was not a very enlightening document, but because part of its purpose was to slide over serious points of disagreement, how could it have been different?

All that remained was for the Japanese to reply. Like each of the other Western proposals to Japan regarding intervention, the American *démarche* produced a great debate within the Japanese government and accentuated the fierce disagreement between the Army, who saw intervention as a pretense for large-scale expansion onto the Asian mainland, and the liberals, who felt that Japan could act successfully only if assured of the support of the United States. The Army felt that no less than seven divisions (150,000 men) would be needed even if operations were confined east of Irkutsk. In a series of heated meetings of the Advisory Council on Foreign Relations a compromise formula was worked out with wording satisfactory to the liberals, but with an easy loophole for the Army.[96]

The Japanese Ambassador in Washington placed this formula

[94] Balfour to Reading, Washington, unnumbered telegram, 22 July 1918; Wiseman MSS.

[95] The text of the memorandum, conveyed orally to the President by Lord Reading on 23 July and formally handed to the State Department on the 30th, is printed in *Foreign Relations, 1918, Russia*, vol. II, pp. 315-17.

[96] The debate within the Japanese government is carefully described in Morley, *Japanese Thrust*, pp. 264-90.

before Polk, the Acting Secretary of State, on 24 July. Ishii assured Polk that Japan did not intend to send a large number of troops, but that for domestic political reasons they could not accept foreign limitations to any fixed number. He intimated that a full division at peace-time strength—about 12,000 men—would be sent, with the understanding that the final number would depend on the opposition they met from the Bolsheviks and the prisoners of war.[97] Ishii also showed Polk a draft declaration to the Russian people stating that the Japanese government was anxious not only to meet the desires of the American government but also "to act in *harmony with the Allies . . .* having regard at the same time to the *special position of Japan.*" The declaration added that although the original Japanese contingents would go to Vladivostok, a further detachment would be sent, if the situation demanded, to operate and maintain order along the Siberian railway.[98] As if to emphasise this point, Foreign Minister Goto, in Tokyo, told the American Ambassador that it was a military necessity to send troops along both the Trans-Siberian and Chinese-Eastern Railways as far as their junction at Karymskaya.[99]

The British government greeted Tokyo's proposed declaration with warm approval,[100] but the implications of Japanese unilateral action which it contained so alarmed President Wilson that he almost withdrew the United States from the whole affair.[101] Acting Secretary of State Polk told Ishii that Japan could have supreme command of the expedition and could send the projected 12,000 men, but he pleaded that an upper limit be set.[102] For their part, the Japanese agreed to strike from their declaration the sections which disturbed the Americans, and they repeatedly gave assurances that no more troops would be sent than necessary "to prevent the slaughter of the Czechs," but they resolutely refused to specify an upper limit.[103]

[97] Polk described his interview with Ishii in a letter to President Wilson, 24 July 1918; *Foreign Relations, 1918, Russia*, vol. II, pp. 301-2.
[98] The draft declaration is printed in *ibid.*, p. 302, n. 1 (italics added).
[99] Morris to Secretary of State, Tokyo, 23 July 1918, 10 p.m.; *ibid.*, p. 300.
[100] As expressed in a telegram from Balfour to Greene, Tokyo, no. 724, 30 July 1918, 3 p.m.; Milner MSS, unfiled folder 32.
[101] Unterberger, *Siberian Expedition*, p. 82, citing the diary of the State Department's assistant counselor, Gordon Auchincloss.
[102] Polk to Morris, Tokyo, 27 July 1918, 4 p.m.; *Foreign Relations, 1918, Russia*, vol. II, pp. 306-7.
[103] Morris to Secretary of State, Tokyo, 1 August 1918, 1 a.m.; *ibid.*, pp. 321-23.

By this time Tokyo had clearly assumed the initiative.[104] On 2 August, without consulting the United States or their European Allies, the Japanese published their declaration of policy. True to their word, it did not contain any references to Japan's "special position" or to action beyond Vladivostok. But neither did it refer to the number of troops to be sent; and it did not mention the goal towards which the whole British diplomatic effort had been directed—the re-establishment of an Eastern Front.[105]

Thus, the long and wearisome Anglo-Japanese-American negotiations over intervention in Siberia were concluded. On 3 August, the day after the Japanese published their declaration, Sir Conyngham Greene, in Tokyo, noted with considerable relief that the issue appeared "at last to have emerged from the diplomatic sphere, and to have passed into the hands of the military."[106] Regrettably, the Ambassador's comment was all too true. Although the negotiations were concluded, they had scarcely resulted in agreement. The very real differences among the powers were still unresolved. Now they were to be passed on to military men whose training and experience had not prepared them for statesmanship. Within a month there were to be over 70,000 Japanese soldiers in Manchuria and Siberia. Virtually none of them were ever to venture west of Irkutsk.

[104] The fact that Japan had the initiative was reflected even in the behaviour of Ambassador Chinda in London. After an interview with Chinda on 31 July, Lord Robert Cecil observed that the Ambassador "altogether took a much stiffer and more independent line, much more definitely resolved on intervention than any which he had hitherto assumed." (Reported by Balfour to Greene in Tokyo, telegram 730, 31 July 1918, 10:30 p.m.; Milner MSS, unfiled folder 32.)

[105] The declaration is printed in *Foreign Relations, 1918, Russia*, vol. II, pp. 324-25.

[106] Greene to Balfour, telegram 846, Tokyo, 3 August 1918, 11 p.m.; Milner MSS, unfiled folder 32.

CHAPTER VIII

THE BEGINNING OF INTERVENTION: THE NORTH

We had committed the unbelievable folly of landing at Archangel with fewer than twelve hundred men.—Lockhart, in "Memoirs of a British Agent"

DURING late June and July, while the American government was reluctantly giving its consent to a limited Allied involvement in Siberia, the position of Lockhart and, indeed, of the entire Allied community in Moscow, grew considerably more precarious. Much of the mounting tension was due not to any action of the Allies, but to two internal crises which befell the Bolshevik leadership on the same day, 6 July. The first of these was the assassination of Count Mirbach, the German Ambassador, in the drawing room of his Embassy, by two Left S-R's who hoped to precipitate renewed hostilities with Germany. The Soviet regime immediately blamed the murder on "agents of Russian and Anglo-French imperialism"; this charge was indignantly denied by the Left S-R's themselves, who announced that their party was fully responsible.[1] Mirbach's assassination was the signal for a general rising of Left S-R's in Moscow, a wild and ill-conceived action easily suppressed by the Bolsheviks.

But on the same day (and apparently completely unconnected with the Moscow events), in the provincial town of Yaroslavl, situated on the Volga between Moscow and Vologda, Boris Savinkov and his Union for the Defence of Fatherland and Freedom began a much more serious insurrection. Battle raged for over a fortnight, and the rebels were defeated only after a heavy bombardment by artillery brought up by Soviet reinforcements from Moscow. In reprisals for the rising the Bolsheviks executed scores of Savinkov's partisans.[2]

[1] Bunyan, *Intervention*, pp. 212-21.
[2] *ibid.*, pp. 179-81, 192-96.

The Allies were blamed for the Yaroslavl uprising, too, but this time with some justification. In fact the Bolsheviks might have blamed the French alone, rather than the British. Balfour had, after all, instructed Lockhart to have nothing whatever to do with Savinkov's plans, and to cease inquiring into them.[3] The French, however, are said to have supported Savinkov with large sums of money transmitted through their consulate-general and military mission in Moscow.[4] Lockhart described these arrangements in the report on his mission which he wrote for the War Cabinet after his return to London in November 1918. In early June, Lockhart said, Noulens sent word to various White leaders that Allied intervention on a large scale would take place before the end of the month, and he held out bountiful promises of both men and money. "There is no doubt," Lockhart wrote, "that the ill-fated adventure of the 'White Guards' at Yaroslavl was due directly to this misleading information."[5] On the very day of the Yaroslavl rising, before news of it had reached Moscow, Lockhart telegraphed that the French had given the National Centre (to which were affiliated both Savinkov's Union and Alekseyev's organisation on the Don) two-and-a-half million rubles, and had told them that intervention was already decided upon. Lockhart warned London that the Whites had committed themselves on the basis of this information; if intervention did not take place, and if they were left to their fate, he said, the Allied position in Russia would be irretrievably damaged.[6]

In mid-July, when National Centre representatives made a desperate request for a million rubles, Lockhart himself gave them this sum, although he lacked authorisation to do so from London. Reporting his action to Balfour, he apologised for acting thus without sanction. Had he not come to their aid, he explained, his ultimate responsibility would have been far greater.[7]

[3] See above, p. 190.

[4] So Savinkov claimed in his trial before a Soviet tribunal ten years later. Fischer, *Soviets in World Affairs*, vol. I, pp. 118-20, quotes extensively from Savinkov's testimony. Noulens, however, denied that he ever gave Savinkov financial aid (Noulens, *Mon ambassade*, vol. II, pp. 109-10).

[5] "Memorandum on the Internal Situation in Russia," 1 November 1918; Milner MSS, box C-2.

[6] Lockhart to Balfour, telegram 323, Moscow, 6 July 1918; Milner MSS, unfiled folder 32.

[7] Lockhart to Balfour, telegram 336, Moscow, 16 July 1918; Milner MSS, box C-1. I have been unable to find Balfour's reply. Since Lockhart made subsequent financial contributions to the Whites, one may assume that the Foreign Secretary gave his approval.

Lockhart was especially impressed by reports from South Russia of Alekseyev's Volunteer Army, the successor to the force formed the previous winter on the Don by Alekseyev and the Cossack Ataman, Kaledin, to which the British government had given £10 million.[8] These funds, however, had done little good. In February, with Red troops advancing on their headquarters at Rostov, Kaledin had shot himself and Alekseyev had led the 3,500-man Volunteer Army on a terribly punishing winter march into the Kuban country to gather recruits and supplies, and then back to the Don. In 50 days this force fought 40 engagements against the Bolsheviks.[9] By late July Alekseyev's A.D.C., meeting Lockhart secretly in Moscow, could report that the Volunteers numbered 20,000 (including, however, some 6,000 to 7,000 Cossacks who would not fight outside their own territories) and had captured considerable quantities of Bolshevik artillery. From the Allies Alekseyev asked for financial and actual military support and also an assurance that they had no intention of restoring Kerensky to power nor, indeed, of interfering in any way in Russian domestic politics. Although they could give no formal assurances, Lockhart and his French colleagues despatched to Alekseyev a courier carrying ten million rubles and the promise of much more money in the future.[10]

In supporting these White forces, Lockhart was, of course, guilty of counter-revolutionary actions against the Soviet regime. As he was to discover six weeks later, his diplomatic immunity offered him little protection. Meanwhile his position was made no easier by his own countrymen. On 22 July there arrived in Moscow a British economic mission headed by Sir William Clark, Comptroller General of the Department of Overseas Trade, and including Leslie Urquhart, chairman of the Russo-Asiatic Corporation (which before the Revolution controlled vast mining interests in the Urals and the Altai region), and two other Britons who had managed firms in Russia. The circumstances surrounding this economic mission are still not entirely clear. Although it reached Murmansk on the same ship which brought Lindley back to Russia in early June, it seems to

---

[8] See above, Chapter II.

[9] For an account of the Volunteer Army during this period, see Stewart, *White Armies*, pp. 25-79.

[10] Lockhart to Balfour, telegrams 341 and 342, Moscow, 21 and 23 July 1918; Milner MSS, box C-1.

have had nothing to do with the Foreign Office.[11] Almost certainly it had its origins in the brief period in April and May when agreement with the Bolsheviks seemed possible. Naturally, its presence in Russia mystified and somewhat alarmed the other Allied governments, which tended to look askance at efforts to come to terms with the Soviet regime. The American Ambassador, Francis, commented that it was especially unfortunate that just when he had been trying to impress upon the Russians that Germany aimed at the economic exploitation of Russia, a mission should come with the avowed purpose of advising British capital on how best to invest in the country.[12] In response to an anxious query from Lord Reading in Washington, Balfour cabled the following explanation:

The economic mission to which you refer is only a small commission of commercial experts sent out with Mr. Lindley to Russia by H.M. Govt. to advise them as to the best means of restoring and developing British trade relations and interests in Russia and of countering enemy schemes of commercial penetration. . . .[13]

Lockhart had complained to London when the mission first reached Murmansk.[14] Now, when it had come to Moscow, armed with a written guarantee from Karl Radek that its members would be able to leave when they wished,[15] Lockhart found that Clark knew nothing of the Allies' plans regarding Russia, while Urquhart was a convinced interventionist. It was Lockhart's unpleasant duty, at a time when his personal relations with the Bolsheviks were severely strained, to take his visitors on a tour of Soviet offices for discussions

[11] Lindley had come back to Russia with the intention of going to Moscow. When he reached Vologda on 7 July, however, he found that the attitude of the Bolsheviks had changed so much since the time he had left England that it would have been compromising for himself or any of his subordinates to go to the Soviet capital. Much the same attitude had been taken, it will be recalled, during the early days of the Bolshevik regime regarding contact by official British diplomatic agents. Lindley felt, however, that the same considerations did not apply to the members of the economic mission, and therefore he allowed them to go on to Moscow (Lindley to Balfour, telegram 43, Murmansk, 30 July 1918, 11:43 a.m.; Milner MSS, box C-1).

[12] Francis to Secretary of State, despatch 1118, Vologda, 11 July 1918; U.S. National Archives, State Department file 861.00/2575.

[13] Balfour to Reading, Washington, telegram 4316, 11 July 1918; Wiseman MSS.

[14] See above, p. 190.

[15] The guarantee is printed as a "Letter from the representative of the People's Commissariat of Foreign Affairs in Vologda to the English representative Lindley," 14 July 1918, in *Dokumenty vneshnei politiki*, vol. 1, p. 396. The treatment accorded Radek in this volume is the same as that given to Trotsky; his name is omitted in every case except where doing so would actually falsify the text of the document.

of trade and commerce. By then the Czechs had taken Simbirsk and were besieging Kazan, Savinkov's forces were holding Yaroslavl, and Lockhart expected Allied landings at Archangel at any moment. Was it any wonder, he asked in his memoirs, that the Bolsheviks later accused him of "Machiavellian duplicity"?[16]

The economic mission stayed only two days in Moscow and accomplished nothing. Scarcely had it left, however, when Lockhart learned that the Allied embassies had suddenly fled Vologda bound for Archangel. Their departure, in the early hours of 25 July, had come after a fortnight of Bolshevik threats and cajolements designed to get them to give up their provincial haven and come to Moscow, where the Soviet government might better protect them. Suspecting that the Bolsheviks wanted them in Moscow so that they could be held as hostages in the event of Allied intervention, the diplomats refused. On 17 July a British officer arrived in Vologda with a message from General Poole in Murmansk saying that his force would land at Archangel at the end of July or the beginning of August and asking the diplomats to be ready to leave Vologda at a moment's notice. This message, combined with a statement from Chicherin on the 22nd that the Soviet government could not be responsible for their safety, once fighting started, unless they were in Moscow, caused the diplomats to decide to leave Bolshevik territory as soon as possible.[17]

The special diplomatic trains reached Archangel early on 26 July. Nearly two more days were spent in negotiating with the Soviet authorities for vessels in which the 132 Allied diplomats, together with some 70 British and French residents, could leave. At last two ships were provided. Just as they were about to weigh anchor, in the early hours of 28 July, another train pulled up to the station and the members of the British economic mission sprinted down the dock and clambered on board, infinitely relieved at their narrow escape from Bolshevik territory.[18]

[16] Lockhart, *British Agent*, p. 306.

[17] The correspondence between the Allied diplomats at Vologda and Chicherin (and also with Radek, who was sent to Vologda to take charge of arrangements there) is printed in *Dokumenty vneshnei politiki*, vol. I, pp. 385, 388-89, 392-97, 402-9. Translations of many of the items, and an account of the events at Vologda, may be found in David R. Francis, *American Embassy*, pp. 245-46. See also Kennan, *Decision to Intervene*, for an account based on the recollections of American Foreign Service officers who were at Vologda (pp. 443-47 and 450).

[18] Lindley described the departure from Archangel in his telegram 43 to Balfour, Murmansk, 30 July 1918, 11:13 a.m.; Milner MSS, box C-1. See also Kennan, *Decision to Intervene*, pp. 451-52.

In Moscow, far behind them, Lockhart and his Allied colleagues had been left as virtual hostages.

❖

The tiny steamers with their diplomatic passengers made their way to the British-held port of Kandalaksha located on the Murmansk-Petrograd railroad at the western end of the White Sea. As soon as they reached shore, Lindley and Francis telephoned General Poole at Murmansk and told him that they had been contacted in Archangel by anti-Bolshevik elements who were planning a *coup d'état* to coincide with the expected Allied landings. Owing to police pressure which threatened to disrupt their organisation, the coup could be postponed no longer, and the plotters anxiously requested Allied action. Lindley and Francis therefore urged that Poole occupy Archangel immediately.[19]

Poole had wanted to await the arrival of promised reinforcements before he attempted a landing at Archangel, but since an anti-Bolshevik coup was a most important element in his plans, he decided to act at once. In his landing party there were roughly 1,200 men—a French battalion, a detachment of Royal Marines, and about 50 American sailors from the cruiser *Olympia*. Admiral Kemp's naval forces were also small: he could spare only the French battleship *Amiral Aube* and the British cruiser *Attentive* and seaplane tender *Nairana* for the operations. These were sufficient to enable him to eliminate the rather formidable Bolshevik defences on Mudyug Island which flanked the entrance to the only navigable channel through the delta of the Dvina River. But the town of Archangel itself lies twenty-five miles up this channel, which is no wider than the Thames at London Bridge. The Allied flotilla would have to steam this distance entirely at the mercy of the defenders hidden in the dense forest which lined both banks. A landing at Archangel itself in the face of organised opposition was therefore scarcely feasible. For this reason Poole and Kemp depended upon a *coup d'état*.[20]

Poole had been organising a coup throughout the preceding month. On 3 July he informed the War Office that the success of not only the landing but of his progress inland depended entirely on the extensive use of secret agents.[21] Two parties of Allied agents,

---

[19] Noulens, *Mon ambassade*, vol. II, pp. 167-68; Newbolt, *Naval Operations*, vol. v, p. 323.

[20] *ibid.*, p. 324.

[21] Poole to War Office, telegram E.109, Murmansk, 3 July 1918, 8:20 p.m.; Milner MSS, box D.4.

landing from the sea near Archangel, were arrested by the Bolsheviks and shipped off to prison in the interior.[22] But a successful rising was organised by Captain Georgi Ermolaevich Chaplin, a young and daring former naval officer who had at one time been attached to the Royal Navy and who was a great admirer of Britain. Chaplin had been told that Poole's forces would reach Archangel on 2 August; therefore he timed his coup for the night of the 1st.[23]

The entire operation was carried out with great efficiency. The fortress on Mudyug Island was forced to surrender on the evening of the 1st after one of the first air-supported troop landings in military history. Two wounded Frenchmen were the only Allied casualties. The next day, after Chaplin's coup, the Allied squadron steamed up the channel to the town unopposed, and Poole's landing was greeted by a large and enthusiastic crowd.[24] Only the American Consul bothered to report that the crowd was composed entirely of the two elements which had suffered most under the Bolsheviks: the bourgeoisie and the wealthier peasantry. "The working class," he reported, "was patently absent. . . . During the march of the Allied officers through the streets to the government building the absence of the city working class was even more conspicuous."[25]

The occupation of Archangel marked the real beginning of Allied intervention in Russia. Completely unheeded went the warning made two months before by the British Consul at Archangel, Douglas Young, that military operations without the consent of the *de facto* rulers of Russia, even if locally successful, could not lead to permanent advantage and would inevitably commit the British government to ever-increasing obligations from which they would be unable to free themselves without discredit and great loss of prestige.[26] Young was to be proved right in every respect.

[22] Reported by the American Consul at Archangel, Cole, to the Secretary of State, despatch 29, 22 July 1918; *Foreign Relations, 1918, Russia*, vol. II, pp. 500-2.

[23] G. E. Chaplin, "Dva perevorota na severe" (Two Coups d'Etat in the North), *Beloye Delo* (White Affairs), vol. IV, Berlin, 1928, p. 19.

[24] Telegram, Poole to War Office, 2 August 1918, quoted in U.S. Office of Naval Intelligence memorandum of 3 August; U.S. National Archives, Naval Records Branch, file WA-6, box 608. Newbolt, *Naval Operations*, vol. v, pp. 324-25. Gen. Sir H. E. Blumberg, *Britain's Sea Soldiers; A Record of the Royal Marines during the War, 1914-1919*, Devonport, 1927, pp. 82-84. See also the report by British Consul Douglas Young, telegram 114 to Balfour, Archangel, 3 August 1918, 7:20 p.m.; Milner MSS, box D-4.

[25] Cole to Secretary of State, despatch 41, Archangel, 10 September 1918; *Foreign Relations, 1918, Russia*, vol. II, p. 527.

[26] Young to Balfour, telegram 75, Archangel, 6 June 1918 (sent 12:5 a.m. 7 June); Milner MSS, box D-4. It seems probable that Young was influenced by the arguments

In the ease with which Bolshevism had been driven from Archangel, such forebodings were naturally forgotten. So successful was
Chaplin's coup that by the time the Allied vessels had reached the
town there was already in being a new government, the Supreme
Administration of the Northern Region, which could formally invite
the troops to land. Chaplin had recognised the immense popularity
of N. V. Chaikovsky, a vigorous old Populist and former member
of the Constituent Assembly who was one of the great figures of
non-Marxist Russian socialism, and had invited him to form a government.[27] Chaikovsky had assured Chaplin that he would create
a "business government," representative of all shades of political
opinion, but he chose six S-R's, all of them members of the dissolved
Constituent Assembly. The fact that the government was composed
solely of socialists infuriated Chaplin, whom Chaikovsky named
Commander-in-Chief of Russian forces, and was immediately to
to bring the government into conflict with the Allies.[28]

From the beginning, General Poole virtually assumed the rôle of a
viceroy, and it was painfully obvious that the new "Supreme Administration" was subordinate to his personal rule. He appointed a French
army officer, Colonel Donop, as Military Governor of the town.
Consistently, on Poole's or Donop's orders, British or French troops
interfered directly in matters which should have been left to the duly-
established Russian government of the town. When a given measure
had been carried out, Poole would simply notify Chaikovsky by
letter. The district was placed under martial law, and Poole decreed
that sedition and any attempts to spread "false rumour calculated to
provoke unrest or disturbance among the troops and population"
would be punishable by death.[29]

---

of a very long and tightly-reasoned despatch written by his American colleague, Felix
Cole, to the Secretary of State on 1 June (printed in *Foreign Relations, 1918, Russia*,
vol. II, pp. 477-84). Cole and Young worked closely together, and the British Consul
must certainly have heard Cole's argument.

[27] Chaikovsky, it is worth noting, could speak English fluently. He had spent
26 years in exile in England and six more in America.

[28] This account of the origins of the Archangel government is drawn from Leonid
I. Strakhovsky, *Intervention at Archangel: The Story of Allied Intervention and
Russian Counter-Revolution in North Russia 1918-1920*, Princeton, 1944, pp.22-23.

[29] The texts of some of Poole's initial decrees are printed in the article "Anglichanie
na severe" (The English in the North), *Krasnyi arkhiv*, vol. 19, 1926, no. 6, pp. 40-42.
They are translated in C. E. Vulliamy, ed., *The Red Archives: Russian State Papers
and Other Documents Relating to the Years 1915-1918*, London, 1929, pp. 302-3. See

In justice to Poole it should be stated that his position was not an easy one. As commander of a very small military force far from its home base and threatened with attack by larger Bolshevik detachments, he naturally felt that he should act to ensure the safety of his men. Moreover, almost immediately after the landing at Archangel he despatched one party of troops down the railroad toward Vologda and another up the Dvina River toward Kotlas. Both of these forces soon became engaged in heavy fighting. The few hundred men Poole had left in the town might not have been sufficient to deal with a major civil disturbance, despite the threatening guns of the Allied warships in the harbour. Undoubtedly he felt that strong measures were necessary to forestall trouble.

Poole's position was further complicated by the arrival from Murmansk on 9 August of the Allied diplomats, who also had ideas as to how Archangel should be administered. From the outset they became a sort of court of appeal to which Chaikovsky could bring his complaints against Poole's high-handed methods. This naturally angered and exasperated Poole, who, as a soldier whose entire experience had been in field operations, was used to direct and simple command relationships. Even his successor, General Ironside—a much more clever man—could complain of the "detached attitude" which the Archangel diplomats took towards military operations. "In many ways," he later wrote, "they regarded themselves almost as neutrals, though their position was so close to our front line."[30]

In reality this was a far from accurate characterisation, for the Allied diplomats themselves were divided by serious differences of opinion. Noulens, because of his marked distaste for socialism, was Poole's uncritical partisan in virtually all matters, and he regarded his position as rather more that of a governing commissioner than that of an ambassador. He and his Allied colleagues, he later wrote, "considered it necessary to exercise supervision and control over the acts of politicians placed for the first time at the head of affairs, in conditions which affected the responsibilities of the Allies."[31] In his

---

also Strakhovsky, *Intervention at Archangel*, pp. 32-36. Poole's interference extended even down to deciding which flags the Russian community would fly. He ordered the suppression of all attempts to fly the red flag, despite the fact that Chaikovsky's government had resolved to fly the red flag of socialism—not the Bolshevik flag, which was marked with the large letters RSFSR—along with the national flag.

[30] Field-Marshal Lord Ironside, *Archangel, 1918-1919*, London, 1953, p. 27.

[31] Noulens, *Mon ambassade*, vol. ii, p. 180.

memoirs, Noulens presents the following idyllic picture of life in the
little northern community:

General Poole and his officers devoted themselves exclusively to their
military task. The Government of the North laboured in complete independence for the regeneration of Russia. At the same time, the rôle we
played was not only that of diplomats accredited to a government . . . we
were anxious to help the new ministers to avoid the pitfalls into which
their inexperience might plunge them. We were for them efficient and
benevolent guides, wholly disinterested in exploiting the situation for the
profit of the countries we represented.[32]

Francis, although prevented by failing health from playing as full
a rôle in the affairs of the region as some of his colleagues, could not
take such a happy view, and was considerably disturbed by the
methods adopted by Poole. In his memoirs he commented:

The Tchaikovsky administration, I think, was well disposed and intended
to administer a very good government. As to the position of General Poole,
I am satisfied he did not want to establish a government of his own, but
British soldiers have been colonizers for so long that they do not know how
to respect the feelings of socialists.[33]

But the strongest opposition to Poole was to come from his own
countryman, Lindley, and it was Lindley who most clearly recognised the real issues at stake. At a later date he set them before his
Allied colleagues in the following terms:

Unless our adventure here is to begin and end with the occupation of a
small district, it is absolutely necessary that a Russian Authority should
exist which the population can regard as their own Government, and
capable of being expanded or absorbed into the government of the whole
country. In order to assure this the existing Government must appear to
have real authority. . . .[34]

Lindley was no uncritical supporter of the local government. Indeed
he was as insistent in criticising it as he was insistent that it receive—
and exercise—genuine responsibility. But he was always aware that the
new Russia which the Allies were seeking to establish could never

[32] *ibid.*, p. 181.
[33] Francis, *American Embassy*, p. 272.
[34] Memorandum by Lindley to Poole and the Allied Ambassadors, Archangel,
8 October 1918; U.S. National Archives, Petrograd Embassy 800 file.

have its roots in a military occupation enforced against the wishes of the Russian people.[35]

By a curious turn of events, the arrival of Allied forces at Archangel coincided with the virtual elimination of the danger they were sent to prevent. On 9 August the British Consul at Helsingfors telegraphed the Foreign Office that German forces were rapidly leaving Finland.[36] The Allies had at last assumed the offensive on the Western Front, and all available German troops were being sent to hold the line in France. The likelihood of a German offensive eastward from Finland through Petrograd had disappeared.

Neither was there any likelihood that the Czech detachments, embroiled as they were on the Volga and in Siberia, would reach Archangel. Yet one of the principal reasons Poole and his men had been sent to Archangel was to receive the Czechs and to train them either for service in the West or on a new Eastern Front. Thus the situation had completely changed. The War Office recognised this change by sending Poole a new set of orders on 10 August.[37] He was to "co-operate in restoring Russia with the object of resisting German influence and penetration" and to help the Russians to "take the field side by side with their Allies" for the recovery of their country. This was hopelessly vague language. The War Office could not bring itself to state that the future of the North Russian expedition would be in fighting Bolsheviks, not Germans.

Poole's immediate aim, according to these new instructions, was to establish communications with the Czechs in central Russia, and with their assistance to secure control of the Archangel-Vologda-Ekaterinburg Railway and the river and rail lines of communication between Archangel and Vyatka. At the same time he was to support any local administration friendly to the Allies and to organise Russian armed forces to resist Germany. The War Office admitted that it

[35] In the following pages many examples of Lindley's attitude will be seen. But at this point it is well to quote Noulens' description of the British Chargé d'Affaires: "The characteristic of his face was a benevolent smile which I never saw depart no matter how disturbed the circumstances. He was served by an imperturbable calm and a perspicacity the more effective because it was so little evident." (Noulens, *Mon ambassade*, vol. I, p. 40.)

[36] A paraphrase of this telegram was given the State Department on 13 August 1918; U.S. National Archives, State Department file 861.00/2473.

[37] War Office to Poole, Archangel, telegram 64052, 10 August 1918; Milner MSS, box D-4. Poole's orders are partially summarised in Newbolt, *Naval Operations*, vol. v, pp. 326-27.

seemed more probable that the Czechs in western Siberia would turn east for safety rather than move west to Poole. If that proved to be the case, he was to concentrate his efforts on organising local armed forces and defending Archangel. Finally, the Supreme War Council would send him no additional troops besides the 5,500 Americans already promised to him.

If Poole's orders skated over the fact that the Allied forces were fighting Bolsheviks, a mimeographed sheet of "Information of general interest to troops arriving in Russia,"[38] distributed by the British command to the landing forces, did not. Under a section headed "The Enemy" there were two categories, Bolsheviks and Germans. The former were described as:

... soldiers and sailors who, in the majority of cases are criminals. Their natural, vicious brutality enabled them to assume leadership. The Bolshevik is now fighting desperately because the restoration of order means an end to his regime, and secondly, because he sees a rope around his neck for his past misdeeds if he is caught.

As for the Germans:

The Bolsheviks have no capacity for organisation but this is supplied by Germany and her lesser Allies. The Germans usually appear in Russian uniform and are impossible to distinguish. . . .

In case this last difficulty might confuse a simple soldier and lead him to write home that he was fighting Russians, the information sheet provided a special warning:

Writers must be guarded in their letters when speaking of the enemy as there is much wilful mis-understanding on this point by peacemongers. We are not fighting Russia nor honest Russians. We are fighting Bolsheviks who are the worst form of criminals. . . .

For the soldier who might think that he was interfering in the internal politics of Russia, the following assurance was offered:

The Bolshevik Government is entirely in the hands of the Germans who have backed this party against all others in Russia owing to the simplicity of maintaining Anarchy in a totally disorganised country. Therefore, we are definitely opposed to the Bolshevik-cum-German party. In regard to other parties we express no criticism and will accept them as we find them

[38] U.S. National Archives, Naval Records Branch, file WA-6, box 609.

provided they are for "Russia" and therefore for "out with the Boche." Briefly, we do not meddle in internal affairs.

It must be realised that we are not invaders but guests and that we have not any intention of attempting to occupy any Russian territory.

And for the guest who wanted to get on with his hosts, the sheet advised, under the heading "Russian Character":

Generally speaking the Russian is exactly like a child—inquisitive, easily gulled, easily offended. He is very clever in a theoretical way but is rarely practical. Consequently two golden rules for dealing with Russians are:—

1. Treat him very kindly, absolutely justly, but absolutely firmly.

2. Never believe him when he says "It is done" or "It shall be done." Go and see for yourself.

These last instructions were doubtless included to help the Allied soldiers in dealing with the many Russians who were confidently expected to flock to the anti-Bolshevik standard. As at Murmansk, where Maynard had started raising a local force as soon as he arrived, Poole also immediately started recruiting. Maynard, however, had met with very little success. In over a month's time, he had been able to enlist only 1,200 men, of whom 300 were fit only for labour details. This experience had forced him to the conclusion (which Lockhart had often voiced) that Russians would join a foreign force only if it were strong and obviously sure of success.[39] To prospective recruits, the tiny forces at Murmansk and Archangel must have seemed anything but powerful.

Poole met with a similar lack of response at Archangel. His first reaction was to cable the War Office asking them to send out a brass band, which he considered "invaluable for recruiting purposes," and some Scottish pipers as well.[40] A few days later, however, he touched upon a much more serious cause of discontent than any lack of martial airs, and urgently requested that London revise the section in his orders which stipulated that Russian troops were to receive rations on the scale used in the old Tsarist Army.[41] In effect, this order meant that the Russian troops received half the food that the

[39] Maynard to War Office, telegram M.I. 93, Murmansk, 2 August 1918 (sent 12:53 a.m.; 3 August); Milner MSS, box D-4.

[40] Poole to War Office, telegram 277, Archangel, 15 August 1918, 9:2 p.m.; Milner MSS, box D-4.

[41] Poole to War Office, telegram E.323, Archangel, 20 August 1918 (sent 12:30 a.m., 21 August); Milner MSS, box D-4. For the War Office's initial directive, see above, Chapter VI.

Allies did. Apparently Poole's cable was overlooked in London, for the regulation went unchanged until November, when the War Office responded with alacrity to a similar request from Ironside.[42]

Under pressure from Poole the local government declared on 20 August the restoration of universal military service, but deferred a call-up until after the harvest. In reporting this measure, Lindley expressed his opinion that it was a mistake: it was virtually unenforceable and would be likely to make the Allies unpopular in any district they occupied. Because the measure obviously originated with the Allies, Lindley said, the odium of conscription would fall upon them.[43]

As it turned out, the call-up did not actually begin until late in the year, again at the instigation of Ironside.[44] For the bulk of the bitter fighting between the first landings and the winter's freeze Poole had to rely upon the small force he had brought with him and the reinforcements—principally an American infantry regiment, engineer company, and field hospital unit—which he received in the first days of September.

These reinforcements meant that for the first months of intervention the Archangel force was predominantly American, with 4,800 men, as opposed to 2,420 British, 900 French, and 350 Serbs.[45] These American troops were, in theory, bound by President Wilson's *aide mémoire* of 17 July which stated that the only "legitimate object" for which they might be employed would be guarding military stores and rendering "such aid as may be acceptable to the Russians in the organization of their own self-defense." They were not "to take part in organized intervention . . . from either Vladivostok or Murmansk and Archangel."[46]

In North Russia these restrictions were forgotten. Within twenty-four hours of their landing at Archangel on 4 September, one American battalion was packed off in boxcars down the railway to the fiercely-held front at Obozerskaya 75 miles to the south, and another, with a battalion of Royal Scots, was sent in river boats some 100 miles

[42] Ironside, *Archangel*, p. 48.

[43] Lindley to Balfour, telegram 106, Archangel, 28 August 1918, 1:20 p.m.; Milner MSS, box C-1.

[44] Ironside, *Archangel*, p. 68.

[45] British Staff paper, "Order of Battle of Allied Troops in N. Russia," U.S. National Archives, Modern Army Branch, Supreme War Council folder 349, item 1.

[46] See above, Chapter VII.

up the Dvina to join the tiny British force of naval monitors and infantry patrols in an effort to seize Bereznik, which Poole had chosen for their winter camp.[47] In these actions the Americans were entirely under British command. Too often, it seems, British officers and soldiers applied their instructions on how to get on with the Russians to their American allies. Nine months later, in a report to Washington, the Brigadier General commanding American troops in North Russia bitterly described this situation in the following terms:

General Poole was in command during the early period of the operations, and he appeared to interpret the decision of the Supreme War Council in Paris that the operations should be under direction of the British to mean that the exercise of the command even down to the smallest units should be by British officers, whatever might be their ability to exercise such command. To meet this situation, the practice was instituted and has been followed throughout, of appointing officers to temporary rank without pay, apparently to insure the seniority of British officers in all cases, but perhaps also as a species of reward.

And the report continued:

More or less friction and irritation developed between the British troops and our junior officers and enlisted men, which exists up to this time [July 1919]. It is interesting to note that the British policy has not been one, in any sense, of co-operation with their Allies, but merely of employing such forces as were obtained from the other Allies, subordinated in every way to British direction. I naturally expected upon my arrival to be taken somewhat into the confidence of the British command as to their plans and policy, but I soon found that I was mistaken in this respect, and found a difficulty even in getting orders issued through these Headquarters for the movements of American troops,—it having been the practice of the British command to ignore the commanding officer of American troops, except to call upon him for support in enforcing orders issued to the troops without his knowledge or concurrence, and for action in matters of complaint against American officers and troops.[48]

[47] Newbolt, *Naval Operations*, vol. v, pp. 327-30; Kennan, *Decision to Intervene*, pp. 426-29. See also E. M. Halliday, *The Ignorant Armies*, New York, 1960, pp. 32-34, 49-56. Halliday draws his account of American military action in North Russia from the published and unpublished reminiscences of many of the American participants.

[48] Report by Brig. Gen. W. P. Richardson to Adjutant General, Archangel, 23 July 1919; copy in the Papers of Frank L. Polk, file 85-69, in the Library of Yale University. The same criticisms about the British system of temporary rank was made by Admiral N. A. McCully, commander of U.S. Naval Forces, North Russia, on

Meanwhile, with Poole's forces fighting the Bolsheviks far in the interior of Russia, mired in the endless swamps, sometimes up to their knees in water, constantly at the mercy of clouds of mosquitoes, the situation at Archangel was becoming more and more critical. The regime of martial law continued. All public meetings of any kind were forbidden—an especially bitter measure to the moderate socialists who made up the majority of the population and who had suffered similar restrictions under the Bolsheviks. Worst of all, no food ships arrived to relieve the population. Because the Allied representatives did not themselves know when food was to be expected, they could not even make promises of relief in the future. The situation was ready-made for Bolshevik propagandists, who could tell the people that the Allies had come only to exploit and not to help them. Finally, when the military expeditions along the railroad and the river bogged down, Allied military prestige among the local citizens suffered a severe blow. Russians enlisted by the British for the so-called Slavo-British Legion began to desert.[49]

Relations between the military authorities and the local government grew increasingly bitter. Only the presence of the Allied ambassadors prevented the government's resignation, which would clearly have made the foreign troops seem like occupiers instead of "guests." Lindley, Francis, Noulens, and Torretta (the Italian Chargé d'Affaires) repeatedly met with Chaikovsky and some of the other ministers in efforts to reach an understanding as to what should be the proper spheres of the military and civil authorities. Gradually, due to the efforts of Lindley and Francis, some progress was made, and Lindley even had hopes that Chaikovsky would drop the more militant and uncompromising socialists from his government.[50] But then disaster came.

Early in the evening of 5 September, as the diplomats and Russian ministers were filing out of Francis' office after a particularly amicable discussion, Noulens told Lindley that he had heard from a

20 December 1918. McCully reported that even non-commissioned officers were sometimes given rank as high as major, so that they would outrank any Allied officers with them. (U.S. National Archives, Naval Records Branch, file WA-6, box 607.)

[49] The Archangel situation was well analysed in a long despatch by the American Consul, Felix Cole, on 10 September 1918; *Foreign Relations, 1918, Russia*, vol. II, pp. 527-30.

[50] Lindley to Balfour, telegram 126, Archangel, 6 September 1918; Milner MSS, box D-4.

secret source (which, it seems, was Colonel Donop, the Military Governor) that Chaplin and some other Russian officers were plotting to kidnap and deport Chaikovsky's government that very evening. Noulens said that he did not credit the report, but Lindley immediately went to see Poole and warned him that such a development would have grave consequences. The general, in his turn, directed an aide to write to Chaplin and tell him that Poole had heard the rumour, but scarcely believed it to be possible and advised him against such a step. As one American observer noted, "Poole's activity seems to have ended there."[51]

Because of the housing shortage in Archangel, all of the government ministers who did not actually come from the city (six out of eight, including Chaikovsky) occupied one house. This house was directly opposite the headquarters of the British Intelligence Bureau, whose chief, Colonel Thornhill, had been Assistant Military Attaché in Petrograd, knew Russian fluently, and had long been a warm personal friend of Chaplin.[52] Somehow, during the night of 5-6 September, there were no guards at the British Intelligence Bureau and no patrols in the streets around it. At 12:30 a.m. some 30 Russian officers dressed as soldiers surrounded the house where the ministers lived, arrested all of them, and deported them to Solovetski Island in the White Sea.

The following morning, when they were reviewing an American battalion together, Poole calmly told Francis that Chaplin had deposed the government. Chaplin himself, also present at the review, freely admitted to the indignant ambassador that he had been responsible. Writing about the incident ten years later, Chaplin said that it was clear that the Allies were losing all patience with the Chaikovsky government and would soon take all power into their own

[51] Report by Professor Archibald G. Coolidge to Secretary of State on events in Archangel, 5-12 September 1918 (written 30 September); U.S. National Archives, State Department file 861.00/2899½.

The account presented here of Chaplin's attempted coup at Archangel is a reconstruction based on a great many separate reports, both contemporary and after the fact. Besides Coolidge's report and Lindley's telegram cited immediately above, they are Francis' telegrams of 6, 7, 8, 9, and 10 September and his despatch of 17 September, printed in *Foreign Relations, 1918, Russia*, vol. II, pp. 521-32; Noulens, *Mon ambassade*, vol. II, pp. 199-202; Francis, *American Embassy*, pp. 269-77; Strakhovsky, *Intervention at Archangel*, pp. 49-80. Except where specific material is cited, it may be assumed that the narrative is based upon these sources.

[52] Chaplin, "Dva perevorota," p. 23.

hands, turning the region into a virtual Entente colony. Therefore, since it was by his action that the government had been formed in the first place, he decided to liquidate it and put into power a Russian general strong enough to earn the respect of the Allies. He did not know which general, but he had heard that General V. Gurko was in the region and intended to contact him.[53] In the meantime he had had posters printed proclaiming a state of siege and nominating a temporary chief of civil administration for the region.

Francis told Poole not to allow Chaplin to issue any proclamations until they had been submitted to the Allied chiefs of mission. When they met a short time later the diplomats agreed that the coup, for which the Allies would inevitably be blamed, could not be tolerated, and they telegraphed to the British naval base at Kem ordering a man-of-war to rescue the deposed government. Lindley urged that Chaplin and his accomplices should be arrested, but Poole refused, maintaining that such an action would have a disastrous effect on the Russian forces then in the course of organisation. Poole was supported by Noulens, and no action was taken.[54]

It is not clear whether or not Poole made any effort to restrain Chaplin, but by the next morning Archangel residents were faced with three proclamations—one by Chaplin, a counter-proclamation by the two members of the government who had escaped arrest, and a third by the Allied diplomats, informing them that the old government was being brought back. The sympathy of the population was overwhelmingly with Chaikovsky; demonstration strikes broke out in many industries. By the 8th they had spread to the tramways and the railway. Poole greeted them—apparently without consulting the diplomats—with a decree that "all essential services and ship handling" were to proceed without interruption or else strikers would be arrested and turned over to military courts. Despite Poole's threats the strikes continued unabated, and the normal life of the city came to a standstill.

Meanwhile, the kidnapped ministers had been freed by the British warship sent from Kem. When the ship arrived in Archangel on the evening of 8 September, Lindley went aboard to confer with Chaikovsky and urged the President to drop some of his more extreme

[53] *ibid.*, p. 27.
[54] Lindley to Balfour, telegram 133, Archangel, 7 September 1918, 7:20 a.m.; Milner MSS, box D-4.

colleagues from the government. Chaikovsky agreed, but after a night on shore he issued a proclamation—without securing the prior approval of the diplomats as he had promised—announcing that all members of the government would remain in office.[55]

With the reinstatement of the government Chaplin's abortive coup was over; superficially, everything was as before. Actually, the coup had been a disaster. As Lindley had feared, the position of the extreme socialists in the government was immeasurably strengthened. They even claimed that the return of the government was entirely due to the general strike and threatened similar action in the future at a moment's notice. As for Chaplin, although Lindley insisted that the only way to restore confidence between Russian officers and their men was to deport him, Poole still refused, and maintained that loss of command and reduction in rank was enough punishment for him. Again Noulens supported Poole. Although thoroughly angry with Chaplin and the coup, the French Ambassador would make no concessions to the strikers or the government. Severely critical of Poole and Noulens, Lindley told London that the Allies at Archangel would have to choose between a policy either of co-operation with the popularly-supported Russian authorities or of military occupation. No longer could they pursue both policies simultaneously.[56] He asked to be relieved from his post unless he were given more control over the employment of British military forces.[57]

As it turned out, the most effective protests were not Lindley's but those made by Francis which had come to the attention of President Wilson. On 9 September Wilson ordered Secretary of State Lansing to tell the British government that unless Poole were to change his whole attitude in dealing with the local government at Archangel, the American troops would be entirely withdrawn from his command.[58] Lansing immediately sent for Colville Barclay, the British

[55] Lindley to Balfour, telegram 142, 9 September 1918, 1:41 p.m., and telegram 151, 10 September, 7:43 p.m.; Milner MSS, box D-4.

[56] Lindley to Balfour, telegram 144, Archangel, 8 September 1918, 8:10 p.m.; Milner MSS, box D-4.

[57] Francis reported that Lindley had told him this confidentially (Francis to Secretary of State, telegram 391, Archangel, 10 September 1918; *Foreign Relations, 1918, Russia*, vol. II, p. 532). There is no statement to this effect in any of Lindley's telegrams in the Milner MSS, but these papers do not contain all of Lindley's telegrams.

[58] So Lansing recorded in his Desk Diary on 9 September (Robert Lansing Papers, Library of Congress, Washington, D.C.).

Chargé d'Affaires (Lord Reading was in London), and relayed the President's message, adding that the United States government insisted on the Russians' being allowed to work out their own salvation without interference by an Allied military governor.[59] The American Ambassador in London was instructed to make similar representations.[60]

The threat that three-quarters of Poole's force would be taken away from him, Lindley pointed out on 15 September, had had more effect on the General's behaviour—and on Noulens' as well—than all that he himself had been able to say during the preceding month.[61] The diplomats, with Poole's assent, removed Colonel Donop from the office of Military Governor and asked Chaikovsky to appoint a Russian Governor-General who would be given full powers and responsibility for the internal security of the city. These steps, Lindley reported, should have been taken from the start. He had never believed that the Allied troops would have been endangered by Russian control in the rear, but Poole had always dismissed his views with the observation that he was not responsible for the troops. Now, Lindley remarked ruefully, the Chaplin coup had made it more dangerous than ever to hand over civil authority to Russians, but such a policy was still far less risky than continuing the old "occupation" regime.[62]

With the end of the crisis brought on by Chaplin, momentary calm came to Archangel. But the coup had underlined a grave dilemma which confronted anti-Bolshevik communities all over Russia—a dilemma which was never to be resolved. Simply stated, it was that in the Russia of 1918, only socialist governments could hope to claim the loyalty of the people, but that the socialists were completely incapable of organising and leading the armies that they needed to defend themselves against Bolshevism.[63] Therefore they were forced

[59] Barclay to Balfour, telegram 4070, Washington, 9 September 1918, 8:25 p.m.; Wiseman MSS.

[60] Lansing to Page, London, telegram 1313, 12 September 1918; *Foreign Relations, 1918, Russia*, vol. II, pp. 533-34.

[61] Lindley to Balfour, telegram 164, Archangel, 15 September 1918, 11:45 a.m.; Milner MSS, box D-4.

[62] *idem*.

[63] It should be noted that these remarks do not apply to the Bolsheviks themselves. Under Trotsky's firm hand, their socialist ideology did not extend to military organisation. Not only did they make far better use of former Tsarist officers than did their opponents (through a well-developed combination of rewards and threats) but they turned out some remarkably able military leaders themselves.

to seek an alliance with the only available source of military experience—former Tsarist officers who were almost uniformly anti-socialist and monarchist by inclination. Chaplin's sentiments, if not his tactics, were not unrepresentative of those of his brother officers. However patriotic and anti-Bolshevik these officers were, they could not hope to resist the Bolsheviks themselves, and they were forced to rely upon the socialists to recruit the armies they needed. Thus each of these normally antithetic groups—the officers and the socialists—had to rely upon the other. In no case was the resulting alliance-of-necessity ultimately satisfactory. Inevitably, in their mutual distrust, each side crippled the other. Thus, at Archangel, when Chaikovsky was invited by the Allies to appoint a Russian Governor-General, he named an officer, Colonel B. A. Durov, who was unacceptable to the other officers because they considered him inexperienced and of too low rank.[64]

Too often, as at Archangel, the intervention of the Allies aggravated, rather than alleviated, these tensions. The Allied officers (though not, as a rule, the Americans) had little more sympathy for socialism than their Russian colleagues. To these men the socialism of Kerensky had caused the ruin of the Russian Army and had needlessly prolonged the fighting in France. Socialism meant disorganisation, the greatest horror of the professional soldier. Moreover, many of the Allied officers who came back to Russia in the Intervention had served there before February 1917 and had formed strong sentimental bonds with what they conceived to be the old Russia. To men such as Thornhill, Chaplin seemed much more likely than Chaikovsky to restore this old Russia.

The week of the Chaplin affair marked a turning point not only in the political ambitions but also in the military fortunes of the British officers at Archangel. On 10 September the Red Army wrested Kazan from the Czechs and began a drive that eventually resulted in the collapse of the whole Volga front. Poole's urgent request, on 8 September, that the War Office should give the Czechs sufficient help so they would push towards him instead of retreating eastward,[65] was in vain: the Czechs had reached the limit of their advance.

---

[64] As reported by Francis to Secretary of State, telegram 426, Archangel, 26 September 1918; *Foreign Relations, 1918, Russia,* vol. ii, p. 547.

[65] Poole to War Office, telegram E.456, Archangel, 8 September 1918; Milner MSS, box D-4.

Poole was also to be disappointed in his many requests for reinforcements. When the War Office passed them on to the Supreme War Council in Paris, the Americans were especially bitter. They had not known before of the War Office's new orders to Poole which included the instructions to seek a junction with the Czechs, and they regarded the whole scheme as a British attempt to involve American troops in a far greater operation than the President had intended. Writing to the U.S. Chief of Staff from Versailles on 3 September General Bliss commented:

. . . I think the British possibly feel that they may have bitten off more than they can chew and want to throw the responsibility elsewhere. This they cannot do if I have anything to say about it.[66]

Bliss did have something to say about it. On 14 September he told his colleagues in the Council Chamber at Versailles that no more American troops would go to North Russia. With victory in the West evidently so close, he said, dividing the Allied effort would result only in delay. The other Permanent Military Representatives agreed with him,[67] and ten days later the War Office had to tell Poole that they found it impossible to send him the reinforcements which they had wanted him to have.[68] On 26 September, the American position was stated in a formal note to the Allied governments:

. . . as it is, in the opinion of the Government of the United States, plain that no gathering of any effective force by the Russians is to be hoped for, we shall insist with the other governments, so far as our cooperation is concerned, that all military effort in northern Russia be given up except the guarding of the ports themselves and as much of the country round them as may develop threatening conditions. . . .
No more American troops will be sent to the Northern ports.[69]

It was, indeed, plain that there would be "no gathering of any effective force by the Russians." By early October the British had

[66] Letter from General Bliss (Versailles) to General Peyton C. March (Washington), 3 September 1918; U.S. National Archives, Modern Army Branch, Supreme War Council folder 366, item 5.
[67] Minutes, 46th meeting of Permanent Military Representatives, Versailles, 14 September 1918, 10 a.m.; U.S. National Archives, Modern Army Branch, Supreme War Council Records.
[68] War Office to Poole, Archangel, telegram 67106, 24 September 1918 (sent 25 September, 9 p.m.); Milner MSS, box D-4.
[69] Secretary of State to Ambassadors in London, Paris, Rome, Tokyo, un-numbered telegram, 26 September 1918, 8 p.m.; *Foreign Relations, 1918, Russia*, vol. II, pp. 394-95.

managed to recruit about 1,600 officers and men for a Slavo-British Legion, while the French had been able to enlist only 200.[70] Poole had not given up hope, however, and on 13 October he pressed on the War Office a plan for an offensive along the Archangel-Vologda railway, through thickly populated country from which he might gather many recruits. For this effort he would need reinforcements which were on their way to Maynard at Murmansk.[71] His plan was firmly rejected in London: the War Office could see no evidence that the presence of British troops would produce the "revulsion of feeling" against the Bolsheviks which Poole predicted.[72] Thus another objective of the northern intervention—the provision of a nucleus around which "loyal Russians" could rally—was implicitly denied.

Poole could justly complain, however, that his resources were much smaller in proportion to his responsibilities than Maynard's were at Murmansk. On 1 September Maynard had made an urgent appeal for reinforcements to protect the port and its outlying garrisons against a German offensive which he expected in the early autumn.[73] Although it was already evident that the Germans were withdrawing from Finland and using all their available manpower on the Western Front, Maynard's request was immediately agreed to by the War Cabinet, and arrangements were made for the despatch as soon as possible of all the reinforcements he had asked—an infantry brigade of four battalions, two machine-gun companies, a mortar battery, and a three-battery brigade of field artillery.[74] The addition of these 5,000 men brought Maynard's force up to the very respectable figure of 15,000—7,400 British, 1,000 French, 1,350 Italians, 1,200 Serbs, and more than 4,000 Russians, Karelians, and Finns.[75]

By 10 October, however, it had become obvious even to the War Office that Germany was in no position to launch an attack through

[70] Francis to Secretary of State, telegram 451, Archangel, 6 October 1918; *ibid.*, p. 553.

[71] Poole to War Office, telegram E.655/6, Archangel, 13 October 1918, 5:45 p.m.; Milner MSS, box D-4.

[72] War Office to General Officers Commanding Archangel and Murmansk, telegram 68752, 16 October 1918, 6 p.m.; Milner MSS, box D-4.

[73] Maynard to War Office, telegram M.582, Murmansk, 1 September 1918 (sent 2 September, 1:33 a.m.); Milner MSS, box D-4.

[74] War Office to British Military Representative, Versailles, telegram 65612, 3 September 1918, and to Maynard and Poole, Murmansk and Archangel, telegram 65639, 4 September, 5:5 p.m.; Milner MSS, box D-4.

[75] "Order of Battle of Allied Troops in N. Russia," cited above, footnote 45. See Maynard, *Murmansk*, p. 132.

some 500 miles of Arctic wasteland, and Maynard was informed that his force was considered more than sufficient for the defence of Murmansk and Pechenga. It could either be withdrawn or employed down the railway in order to open up winter communications with Archangel through Soroka and Onega, and to maintain forward bases for operations against the Bolsheviks. The War Office favoured the latter alternative—Maynard was to keep all his force.[76] In matter-of-fact orders like this, intervention was transformed from an anti-German to an anti-Bolshevik venture.

Maynard's military task, during the months of the late summer and autumn of 1918, was much easier than Poole's. Fighting in the Murmansk region consisted mostly of desultory clashes between patrols of White Finns and British-led Red Finns. The Bolsheviks had made no move up the railway, and Maynard's troops had not gone south to meet them. There were no "fronts" like those on the railway and the Dvina River in Poole's sector.

Maynard's political task was also much easier than Poole's. Relations between the Allies and the local population had been established longer and were on a surer footing. If Maynard had been provided with some cash when his expedition left England in June, and if shipments of food had reached him in good time, he would have had very little trouble. The break between the Murmansk Soviet and the Bolshevik central government had made the region entirely dependent upon the Allies, who had undertaken in the 6 July agreement "as far as possible" to feed the entire population of the region, including the railwaymen who formed a large proportion of it. After the cutting of the rail link with the south, virtually the only function remaining to the railway was hauling goods and troops between the Allied bases on its northern section. The railway workers naturally expected to be paid for their work. When Maynard could not pay them, they went out on strike.

Maynard had strongly appealed for money and provisions before he left England, and during the summer, as the situation became more and more serious, his telegrams grew increasingly urgent. London simply would not send him any money, and instead of adequate provisions for the population he was promised only flour.

[76] War Office to Maynard and Poole, Murmansk and Archangel, telegram 68337, 10 October 1918, 9:15 p.m.; Milner MSS, box D-4.

Maynard put on a brave front before the strikers, but with justice he told London on 18 August:

It must be realised in the first place that the feeling against the Allies in this district is not confined to a few. The majority of workmen and many others blame us for shortage of food and for the loss of their pay. . . . I do not think it is realised that in two months from now except for some flour there will be no food at all for a population in this district of over 100,000. . . . Refusing sufficient food is the most certain means of making our mission on this side a failure. I am doing all I can to get rid of useless mouths and have told strikers I do not mind at all if they leave the district; but it must be remembered that every man thus sent south will be a man against us.[77]

And on 1 September, when he had still received no money and by which time the strike had paralysed the railroad and made communication with British bases to the south extremely difficult, Maynard telegraphed:

Had my request [for cash] been met, all this trouble at most critical time would have been avoided. Surely this question of a few pounds does not compare with risks my troops are running.[78]

Lindley, in Archangel, strongly supported Maynard's appeal. Poole, he reported, had urged Maynard to fight the strikers "ruthlessly," but he himself thought that food and money, and not force, would be the only way to get the railway running again.[79] Some food did arrive in September and October, but lack of a sound currency was the basic problem. The situation was resolved only in December when Maynard, in desperation, took a destroyer to England and made his appeal in such strong terms that the treasury finally gave him permission to distribute £150,000 in British bank notes.[80]

Meanwhile, Murmansk had been taken under the political authority of Archangel. Administration was placed in the hands of a Deputy-Governor appointed by and responsible to the Governor-General in Archangel. The Murmansk regional Soviet was dissolved,

[77] Maynard to Poole (Archangel) and War Office, telegram M.372, Murmansk, 18 August 1918, 3:34 p.m.; Milner MSS, box D-4.

[78] Maynard to War Office, telegram M.584, Murmansk, 1 September 1918 (sent 2 September, 2 a.m.); Milner MSS, box D-4.

[79] Lindley to Balfour, telegram 117, Archangel, 3 September 1918, 7:50 p.m.; Milner MSS, box D-4.

[80] Maynard, *Murmansk*, pp. 158-60.

but its principal members were retained as an advisory council until elections for a District Zemstvo could be held.[81] This return to a system of local government which had been characteristic of the last decades of the Tsarist regime was preceded by the reconstitution on bourgeois lines of the Archangel government itself. The so-called Supreme Administration of the Northern Region had never recovered from the severe loss of prestige it had suffered at the hands of Chaplin. In late September, in an effort to create an authority which would be more respected by the Allies (precisely Chaplin's objective, it will be recalled), Chaikovsky sent three of his most militantly socialist colleagues to Samara, where some seventy other S-R members of the Constituent Assembly had taken advantage of Czech military success to form (in name alone) an "all-Russian" government.[82]

With these three safely disposed of, Chaikovsky announced on 7 October the formation of the Provisional Government of the Northern Region. He himself, as President and Minister for Foreign Affairs, was the only socialist included. Colonel Durov remained Governor-General, in charge of internal security and military affairs, while leaders of various bourgeois parties took over the Ministries of Finance, Commerce, Justice, and Posts and Telegraphs. From the point of view of Allied interests, Lindley reported, the new government seemed most satisfactory. But he feared that its non-socialist composition might alienate it from the local population.[83]

At least the new ministers did not have to contend with General Poole. On 14 October he left for England to talk over the North Russian situation with the War Office. Although he told the ambassadors he would be away for only thirty days, he was never to return. Poole's recall was not unexpected. But no-one expected that he would have the temerity to call on Chaikovsky and ask the old President to write to London requesting that he be sent back to Archangel. Chaikovsky confided to Francis that he found Poole's visit acutely embar-

[81] Lindley to Balfour, telegram 262, Archangel, 10 October 1918, 1:56 p.m.; Milner MSS, box D-4.

[82] Information of events in Central Russia and Siberia was slow in getting to Archangel. By the time Chaikovsky had despatched his colleagues to Samara, the government there was already defunct, having transferred its power to the so-called Ufa Directorate, formed as a result of a conference of the various Siberian "governments" from 8 to 23 September 1918. See below, Chapter IX.

[83] Lindley to Balfour, telegram 256, Archangel, 9 October 1918, 2:10 p.m.; Milner MSS, box D-4.

rassing after all that had passed, but that nevertheless he had given the general a personal letter of thanks.[84]

With Poole gone, Major-General Edmund Ironside took command of all the Allied forces.[85] He was surely one of the most extraordinary officers in the British Army. Only thirty-seven years old, he looked even younger. He was of immense size—over six feet four inches tall and nearly twenty stones in weight. Apparently, he was an expert linguist. Ambassador Francis, who was highly impressed with him, recorded that he was fluent in Russian, French, German, Italian, and Swedish and that he knew something of eleven other languages.[86] But his greatest difference from Poole was that although he was an able leader in the field (he had been commander of an infantry brigade in France when he was picked for the Russian assignment), he had also had extensive experience as a General Staff officer and was capable of handling great quantities of intricate administrative detail—an ability vitally necessary in an isolated command, such as North Russia, and one that Poole totally lacked.

When Ironside took over in North Russia, the war in the west was entering its final stages. Even to the troops in North Russia, cut off as they were from information about the rest of the war, it was obvious that Germany would soon surrender. On 17 October Ironside was forced to report that his battalion of French infantry had been seriously affected by rumours of a German armistice and were inclined to insubordination. It was clear, he said, that when an armistice did come the battalion would fight no longer. The Americans, too, had definitely told him that in case of an armistice they would no longer engage in offensive operations. In view of the American regimental commander's instructions from Washington, Ironside could apply no pressure to him.[87] The same attitudes were reported

---

[84] Francis to Secretary of State, telegram 1230 (?), Archangel, 16 October 1918; U.S. National Archives, Petrograd Embassy 800 file.

[85] When Ironside reached Russia, on 1 October, he was a Brigadier-General and Chief of Staff to Poole. With Poole's departure Ironside became acting commander and, on 19 November, Commander-in-Chief, with the temporary rank of Major-General.

[86] Francis, *American Embassy*, p. 295. *The Times* correspondent in Archangel, William Soutar, in his book, *With Ironside in North Russia*, London, 1940, p. 88, also recorded that Ironside was fluent in Russian, and that he was "an uncommonly good linguist."

[87] Ironside to War Office, telegram E.672/6, 17 October 1918, 3:15 p.m.; Milner MSS, box D-4.

by the American naval attaché when he returned from a visit to the railroad front. The French, he said, claimed that further service in the north was solely in Britain's interest.[88]

Less than a month later, on the day of the Armistice, news reached Archangel of renewed and much more vigorous Bolshevik attacks on the Dvina front. "The enemy had shown that they could attack," Ironside wrote of the events of 11 November, "and had no intention of allowing us to remain in peaceful occupation of any Russian territory, however small it might be."[89] On the following day, to a gathering of Russian officers, Ironside declared: "The Germans have accepted all conditions. . . . Now the task of the Allies is to restore order in Russia. . . ."[90]

[88] Reported by Francis to Secretary of State, telegram 491, 18 October 1918; *Foreign Relations, 1918, Russia,* vol. ii, p. 559.
[89] Ironside, *Archangel,* p. 51.
[90] Strakhovsky, *Intervention at Archangel,* p. 106 (from an Archangel newspaper).

CHAPTER IX

THE BEGINNING OF INTERVENTION:
SIBERIA

> To re-establish order in Russia will be a herculean task. No half-baked constitutionalism could possibly succeed in it. The only possible way out seems to be a provisional military Government....
>
> —*Lord Robert Cecil to the War Cabinet, September 1918*

WHILE the small British, American, and French detachments were establishing themselves at Archangel during the late summer of 1918, much larger forces—principally Japanese—were moving into eastern Siberia. This was the result of the protracted Anglo-American-Japanese negotiations of June and July. President Wilson had agreed to intervention in order that Allied forces at Vladivostok and along the railways might free Czech troops from garrison duties and enable them to go to the rescue of their beleaguered colleagues then in combat with Red Army detachments on the Volga, in the rugged terrain around Lake Baikal, and on the Ussuri River. From the outset, however, the President's plan for a strictly limited intervention was severely criticised in the other Allied capitals; military leaders in London, Paris, and Tokyo were afraid—or they professed to be afraid—that the American programme for assisting the Czechs could not save them from extermination at the hands of the Bolsheviks. Before the initial American and Japanese troops had all landed at Vladivostok, the British and Japanese governments, each for its own reasons, began working to have their numbers vastly increased.

Thus, on 9 August the Chief of the Imperial General Staff, General Sir Henry Wilson, addressed a memorandum to the French and Japanese General Staffs supporting the estimate of the Czech commander at Vladivostok that no less than eight battalions of Allied troops were needed to assist the Czech detachment on the Ussuri front, while three divisions were necessary to force a way through to the Czechs at Lake Baikal. In the opinion of the British General Staff these estimates were reasonable, and, therefore, all of the troops earmarked for Siberia under the American proposals would be required for the Ussuri offensive. The C.I.G.S. suggested that in those circumstances Japan should supply the three divisions needed at Lake Baikal, perhaps routing them through Manchuria to save time.[1]

Sir Henry Wilson's memorandum was a "suggestion," not a formal request. Before a formal request could be made, London still felt that Washington's permission was necessary. Implicit in the original American proposal for intervention by 7,000 Americans and 7,000 Japanese was the possibility that these numbers might be modified in the event of an emergency.[2] On 12 August, therefore, the British Embassy in Washington gave the State Department a memorandum asserting that the Czech position was "clearly one of emergency," asking the Americans formally to request that the Japanese should send all the military assistance Tokyo felt necessary, and stating that unless the United States government had "grave objections," the British government would make such a request themselves.[3]

It is somewhat surprising that this overture was even made. Only three days before, when Colville Barclay, as Chargé d'Affaires, had informally raised the same question, Acting Secretary of State Polk indignantly expressed his amazement that the British government should claim an "emergency situation" at so early a date. Polk stated that the U.S. government would not consider any change in plans until the American troops then still en route arrived in Vladivostok.[4] Chastened by this interview, Barclay warned Balfour against putting too much pressure on President Wilson, recommending that in the future Britain should avoid giving the appearance of "pulling the chestnuts out of the fire for the Japanese" and let them make their own requests to Washington.[5] But this advice was not heeded and

[1] A detailed summary of Wilson's memorandum was sent to the British Military Representative in Washington as telegram 63995, 9 August 1918, 11:30 p.m.; Milner MSS, box E-2.

[2] This was indicated in paragraph 7 of President Wilson's initial memorandum on intervention on 6 July. See above, Chapter VII.

[3] *Foreign Relations, 1918, Russia*, vol. II, pp. 341-42.

[4] Barclay to Balfour, telegram 3604, Washington, 9 August 1918, 9:10 p.m.; Wiseman MSS.

[5] Barclay to Balfour, un-numbered personal telegram, 10 August 1918; Wiseman MSS.

Barclay was instructed to make the formal *démarche*. London could not reasonably have expected any other reply than Secretary Lansing's formal statement on 14 August that the American government "would be gravely embarrassed if the British Government should take the action suggested" and approach the Japanese.[6]

Lansing's frigid reply produced another round of worried communications between the Foreign Office and British embassies in the Allied capitals, between Lord Reading (who was in London) and Wiseman, and between Wiseman and Colonel House, all on the subject of how not to provoke the President.[7] Sir Henry Wilson even sent a special message to Foch, calling the situation "one of those impasses between political and military opinion which, were it not fraught with so grave dangers, would be considered ridiculous," and asking the Marshal to use his great influence to secure the President's approval. The C.I.G.S. added bitterly:

. . . although the resources of diplomacy are exhausted, in the event of disaster it will be no satisfaction for the Allies to ascribe the massacre of a brave ally [the Czechs] to the President of the United States.[8]

Sir William Wiseman, who best understood the President's attitude, described it thus in a telegram to Reading on 23 August:

The danger now is—to be quite frank—that he is beginning to feel that the Allies are trying to rush, even trick, him into a policy which he has refused to accept. He is well aware that he is committed to the task of rescuing the Czechs, but thinks the Allies are already trying to change the character of the expedition into a full-fledged military expedition with the object of reconstituting the Eastern Front.[9]

Wiseman's message—like all the others—urged that the Japanese, as the power nearest the scene, should make their own appeals to America and not leave this unpleasant task to the British.

[6] Secretary of State to the British Chargé, 14 August 1918; *Foreign Relations, 1918, Russia*, vol. II, pp. 345-46.

[7] See, for example, Reading's telegram CXP 738 to Wiseman from London, 20 August 1918; Arthur Murray's personal letter to Wiseman of the same day; Balfour's telegrams 806 to Greene in Tokyo, 1749 to Lord Derby in Paris, and 5157 to Barclay in Washington—all on 21 August; and Wiseman's telegram 706 to Reading in London, 22 August. All of these are in the Wiseman MSS.

[8] C.I.G.S. to Foch (through General DuCane in Paris as telegram 64854), 22 August 1918, 11 p.m.; Milner MSS, unfiled folder 32.

[9] Wiseman (New York) to Reading (London), telegram CXP 708, 23 August 1918; Wiseman MSS.

But the Japanese had no need to consult America. The terms of the initial American proposal had clearly put the initiative into their hands, and messages like Sir Henry Wilson's memorandum of 9 August had indicated that the more troops Japan put into the field in Siberia the more fervent would be the approval of the Entente Powers. This was made quite explicit by Balfour in an interview with the Japanese Ambassador on 25 August. Chinda told the Foreign Secretary that Japan had decided to send reinforcements to Siberia and hoped that the British government would approve. Balfour expressed his great pleasure at the news and told Chinda (as he later cabled Barclay in Washington) that it seemed to him

... that the amount of forces required to achieve our objects in Siberia was *entirely a military question* and His Majesty's Government would approve anything which the High Command in Tokyo thought necessary.[10]

Three days later Chinda called on Balfour again. Worried that he had not made himself clear on the 25th, he explained that the purpose of his visit on that day had been rather to intimate the intentions of his government than to apply for approval or support.[11] Nothing could have demonstrated more clearly the confidence the Japanese had in the strength of their position.

Japanese troops began to flood into Siberia and Manchuria. The original contingent of 12,000 landed at Vladivostok between 3 and 10 August. By the 21st, 12,000 additional troops had moved into the zone of the Chinese-Eastern Railway. The Japanese announced that this movement was made under the Sino-Japanese Military Agreement of 16 May 1918, but it was soon learned that the Chinese, who strenuously objected, had not even been consulted.[12] On 26 August the Japanese General Staff told the Allied military attachés in Tokyo that 10,000 additional troops had embarked for Vladivostok, and that another 20,000 had been mobilised and would be sent to northern Manchuria.[13] By the Armistice there were more than 70,000 Japanese soldiers in Siberia.

[10] Balfour to Barclay, Washington, telegram 5257, 25 August 1918, 6 p.m.; Milner MSS, unfiled folder 32 (italics added).
[11] Balfour to Barclay, Washington, telegram 5315, 28 August 1918; Wiseman MSS.
[12] Memorandum of a conversation between the Third Assistant Secretary of State and the Chinese Minister, 21 August 1918; *Foreign Relations, 1918, Russia*, vol. II, p. 353.
[13] Morris to Secretary of State, 26 August 1918, 4 p.m.; *ibid.*, pp. 355-56.

Meanwhile, the British battalion sent to Vladivostok from Hong Kong had gone into combat against the Bolsheviks on the Ussuri front. The 25th Middlesex was a garrison battalion composed of men physically unfit for duty in France. Its commander, Lieutenant Colonel John Ward, was a trade union leader and Labour M.P. Since the battalion was not intended for front-line service, it lacked such basic field equipment as tents and mosquito netting.[14] Nevertheless, because it was the first Allied infantry detachment to reach Siberia, the War Office—on the advice of Colonel T. A. Robertson, the British Military Representative at Vladivostok—agreed that half of it should go to the Ussuri front to help the Czechs hold the line until the Japanese could arrive.[15] Robertson arranged with the Czech commander that the 500 British infantrymen and 43 machine-gunners would be used only defensively and in reserve.[16] As a result they did little actual fighting, most of the time remaining idle spectators of the action between Czechs and Bolsheviks. On 25 August several Japanese battalions arrived and, together with the Czechs, completely defeated the Bolshevik forces.[17] Thus the danger facing the Czechs on the Ussuri front was eliminated. The only real area of danger left was Trans-Baikalia.

It was soon apparent, however, as the Americans had predicted, that the danger to the Czechs around Lake Baikal had been vastly over-estimated. Unaided by foreign forces the Czechs easily overcame the Bolsheviks, and in the first days of September the central and eastern parts of the Czech Corps met near Chita.[18] By 10 September B. F. Alston, the British Consul at Vladivostok, could report that the railway was open and in the hands of the Czechs all the way from the Pacific to beyond the Urals.[19] As soon as this news reached London, Lloyd George despatched a letter of congratulation to Beneš,

[14] Ward, *"Die-Hards,"* p. 16.

[15] War Office to Robertson, Vladivostok, telegram 63595, 3 August 1918; summarized in "Diary, Short History of Events," cited above, Chapter v, footnote 30.

[16] See Robertson's telegrams 7 and 9 to Director of Military Intelligence, 5 August 1918, 5:5 p.m. and 7 August, 11:45 p.m., and the War Office's telegram 63736 to Robertson, 5 August, 7 p.m.; Milner MSS, box E-2.

[17] Ward, *"Die-Hards,"* pp. 16-52.

[18] Morris to Secretary of State, Tokyo, 5 September 1918, 6 p.m.; *Foreign Relations, 1918, Russia,* vol. II, p. 368.

[19] Alston to Balfour, telegram 32, Vladivostok, 10 September 1918; Wiseman MSS (as no. 5614 Balfour to Barclay, 13 September).

the President of the Czecho-Slovak National Council in Paris, calling the Czech achievement "one of the greatest epics of history."[20]

The opening of the railway, so that the Czechs scattered across Siberia could collect at Vladivostok and from there leave Russia, was one of President Wilson's principal aims when he agreed to limited Allied intervention. As it happened, the bulk of the American troops assigned to Siberia—8,763 men in all—did not arrive until after the Czechs had already achieved this goal. Under the President's plan the only task remaining for the foreign forces was to protect the Czechs while they were being evacuated.

For the British, on the other hand, the quick Czech success opened up prospects for the immediate establishment of a new Eastern Front on the Volga along the Czech forward positions at Kazan and Simbirsk. It was at this time, it will be remembered, that General Poole in Archangel was urging that all possible aid be given the Czechs so they could effect a junction with his forces at Kotlas.[21] But it was also at this time that the tide began to turn against the Czechs and the White Russian forces which had joined with them. On 5 September strongly reinforced Bolshevik armies, under Trotsky's personal leadership, began a counter-attack. Kazan fell to them on the 10th, Simbirsk three days later.[22] General Knox, who had just arrived in Siberia, cabled from Vladivostok on the 16th that there was no doubt that the Czechs on the Volga were "at their last gasp." Only the Japanese and the Americans, he said, had the means to save them. If they did not act at once the Allies would lose their last chance of preserving a front in European Russia, and the opportunity offered by the opening of the Trans-Siberian Railway would be wasted. Knox concluded his appeal by asking:

Can nothing be done to make the Japanese despatch even two divisions to save the situation? The despatch of a division now would alter the whole situation in European Russia, before winter sets in. The holding back of the assistance asked for will probably involve the Allies in the spring in a long and costly campaign. It allows the enemy to drain European Russia of supplies during the winter and may force decent elements in despair to invite German protection. It seems that the Allies are deliberately throwing away a rare opportunity.[23]

[20] Masaryk, *Making of a State*, p. 256, n.   [21] See above, Chapter VIII.
[22] Stewart, *White Armies*, p. 116.
[23] Knox to Director of Military Intelligence, telegram 45, Vladivostok, 16 September 1918, 1:45 p.m.; Milner MSS, box E-2.

There was certainly no chance that the Americans would help the Czechs in western Siberia. Poole's efforts to get the Czechs to push towards Archangel, so President Wilson wrote to his Secretary of State on 8 September, illustrated "in the most striking way the utter disregard of General Poole and of all the Allied governments" of the policy to which the United States government "expressly confined" itself. It was "out of the question," said the President, to send the Czechs reinforcements from eastern Siberia; they would receive American aid only if they were brought out eastward, not westward. In despair, the President asked: "Is there no way—no form of expression—by which we can get this comprehended?"[24] His concern led to the general statement of American policy issued to the Allied governments on 27 September, which stated, as we have seen, that U.S. troops would not take part in operations into the interior from Archangel.[25] It also stipulated that the Czechs would receive no more American support unless they retired east of the Urals. And although it pointed out that the limitations upon American action were not meant as criticism of the policies of the Allies, a confidential message sent at the same time to American ambassadors said:

> The ideas and purposes of the Allies with respect to military operations in Siberia and on the "Volga front" are ideas and purposes with which we have no sympathy. We do not believe them to be practical or based upon sound reason or good military judgement.[26]

It is doubtful that the British government ever seriously thought that America would come to the aid of the Czechs on the Volga. But they were certainly counting upon the Japanese, who had so eagerly sent 70,000 soldiers to Siberia. During the Anglo-Japanese discussions of June and July the Japanese government had made it quite plain that they did not intend to send troops west of Lake Baikal. Yet the British had dismissed so disagreeable a fact from their calculations; persistently they had conjured up images of a Japanese blow at Germany from the east.[27]

By mid-October, however, when 9,000 Czechs were forced to

[24] Wilson to Lansing, 8 September 1918; U.S. National Archives, Department of State file 861.00/2617.

[25] The American statement is cited above, Chapter VIII, footnote 69.

[26] Secretary of State to Ambassadors in Tokyo, London, Paris and Rome, 26 August 1918; *Foreign Relations, 1918, Russia*, vol. II, p. 393.

[27] See above, Chapter VII.

evacuate Samara in the face of 25,000 Bolsheviks,[28] it had become obvious that the Japanese were firmly entrenching themselves exactly where they said they would—in the Maritime Provinces and in northern Manchuria. On 16 October, therefore, Balfour ordered Sir Conyngham Greene to make a formal appeal in Tokyo. The British note recited all the arguments for helping the Czechs—that their withdrawal would mean a serious blow to Allied prestige, a great extension of Bolshevik authority, the loss to the Central Powers of the year's exceptionally bountiful harvest in the Urals, and the abandonment of Alekseyev and his loyal forces in the south. The note then continued, not a little disingenuously:

To give no further help to the Czecho-Slovak forces would seem to His Majesty's Government to be a grave mistake on political, economic and military grounds. They are also deeply sensible of the point of honour involved. Happily, they are informed by their military advisers that there is no technical military reason to render such a decision necessary.

The British government was confident, the note concluded, that the Japanese, as loyal Allies, would not "withhold their hearty co-operation. . . ."[29]

The Japanese refusal, in a memorandum handed to Greene on 23 October, was polite but categorical. Subsequent events, it said, had not caused the Japanese government to modify their prediction of 24 June that grave difficulties would accompany a military expedition beyond eastern Siberia. After long and careful consideration, and despite their strong sympathies for the Czechs, they had decided that no further westward advance would be attempted by the Japanese forces then operating east of Lake Baikal.[30] As for the Czechs, Foreign Minister Goto told Greene in conversation, the Japanese thought they should withdraw of their own accord to Omsk or any other place of safety rather than take the risk of further fighting, especially in view of the almost certain surrender of Germany in the near future.[31]

[28] Stewart, *White Armies*, p. 117. Samara was evacuated on 8 October.

[29] Balfour to Greene, Tokyo, telegram 988, 16 October 1918, 7 p.m.; Milner MSS, box E-2.

[30] Greene to Balfour, telegram 1094, Tokyo, 23 October 1918, 1:10 p.m.; Milner MSS, box E-2.

[31] Greene to Balfour, telegram 1093, Tokyo, 23 October 1918, 10:40 p.m.; Milner MSS, box E-2.

Ambassador Greene made no comment on Goto's linking of Japanese aid to the Czechs with Germany's fortunes. But a fortnight later the British Military Attaché, Brigadier-General C. R. Woodroffe, submitted his own analysis, written on the basis of information furnished him by "reliable sources" within the Japanese government. In the light of subsequent developments it is worth quoting:

At the time Japan agreed to send troops to Siberia the issue of the war was still gravely in doubt; they went there hoping that Germany would win or that it might prove a draw with both sides thoroughly exhausted. In that case they would have established themselves in eastern Siberia and none of the Powers would be in a position to turn them out. They still hope to prolong by one excuse or another their occupation in the course of which economic claims may be established which may be eventually converted into political possession.[32]

❖

The refusal of the United States and Japan to support the Czechs on the Volga front meant that if Siberia (and, indeed, Russia) were to be saved from Bolshevism, such a result would have to be effected by the Russians themselves. The Czechs were rapidly growing weary and disillusioned. From 28 October—the day Czechoslovak independence was declared in Prague—they had a country of their own. The defeat of the Central Powers left them no further reason to fight on in Siberia. They wanted to go home. At the end of October, completely disheartened by the complete failure of the Allies to come to their aid, the Czech command ordered a retirement along the entire front.[33]

Meanwhile, White Russian forces were gradually being raised to take the place of the Czechs. The internal political situation in Siberia was so complicated—one enterprising scholar has counted no less than 19 separate "governments" between the Volga and the Pacific at this time, each hoping to succeed the Bolsheviks as the recognised government of Siberia[34]—that the present narrative cannot even attempt adequately to describe it.

[32] A copy of this analysis, given to the American Military Attaché, was forwarded to the Secretary of State by Ambassador Morris in an unnumbered telegram on 10 November 1918, 3 p.m.; U.S. National Archives, Department of State file 861.00/3194.

[33] As reported by Knox's assistant, Col. J. M. Blair, to War Office, telegram 144, Vladivostok, 29 October 1918, 3:45 p.m.; Milner MSS, box E-2.

[34] White, *Siberian Intervention*, p. 95.

The various attempts by Horvat, Peter Derber, and Cossack leaders like Semenov to establish political authority in eastern Siberia have already been briefly mentioned. The centre of anti-Bolshevik political life, however, lay far to the west in the rich plains on both sides of the Urals. In this area, after the Czechs had driven out the Bolsheviks in June 1918, there existed two principal centres of authority.[35] One was west of the Urals at Samara. Established by a group of seventy Socialist-Revolutionary members of the Constituent Assembly, the Samara government (or "Komuch" as it came to be called from the initials of its Russian name) was a committee, headed by Viktor Chernov, the President of the short-lived Constituent Assembly, who regarded themselves as the temporary rulers of Russia until that body could meet again. The Komuch adopted intact the rather extreme programme of the Left S-R's and by doing so denied themselves the support of most of the region's prosperous wheat-farmer population. Nevertheless, they managed to build up a People's Army of volunteers and conscripts which by August numbered over 10,000. This force was the principal ally of the Czech Corps in the fighting on the Volga front.

The other government was the five-man Siberian Provisional Government at Omsk. Thoroughly bourgeois, they based their authority at first on the Siberian Regional Duma which had also been dispersed by the Bolsheviks. The Siberian government duly resuscitated the Duma, but when they found that this predominantly S-R body intended to have a voice in governmental affairs, they once again dissolved it—an action which resulted in the killing of one of the Duma leaders. These tactics and the restoration of many of the old institutions and practices abolished by the Bolsheviks earned the Siberian government the support of many former Tsarist Army officers, as well as that of the wealthier peasantry.

Politically the Komuch and the Siberian government were poles apart, and they quickly came into conflict. Chiefly as a result of the urgings of the Czechs, who were sickened by the spectacle of anti-Bolshevik Russians quarrelling among themselves at a time of such great danger, representatives of the two groups, as well as those of other, lesser groups which also claimed some sort of political author-

[35] This account of the development of anti-Bolshevik movements in Siberia is drawn from Bunyan, *Intervention*, pp. 324-73; Stewart, *White Armies*, pp. 144-51; and White, *Siberian Intervention*, pp. 99-107.

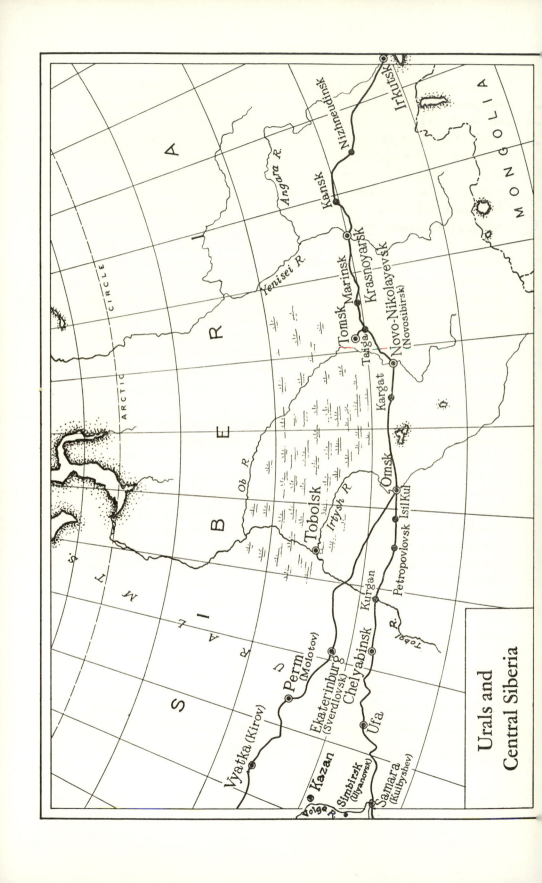

Urals and
Central Siberia

ity, agreed to meet together to resolve their differences. The principal meeting was the so-called State Conference which met at Ufa, barely beyond the range of Bolshevik guns, from 8 to 23 September. Out of this conference, as the result of a most unwieldy compromise, there came an All-Russian Provisional Government basing its authority on the Constituent Assembly. In addition to two S-R's[36] its five-member Directorate contained General V. B. Boldyrev, a capable and liberally inclined officer, and P. V. Vologodsky, the premier of the Omsk Siberian government, which continued to exist as a regional authority.

The Directorate also decided to establish itself at Omsk and when it did so, on 9 October, the town became the seat of two governments, one claiming authority over Siberia, the other over all Russia, including Siberia. The monopoly of force, however, was in the hands of the Siberian government. For a month these two bodies maintained an uneasy coexistence, the three socialists on the Directorate being eyed with considerable suspicion. Finally, on 5 November an agreement was reached whereby the two governments were amalgamated. This process was in reality a farce: the entire 13-member Council of Ministers of the Siberian government became the administrative organ of the new All-Russian Provisional Government, while the Directorate remained as little more than a figure-head. In this arrangement conflict was inevitable.

In the explosive mixture of bombast, idealism, and intrigue which comprised the politics of anti-Bolshevik Siberia, the Allied powers— particularly the British but also the Japanese—played an often decisive part. From the time of the initial American decision to intervene the British government emphasised the importance of the political side of intervention. Responsible for this emphasis was Milner, who foresaw that military intervention would raise difficult political problems demanding solution by Allied representatives on the spot. Milner wanted to send to Siberia an Allied commission of senior officials possessed of considerable discretionary powers. In order to assure U.S. participation, he was willing to see an American as its head and suggested Herbert Hoover for the position.[37]

[36] Chaikovsky was originally named to the Directorate. Because he could not leave his post at Archangel, an S-R was named to take his place. It was also hoped that General Alekseyev could come to Omsk to take part in the new government, but he died on 8 October.

[37] Milner's views on this point were summarised to Wiseman in New York in Arthur Murray's telegram CXP 692, 13 July 1918; Wiseman MSS.

When it became clear, as July passed into August, that the American idea of intervention was very different from the British, Milner nevertheless pressed the Cabinet to send out a British political commissioner even if the other Allies did not.[38] Accordingly, on 2 August, the position of British High Commissioner for Siberia was offered to Sir Charles N. E. Eliot, the 54-year-old Vice-Chancellor of Hong Kong University. Eliot was a sound choice: after a Fellowship at Trinity College, Oxford, he had spent seventeen years in the diplomatic service, including five years at St. Petersburg, and had capably carried out many difficult assignments. In Siberia he was to represent the British government in all political questions and have direct control over and be responsible for all British agencies other than the military and naval commands, including any that might be established for economic relief.[39] When Eliot had accepted the post, the government informed the Allies of his selection and urged them to make similar appointments.[40]

The reactions of the various governments to the British overture were characteristic of their attitudes towards intervention. To the Americans, political commissioners smacked of political interference, and they refused to appoint one.[41] The Japanese government also refused to appoint a High Commissioner. Instead, they established a Department of Political Affairs in the general headquarters of their expeditionary force at Vladivostok.[42] So far as Japan was concerned, the Army was running intervention; the Army would also take charge of its political aspects. Only the French welcomed the British overture as, indeed, they had welcomed the idea of intervention, and they appointed their Ambassador in Japan, E. L. G. Regnault, as their High Commissioner. But because the French made only a very small material contribution to Siberian intervention, Regnault's actual influence proved to be slight.

In the tangle of Siberian events it was impossible to separate the political aspects of intervention from the military. This was especially

---

[38] Murray to Wiseman, New York, telegram 713, 3 August 1918; Wiseman MSS.

[39] Balfour to Sir Charles Eliot, Hong Kong, through Sir J. Jordan, Peking, telegram 411, 2 August 1918, 4 p.m.; Milner MSS, unfiled folder 32.

[40] British Chargé to the Acting Secretary of State, 11 August 1918; *Foreign Relations, 1918, Russia*, vol. II, pp. 339-40.

[41] Secretary of State to the French Ambassador, 31 August 1918; *ibid.*, p. 362.

[42] Greene to Foreign Office, unnumbered telegram, Tokyo, 22 August 1918, 10:30 a.m.; Milner MSS, unfiled folder 32.

the case because one of the primary objects of both the British and the French was to organise and equip a new Russian Army for service on a restored Eastern Front. From August 1918 onwards large British and French military missions began to arrive in Siberia to carry out this programme. These missions were necessarily swept right into the heart of Russian political intrigue. They could not help but exercise a decisive influence on internal politics because it was their task to determine which Russian factions should receive Allied support and material assistance and thus become the new Russian Army. This is what Balfour meant when he wrote in July that "however strong and genuine" was the British government's desire "to keep out of Russian politics" it would "probably be in practice almost impossible to prevent intervention having some (perhaps a great) effect on Russian Parties."[43] For the politics of civil war are naturally power politics in the rawest sense of the term. This fact can be stated in no better terms than those used by Admiral Aleksandr Vasilevich Kolchak in conversation with General Knox when they met in Tokyo in August 1918. "I said," Kolchak later related,

that the organization of a government in such circumstances was possible under one condition only: this government must lean on an armed force at its disposal. This factor determines the question . . . for without it government will be a fiction and anyone else who has an armed force at his disposal can take power into his hands.[44]

When Kolchak put these views to Knox, the two were meeting for the first time. At 45, Kolchak was three years the younger. His career had been highly distinguished not only as a naval officer (he had achieved considerable success as commander of the Black Sea Fleet in 1916) but also as an oceanographer and Arctic explorer. In April 1917 he was invited to America to advise the U.S. Navy on the use of mines. Returning to Russia via the Far East, he arrived in Tokyo on the fateful day of 8 November 1917. Immediately he called upon Sir Conyngham Greene and volunteered for service in the British Army (he felt that his high rank might embarrass the Royal Navy). His offer was gratefully accepted, but before he could report for staff

[43] Cited above, Chapter VII, footnote 89.
[44] Elena Varneck and H. H. Fisher, eds., *The Testimony of Kolchak and other Siberian Materials*, Stanford University, California, 1935, p. 142. This volume contains the transcript of Kolchak's interrogation by a Bolshevik commission before his execution in February 1920.

duty on the Mesopotamian front, the Russian Minister at Peking asked London for his services in re-organising Russian forces in the Far East.[45]

Kolchak then went to Harbin and became commander of Horvat's forces. But instead of employing them against the Bolsheviks, he had to use them simply to keep order and to threaten marauders like Semenov who consistently encroached on Horvat's domains. Kolchak quickly grew disgusted with Harbin and its atmosphere of intrigue and plotting. He was especially troubled by the Japanese officers in Manchuria who, while professing their support for his efforts, constantly worked to frustrate them. In late June he told the British Military Attaché of his conviction that Japan's policy was to oppose any attempts like his own to establish a strong Russian central authority, and to support instead a number of weak Russian forces, such as Semenov's, which could serve as façades for Japanese entrenchment in Siberia.[46]

In his behaviour and bearing Kolchak was an attractive and honourable man. His military record in the past had shown that he was capable of acting with vigour and intelligence. The contrast between him and most of the other Russian officers in the Far East was immense. It was no wonder, therefore, that after their interview on 31 August Knox should report: ". . . there is no doubt he is the best Russian for our purpose in the Far East. . . ."[47] At this meeting Kolchak presented Knox with a memorandum he had drafted on the re-organisation of a Russian Army. The two men agreed that only with British supervision, instructors, and materials could the immense task be undertaken. They would have to start at the beginning, even retraining the existing officers and non-commissioned officers, so completely had the rot of indiscipline set in.[48]

Shortly after this meeting Kolchak left Harbin, convinced that the regeneration of Russia would never come from the Far East. On his way to the south, where he hoped to join Alekseyev, he stopped in Omsk. There he was pressed by Boldyrev into accepting the port-

[45] There exists no better account of Kolchak's background than his own striking testimony in *ibid.*, pp. 9-148.

[46] Reported by Jordan to Balfour, telegram 541, Peking, 27 June 1918, 9:45 p.m.; Milner MSS, box E-1.

[47] Knox to Director of Military Intelligence, telegram 9, Vladivostok, 31 August 1918, 12:40 p.m.; Milner MSS, unfiled folder 32.

[48] *idem.* See also Varneck and Fisher, *Kolchak*, p. 142.

Parade marking arrival in Vladivostok of Japanese and American troops in
August 1918. In the foreground is a unit of Czechs; behind them along the
town's main street comes the British 25th Middlesex Battalion

Major-General Alfred Knox (seated) in his headquarters in the British Military Mission, Vladivostok; beside him is his assistant, Lieutenant-Colonel J. M. Blair

Admiral Aleksandr V. Kolchak shortly after assuming the position of Supreme Ruler in November 1918

Kolchak's headquarters at Omsk, November 1918

folio of Minister of War in the Siberian government and was given the task of organising that body's 200,000 raw recruits into an army. It was then mid-October. Word had just reached Omsk that Alekseyev had died.

Meanwhile, within the British government there was considerable concern at the weakness and lack of unity among the various anti-Bolshevik factions in Russia. Lord Robert Cecil raised the problem in a short note to his Cabinet colleagues in early September. He doubted whether it would be possible for a democratic republic to become established in the Russia of that time. But he also felt that if Allied intervention became identified with restoration of the monarchy, the results would be disastrous. And he continued:

To re-establish order in Russia will be a herculean task. No half-baked constitutionalism could possibly succeed in it. The only possible way out seems to be a provisional military Government to be followed when order has really been re-established by a constitutional assembly. Whether the military dictatorship, once in power, will be content to abdicate seems very doubtful—indeed, one may say it certainly will not unless under the influence of the Western democracies. We should therefore aim at securing military chiefs whom we can trust, supporting them financially as well as by armed force and making ourselves indispensable to them. . . . It should be remembered that a permanent military despotism in Russia would be a very serious menace to the peace of the world.[49]

On 9 September, the same line of argument was set forth by Balfour in a telegram of "general considerations" for the guidance of Sir Charles Eliot. The Foreign Secretary was much concerned that the apparent success of Allied military intervention was accompanied by increased quarrelling among the anti-Bolshevik elements themselves. Unless they could compose their differences, they would inevitably meet with disaster. The British government, Balfour said, very much disliked having to intervene in Russian internal politics and naturally hoped that the Russian people themselves would establish an administration sufficiently reliable to enable the Allies to avoid the alternatives either of imposing one section of Russian political opinion as the

[49] Cecil's note was written to accompany a paper by Polyakov, the London correspondent of the newspaper *Russkoye Slovo*, giving the case for moderate republicanism in Russia. Polyakov's paper is worthless, and it is surprising that Cecil took up his colleagues' time with it, especially as he disagreed with its premises. Both are undated, but textual evidence and their position in box C-1 of the Milner MSS indicates that the time was early September 1918.

ruling authority or of having to set up a military occupation of their own.

Although these were the government's hopes, the telegram continued, the outlook did not seem very promising, and it might well happen that the various rival Russian factions could be reconciled only under a provisional military government. Such a government "would have to be presided over by a Russian who has won his position by his own personality" and whose strength rested on Russian, not Allied support, although of course the Allies would help him. Unfortunately, however, there seemed to be no outstanding Russian who was clearly suitable. The "nearest approach" seemed to be Alekseyev. Therefore, while Eliot was to do nothing to suggest Alekseyev for such a position, he should support him if there were indications that a movement under his leadership, with Allied help, seemed likely to succeed.[50]

If the idea of a military dictatorship seemed attractive from the detachment of London, it was infinitely more appealing to British representatives faced with the actual chaos of Siberia. As September wore on into October, these representatives seized upon the Siberian Provisional Government at Omsk because it seemed much stronger than the various other "governments" in Siberia. Moreover, its western location meant that it was removed from the choking intrigue of Vladivostok and Harbin, and out of the reach of Japan. Yet the Omsk government was also an object of despair: it seemed ultimately incapable of instituting the real discipline and efficiency that would be necessary to save Russia.

General Knox, the most important of the British representatives, devoted himself to the reconstruction of a Russian Army. His position was an extremely difficult one because of the confused relations among the intervening Powers themselves. Knox's precise status was only that of Chief of the British Mission attached to the staff of General Otani, the Japanese Supreme Commander of all Allied forces in Siberia. The Japanese, it will be remembered, had insisted upon the supreme command because of their "special position," and both the British and the Americans had assented. There was no formal agreement to this effect, but the *de facto* situation was recognised by the Japanese appointment of a full general to command their forces,

[50] Balfour to Eliot, Vladivostok, telegram 26, 9 September 1918, 7:30 p.m.; Milner MSS, box E-2.

while both Knox and Graves, the American commander, were major-generals.

From the outset the relations between the British and the Japanese in Siberia were frigid to a point of hostility, despite the warm tones in which London and Tokyo assured each other of the strength of the Anglo-Japanese Alliance. Not only would the Japanese move no farther west than Harbin (only one Japanese battalion ever got as far as Irkutsk) but they persisted in supporting Horvat and Semenov, each of whom was much more concerned with carving out little personal spheres of power than with reconstructing a Russian Army. Semenov especially, whom the British government had once been so eager to support, had proved to be little more than a bandit.[51] His Mongol troops even went so far as to hold up traffic on the railroads and rob and murder travellers. They were, moreover, unspeakably brutal in their methods, often machine-gunning all of their prisoners *en masse*.[52] In mid-October, Knox reported that Semenov was wholly in the pay of the Japanese and that General Otani had offered him the command of all Cossacks east of Lake Baikal. This move infuriated Knox, who had been working to place all Russian forces under the authority of Omsk; he strongly contended that Otani's position as the commander of Allied forces did not give him the power to take such a step without the consent or even the knowledge of the other Allies.[53] And in early November it was learned that the Japanese General Staff had completed arrangements with Semenov and Kalmykov, a lesser Cossack ataman whose methods were perhaps even more brutal than Semenov's,[54] for them to organise their own 20,000-man army entirely financed and equipped by Japan.[55]

The British complaints against the Japanese were not simply that

[51] Knox to War Office, telegram 41, Vladivostok, 2 October 1918, 10:40 a.m.; Milner MSS, box D-3.

[52] The papers of the American Ambassador in Japan, Roland S. Morris, in the Library of Congress contain documentary evidence (mostly eye-witness reports by U.S. Army officers) of Semenov's incredible bestiality. Morris' papers also contain many similar accounts of equally barbaric acts by Japanese troops.

[53] Knox to War Office, Irkutsk, 18 October 1918 (transmitted as telegram 106 from Blair, Vladivostok, 22 October, 2:50 p.m.); Milner MSS, box E-2.

[54] The chronicler of the White Armies writes: "Kalmykov not only ordered the sacking of villages and wholesale robberies, but beat and killed with his own hands." (Stewart, *White Armies*, p. 141; see also pp. 258-61, 312-14.)

[55] Morris to Secretary of State, Tokyo, 7 November 1918, 4 p.m.; *Foreign Relations, 1918, Russia*, vol. II, p. 428.

they were promoting division instead of unity in Siberia. Report after report emphasised their total disregard of the Russian population; Knox telegraphed that they treated all Russians "as swine."[56] In the words of a Foreign Office memorandum circulated to the Cabinet at the end of 1919, summarising all that had happened in Siberia since the Bolshevik Revolution:

The Japanese accompanied their entry into Siberia with the usual proclamation of disinterestedness. The proclamation affirmed the constant desire of Japan to promote relations of enduring friendship with Russia and the Russian people, and reaffirmed her avowed policy of respecting the territorial integrity of Russia and of abstaining from all interference in her internal politics. . . . Nevertheless a self-seeking and obstructive attitude on the part of the Japanese became evident at once. Their first action on arrival in Vladivostock and in Khabarovsk was to occupy high-handedly a huge number of public and private buildings at enormous cost without any reference to the Russian authorities. . . . The Amur steamers they seized as prizes of war. Their progress through the country was marked by utter contempt of the population, and they proceeded to occupy pacified territory in the rear with a force five times stronger than was required, while doing nothing to help the half-armed and half-clothed Russians and Czechs to fight. The immediate impression created was that they were endeavouring by every means in their power to prevent the establishment of a strong Central Government with a single army, and their behaviour was generally described as that of a people who intend to annex what they have occupied.[57]

In mid-October Japanese soldiers guarding the Amur Railway detained a train carrying Colonel Ward and his battalion to Omsk and held up a later train on which Knox was travelling and tried to arrest him.[58] Both Ward and Knox were eventually allowed to

[56] In addition to Knox's telegram of 18 October, cited above, from which this phrase is taken, see Col. Blair's telegram 97 to War Office, 21 October, 2:10 p.m., and Alston's telegram 199 to Balfour, 31 October, 4:5 p.m. (both from Vladivostok); Milner MSS, box E-2.

[57] Memorandum on Siberia by J. D. Gregory, chief of the Foreign Office's Northern Department, circulated to the Cabinet on 20 December 1919; printed, with some abridgements, in *Documents on British Foreign Policy 1919-1939*, series I, vol. III, London, 1949, pp. 700-32. The section quoted here, on p. 727, is followed immediately by the statement: "It must not, however, be forgotten that military occupation even in a friendly area is inclined to be uncompromising, and even General Poole treated Archangel and the surrounding territories as a conquered country."

[58] Sir Charles Eliot to Balfour, 23 October 1918, Omsk (through Alston, Vladivostok, as telegram 184, 25 October, 8:20 a.m.); Milner MSS, box E-2.

continue on their way, but no incidents could better have characterised Anglo-Japanese relations in Siberia.

Ward's 25th Middlesex Battalion was on its way to Omsk to serve
on garrison duty and help preserve order in the town. Knox was on
an urgent mission to convince General Boldyrev, the Supreme Commander of the troops at Omsk, that he had to make drastic changes if
he were ever to raise an effective army. Before he set out for Omsk,
Knox had reported:

> I know shortcomings of these people, but fear that to find any real states-
> men in Russia is impossible. If this Government falls we may have anarch-
> ists or at best a Government of sentimental socialists that will never allow
> an army to be raised and will prepare way for the return of Bolshevism
> and the Germans.[59]

Knox wanted Boldyrev to cut down drastically on the number of
men the Siberian government had called up, for there were neither
enough officers to lead them nor enough funds to pay them. If these
measures were not taken and discipline not drastically tightened,
Knox predicted, there would be only an armed rabble instead of
an army.[60]

Knox's talks with Boldyrev and Kolchak, the Minister of War,
resulted in an agreement signed on 24 October. Knox promised to do
all in his power "to assist the Russian Government in organising a
Russian army" if several conditions were fulfilled: full control was
to be in the hands of the officers with no committees or commissars
of any kind among the rank and file; neither officers nor men were
"to mix in politics"; the Omsk government was to demand that the
Allies (i.e. the Japanese) give all aid through Omsk and none to
Semenov or Kalmykov; all promotions and appointments (i.e., Semenov's by the Japanese) were to be made only from Omsk; and
Horvat's troops were to be disbanded.[61]

Knox left Omsk for Vladivostok before the merger on 5 November
of the Directorate and the Siberian government. During his stay he

[59] Knox to War Office, telegram 31, Vladivostok, 29 September 1918, 6:40 a.m.;
Milner MSS, box D-3.
[60] Knox to War Office, telegram 70, Vladivostok, 9 October 1918, 3:5 p.m.; Milner
MSS, box D-3.
[61] The text of the agreement is in V. Boldyrev, *Direktoriya, Kolchak, Interventy.
Vospominamiya* (The Directorate, Kolchak, and the Interventionists. Reminiscences),
Novonikolaevsk, 1925, p. 524; a translation appears in Bunyan, *Intervention*,
pp. 365-66.

had been troubled by the division between the two groups, for it obviously weakened their armed forces. He clearly favoured the Siberian government because it was not socialist, and he ostentatiously paid no official call on Avksentiev, the S-R chairman of the Directorate, and had no contact with its members as a body. Boldyrev (who, after all, was a member of the Directorate and was responsible to it, not to the Siberian government) repeatedly emphasised to Knox that the leadership of the anti-Bolshevik movement belonged not to any general or generals, but to the government—the Directorate. The British officer, Boldyrev wrote, refused to admit any point of contact between a general and a socialist. On 25 October, at tea, Knox jokingly warned Boldyrev that if the Directorate did not come to terms with the Siberian government, he would organise a gang and overthrow them.[62]

By this time, after Alekseyev's death, London had also focussed attention upon Omsk. On 27 October Balfour telegraphed Eliot the government's opinion that the situation seemed to depend entirely upon the formation at Omsk of a really strong Russian government, with disciplined armed forces. The Foreign Secretary asked if Eliot and Knox agreed, and cautioned them to remember that in view of the attitudes demonstrated by Japan and America almost all of the task of providing and shipping war materials to Russia would fall upon Britain and France.[63]

From Irkutsk, on 3 November, Eliot replied that he and Knox agreed that it would be disastrous to stop active co-operation with Omsk at that moment, and that the arrangements at Omsk, although far from perfect, represented an honest attempt to restore order which certainly deserved support if the present difficulties—the division between the Directorate and the Siberian government—could be surmounted. And Eliot added a special message from Knox:

. . . Large forces and material aid are not required but what we want is immediate decision enabling us to inform Russian Government what they may expect and when; as it is, everyone is naturally losing faith. If we retire now, re-establishment of Bolshevism will mean general massacre.[64]

[62] Boldyrev, *Direktoriya*, p. 84.

[63] Balfour to Eliot (as telegram 128 through Alston at Vladivostok), 27 October 1918, 5 p.m.; Milner MSS, box E-2.

[64] Eliot to Balfour, 3 November 1918, Irkutsk (sent through Alston at Vladivostok as telegram 213, 6 November, 9:35 a.m.); Milner MSS, box E-2.

Amidst considerations of this sort London received the news that the Directorate and the Siberian government had finally come to terms with each other and established a unified authority. Moreover the war in Europe had just ended; the time was ripe for a Russian policy which involved, perhaps, a few more risks. On 14 November, therefore, the War Cabinet made the momentous decision to recognise the new amalgamated government as a *de facto* government.[65]

News of this recognition, however, was never made public nor even conveyed to the authorities at Omsk. For on the night of 17 November a group of officers arrested and kidnapped four socialist ministers of the amalgamated government, including Avksentiev and Zenzinov, the two S-R members of the Directorate. From early the next morning until shortly after noon the Council of Ministers met in extraordinary session and at last decided to dissolve the government and offer all civil and military power to Admiral Kolchak, who would be called Supreme Ruler. Kolchak accepted the position; the military dictatorship which London had thought so necessary had come.

These are the bare facts. They would be sufficient for our narrative but for the many accusations which have linked the British government in general, and General Knox in particular, with the plot that brought Kolchak to power. The most specific accusations were made by General Maurice Janin, who had been commander-in-chief of all Czech forces and who, at the time of the Kolchak coup, had just arrived in Vladivostok to take personal command of the Czech troops in Siberia and to head the French Military Mission. In a report to the French Ministry of War in June 1920, Janin wrote that the British wanted "a government to themselves" in Siberia so that they could demand from it the concession of Turkestan and all its riches as the price for their intervention. Therefore, Janin said, they recalled Kolchak after he had set out for the Mesopotamian front and sent him to Omsk, where "with the experience that they had acquired at Petrograd and at Archangel of Russian coups d'état, the English organised, with a band of Russian monarchist officers, a coup

---

[65] "Diary, Short History of Events," cited above, Chapter v, footnote 30. The fact of this recognition is also stated in Winston S. Churchill, *The Aftermath*, London, 1929, p. 164. Neither of these sources say what it was recognised *as*. Presumably, it was as the government of Siberia.

d'état whose consequences were the ruin of Siberia."[66] In his memoirs, written much later, Janin wrote that Knox had organised the coup during the ten days or so he spent in Omsk at the end of October before he left for Vladivostok (where he was going, as a matter of fact, to meet Janin). Knox wanted the plot carried out before Janin's arrival in Omsk, the French general wrote, because of Janin's friendship with General Boldyrev. Janin further stated that a British officer on Knox's staff, Captain Steveni, was present at the meeting of Russian officers in which the actual workings of the plot were planned.[67] One of Janin's assistants, General J. Rouquérol, has made this same statement, although he did not mention Steveni by name.[68] And Noulens (who was in Archangel at the time) wrote that the officers of Knox's entourage were "seduced by the sporting side" of their general's adventure and hence took part in it most willingly.[69]

Russian accounts are much more circumspect than these French memoirs. Subbotovsky, the Soviet historian who wrote from the captured archives of the Kolchak government, merely states (without citing any evidence) that Knox "was one of those military foreigners to whom Kolchak owed his elevation to the post of Supreme Ruler."[70] Boldyrev, who was at the front at the time of the actual coup, makes no specific accusations against Knox, but states that he was the "primary inspiration" (glavnim vdokhnovitel'em) of the change in government.[71] Milyukov, writing in 1922, states only that it was

[66] Janin's report to the Ministry of War is printed in L. H. Grondijs, *Le Cas-Koltchak—Contribution à l'histoire de la Révolution Russe*, Leiden, Netherlands, 1939, p. 233. In his reference to Petrograd Janin presumably meant the Kornilov affair.

[67] General Maurice Janin, *Ma mission en Sibérie*, Paris, 1933, pp. 30-31.

[68] General J. Rouquérol, *L'Aventure de l'Amiral Koltchak: La Guerre des Rouges et des Blancs*, Paris, 1929, p. 44.

[69] Noulens, *Mon ambassade*, vol. II, p. 255. Another member of the French military mission, Lt.-Colonel Pichon (who was in Chelyabinsk at the time of the coup), wrote that there was "no doubt" that Kolchak was "the man of General Knox." Pichon makes no specific allegations, however, and is mainly concerned with showing that the French had no connection with the affair. ("Le coup d'État de l'amiral Kolčak," *Le Monde Slave*, Paris, 1925, no. 2, p. 259.)

[70] I. Subbotovsky, *Soyuzniki, russkie reaktsionery i interventsiya; kratkii obzor (Iskliuchitelno po offitsial'nym arkhivnym dokumentam Kolchakovskogo pravitel'stva)* (The Allies, Russian Reactionaries and Intervention; a Brief Outline. Exclusively from Official Archive Documents of the Kolchak Government), Leningrad, 1926, pp. 25-26.

[71] Boldyrev, *Direktoriya*, p. 523, n. 77.

known that Knox approved of the arrest of Avksentiev.[72] G. K. Guins, a civil servant under the old regime who became a minor member of Kolchak's government and who left a surprisingly dispassionate account of his experiences, wrote that the "legend that Kolchak was the creature of Knox" grew simply from Knox's warm welcome of the Admiral's selection as Minister of War in the Siberian government, and his statement that this selection assured the assistance of Great Britain.[73] And even recent Soviet accounts, although filled with dark accusations against the Allies, do not suggest that they had any direct connection with the events which brought Kolchak to power.[74]

What part, then, did the British government and General Knox have in the coup? So far as the government was concerned, none whatsoever. We have seen that on 14 November the War Cabinet decided to recognise the Provisional Government headed by the Directorate as a *de facto* government. Such a step would hardly have been taken if London had had any inkling of the forthcoming events. Indeed, on the very eve of the coup the Foreign Office was drafting a telegram to Omsk announcing the recognition.[75]

As for Knox, it is impossible to say for certain, but it is most probable that his part in the affair was no more than that of a warm sympathiser.[76] He had arrived in Omsk in mid-October with the task of restoring military efficiency to the Russian Army. Obviously this task was made much more difficult by the weakness of the governmental arrangements at Omsk—a weakness due to the tension be-

---

[72] Paul N. Milyukov, *Russia Today and Tomorrow*, New York, 1922, p. 152.

[73] G. K. Guins, *Sibir, soyuzniki i Kolchak. Povorotnyi moment russkoi istorii. 1918-1920 g.g.: Vpechatleniya i mysli chlena Omskago pravitel'stva* (Siberia, the Allies and Kolchak. The Turning Point of Russian History, 1918-1920: Impressions and Thoughts of a Member of the Omsk Government), Peking, 1921, vol. I, p. 276.

[74] Volkov, *Krakh angliiskoi politiki*, although giving an account of British aid to Kolchak subsequent to the coup, does not even discuss the actual coup. *Istoriya grazhdanskoy voiny*, vol. III, indicates that the coup was both conceived and executed entirely by reactionary Russian officers (p. 334).

[75] So says Nabokov, the White Chargé d'Affaires in London, who was told of the telegram by Lord Robert Cecil in an interview on 19 November (Nabokoff, *Ordeal*, p. 276).

[76] Knox himself has naturally denied any connection with the coup. In his only published statement on the matter he wrote: ". . . the *coup d'état* which placed Kolchak in power . . . was carried out by the Siberian Government without the previous knowledge, and without in any sense the connivance of Great Britain." (*Slavonic Review*, vol. 3, no. 9, March 1925, p. 724; Knox was reviewing General Janin's "Fragment de Mon Journal Sibérien," *Le Monde Slave*, December 1924—the "Fragment" later was incorporated into Janin's memoirs.)

tween the conservatives of the Siberian government and the socialists of the Directorate. During Knox's stay, on 24 October, the Central Committee of the Socialist-Revolutionary Party published a manifesto by Chernov, the former President of the Constituent Assembly, denouncing as reactionary the Siberian government and the many officers who had flocked to its colours, severely criticising the Directorate for its failure to assert socialist principles, and calling upon all S-R's to arm themselves to fight the counter-revolution.[77] Naturally this proclamation aroused enormous indignation in military circles, an indignation heightened by the fact that the socialist members of the Directorate refused to sanction any measures against Chernov and the others responsible for it. Knox is reported to have warned that if such socialist agitation were continued the Directorate could expect no further help from the Allies, and to have recommended that Chernov be shot.[78]

While Knox was in Omsk he mingled and talked freely with the higher Russian officers—he got on particularly well with their type—and he certainly did not hesitate to say exactly where his sympathies lay.[79] It is doubtful whether he ever took part in any active plotting, however; if he went so far as to suggest a coup, it seems highly unlikely that he would have done so in any way except informally—certainly not in the name of the British government. As for Captain Steveni, it is not inconceivable that he did take part in the meeting at which the plot was formulated. Steveni was from an old British St. Petersburg family. Since the early summer of 1918 he had been used for liaison with various anti-Bolshevik groups in Siberia. His telegrams to the War Office leave no doubt as to his political views: he was a bitter anti-socialist and, indeed, a thorough-going reactionary who desired a complete restoration of the Tsarist regime.[80] There is no way of telling whether he actually took part in the plot, but if he

[77] The manifesto is printed in Bunyan, *Intervention*, pp. 362-65.

[78] Cited by Varneck and Fisher, *Kolchak*, p. 247, n. 188, from V. M. Zenzinov (ed.), *Gosudarstvennyi perevorot Admirala Kolchaka v Omske 18 noyabrya 1918 goda. Sbornik documentov* (Coup d'état of Admiral Kolchak at Omsk, 18 November 1918. Collection of Documents), Paris, 1919, p. 191.

[79] Boldyrev, *Direktoriya*, p. 79.

[80] See Steveni's telegram 17 to Director of Military Intelligence from Harbin, 16 July 1918, 2:35 a.m., strongly urging Allied support of Horvat as an alternative to socialism and a way to restore order and discipline on a pre-revolutionary basis; Milner MSS, box E-2. Steveni's other telegrams in this box are in a similar vein.

did, it was in all probability on his own initiative and not under Knox's orders.

All this has been conjecture. But there is one way in which there is no doubt that the plotters were significantly assisted by British soldiers. It will be recalled that Colonel Ward's 25th Middlesex Battalion had come to Omsk in mid-October to help keep order in the town. During the night of 17-18 November, after he had learned that the socialist ministers had been kidnapped, he alerted all his troops. As it happened, his cantonment was directly next to the building where the Council of Ministers met on the 18th in the long session which eventually resulted in Kolchak's nomination as Supreme Ruler. Ward's machine guns covered every street in the surrounding neighbourhood. Their presence during these crucial hours was enough to discourage the interference of any other armed force, such as the Czechs who were garrisoned on the outskirts of the town. The Czechs were extremely hostile to the reactionary Russian officers; had they known that the ministerial session was going to result in a dictatorship, they might well have acted to prevent it. Ward wrote of his actions:

That these arrangements gave the Ministers greater confidence to proceed with their policy I have no doubt. That was one of the inevitable consequences of the preparations for our own defence . . . it did steady the situation.[81]

Ward also performed one other important service for the new government. He warned Kolchak that although he himself felt that the circumstances justified the arrest of the four socialists, their execution would make it impossible for the Admiral's regime to obtain aid or recognition from the British government. Kolchak fully agreed, and it was arranged that the prisoners would travel with a guard of British soldiers to Vladivostok, and from there leave Russia for Paris.[82]

Ward remained one of Kolchak's staunchest supporters throughout his tour of duty in Siberia and afterwards when he had returned to the House of Commons. His enthusiasm was shared by another British officer in Omsk, Colonel Nielson, a member of Knox's staff, who supplied London with the first reports on the *coup d'état*. Nielson was firmly convinced, he telegraphed the War Office, that the

[81] Ward, *"Die-Hards,"* p. 130.
[82] *ibid.*, pp. 135-38.

coup represented an "absolutely honest attempt to restore order" and that if it had not taken place, there soon would have been "Bolshevik S-R risings." He was also convinced that the arrested members of the Directorate were fully in sympathy with the Chernov manifesto. Kolchak, he reported, had no intention of restoring the monarchy—his only policy was "salvation of Russia." Nielson commented: "I believe him to be sincere and I am prepared to guarantee this."[83]

Sir Charles Eliot, however, was less sanguine. From Vladivostok, where he learned of the coup, he telegraphed that Kolchak had many estimable traits, but that he was said to be an indifferent administrator and to suffer from nervous irritability which at times amounted almost to a disease. It did not seem probable, Eliot thought, that Kolchak could continue long in office or compete with Denikin (who had taken Alekseyev's place in the south) as the leader of all Russia when communications were restored between Siberia and Europe. And he warned that while Kolchak would have considerable support from all the moderate parties of Siberia, he would have to count on the opposition both of the Japanese, who were hostile to him personally as well as to all attempts to establish a strong central government, and of the Czechs, who were bitterly resentful that their sacrifices on the Volga front had resulted only in the establishment of a dictatorship.[84]

In London, the government's reaction to the events in Omsk was to take a much more cautious view of anti-Bolshevik politics. Britain had been ready to recognise the Directorate, only to find it had been swept away. Who could tell, Lord Robert Cecil asked Nabokov when they met on 19 November, whether the same thing would not happen again within another three weeks? How was the government to be expected to arrive at any decisions on Russia in such circumstances? The only course would be to wait and see what happened.[85]

[83] Nielson to War Office, Omsk, 19 November 1918 (through Knox in Vladivostok as telegram 253, 20 November, 5:5 p.m.); Milner MSS, box E-2.

[84] Eliot to Balfour, telegram 252, Vladivostok, 19 November 1918, 5:50 p.m.; Milner MSS, box E-2.

[85] Nabokoff, *Ordeal*, p. 277.

CHAPTER X

THE BEGINNING OF INTERVENTION:
REPERCUSSIONS IN MOSCOW

We had been caught like rats in a trap.—*Lockhart, in "Retreat from Glory"*

INEVITABLY, intervention in North Russia and Siberia had grave repercussions upon Lockhart and the other British officials and private residents still remaining in Russia. For all of them, intervention meant constant fear; for a large proportion it meant arrest and imprisonment; and for one it meant violent death.

Curiously, there was never a definite breaking-off of relations between Britain and the Bolshevik regime. On 29 July, before the landings at Archangel or Vladivostok, but with Maynard's force firmly entrenched at Murmansk, Czech troops on the Volga, and the Yaroslavl revolt just quelled, Lenin told a meeting of the Moscow Soviet that war had come once again, and the enemy was Anglo-French imperialism.[1] Puzzled and worried, Lockhart, together with the French, American, and Italian consuls-general, called on Chicherin to ask if Lenin's speech was, in fact, to be regarded as a declaration of war, with the consequent rupture of *de facto* relations and the departure of all the Allied officials. Chicherin's reply was evasive; there existed, he said, not a state of war but a "state of defence" which did not necessarily imply a rupture of relations. The Soviet government, said the Commissar, desired, indeed, to continue its relations with the Entente Powers.[2]

Neither did London desire a break. For a break would imply that intervention was aimed against the Soviet regime as well as against Germany. When Balfour received Lockhart's report of Chicherin's

---

[1] Lenin's speech is printed in his *Sochineniya*, vol. XXIII, pp. 151-64.

[2] Lockhart to Balfour, telegram 347, Moscow, 1 August 1918; Milner MSS, unfiled folder 23. See also *Foreign Relations, 1918, Russia*, vol. I, p. 641.

explanation, the troops had already landed at Archangel. Nevertheless on 8 August he sent the following instructions in reply:

You should, as far as possible, maintain existing relations with Bolshevik Government. Rupture, or declaration of war should come, if come it must, from Bolsheviks not from Allies.[3]

Moscow learned of the Archangel landings on 4 August. Initial reports were wildly exaggerated. The lowest estimate stated that two divisions had landed; some reports put the figure as high as 100,000 men. The Japanese were said to be sending seven divisions through Siberia to help the Czechs on the Volga. Even the most optimistic Bolsheviks saw the end of their regime in sight.[4] In this atmosphere of despair Chicherin addressed a letter to the American Consul-General, DeWitt C. Poole, implying that Britain was the guiding spirit behind intervention and asking just what Poole thought Britain wanted from the Bolsheviks. Chicherin asked:

Is it Britain's aim to destroy the most popular Government that the world has ever known, the Soviets of the poor and the peasants? Is its aim counter-revolution? . . . I must assume that this is so. We must assume that Great Britain intends to restore the worst tyranny in the world, odious Tsarism. Or does it intend to seize certain towns, or a part of our territory?[5]

Before dawn on 5 August, in retaliation for the landings, the Cheka arrested and interned some 200 British and French residents of Moscow. Chicherin stated that they were being held as hostages; if Allied troops in North Russia continued to shoot Bolshevik prisoners the Soviet government could not be responsible for the fate of Allied residents.[6] Despite Chicherin's assurances that consular officials would not be included, the police descended on the British Consulate-General and arrested every member of the staff except Consul-General Oliver Wardrop, who quietly burned confidential papers in his locked office while the arrests were being made. Lockhart and Hicks, as diplomatic officials, were also spared. A few hours later, the French consulate suffered a similar raid.[7]

[3] Balfour to Lockhart, Moscow, telegram 233, 8 August 1918, 7:30 p.m.; Milner MSS, box C-1.

[4] Lockhart, *British Agent*, pp. 308-9.

[5] Chicherin's letter to Poole, 5 August 1918, is in *Dokumenty vneshnei politiki*, vol. I, pp. 418-19. A translation is in Degras, *Soviet Documents*, vol. I, pp. 93-95. Poole did not reply.

[6] So Chicherin told U.S. Consul-General Poole on 5 August. See Poole's report in *Foreign Relations, 1918, Russia*, vol. I, p. 642.

[7] Wardrop to Balfour, 5 August 1918. This despatch and others from Wardrop concerning the closing of the British Consulate-General were printed in the White

The internment of the consular staffs lasted only a few days. By 9 August all British officials and all except twenty-five private residents had been released;[8] Moscow had learned how small, in fact, were the forces landing in Archangel. All the dejection of the previous few days had gone, Lockhart recorded. The Bolsheviks could afford to relax their measures against the Allied communities.[9] Nevertheless, the Allied consuls had learned how powerless they were in the face of rising Soviet anger, and on the 9th they all took down their flags and handed over their premises and the task of representing their national interests to their neutral colleagues. Britain's interests were entrusted to the Netherlands. Wardrop relinquished his responsibilities with a heavy heart. To Balfour he wrote:

For many months I have done my best to induce British subjects to leave, and have publicly warned them of the risks they incurred, and denied all responsibility for the consequences if my warnings were neglected; nevertheless I cannot entirely overcome my feeling of discomfort. My only consolation is that I can be of no further use to my nationals here, and a neutral will be infinitely better able to help them.[10]

Wardrop's nationals, although most of them had been released, were far from out of danger. As the consuls set about making arrangements to enable themselves and their countrymen to leave Russia, Chicherin announced that the British would not be allowed to leave until Litvinov and all his staff had left England, and that the French would be held until all Russian soldiers serving in France had been permitted to return to Russia.[11]

So far as the British were concerned these conditions did not seem onerous. Lockhart told Chicherin he felt sure they would be acceptable: he knew of no limitations on the departure from England of Litvinov or his staff.[12] The immediate problem in securing British assent was simply that communications between the two countries were so difficult. The Allied representatives, having closed their consulates, had to communicate both with their own governments

---

Paper, Miscellaneous No. 30 (1918), *Despatches from His Majesty's Consul-General at Moscow, August 5 to 9, 1918.* (Henceforth cited as "Wardrop Despatches.")

[8] Wardrop to Balfour, 9 August; *ibid.*

[9] Lockhart, *British Agent*, p. 310.

[10] Wardrop to Balfour, 6 August; in "Wardrop Despatches."

[11] Agreement between the Soviet government and the Neutral Powers concerning the exchange of officials and soldiers, 9 August 1918, *Dokumenty vneshnei politiki*, vol. I, p. 422.

[12] As related in a Memorandum for the Swedish Consul-General from the Allied Consuls, 9 August 1918; in "Wardrop Despatches."

and with the Bolsheviks through the neutrals. Lockhart's report of Chicherin's conditions, for instance, had to be taken out of Russia by Swedish courier (telegraphic communication being so haphazard) and did not arrive in London until 28 August.[13]

London had learned of these conditions earlier, however, from Lindley, who had been informed of them in Archangel by Soviet wireless. By 23 August the Dutch Minister in Petrograd, Oudendijk, was able to send Chicherin Balfour's reply that Litvinov could leave England when he wished. Yet on the next day, the Soviet government added to its conditions the requirement that the release of interned British and French residents should coincide with the ending of repressive measures against Soviet officials and sympathisers in the Allied countries and in the territories occupied by the Czechs and by British and other Allied troops. That this had been done was to be certified by International Red Cross observers who were to be sent to the occupied regions.[14] The internees were, in fact, being held as hostages. On 26 August these conditions were rejected out of hand by the neutral ministers in Petrograd.[15] The negotiations had effectively come to a standstill.

There was never time to re-open them. On the morning of 30 August the head of the Petrograd Cheka, M. S. Uritsky, was shot dead in front of his headquarters by a military cadet; that evening, after Lenin had addressed a workers' meeting in a Moscow suburb, he himself was shot and gravely wounded by a young Left S-R named Dora Kaplan. These two unconnected events unleashed from the Bolsheviks a ruthless reign of terror. In Petrograd alone, during the next two days, over 500 political prisoners were taken out and shot. Cheka units all over Soviet territory were instructed to seize hostages and shoot them in reprisal for any opposition activities. All "White Guards" were to be shot on sight.[16]

The impact of the Terror was quickly brought home to the little British community. On 31 August, the day after the shooting of Uritsky and Lenin, an armed mob stormed into the British Embassy in Petrograd. When their way was blocked by the Naval Attaché,

[13] It is in the Milner mss, box C-1, as telegram 2435 from Stockholm, 27 August 1918, 9:20 p.m.

[14] Telegram, Chicherin to Oudendijk, Petrograd, 24 August 1918; *Dokumenty vneshnei politiki*, vol. 1, p. 437.

[15] Memorandum from the Neutral Ministers to Chicherin, Petrograd, 26 August 1918; *Foreign Relations, 1918, Russia*, vol. 1, pp. 664-65.

[16] Chamberlin, *Russian Revolution*, vol. ii, pp. 64-67.

Captain F. N. A. Cromie, the senior of the few British officials remaining in the building, he was told to stand aside or be shot down. Cromie drew his pistol and killed two of the mob before their bullets killed him. The Embassy was then searched, its archives and documents taken, and the other British officials imprisoned in the Fortress of Peter and Paul, where they were crowded together with Russian prisoners, twenty or more to a tiny unfurnished cell, and fed only with what could be brought them by the neutral legations.[17]

On 4 September, five days after Cromie's death, the Dutch Minister, Oudendijk, returned from Moscow to find Cromie's corpse, horribly mutilated, lying still unburied in the English church. Despite the protests of some of the British officials still at large that a public funeral would provoke hostile demonstrations, Oudendijk was adamant, and the neutral diplomats gave Cromie what amounted to a state funeral; as the procession slowly crossed the Nicolai Bridge on its way to the cemetery on the opposite side of the Neva, sailors lolling on the unpainted decks of destroyers moored below—all that was left of the Russian navy—rose in respect.[18] Even the German and Austrian Consuls-General were moved to join the neutral diplomatic

---

[17] See the memorandum by the Dutch Minister, Oudendijk, undated but written immediately after these events, in *Foreign Relations, 1918, Russia*, vol. i, pp. 675-77. The most graphic account of Cromie's death, by the Petrograd Correspondent of *The Times* who was in the Embassy at the time and was himself imprisoned, appeared in *The Times*, 24 October 1918.

The Soviet version of the raid on the British Embassy is vastly different. According to *Izvestiya*, 5 September 1918 (translated in Bunyan, *Intervention*, p. 147), the British "murdered Comrade Uritsky because he brought together the threads of the English conspiracy in Petrograd." The Embassy was raided by Cheka agents looking for "traces of the vile plot." In the building they found "one of the principal groups of the English conspirators"; they arrested "five Russian counter-revolutionists, including Prince Shakhavskoi, Jr. [a boy of 15], and about twenty-five English agents." Cromie was killed because he forcibly resisted the Cheka.

The Bolsheviks fully realised that in violating the Embassy they had committed a serious breach of international law. In ordinary circumstances, the report said, they would never have resorted to searching the premises. But they could not remain silent "when the embassy is converted into quarters of conspiracy for plotters and murderers, when officials living in our territory weave . . . a net of bloody intrigue and monstrous crime."

Like so many other incidents of this turbulent period, the exact circumstances of this one will probably never be established. There is no evidence whatsoever to lead one to think that the British had anything to do with Uritsky's death. Cromie himself was involved in a "plot" of sorts—he had stayed in Petrograd with the express purpose of blowing up the remains of the Russian fleet if the city seemed menaced by a German advance. At the date of his death his plans for this destruction were far advanced, but there was nothing specifically counter-revolutionary about them. They were wholly connected with Britain's war against Germany.

[18] Oudendyk, *Byways in Diplomacy*, pp. 296-98.

corps in vigorously protesting, in the name of humanity, against the Terror.[19]

The news of Cromie's death reached London on the very day that the government had planned, as a unilateral gesture of good will, to start on their homeward journey twenty-five Russians specially selected by Litvinov.[20] Now this order was cancelled, and Litvinov and his staff were placed under preventive arrest in Brixton Prison until all British representatives in Russia were allowed to leave the country. To Chicherin, Balfour sent a demand for immediate reparation and for prompt punishment of all persons connected with "this abominable outrage." And the message continued:

Should the Russian Soviet government fail to give complete satisfaction or should any further acts of violence be committed against a British subject His Majesty's Government will hold the members of the Soviet government individually responsible and will make every endeavour to secure that they shall be treated as outlaws by the governments of all civilized nations and that no place of refuge shall be left to them.[21]

This was no idle threat. In Tokyo, Foreign Minister Goto told the American Ambassador that on 9 September the British government had requested Japanese co-operation in exacting reprisals for Cromie's death upon Bolshevik prisoners in eastern Siberia. Goto had refused; he told the American Ambassador that he found the British proposal most extraordinary, and that he could not conceive of taking reprisals upon Bolsheviks thousands of miles away for the actions of a mob in European Russia.[22]

Meanwhile, the Cheka had arrested Lockhart. Actually, they arrested him twice. The first time was at 3:30 a.m. on 31 August, the day after the attempt on Lenin's life. Lockhart and Hicks were taken to 11 Lubyanka Street (the Cheka headquarters), where Peters, the head of the Cheka, tried to implicate Lockhart in the plot against Lenin. They were then kept overnight and released, apparently on the instructions of Chicherin, who had protested against their arrest.[23]

Two days later, on 3 September, the Moscow press announced the liquidation of a conspiracy, headed by Lockhart, which by bribing

---

[19] See Oudendijk's memorandum cited above, footnote 17.
[20] *The Times*, 5 September 1918.
[21] *ibid*. The telegram was despatched on 4 September.
[22] Morris to Secretary of State, unnumbered telegram, Tokyo, 11 September 1918, 1 a.m.; U.S. National Archives, State Department file no. 861.00/2663.
[23] Lockhart, *British Agent*, pp. 317-21.

Soviet troops had sought to capture the Bolshevik leaders and proclaim a military dictatorship in Moscow. One of the objects of the
coup, had it been successful, would have been the renewal of war with
Germany; an atmosphere suitable for renewed war would have been
generated by the publication of forged German-Soviet treaties.[24] Subsequent accounts added that a whole supporting structure of espio-
nage had been uncovered, including Allied plots to blow up bridges
and railways leading into Moscow and Petrograd. The Cheka was
reported to have found papers signed by Lockhart guaranteeing the
conspirators the protection of the British Military Mission in Moscow.[25] The next day Lockhart was again arrested.

[24] The official announcement of the liquidation of the plot, dated 2 September
1918 and printed in *Izvestiya*, 3 September, is printed in *Dokumenty vneshnei
politiki*, vol. 1, pp. 462-63. A translation is in Degras, vol. 1, *op.cit.*, pp. 98-99.

[25] Published accounts of what came to be called the "Lockhart plot" have suffered
from the shifts and slants of Soviet historiography. In 1920, a high official of the
Cheka, M. Ya. Latsis, in his book, *Dva goda borby na vnutrennem fronte* (Two
Years of Struggle on the Internal Front), Moscow, 1920, pp. 19-22, described the plot
in great detail, listing dates and amounts of money transferred as bribes to the
commander of a Soviet regiment, and stating that the principal object of the plot was
the murder of Lenin and Trotsky. The First Edition of the *Bolshaya Sovetskaya
Entsiklopediya* (Great Soviet Encyclopedia), vol. 37, Moscow, 1938, under the heading "Lockhart," briefly summarises these facts, but omits the name of Trotsky, leaving
only Lenin as the prospective murder victim (p. 362).

In the second edition of the *Entsiklopediya*, vol. 25, Moscow, 1954, under the heading "Lockhart Conspiracy," the account reaches fantastic proportions (p. 364). The
plot becomes Anglo-American, and an equal part is alleged to have been played by
the American Consul-General, DeWitt C. Poole; Lockhart, Poole, and other Americans are said to have allied themselves with "the White Guards, the Socialist-
Revolutionaries, the Mensheviks and Trotsky and Bukharin." Using their diplomatic
privileges, the Allied representatives are said to have organised the "White Guard
risings in Yaroslavl, Rybinsk, Murom and other towns, the mutiny of the Czechoslovak corps in the Povolzhe and in Siberia, and the mutiny of the Left S-R's in
Moscow and Samara." They are also accused of plotting Dora Kaplan's abortive
attempt on Lenin's life, and the murder of Uritsky. Finally, it is stated that after the
failure of the Left S-R rising in Moscow, Lockhart and his fellow conspirators secured
the support of Trotsky and Bukharin for another anti-Soviet plot, aimed at killing
Lenin, arresting the rest of the Soviet government, and turning them over to the
"Anglo-American interventionists" in Archangel.

Volkov (*Krakh angliiskoi politiki*, p. 51), also writing in 1954, gives a brief
summary of this last version, omitting the references to Trotsky and Bukharin, but
adding the names of Stalin and Sverdlov to Lenin's as prospective murder victims.

Finally, the most recent account (1957) is a long note (no. 58) appended to
Dokumenty vneshnei politiki, vol. 1, pp. 724-26, quoting the "Bulletin of the Press
Bureau of the All-Russian Central Executive Committee," 2 September 1918. This
account is very similar to that of Latsis, including the same figures, dates, addresses,
and other facts, and making the plot Anglo-French instead of Anglo-American. It
would seem that the full circle had indeed been turned except for the fact that only
Lenin, and not Trotsky, is stated to have been singled out for murder. Curiously, this
section on the murder is the only part of the original Press Bureau bulletin which is
paraphrased; all the rest is quoted directly.

It is difficult to know what to make of the allegations against Lockhart. He had certainly been sending money to the White forces in South Russia. During August, following the breach in Anglo-Soviet relations produced by the beginning of intervention, he had considerably increased his financial support of Alekseyev's armies.[26] However, he was not charged with these activities, but rather with having bribed Soviet troops to overthrow their government. As he explained in his memoirs, he *had* been in contact with the commander of a Lettish regiment and *had* given him a signed slip of paper—not offering the protection of the British Military Mission but asking British front-line troops near Archangel to allow a messenger to pass through to General Poole. For the Letts wanted to return to their homeland rather than stay in Soviet service, and they told Lockhart that they planned to get posted to the Archangel front and then defect by passing through the British lines. Lockhart was confronted with his signed message when he was first arrested on 31 August.

According to Lockhart, he himself saw the Letts only twice—on 15 and 16 August—and since at that time it looked as if he would soon be leaving Russia, he passed them on to a British intelligence officer named Sidney Reilly. Lockhart never found out whether Reilly did in fact offer the Letts money; once Reilly suggested that after the departure of the diplomatic communities he and the Letts might be able to stage a counter-revolution, but this suggestion was turned down categorically by Lockhart and his French colleagues, and Reilly was warned to have nothing to do with so dangerous and doubtful a plan. After this warning, Reilly went into hiding, and Lockhart did not see him again until he later escaped to England.[27]

We will never know what evidence the Soviet government had for the sweeping allegations against Lockhart. Neither will we know the scope of Reilly's activities after he had vanished into the conspiratorial underground of Moscow. We can, therefore, say little more about the

[26] Lockhart, *British Agent*, p. 312. Lockhart described the way in which he obtained currency for shipment to Alekseyev as follows (p. 313): "There were numerous Russians with hidden stores of roubles. They were only too glad to hand them over in exchange for a promissory note on London. To avoid all suspicion, we collected the roubles through an English firm in Moscow. They dealt with the Russians, fixed the rate of exchange, and gave the promissory note. In each transaction we furnished the English firm with an official guarantee that it was good for the amount in London. The roubles . . . were handed over to Hicks, who conveyed them to their destined quarters."
[27] Lockhart's account of these incidents is in *ibid.*, pp. 314-16, 322-23.

"Lockhart plot" than that if, indeed, there was one, Lockhart's own complicity was probably minimal. Minimal or not, his second imprisonment, unlike his first, was not a mere day's detention. On the evening of 4 September, just after Lockhart had again been arrested, Oudendijk (who was visiting Moscow) went to Chicherin and found that the Commissar for Foreign Affairs did not even know that the Cheka had acted. Although Chicherin protested that he was powerless to interfere with the affairs of the police, he finally telephoned the Cheka and pleaded with them to do nothing with Lockhart until the next morning. The Dutch Minister felt that this intervention saved Lockhart's life by preventing precipitous and irresponsible action by the police.[28] Lockhart's own account, however, does not indicate that he felt he was in such acute danger. He was not badly treated. After five days at 11 Lubyanka Street he was transferred to solitary confinement in a tiny flat inside the Kremlin, formerly the quarters of a lady-in-waiting.[29]

Meanwhile, Lenin was rapidly recovering from his bullet wounds and the first frightening excesses of the Terror had largely been curbed. Through the medium of Oudendijk the Anglo-Soviet negotiations for the exchange of detained persons began once again. On 15 September Oudendijk informed Chicherin of the British government's decision to allow Litvinov and his staff, as well as all other Russians who so chose, to return to Russia as soon as the Soviet government had released all British subjects including diplomats, consular officials, officers of the Military Mission, and civilians.[30] Replying on the 16th, Chicherin agreed that an immediate exchange should take place, but insisted upon retaining in internment all British and French "bourgeois" male civilians between the ages of 15 and 48. They would not be able to leave Russia, he said, until the Allies stopped all repressive measures against Soviet sympathisers both in British and French territory and in the occupied regions of Russia.[31] Chicherin reiterated this condition in another telegram on the 18th: women, children, old men, and all working-class males would be allowed to leave Russia along with diplomats, consuls, and the like as

[28] Oudendyk, *Byways in Diplomacy*, pp. 293-94.
[29] Lockhart, *British Agent*, pp. 326-29.
[30] Oudendijk to Chicherin, 15 September 1918; *Dokumenty vneshnei politiki*, vol. 1, p. 484.
[31] Note from Chicherin to the Representatives of the Northern Neutrals, 16 September 1918; *ibid.*, pp. 482-83.

soon as Litvinov had telegraphed that he and his staff were leaving England. But the bourgeois males of military age would have to stay.[32] Finally, on 19 September Chicherin made his conditions even more stringent by demanding that along with Litvinov there be returned twenty-six Bolshevik commissars who had fallen into Menshevik hands while fleeing from a British force which had just occupied Baku.[33]

Chicherin's demands put the British government in a dilemma. It was obvious that they could not continue military intervention and yet cease repressive measures against Bolsheviks and Bolshevik sympathisers. Nor did they have any means of putting pressure on the Soviet regime other than intervention. By mid-September, however, after the Chaplin affair at Archangel, it was already apparent that Allied forces of the magnitude of those being sent to North Russia would make no very great progress towards Moscow during the coming winter. Hence the government was forced to make the best of a clearly unpromising situation and leave the military-age male civilians in Bolshevik hands while exchanging the officials, the members of the military missions, and the other civilians. Had they insisted upon all British citizens being released, the Soviet government would simply have let Litvinov stay where he was; then the much larger staff of British officials in Russia would have had to stay where they were, too.

Once the government had decided to settle for this compromise, Balfour called in Reginald Leeper, who had been one of the strongest advocates of such a policy, and asked him how he thought the exchange should be effected. Leeper replied that he was convinced that if the Bolsheviks were treated as brigands, they would certainly behave like brigands, but if they were treated as gentlemen, they might behave like gentlemen. Therefore he proposed that the British government should first release Litvinov and the other Russians and allow them to get to neutral soil before the Bolsheviks released Lockhart and his colleagues. Balfour agreed, and insisted that Leeper should place his views before the War Cabinet.[34]

The two men immediately went over to 10 Downing Street. In

[32] Telegram, Chicherin to Oudendijk, Petrograd, 18 September 1918; *ibid.*, p. 489.
[33] Telegram, Chicherin to Oudendijk, Petrograd, 19 September 1918; *ibid.*, p. 489. For the affair of the twenty-six Baku Commissars, see below, Chapter xi.
[34] Interview with Sir Reginald Leeper.

Lloyd George's absence, Bonar Law was in the chair for a Cabinet session which was just beginning. With trepidation, Leeper put his views before the Cabinet. Despite Balfour's support, they were rejected; the Cabinet decided to require that the British subjects should cross the Russian frontier before Litvinov and his companions were freed. Leeper was instructed to go straight from the meeting to Brixton Prison to put the government's views before Litvinov. At Brixton, the prison governor insisted that an armed guard should accompany the young man into Litvinov's cell; the prisoner was regarded as dangerous. Leeper adamantly refused, and only after prolonged argument was he allowed to proceed alone.[35]

As soon as he had heard the government's proposals, Litvinov called them ridiculous; he was sure that Moscow would never accept. Leeper agreed, and asked what Litvinov could suggest. Litvinov replied that he and the other Russians should be allowed to get as far as Oslo before the British prisoners crossed the Finnish frontier. He said that he would give the British government a written guarantee that he would return to England if the Bolsheviks did not carry out their part of the agreement.

Leeper took Litvinov's proposal back to Balfour. The Foreign Secretary thought that it was quite fair, but was sure that his colleagues would never agree. Therefore he decided to go ahead with the exchange on his own authority, without telling the rest of the government. Balfour managed to effect the release of the prisoners only with the greatest difficulty, but on the following evening Leeper and a man from Scotland Yard accompanied the fifty or so Russians on the night train to Aberdeen. Not until after the party reached Aberdeen did Litvinov have time to telegraph Chicherin that he was coming. Only one barrier remained to be crossed: the Army guard at the Aberdeen quay refused to let the Russians through without orders from the War Office. By then, however, Balfour had informed his colleagues of his *fait accompli*; when the guard telephoned London, he was told to let the Russians board the waiting Norwegian steamer.[36]

By the time Litvinov reached Oslo, Lockhart, Hicks (and his newly

---

[35] *idem.* Leeper says that Litvinov greeted him with the remark that he far preferred his old cell at Kiev to Brixton; at Kiev he could read anything he wished, while at Brixton he was allowed only the Bible.

[36] *idem.*

acquired Russian wife), Wardrop, and twenty-seven other members of the British official community in Moscow had been allowed to cross the Finnish frontier.[37] On 9 October they reached Stockholm, where they were joined five days later by twenty-six members of the official colony in Petrograd. In succeeding days, some 130 non-official British residents were permitted to leave Russia.[38] Behind them forty-five of their countrymen were still imprisoned in Petrograd's Fortress of Peter and Paul and twenty more were imprisoned in Moscow. Most of them were to remain interned for over a year until the advent of a slightly happier period of Anglo-Soviet relations.

❖

The returning English prisoners reached London on 19 October. Within a few days, Balfour received Lockhart at the Foreign Office. Their interview lasted two hours. Lockhart later described it as "entertaining but curious."[39] The Foreign Secretary showed little interest in any of the younger man's information about the Soviet regime and conditions within Russia. Such matters as the relative strength of the Bolsheviks and their enemies were not even mentioned. Instead, Balfour questioned Lockhart at length on Lenin's ideology, and took great pains to refute it point by point.[40]

Balfour did, however, ask Lockhart to draft a report on the Russian situation for the War Cabinet. Accordingly, on 7 November, the first anniversary of the Bolshevik Revolution, Lockhart delivered a long memorandum to the Foreign Office.[41] He began by stating his opinion that the Soviet regime was stronger than at any time during its brief history. It possessed the one fundamental attribute of any real government—physical power to enforce its decrees. Moreover, the Bolsheviks

[37] Chicherin evidently did not insist upon his demand that the twenty-six Baku Commissars should be returned before the British officials were released. Had he done so his efforts would have been to no avail: all twenty-six were executed on 20 September, the day after Chicherin had demanded their release. But Moscow was not to learn of their fate until the following spring. See below, Chapter xi.

[38] *The Times*, 18 October 1918.

[39] R. H. Bruce Lockhart, *Retreat from Glory*, London, 1934, p. 12.

[40] *ibid.*, p. 13.

[41] "Memorandum on the Internal Situation in Russia," dated 1 November 1918 but forwarded to Balfour on 7 November. A copy, printed for the War Cabinet, is in the Milner MSS, box C-2. In a covering letter submitted with his report, Lockhart wrote: "I feel that in many respects my mission has not succeeded. I trust, however, that the valuable material and information which we have been able to obtain concerning a movement that constitutes a menace to the whole civilised world may redeem it from being considered altogether as a failure."

were considerably stronger than any of their domestic opponents. For that reason, Lockhart said, it was a mistake for the Allies to count on such anti-Bolshevik elements as the peasantry to fight against the regime. The peasants might welcome a deliverer who would relieve their wants, but they could not be induced again to undergo the horrors of war.

Lockhart saw three possible courses which the Allies might follow in regard to Russia. The first would be to abandon intervention altogether, secure the free and unhindered exit of the Czech troops, and come to some sort of working arrangement with the Bolsheviks. The advocates of such a policy, Lockhart said, pointed out that it would absolve the British government from the charge of suppressing an anti-capitalist revolution; that Bolshevism could not be killed by bayonets, but should be allowed to die a natural death; that by not sending troops to Russia to fight the Bolsheviks after the conclusion of hostilities in Europe, the British government would help to avoid the possibility of serious labour unrest at home; and that once freed from the constant menace of outside interference, the Soviet regime would become more moderate because the Bolshevik leaders would not be able to use Allied intervention as an excuse for internal repression.

Lockhart saw serious objections to such a policy. Before Bolshevism died a natural death, it might spread and cause untold suffering in rich and fertile districts of Europe. An Allied withdrawal would be seen by the Bolsheviks only as a sign of weakness, and would stimulate their revolutionary efforts in other countries. Any agreement with the Bolsheviks could only be a temporary one; as soon as they felt themselves strong enough they would break it. Finally, even though the Allies had not given concrete pledges to the counter-revolutionary movements in Russia, they had certainly led them to expect help. To desert these movements at the eleventh hour would gain the Allies doubtful popularity with the Bolsheviks and assure them of the lasting ill will of every other element of Russian society.

At the other extreme from this first policy, Lockhart saw immediate intervention on a "proper scale"—adding to the Allied forces already in Siberia and North Russia, while at the same time taking advantage of the defeat of Turkey to send an expeditionary force through the Black Sea to join Denikin's forces and march immediately upon Moscow. This was the course Lockhart himself preferred.

The Terror, he felt, justified any measures that might be taken against the Bolsheviks. "Bolshevism," he wrote, "or rather the Bolshevik in Russia, can be destroyed, not, however, by gnawing at the outside . . . but by digging at the core."

Lockhart recognised that there were serious objections to this plan. A large number of troops would have to be employed, not only to destroy the Bolshevik armies but also to restore peace and order in Russia. Successful intervention would require 50,000 Allied soldiers in the south and at least the same number advancing through the Urals from Siberia. Lockhart's French colleague in Moscow, General Lavergne, had put the figures even higher; in any case, Lockhart said, it was certain that the more troops the Allies sent the more help they would get from the Russians themselves. He admitted that it might well prove impossible to maintain so many men in Russia after four years of European war, and that the support of America would probably be an absolute necessity. And he added that if the operations proved to be more difficult than they then appeared, the Allied troops might have to remain in Russia for a considerable period of time.

Despite these objections, Lockhart favoured such a policy of massive intervention over the only other policy he thought possible—the first one of abandoning intervention and coming to terms with the Bolsheviks. There remained a middle course which he felt would be certain to end in disaster for the Allies: abandoning intervention or continuing it on the same scale which then existed, but at the same time supporting with arms and money all the various anti-Bolshevik organisations in Russia and also creating a chain of independent states (which would later be called the *cordon sanitaire*) on Russia's western frontier as a barrier against the spread of Bolshevism. Of this middle course, Lockhart wrote:

Without the active support of foreign troops the counter-revolutionary forces in Russia are not strong enough to overcome the Bolsheviks. By financing these organisations, and yet not supporting them actively, we lay ourselves open to the same charges as if we were intervening in force, and at the same time we are only prolonging civil war and unnecessary bloodshed in Russia. The result of our present intervention would seem to show the danger of half measures against the Bolsheviks. Finally, nothing seems more difficult of attainment than the plan of erecting a ring of border-States around Bolshevism, unless these States are supported by

Allied forces. Both Poland and the Ukraine, not to mention the Baltic Provinces, will have enough to do to combat Bolshevism in their own territories. All of these States are far more likely to become Bolshevik themselves, than to be able to exert any healthy influence on Bolshevism from the outside.

This middle course, Lockhart did not have to add, was roughly the policy that the Allies were then pursuing in Russia.

Lockhart concluded his memorandum with the following observations:

1. . . . our intervention is justified on humanitarian grounds, and . . . we should do more by proceeding openly against the Bolsheviks than by trying to suppress them surreptitiously.

2. . . . for the success of such an intervention American co-operation is essential, and operations should commence at once. . . . If America would agree to send the bulk of the required troops it would be possible to secure the necessary complement of French and British troops voluntarily.

3. . . . whatsoever Government we support should make immediately some declaration which will promise the land to the peasants—not necessarily as a socialistic measure, but as an economic remedy which is long overdue. Without a clear pronouncement on this subject we shall have the peasants against us.

4. . . . however difficult it may seem we should proceed cautiously in supporting any one anti-Bolshevik party against another, and in particular, we should beware of a renascence of sentimentalism for the old regime, which is already manifest in some sections of the English press.

5. No intervention can be really successful unless it is accompanied by large supplies of foodstuffs and manufactured goods for the starving population, and no economic relief can be given without a military occupation.

6. A successful intervention will give the Allies a predominant economic position in Russia. It will be more than paid for by economic concessions which will in time repay us for some of the sums we have advanced to Russia.

No other policy can promise the same results, or the same security.

These, then, were the views of the man who had been more closely in contact with the Soviet regime than any other Allied official. It is easy to dismiss them by pointing out that Lockhart was unrealistic in advocating massive intervention and then basing his whole policy on large-scale American participation. But such quick rejection will not

[299]

do. Lockhart had, after all, been in Russia during all the critical Anglo-American negotiations and probably did not realise how final was the American refusal to become involved in large-scale intervention. The importance of Lockhart's memorandum, however, does not lie in its forceful advocacy of the total destruction of Bolshevism. His memorandum was important because it so clearly warned that the various anti-Bolshevik elements in Russia, even if supported by Allied arms and money, were not strong enough to conquer Bolshevism. The Allies, Lockhart said, were faced with the choice of either coming to terms with the Soviet regime or using their own military forces to destroy it. Half-measures would inevitably fail to achieve their object and would only increase the hostility which the Bolsheviks felt for the bourgeois world.[42]

Lord Hardinge, the permanent under-secretary at the Foreign Office, marked Lockhart's paper with an "H." when he read it; he had no other comments to make. Lord Robert Cecil found it "very interesting." Balfour scrawled that it was "a very able document whatever one may think of the conclusions."[43] There is no available record of what the War Cabinet thought of the memorandum, but it seems doubtful whether any great notice was taken of it.

Lockhart remained in London only a few weeks after he had written his memorandum. During that time he frequently saw Milner, and found him as warm and interested as he had always been. He also had an hour's audience with the King, whom he found better informed on the Russian situation than anyone except Milner. The King had, in fact, read nearly every telegram which had passed to and from Russia.[44]

[42] Lockhart later wrote that his memorandum was "a rather feeble attempt to adapt my views to those which I believed were popular in Whitehall" (*Retreat from Glory*, p. 16). This observation must be regarded with some scepticism. Lockhart offered the government a firm choice between large-scale intervention or none; he deliberately ruled out the middle course, the one which surely must have seemed to him the favourite of Whitehall.

[43] *ibid.*, p. 16. Lockhart was later shown these comments in the Foreign Office.

[44] *ibid.*, pp. 18-19. Partly responsible for the King's great interest in events in Russia was, undoubtedly, the deep affection which he had felt for his late cousin, Tsar Nicholas II, who, with his immediate family, had been murdered by the Bolshevik authorities in Ekaterinburg on 16 July 1918. The murder had a profound effect upon George V, and as late as 1930 he recoiled at having to receive at Court a Soviet ambassador. See Harold Nicolson, *King George the Fifth, His Life and Reign*, London, 1952, pp. 57, 385, and 441. For the circumstances of the murder of the Imperial family, see Chamberlin, *Russian Revolution*, vol. II, pp. 84-95.

Before the end of the year, Lockhart went off to Scotland on an indefinite leave of absence at a vice-consul's half pay. After some twelve months of enforced idleness, he became Commercial Secretary to the British Legation in Prague. As he later wrote: "There is no one more quickly neglected than the man on the spot whose policy becomes discredited."[45]

[45] Lockhart, *British Agent*, p. 347. For the details of Lockhart's very distinguished subsequent career, see his *Giants Cast Long Shadows*, London, 1960, particularly pp. 58-70, 92-99, and 233-39. Like many collections of writings about a man's friends, these sketches tell as much about the author as they do about his companions.

CHAPTER XI

THE DEFENCE OF INDIA: THE CAUCASUS AND TRANSCASPIA

LOCKHART's departure from Russia marked the end of the first phase of Anglo-Soviet relations. Diplomacy had failed; now armed force would seek a different solution. When Lockhart was imprisoned, British troops were fighting not only in North Russia and Siberia but also in two other areas of Russia which we have not yet considered: the Caucasus and that vast desert region bounded by the Caspian Sea and the frontiers of Persia and Afghanistan known as Transcaspia. These areas lay directly in the path of Turkish and German forces aiming at the invasion of India; to the British government they were therefore of immense strategic importance. They have not been considered until the present point in this narrative, however, because during the war London viewed them solely in terms of India's defence, and British policy toward both the Caucasus and Transcaspia was only remotely connected with British policy toward the Bolshevik regime or, indeed, with British policy toward the rest of Russia. But in the autumn of 1918, as the end of hostilities in Europe grew closer, the Caucasus and Transcaspia presented problems which further exacerbated the already bitter relations between Britain and the Soviet government. Like the problems of North Russia and Siberia, although not to the same degree, they contributed to bringing about the rupture which occurred in Moscow.

❖

Germany and Turkey had only lately come to menace Britain's Indian Empire; throughout the latter half of the 19th Century the menace had been Russia. From the time of their conquest of the Khirghiz Steppe in the 1840's, the Russians had steadily advanced into Turkestan. The conquest of the Khanates of Kokand, Bokhara and Khiva in the late 1860's and early 1870's had been followed in 1881 by Russian annexation of the entire Transcaspian region and the start of work on a railway link with European Russia to tap the resources of northern Persia and to make further expansion even easier. In 1884 the occupation of Merv brought Russian forces within reach of Afghanistan, a buffer state whose neutrality was considered in London to be vitally important to the defence of India. The British government's alarm flared to anger in March 1885 when the Russians defeated an Afghan force at Penjdeh, inside the territory claimed by the Amir of Afghanistan. Although Britain and Russia reached a compromise agreement over the Afghan frontier the following September, war between them had been only narrowly averted.

In the following two decades the threat of Russian expansion towards India seemed only slightly diminished. But the steadily growing menace of Germany moved the British government to settle their outstanding disputes with Russia as they had with France. The result of overtures which began in 1903 was the Anglo-Russian Convention of 1907 aimed at eliminating Russian influence in the territories immediately bordering India. Russia formally recognised Britain's special interest in Afghanistan and agreed that no Russian agents were to enter the territory. And Persia—the root of the Anglo-Russian antagonism—was divided into spheres of influence, with Russia getting a large and valuable sphere in the north and Britain getting the strategically important eastern province of Seistan and, indeed, the whole region bordering the Indo-Persian frontier and almost all of that bordering the Persian-Afghan frontier.[1]

The convention served its purpose of facilitating a closer relationship between Britain and Russia and, during the few remaining years of peace, of safeguarding India. The coming of the war replaced the Russian menace with that of Germany and Turkey. So long as Russia remained in the Alliance, however, the enemy was contained in Mesopotamia. But in early December 1917, when the Russian commander in the Caucasus agreed to an armistice with the Turks,[2] the barrier collapsed. The armistice did little for the Menshevik government of the Caucasus, the so-called Transcaucasian Commissariat. From the outset the Turks kept pushing forward into Caucasian territory. When the Transcaucasian Commissariat refused to recog-

---

[1] For an excellent account of the negotiation of the Anglo-Russian Convention see Harold Nicolson, *Lord Carnock: A Study in the Old Diplomacy*, London, 1930, pp. 206-57.

[2] See above, Chapter II.

nise the Brest treaty (which ceded to Turkey the districts of Kars, Ardahan, and Batum) and declared their complete independence of Russia and their desire to make their own peace with the Central Powers, the Turks considered themselves freed from the obligations they had undertaken at Brest-Litovsk.[3] Immediately, their newly formed "Army of Islam," under the command of General Nuri Pasha, a half-brother of Enver, moved further into the Caucasus. Their immediate object was to absorb all of Armenia and to establish an independent Moslem republic of Azerbaijan; their eventual intention was to seize the Caspian coast of Persia, rally the large Moslem population of the Caucasus, Transcaspia, and Turkestan, and threaten India from the north and north-west.[4]

Although the distances involved in these grandiose Turkish plans were immense and the Turkish forces ill-equipped, badly trained, and poorly led, the British War Office viewed the situation with considerable foreboding. On 25 March a General Staff memorandum conjured up the following image:

. . . [Germany] will make use of the Pan-Turanian movement and of Mahommedan fanaticism to fan into a flame the ever glowing embers of a religious war, in order to let loose on India the pent-up tide of a Moslem invasion. . . . While Russia was healthy and while Persia was under control we were able to deal with this difficulty, but if German Agents had free access to the lawless tribes of Afghanistan and the frontiers of India, bred as they have been on tales of the legendary wealth of loot which might be theirs, innumerable hordes of savage warriors would swarm into the plains, ravaging, murdering, destroying. The institutions built by long years of careful government would be swept away in a few short weeks and the attenuated garrison of the country would have to be largely reinforced from troops badly needed elsewhere. None but White troops could be trusted . . .

The only way to forestall such a fate, according to the author of this paper, was for Japan immediately to intervene in Siberia and to move troops down into Transcaspia to meet the Turks.[5]

[3] Kazemzadeh, *Transcaucasia*, pp. 86-117.
[4] C. H. Ellis, "Operations in Transcaspia 1918-1919 and the 26 Commissars Case," *St. Antony's Papers, No. 6: Soviet Affairs, Number Two*, London, 1959, p. 131.
[5] Brig.-Gen. H. W. Studd, "A" Branch, British Section, Supreme War Council, "Allied Intervention in Siberia, its Importance from a Military Point of View," 25 March 1918; U.S. National Archives, Modern Army Branch, Supreme War Council Records.

Part of Major-General L. C. Dunsterville's column of Ford cars halted on a
road in Persia on the way to the Caspian Sea

or-General Dunsterville inspecting
uipment of an Armenian soldier
at Baku

British troops advancing towards Turkish positions north of Baku.
In the distance are the oil fields of Bingadi

British troops taking up positions for defence of Baku

These were not simply the isolated views of one British general. Both the estimate of the danger to India and the suggested solution of Japanese intervention were adopted by the Military Representatives at Versailles and incorporated into their Joint Note No. 20 on 8 April.[6] And on 25 July in a long memorandum to the War Cabinet entitled "British Military Policy 1918-1919," the C.I.G.S. wrote:

Unless by the end of the war democratic Russia can be reconstituted as an independent military power it is only a question of time before most of Asia becomes a German colony, and nothing can impede the enemy's progress towards India, in defence of which the British Empire will have to fight at every disadvantage.[7]

At a time when the soldiers were predicting that German troops would over-run Siberia, it was perhaps no more unreasonable to imagine Turks and Germans reaching the frontiers of India.

The extraordinary difficulty of moving troops and their supplies through northern Persia meant that British forces could reach neither the Caucasus nor Transcaspia in any strength, but in late December 1917 the War Office decided to despatch via Bagdad, Enzeli, and the Caspian an armoured-car detachment and a number of British officers to serve as a training mission for local Georgian and Armenian forces in the Caucasus.[8] On 14 January 1918, Major-General L. C. Dunsterville was appointed Chief of the British Mission to the Caucasus and British Representative at Tiflis; his sphere of operations was to extend over all Russian and Turkish territory, south of the main chain of the Caucasus, over which the Transcaucasian Commissariat claimed control. He was to cooperate with a Russian force under a Colonel Lazar Bicherakhov, who had refused to recognise the armistice. Dunsterville's task was to maintain an effective force on the Caucasian front in order to protect the Russian-occupied portions of Turkish Armenia and so to prevent the passage through the Caucasus of Turkish armies.[9] In late January, Dunsterville, a small group of officers and forty-one Ford cars and vans set out from

---

[6] Joint Note No. 20 was not signed by Bliss, the American representative. The text is in U.S. National Archives, Modern Army Branch, Supreme War Council Records.

[7] General Sir Henry Wilson, "British Military Policy 1918-1919," 25 July 1918; Milner MSS, box AF-2.

[8] C.I.G.S. to General Officer Commanding, Mesopotamia, and Commander in Chief, India, telegram 48487, 22 December 1917, 1:25 p.m.; Milner MSS, box G-1.

[9] *Official History: Mesopotamia Campaign*, vol. IV, pp. 104-5.

Bagdad. But they were immediately beset by difficulties and were not able to move to the Caspian until early June.[10]

By then the situation had totally changed. The Turks had taken Elizavetpol and had set up an "independent" republic of Azerbaijan.[11] The Black Sea coast was completely in the hands of the Germans, and the Georgians, afraid of Turkish subjugation, had proclaimed their own independence and had entered into an agreement with the Germans which reduced Georgia virtually to the status of a German protectorate.[12] At the same time, Georgia made peace with Turkey. The treaty, signed on 4 June, gave the Turkish Army full transit rights on Georgian railroads.[13] Also on 4 June, the Turks signed a similar but much more severe treaty with the part of Armenia which they had not already absorbed. Turkish troops were now free to march with their new allies, the Azerbaijanis, against Baku and the surrounding oil fields, the only area of the Caucasus still in the hands of the Bolsheviks.[14] Bolshevik control also extended over most of the shores of the Caspian and to its shipping.

In this situation the immediate objectives of the Bolsheviks and of the British government were much the same: to keep the Turks from capturing Baku and the rich oil deposits and from gaining mastery over the inland sea. If the Turks took Baku and gained command of the Caspian, they could easily ferry their armies across and thus be in a position to go forward along the Transcaspian Railway to the Afghan border. Therefore, on 26 May Dunsterville asked his superiors for permission to take a British detachment to Baku to serve as a nucleus for the reorganisation of local Bolshevik forces.[15]

In London, Dunsterville's request met with sharp opposition in the

[10] *ibid.*, pp. 106-7, 116-20. See Major-General L. C. Dunsterville, *The Adventures of Dunsterforce*, London, 1920, pp. 11-67.

[11] Kazemzadeh, *Transcaucasia*, p. 124. See the Azerbaijan government's collection of documents, *Le 28 Mai, 1919: Le jour du premier anniversaire de l'indépendance de la République d'Azerbeidjan*, Baku, 1919, pp. 8-9.

[12] Kazemzadeh, *Transcaucasia*, pp. 121-23. See also Zourab Avalishvili, *The Independence of Georgia in International Politics, 1918-1921*, London, n.d.—circa 1941, pp. 57-59.

[13] Kazemzadeh, *Transcaucasia*, pp. 125-27.

[14] Bolshevism survived in Baku because nearly half of the town's population were Armenians who supported the Bolshevik policy of restoring Russian dominion over Transcaucasia. The alternative to Bolshevism was incorporation into the Moslem state of Azerbaijan—a grim fate indeed for Armenians.

[15] Dunsterville to War Office and to G.O.C., Mesopotamia, telegram G. 572, Hamadan, 26 May 1918, 6 p.m.; Milner MSS, box G-2.

War Cabinet's Eastern Committee, which had been established in late March to deal with all policy decisions affecting the Middle East and Central Asia.[16] At the time (late May) it was just becoming apparent that Lockhart's efforts in Moscow to secure Soviet co-operation would be fruitless, but such political factors had little to do with the Eastern Committee's refusal to allow British troops to go to Baku. Rather, the Committee feared that once the troops had gone there, they would inevitably be overwhelmed by the vastly more numerous Turkish forces. As Lord Curzon, the Committee's chairman, insisted to his colleagues, the foundations of their policy had been to build a barrier against the Turks in northern Persia. If Dunsterville transferred any of his forces to Baku, the Persian barrier would be weakened.[17] As it happened, this decision of the Eastern Committee coincided with Bolshevik policy in Moscow. On 5 June, the head of the Baku Soviet, Stepan Shaumian, told the British vice-consul that he had received instructions from Moscow categorically forbidding any British forces to set foot on Russian soil.[18] This was, perhaps, the Bolshevik reaction to Lockhart's sharp *démarche*, made on 4 June, concerning the Soviet efforts to disarm the Czechs.[19]

Thus, Dunsterville's force spent June and July in northern Persia. In late June the War Office redefined his ultimate objectives according to the changed military and political situation in the Caucasus. He was to bear in mind that a permanent occupation of Baku was out

[16] The Eastern Committee was formed as the result of Milner's urgings in a letter to Lloyd George on 20 March 1918 (Milner MSS, Private Letters, vol. VIII). Milner felt that the problems in the Middle East and Central Asia that had been raised by Russia's defection from the Alliance were so grave that the several Cabinet committees which had "been pothering over Asian problems" should be merged into one. When the question was raised at the Cabinet the next day, the Eastern Committee was formed.

The Committee's membership fluctuated, but those present at nearly all of its important sessions included Curzon (chairman), Smuts, Balfour or Cecil (sometimes both), Lord Hardinge (the permanent under-secretary at the Foreign Office), Sir Henry Wilson, Edwin Montagu (Secretary of State for India), and Major-General Sir G. M. W. Macdonogh (Director of Military Operations). It is interesting to note that neither Milner nor Lloyd George were members of the Committee, nor did they attend its sessions. Presumably they were both too busy with the conduct of the war in the west.

[17] Minutes, Eastern Committee 10th and 11th meetings, 28 May 1918, 3:15 p.m., and 31 May, 3 p.m.; Milner MSS. Unless otherwise noted, meetings of the Committee were held in Lord Curzon's room at the Privy Council Office.

[18] As reported in a letter from the vice-consul at Baku (McDonell) to Dunsterville, 5 June 1918, and summarised to London by Major-General Marshall (G.O.C., Mesopotamia) in his telegram X9448, 12 June, 12:30 p.m.; Milner MSS, box G-2.

[19] See above, p. 189.

of the question; the government's objects would be achieved if he could get complete control of the Caspian shipping and destroy the Baku oil pumping plant, pipe lines, and oil reservoirs.[20]

Meanwhile, Colonel Lazar Bicherakhov, the Russian leader with whose thousand-man force Dunsterville had been co-operating, had decided that the only way he could gain a foothold in the Caucasus was to pretend that he had come to sympathise with Bolshevism and to offer his troops to the Baku Soviet. Despite his record of anti-Bolshevik activities, his offer was accepted.[21] But he did not long remain in Bolshevik service; soon after he had brought his force to Baku, he marched them northwards and united with an anti-Bolshevik force in Daghestan.[22] During all this time the Turks were rapidly nearing Baku. The closer they came, the more willing grew the Armenian population to abandon the Bolshevik policy of accepting no outside assistance[23] and to invite the British to help them. On 16 July, the S-R's and Dashnaks (members of the Armenian party) in the Baku Soviet proposed that an invitation be extended to the British. The proposal was narrowly defeated,[24] but it had received so much support that Shaumian decided to ask for instructions from the Bolshevik central authorities. From Tsaritsin on 21 July, Stalin, as Commissar for Nationalities, replied in the name of the Sovnarkom strongly condemning the S-R's and the Dashnaks and absolutely forbidding the Soviet to seek support from the "Anglo-French imperialists."[25] The following day, Lenin telegraphed from Moscow endorsing Stalin's instructions.[26]

But stout resolution of this kind could not stem the Turkish advance. As Shaumian told Lenin in a plaintive telegram on 27 July, the situation at the front was daily growing more desperate. The

[20] *Official History: Mesopotamia Campaign*, vol. IV, p. 187.
[21] *ibid.*, p. 183. See also Kazemzadeh, *Transcaucasia*, pp. 133-34.
[22] *ibid.*, pp. 134-35.
[23] Shaumian stoutly affirmed his adherence to this policy in a telegram sent on 21 June to various neighbouring Soviets and to Lenin in Moscow. No British troops would be allowed in Baku, he maintained. (*Dokumenty vneshnei politiki*, vol. I, p. 371.)
[24] *ibid.*, p. 723, n. 51. See also Kazemzadeh, *op.cit.*, p. 136. The British vice-consul in Baku, A. E. R. McDonell, received the impression that the Baku Soviet had voted on 16 July to invite the British, and he so reported to British headquarters in Mesopotamia (*Official History: Mesopotamia Campaign*, vol. IV, p. 198).
[25] *Dokumenty vneshnei politiki*, vol. I, pp. 401-2.
[26] *ibid.*, p. 402. See Kazemzadeh, *Transcaucasia*, p. 136.

Turks had reached Alyat, on the coast a short distance to the south, and were menacing the heights overlooking the city. On the evening of the 25th, Shaumian related, the demoralised S-R's, Dashnaks, and Mensheviks in the Soviet had again proposed an invitation to the British; this time it was carried by a vote of 259 to 236. He had tried, he said, to follow the policy laid down by Stalin and the central authorities. After the passage of the resolution, the atmosphere was charged with tension. Shaumian said that he and his Bolshevik colleagues anxiously awaited either the despatch to Baku of Red Army troops or further instructions as to how he should treat the resolution to call in the British. Meanwhile, he added, "it smelled of civil war."[27]

Shaumian's own response to the Soviet's resolution was to issue a proclamation disbanding the body and declaring that there no longer existed a revolutionary war in Baku, but simply a struggle between the rival British and German-Turk imperialisms. He thereupon loaded all of his colleagues of the Baku Sovnarkom onto a ship and on 31 July, with Turkish troops in sight of the city, they embarked for Astrakhan. They did not get far, however; a gunboat manned by anti-Bolshevik sailors forced them to return to Baku. As soon as they landed they were arrested by the new government, the so-called Centro-Caspian Directorate, which had assumed power as soon as the Bolsheviks had relinquished it.[28] The first formal action of this new body, which had been organised by S-R's and was composed mostly of Russians and Armenians, was to extend a formal invitation to the British to assist in the defence of the city.[29]

Although it seemed certain that Baku would fall to the Turks before any British troops could arrive, the Turks unaccountably did not press their advantage. On 31 July their progress was halted by an Armenian counter-attack. Meanwhile, Dunsterville had apparently persuaded the War Office that his force (which by that time had been considerably reinforced) could keep the city from the Turks, and he was given permission to send a total of two British battalions, with supporting artillery. The first British battalion arrived on 4 August and immediately went up to the front lines. By the time of the British defence of Baku, intervention at Archangel and in Siberia had already

[27] *Dokumenty vneshnei politiki,* vol. I, pp. 411-12.
[28] Kazemzadeh, *Transcaucasia,* pp. 137-38.
[29] *ibid.,* p. 139.

begun; Dunsterville was instructed not to hesitate to dispose of any remaining Bolshevik influence he might find at Baku.[30]

Dunsterville's defence of Baku was doomed from the start.[31] Against his own 900 men and some 8,000 local Russian and Armenian troops (of whom only 1,000 were at all reliable in combat), there were ranged some 6,000 Turkish regulars and 8,000 irregulars. Despite Dunsterville's pleading, the new Baku government would not place the local troops under his command; the S-R's distrusted the British almost as much as the Bolsheviks did. As a result there was virtually no co-ordination among the various defending forces. The majority of the Armenians were worse than useless to the British; often they would simply retire from a battle as soon as the enemy approached. In such circumstances, Dunsterville had no choice but to evacuate his troops or see them wiped out. When he informed the Centro-Caspian Directorate of his decision, they accused him of treason and desertion, and threatened to use their force to prevent the British withdrawal. On 14 September, six weeks after the first British troops reached Baku, the Turks broke through the city's final defence perimeter. That night, utilising the darkness so that the Russians and Armenians would not interfere, Dunsterville successfully embarked all of his remaining British troops for Enzeli. He had lost 125 men and had failed to hold Baku, but he had delayed by six important weeks the enemy's access to the rich oil fields. The next day, Azerbaijani troops burst into the city. The Turks remained outside for three days while their allies, it is reported, massacred 9,000 Armenians.[32]

❖

Dunsterville's troops were the last British soldiers to be in the Caucasus until after the Armistice in November.[33] They had been involved in bitter fighting, but it should be noticed that at no time were they fighting Bolsheviks. If the Bolsheviks had been willing to

[30] *Official History: Mesopotamia Campaign*, vol. IV, p. 213.

[31] The story of the siege of Baku has been so well told by Dunsterville himself and by the Army's historians that there is no point in retelling it here. See Dunsterville, *Dunsterforce*, pp. 218-317, and *Official History: Mesopotamia Campaign*, vol. IV, Chapter XLIII, "The Fall of Baku," pp. 215-57.

[32] Kazemzadeh, *Transcaucasia*, pp. 143-44. Kazemzadeh draws his figures from a report made by the Armenian National Council; he doubts, however, whether they are much exaggerated.

[33] British activities in the Caucasus after the Armistice will be discussed in the second volume of the present work.

invite them to Baku in August, the British would have fought as gladly in partnership with them as with their S-R and Menshevik successors. Meanwhile, in Transcaspia, on the other side of the Caspian from Baku, other British soldiers were in combat with Bolshevik forces. These were the various detachments under the command of Major-General Wilfred Malleson.

Malleson, an Indian Army intelligence officer, was sent from Simla in June 1918 to establish an outpost at Meshed, in Persian Khorasan, from where he and the six officers who accompanied him were to watch developments in Transcaspia and establish contacts which might be useful in the event that the Turks successfully penetrated so far east. If the Turks did reach Transcaspia, Malleson was to do everything he could to render unusable the Transcaspian Railway, which ran from Krasnovodsk into the interior, and to prevent the large stocks of cotton which had been stored along the railway from falling into enemy hands.[34]

At this time, insofar as there was any authority at all in Transcaspia and Turkestan, it was in the hands of the Bolsheviks. The situation was complicated by the presence there of some 35,000 German and Austro-Hungarian prisoners of war. Like their comrades in Siberia, they had been put at liberty after the treaty of Brest-Litovsk. Their presence caused the government of India considerable concern, and an intelligence officer, Major Redl, was sent into Turkestan to investigate. In mid-May, Redl reported that the Bolsheviks had armed 3,000 of the former prisoners at Tashkent, and that they had another force the same size, half composed of armed prisoners, on the Afghan frontier at Kushk.[35] At the end of the month, Redl reported that the Turkestan Bolsheviks had moved additional troops to the Afghan frontier; they had done so, he said, because they seemed genuinely afraid of a combined Anglo-Afghan invasion. The Bolshevik leaders of the Tashkent Soviet had told Redl

---

[34] Ellis, *St. Antony's Papers*, pp. 133-35. Of the danger of enemy penetration of Transcaspia, Malleson later wrote: ". . . the opinion of those in high places at Simla was that it needed the appearance of but a detachment of German or Turkish troops on the Northern frontiers of Afghanistan to precipitate a *jihad* against us . . ." (Major-General Sir Wilfred Malleson, "The British Military Mission to Turkistan, 1918-1920," *Journal of the Central Asian Society* [London], vol. ix, 1922, part 2, p. 96).

[35] C.G.S., India, to D.M.I., telegram 38229, 16 May 1918, repeating Redl's telegram M.D. 67, 15 May; Milner mss, box H-3.

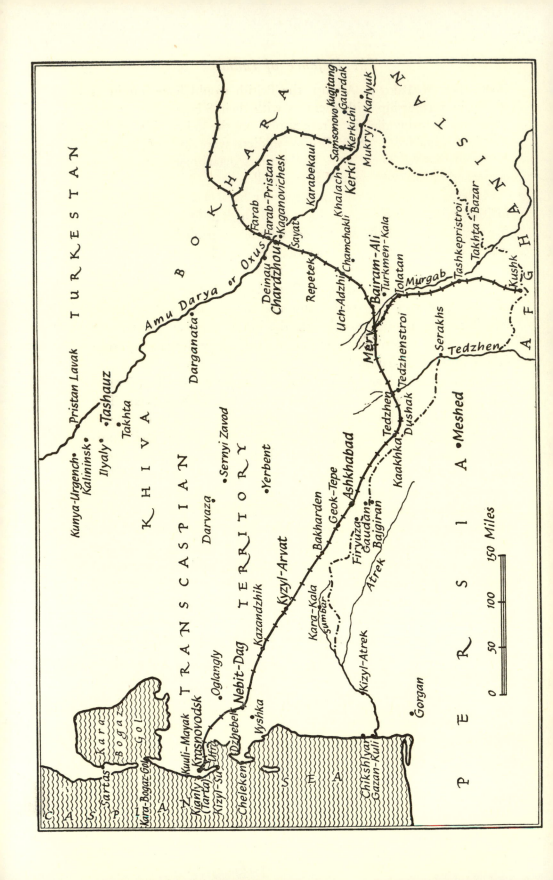

that their principal military objective was to block any Turkish attempts to penetrate into Turkestan. Since Britain's objectives were so much the same, Redl commented, it seemed to him particularly unfortunate that the Bolsheviks misunderstood British policy so much that they feared an invasion from Afghanistan.[36]

The Bolshevik misunderstanding of British policy toward Turkestan, however, was not as great as Redl had thought. On 21 June the General Staff raised the whole question of Turkestan, Afghanistan, and the defence of India in a memorandum to the War Cabinet.[37] The policy of the government of India toward Afghanistan, the memorandum stated, had always been to encircle the country in order to keep it strictly neutral and thus to prevent the entry of any disturbing influences.[38] This policy had proved successful, but with the advent of Bolshevism the northern part of the fence around Afghanistan had been torn down. The country was now open to all evils; the General Staff greatly feared the consequences of the influx of German and Turkish agents and smuggled arms. In the existing situation, the memorandum continued, the Afghan army was the only barrier to a German advance into India. Therefore, the co-operation of the Amir of Afghanistan should be invited against a menace which affected his interests as much as it did Britain's. The Amir should be encouraged to occupy the Murgab Valley from Merv to Kushk. This territory included Penjdeh, which had been lost to the Russians in 1885; to the General Staff there was no question but that it would prove an attractive bait to the Amir.

It could be argued, the memorandum admitted, that such a policy might turn the Bolsheviks of Turkestan against Britain. But this argument was rejected: why should the Bolsheviks be given any consideration in a region over which they had not even the most shadowy claim of *de facto* authority? Tenderness toward the Bolsheviks had already placed European Russia in German hands; Siberia was now within their reach. Should the Allies adopt a similar policy toward Turkestan, Afghanistan would soon be within the grasp of the Central Powers.

[36] C.G.S., India, to D.M.I., un-numbered telegram, 1 June 1918, 12:15 p.m., repeating Redl's H.D. 99, 30 May; Milner MSS, box H-3.

[37] The General Staff's memorandum, dated 21 June 1918, is appended to the minutes of the 16th meeting of the Eastern Committee, 24 June, 3:30 p.m.; Milner MSS.

[38] As we have seen, this was one of the purposes of the Anglo-Russian Convention of 1907.

Not only should the Bolsheviks be disregarded, said the memorandum, but the Allies should not be deterred by false sentiments toward other segments of Russian opinion. All loyal and educated Russians would recognise that their country must pay a price for salvation from further German destruction; no loyal Russian would begrudge the Amir this small piece of Russian soil as a reward for Afghan assistance. In any case, if the Germans once occupied Turkestan, they would offer the Amir a much larger slice as a reward for his co-operation. Moreover, the memorandum concluded, once the wild tribesmen of the Afghan army were committed to a campaign in Turkestan, all of their energies would be occupied and the danger of Afghan attacks on the Indian frontier would disappear.

The General Staff's memorandum was brought before the War Cabinet's Eastern Committee on 24 June. Immediately, the objection was raised that the British government, by adopting the suggested policy, would be taking part in the dismemberment of Russia—exactly what the Germans were doing. After protesting that Russia's territorial integrity could never be violated, it would be impossible for the government to justify taking a large slice of Russian territory and handing it over to Afghanistan.

This argument was countered from another quarter with a sharp reminder: were not the British government in effect trying to do the same sort of thing in Siberia? It was not unlikely that if the Japanese went into Siberia they would stay there. (The time, it will be remembered, was that of the British negotiations with Japan over intervention, during the fortnight preceding the American decision to take action.) The object of British policy in Central Asia, this member of the Eastern Committee continued, was to set up a nexus of Moslem states to stop the German and Turkish advance. In those circumstances, was it wrong to encourage the Afghans to recover territory which the Tsar's government had taken from them years before?[39]

This question was never answered by the Eastern Committee. No definite decision was taken at this meeting, but the General Staff's proposal was put before the government of India, which emphasised in reply that active intervention could neither be expected nor asked

---

[39] Minutes, Eastern Committee 16th meeting, 24 June 1918, 3:30 p.m., in Balfour's room at the House of Commons; Milner MSS.

from the Amir. The latter's policy was strict neutrality; intervention on the side of Britain might well cost him his throne.[40]

✦

These discussions took place before Malleson had even arrived at his base at Meshed. By the time he got there, in mid-July, the power of the Tashkent Soviet over Transcaspia had been radically circumscribed by a successful anti-Bolshevik revolt. Dissatisfaction had been growing for some time owing to an acute shortage of food; in early July, when there were protest meetings in towns along the Transcaspian Railway, the Tashkent Soviet sent a detachment of Red Guards with instructions to liquidate all opposition. But at Kizyl-Arvat, between Krasnovodsk and Ashkhabad, the railwaymen revolted. The Red Guards joined them; together, they seized and executed the commissars who had been leading the punitive expedition. On 14 July a Menshevik and S-R government of Transcaspia was established at Ashkhabad. Calling themselves the "Ashkhabad Committee," the new government rapidly extended their authority along the railway to Krasnovodsk and Merv. Hastily, they organised a force of irregulars and took up a defensive position against attacks from Red troops and prisoners of war some thirty miles east of Merv. Although they managed to hold this position, their situation was extremely critical. In early August they sent representatives to Meshed to ask General Malleson for help.[41]

Malleson had seen that their request would be forthcoming, and on 1 August he asked the War Office for instructions. To assist his superiors in arriving at a policy, he put forward a number of considerations which he felt should be taken into account. By assisting the Ashkhabad Committee, he said, he would be openly opposing the Bolsheviks. Such a policy might or might not be in accord with the declared policy of His Majesty's government. It might also mean "putting money on the wrong horse," as the Bolsheviks in Turkestan were far from defeated. If the Bolsheviks should

---

[40] The reply of the government of India was cited in the minutes, Eastern Committee 27th meeting, 20 August 1918, 3 p.m.; Milner MSS.

[41] Malleson, "Mission to Turkistan," p. 97. See also Alexander G. Park, *Bolshevism in Turkestan, 1917-1927*, New York, 1957, pp. 26-28, and Ellis, *St. Antony's Papers*, pp. 135-36. Ellis was himself a member of Malleson's mission; his article is based not only on his personal experiences but also on a careful survey of published materials, both in English and in Russian.

win, their rage against the British might induce them to offer every possible facility to a German-Turkish advance into Central Asia. Britain would also suffer a great loss of prestige, and her "numerous enemies in these parts of the world might throw off their mask" and openly act against her.

On the other hand, Malleson said, his information led him to think that the forces throughout Asia against the Bolsheviks were so large that the Bolsheviks would eventually be defeated. In his opinion, the advantages of direct association with the leaders of the Transcaspian anti-Bolshevik movement would be great. He would be able to prevent the Turks from having access to Krasnovodsk, the only port on the eastern shore of the Caspian, and keep them from the lines of communication into the interior as well. The government would have to choose between these two courses of action, Malleson said. The third possibility, doing nothing and sitting on the fence, would be disastrous; it would only alienate both sides. He requested immediate instructions, for he wanted to be able to give the Ashkhabad Committee a definite answer when he received their request.[42]

The reply to Malleson's telegram came not from the War Office but from General Sir C. C. Monro, the Commander-in-Chief of the Indian Army. (For London to have replied, Monro said, would have taken too much time.) Monro gave Malleson a free hand; so complex a situation, he said, could be evaluated only by the man on the spot. But he added his opinion that the fall of the Bolshevik regime at Baku, only a few days before, had already identified Britain with the cause of anti-Bolshevism.[43] Malleson was grateful for the freedom of action which Monro gave him, and he telegraphed his own opinion that the situation presented a unique opportunity to occupy Krasnovodsk, and that he should openly espouse the cause of anti-Bolshevism and secure from the Ashkhabad Committee the right to post a British garrison at that strategically important port.[44]

Accordingly, acting on his own authority, Malleson sent an Indian machine-gun section to help the Transcaspian irregulars meet a new Bolshevik attack. But the Soviet forces had been considerably rein-

[42] Malleson telegram MD 128, Meshed, 1 August 1918, repeated by C-i-C, India, to War Office as telegram 6054, 2 August, 1:25 p.m.; Milner MSS, box H-3.

[43] Monro to Malleson, Meshed, repeated to War Office as telegram 60743, 2 August 1918, 9:25 p.m.; Milner MSS, box H-3.

[44] Malleson to Monro, telegram MD 146, Meshed, 3 August 1918, 8:45 a.m., repeated by Simla to War Office as telegram 61001, 6:30 p.m.; Milner MSS, box H-3.

forced, and they drove the Transcaspian troops back through the Merv Oasis to Dushak, a point nearly 100 miles to the west. The retreat was saved from becoming a total rout only by the steady action of the Indian machine-gunners.[45] Malleson then sent 300 Indian infantry to reinforce the Transcaspians, and on 28 August they beat back a heavy Bolshevik attack at Kaakhka.[46]

Meanwhile, on 19 August, Malleson and the Ashkhabad Committee's representative in Meshed signed the protocol of an agreement between the Committee and the British government. As is made quite clear by the recently published Russian version of the text,[47] the agreement got no further than the protocol stage. It never received the formal sanction of the British government, although the government was to feel certain moral obligations toward fulfilling the promises that Malleson had made. The document was, in fact, simply an agreement for co-operation between the Ashkhabad Committee and the British Mission at Meshed.

The signatories agreed, "in view of the common danger from Bolshevism and Turko-German invasion," to act together for the restoration of peace and order in Transcaspia and Russian Turkestan, and to resist all German or Turkish attempts at military or political penetration. For their part, the Committee pledged themselves to give the British facilities for the use of ships on the Caspian, free use of the port of Krasnovodsk, assistance in putting the port in a "state of defence," and all facilities in the use of the railway and telegraph. They promised to raise and train further contingents for military service. In addition, the Russians promised to take steps toward rendering the railway useless to the enemy in the event of a Turkish

[45] *Official History: Mesopotamia Campaign*, vol. IV, pp. 209-10.

[46] *ibid.*, p. 231. For a detailed account of the military operations, see Lt.-Col. D. E. Knollys, "Military Operations in Transcaspia, 1918-1919," *Journal of the Central Asian Society*, vol. XIII, 1926, part 2, pp. 89-110. Col. Knollys commanded the troops from the 19th Punjabi Regiment which took part in the operations.

[47] The text of the agreement of 19 August is printed in the book, *Turkmenistan v period inostrannoy voyennoy interventsii i grazhdanskoy voiny 1918-1920 gg.—sbornik dokumentov* (Turkmenistan in the Period of Foreign Military Intervention and Civil War 1918-1920—Collection of Documents), ed. Sh. Tashlieva, Ashkhabad, 1957, pp. 93-96. An English translation appears in the article, "The Revolt in Transcaspia 1918-1919" by "A Correspondent" (C. H. Ellis), *Central Asian Review* (London), vol. VII, 1959, no. 2, pp. 122-25. Mr. C. H. Ellis has been able to compare this Russian version with the original English language version in the archives of the Foreign Office. He informs me that the two versions are identical in substance, differing only on slight stylistic points which do not affect the sense.

invasion—first withdrawing all rolling stock, next destroying all oil and water tanks, and finally destroying bridges and the track itself. They also promised to withhold their cotton crop from export so long as there was a chance that it might reach the enemy.

On his part, Malleson promised that the British government would defend Baku by all available means as long as possible, would send oil and petrol in as large a quantity as possible from Baku to Krasnovodsk,[48] would defend Krasnovodsk with artillery and infantry against any attacks from the sea, and would make available certain additional small Indian Army military units for service with the Transcaspian forces. But Malleson stipulated that if the British troops were made available for a particular purpose, such as the defence of Krasnovodsk, they could not be diverted elsewhere without the permission of the British government. Those British troops assigned to the eastern front, opposing the forces of the Tashkent Soviet, would be under the command of the Russian officer commanding the Transcaspian forces, but British troops defending Krasnovodsk, because of the technical difficulties of their task, would be under British command. In addition, Malleson promised to provide British instructors and certain rather small quantities of weapons and ammunition for the Transcaspian forces.

Finally, the protocol declared that the British government agreed "in principle" to furnish the Transcaspian government with financial assistance, provided that there might be joint control over the disbursement of British funds. The amount and method of assistance would be the subject of further discussion. The protocol closed, however, with the following declaration:

On behalf of His Majesty's Government, I, Major-General Malleson representing His Majesty's Government, guarantee the continuance of military and financial help so long as the Transcaspian government remains in power and continues to place at the head of its political programme the restoration of order and the suppression of Bolshevik and Turko-German intrigue and plans for invasion.

This pledge, set apart from the body of the protocol, was the real basis of the British obligation to the Transcaspian government.

[48] At the time of the signing of the protocol, it will be remembered, Dunsterville's forces had just taken up the defence of Baku. Nevertheless, this was a rather unusual promise for Malleson to make, for Baku was no concern of his.

It is obvious that the protocol of 19 August was not the agreement for the colonial enslavement of Transcaspia and Turkestan which Soviet historians long represented it as being.[49] In signing it Malleson was hoping to erect not a colonial regime but simply one more barrier against the Turks and Germans in their march toward India. So far as the British government were concerned, the most important objectives of policy in Transcaspia were to secure control of shipping on the Caspian Sea (in order to deny it to the enemy) and to occupy and fortify Krasnovodsk.[50] The protocol specifically enabled Malleson to achieve these objectives. Opposition to the Tashkent Soviet was a strictly secondary objective for the British,[51] but for the Ashkhabad Committee it was much more important than standing guard against Turks and Germans who were hundreds of miles away. Fighting the Bolsheviks at Merv was the *quid pro quo* for which the British got the Transcaspian government's co-operation on the Caspian. In any case, it was obviously in the interests of India to secure the suppression of Bolshevism in Turkestan. Malleson himself regarded the agreement as a strictly temporary military measure. On the day on which he

[49] The publication by the Soviet government of the text of the agreement is especially interesting because it so clearly puts the lie to the account of the agreement that was previously current in Soviet historical writing. An extreme, but not untypical, example of the previous approach is in Volkov's work, published in 1954 (*Krakh angliiskoi politiki*, p. 39). Citing a Soviet archive as his source, Volkov wrote as follows: "On 19 August 1918 Malleson signed an agreement with the S-R-Menshevik government of Transcaspia, transforming Turkestan into an English colony. The S-R-Menshevik traitors handed over to the English imperialists Baku, Krasnovodsk, the Caspian fleet and the Central Asian Railway. The English imperialists carried with them a plan for the creation of a colonial government—the 'Republic of Turkestan.' This puppet republic they intended to convert into an ordinary colony like their colonies in Africa." Volkov then went on to give his readers what he alleged was a quotation from the agreement: " 'This republic,' declared the agreement, 'will find itself under the exclusive influence of England, and will enjoy such independence as that of the English African colonies, the Transvaal and the Orange Free State.' "
For other examples of previous Soviet interpretations, see Ellis, *St. Antony's Papers*, p. 139, n. 9.
[50] On 3 August 1918 the War Office telegraphed to the Mesopotamian Command: "To gain control of the fleet and mount as many guns as become available is the first essential . . . we . . . regard as vital the occupation of Krasnovodsk" (telegram 63605, 5:35 p.m.; Milner MSS, box G-2).
[51] On 10 August, repeating to the War Office a telegram from Malleson urging that he be given more troops to stop the Bolsheviks near Merv, General Monro commented that the primary objective of British policy in Transcaspia was to block the enemy road from the Caspian eastwards, and that for that purpose Merv was of secondary importance (telegram 63117 from C-i-C, India, to War Office, 10 August 1918, 6:15 p.m.; Milner MSS, box H-3).

signed it, he telegraphed to his superiors: "If they [the Transcaspian government] stand, it is worth millions to us. If they fall our liabilities are nil."[52]

After the defeat of the Bolsheviks at Kaakhka on 28 August, Malleson reinforced the Transcaspian forces with a British field artillery battery and company of infantry from Enzeli, and two squadrons of Indian light cavalry. Added to the three companies of Punjabi infantry already at Kaakhka, these reinforcements brought the total of British and Indian troops taking part in the Transcaspian operations to only 1,000 men, a very small commitment by any standards.[53] But this force was sufficient to retake the Merv Oasis on 1 November after extremely heavy fighting.[54]

By this time, the Caspian Sea had also been brought under British control. Since mid-August a small British naval detachment under Commodore D. T. Norris had been working to organise naval bases at both Enzeli and Krasnovodsk. They also worked to mount naval guns (dragged overland through Persia) on a small squadron of motor vessels they managed to acquire at Enzeli. By the end of October five armed vessels were ready for service. They were commanded by officers of the Royal Navy, assisted by British ratings, but the crews were almost entirely Russian.[55] On 29 October, the Cabinet's Eastern Committee laid down that the squadron was to keep any forces hostile to Britain from using the sea and to assist any forces friendly to Britain. They were to capture or sink Russian ships only if they showed active hostility. And the ships with British commanders were directed to fly the Naval White Ensign.[56]

Meanwhile, in mid-September, the fall of Baku to the Turks brought about an incident in Transcaspia which has become a *cause célèbre* in Anglo-Soviet relations: the execution by the Ashkhabad Committee of the twenty-six Bolshevik commissars who had, until the end of July, ruled Baku. They had been jailed by their successors, the Centro-Caspian Directorate, but in the panic that preceded the

[52] Malleson telegram MD 276, Meshed, 19 August 1918, repeated by C-i-C, India, to War Office, telegram 65558, 19 August, 5:40 p.m.; Milner MSS, box H-3.
[53] See the Appendix, "British and Indian troops taking part in operations in Transcaspia, August 1918 to April 1919," in Ellis, *St. Antony's Papers*, p. 151.
[54] *Official History: Mesopotamia Campaign*, vol. IV, p. 331.
[55] Captain David Norris, "Caspian Naval Expedition, 1918-1919," *Journal of the Central Asian Society*, vol. X, 1923, part III, pp. 216-40. See also *Official History: Mesopotamia Campaign*, vol. IV, pp. 250, 329, and Blumberg, *Sea Soldiers*, pp. 271-74.
[56] Minutes, Eastern Committee 37th meeting, 29 October 1918, 3 p.m.; Milner MSS.

arrival of the Turks they were released and were allowed to take a ship for Astrakhan, the only Caspian port still in Bolshevik hands. The ship's crew, however, were afraid that they themselves would be arrested in Astrakhan, and on the pretext of insufficient fuel they headed for Krasnovodsk.[57]

On their arrival, at dawn on 15 September, the twenty-six commissars were placed under arrest by the town commandant, Kuhn, a Caucasian cossack officer with a reputation for ruthlessness. He immediately notified the Ashkhabad Committee and asked for instructions. At the time there were no members of Malleson's mission in Krasnovodsk, and the only British officer in the vicinity, a member of Dunsterville's staff, was told nothing about the commissars. On 18 September, Dokhov, the Ashkhabad Committee's representative in Meshed, informed Malleson of the presence of the prisoners in Krasnovodsk, and asked the British general what he thought should be done with them. Malleson urged that they should be handed over to him, and that they should be confined in India as hostages for the British citizens who were at the time being held by the Soviet government in Moscow and Petrograd. He offered to send British troops to escort the commissars to India.[58]

Malleson then contacted his liaison officer in Ashkhabad, Captain Reginald Teague-Jones, and asked him to press the Transcaspian government to hand the prisoners over to the British. Kuhn, meanwhile, had urgently requested that the commissars be taken off his hands; he had no space for them in his Krasnovodsk jail, and he feared that Bolshevik sympathisers in the town might try to effect their release. On the evening of 18 September, the President of the Ashkhabad Committee, Funtikov, asked Teague-Jones to attend the committee session in which the matter was discussed. According to Teague-Jones, Funtikov showed up at the meeting drunk and informed his colleagues that he had heard from Meshed that Malleson had refused to take over the twenty-six commissars. Funtikov argued that since the Ashkhabad prison was also full, the commissars should be shot.[59]

[57] Kazemzadeh, *Transcaucasia*, pp. 144-45.

[58] Ellis, *St. Antony's Papers*, pp. 143-44. Ellis was in Meshed as a member of Malleson's staff when this incident occurred.

[59] Teague-Jones's version of the whole affair of the twenty-six Baku commissars is given in his letter of 12 November 1922 to the Under-Secretary of State at the Foreign Office, printed in Cmd. 1846 (Russia No. 1 [1923]), *Correspondence*

From Teague-Jones's own account of this meeting, it seems that he did not bother to contradict Funtikov's statement that Malleson had declined to take responsibility for the prisoners. It is certain, however, that Teague-Jones had already received Malleson's telegram sent after the conversation with Dokhov. In any case, Funtikov's contention that the commissars should be shot precipitated a long argument among the committee members, and Teague-Jones did not stay until its conclusion. The next evening, on closely questioning Funtikov, Teague-Jones learned that the committee had decided to have the prisoners shot, but he could elicit no information as to where or when the executions would take place. Only three days later did he learn that during the night of 19-20 September, on Funtikov's orders, Kuhn and his men had loaded the commissars on board a train, taken them some 120 miles into the desert east of Krasnovodsk, and shot them all.

Malleson first learned of the shootings on the 23rd. The report which reached him (presumably from Teague-Jones) said, incorrectly, that five or six of the less important commissars had been spared. Malleson's first comment to General Monro in India was: "Apart from question of justice as to which I can express no opinion, politically this alleged execution . . . means Askabad Government have burnt their boats as regards Bolsheviks." So long as Shaumian and his colleagues were alive, Malleson said, the Transcaspian government could have used them to save their own skins.[60]

To the Ashkhabad Committee, Malleson despatched a telegram strongly protesting against the executions. His protest had the full concurrence of his superiors in Simla, who had previously agreed to his proposals for sending the commissars to India for internment as hostages.[61] But the Ashkhabad Committe never offered any explanation of the shooting to the British.

Meanwhile, the Soviet government in Moscow had received a first inkling of what had befallen the Baku commissars. On 19 September, in a note to Oudendijk, the Dutch Minister, Chicherin stated that in the evacuation of Baku, the British had taken with them the mem-

---

between H.M. Govt. and the Soviet Govt. respecting the murder of Mr. C. F. Davison in Jan. 1920, pp. 6-11.
[60] Malleson telegram MD 581, Meshed, 23 September 1918, repeated by C-i-C, India, to War Office as telegram 76707, 25 September, 2:30 a.m.; Milner MSS, box H-3.
[61] Ellis, *St. Antony's Papers,* pp. 144-45.

bers of the former Baku Soviet government. It was the time, it will be remembered, of the negotiations between London and Moscow for an exchange of prisoners, and Chicherin named the Baku commissars as one of the categories of prisoners whose return the Bolsheviks demanded before they would release the interned British civilians.[62]

Moscow learned nothing more about the twenty-six commissars until the following March, when an S-R journalist named Vadim Chaikin published in a Baku newspaper an article stating that the British were responsible for bringing the commissars to Krasnovodsk and that Teague-Jones and certain members of the Ashkhabad Committee, fulfilling the wishes of the British Military Mission, decided to have them secretly shot.[63] Chaikin's version of the affair was summarised by Chicherin in a note of protest sent by wireless to the British government on 21 April 1919.[64] Stalin, in an article published two days later, wrote that the affair "shouted of the lawlessness and savage debauchery with which the English agents settled accounts with the 'natives' of Baku and Transcaspia, just as they had with the blacks of Central Africa."[65] Soviet historians up to the present day continue to hold the Malleson mission, and by inference the British government, entirely responsible for the killings,[66] and paintings of the episode, such as the famous canvas by I. I. Brodski, show British officers directing the firing squad.[67]

Although the Soviet charges are flimsy indeed,[68] they will probably

[62] Chicherin's note is cited above, Chapter x, footnote 33.

[63] Teague-Jones, in his statement of 12 November 1922 (cited above, footnote 59), said that Chaikin interviewed Funtikov when the latter was a prisoner in the Ashkhabad jail early in 1919, and that Chaikin's story originated with Funtikov. In order to escape Bolshevik reprisals, Teague-Jones said, Funtikov was anxious to shift the blame for the shooting from himself to the British and Chaikin, a fellow S-R, was anxious to help him.

[64] Chicherin to Balfour, 21 April 1919; *Dokumenty vneshnei politiki*, vol. ii, Moscow, 1959, pp. 141-42.

[65] Stalin's article, "*K rastrelyu 26 bakinskikh tovarishchei agentami angliiskogo imperializma*" (On the Shooting of the 26 Baku Comrades by the Agents of English Imperialism), appeared in the Moscow *Izvestiya*, 23 April 1919, and is reprinted in his *Sochineniya* (Complete Works), vol. iv, Moscow, 1947, pp. 252-55. The above passage is on p. 255.

[66] The recently-published *Istoriya grazhdanskoy voiny*, vol. iii, calls the incident "one of the blackest and most infamous pages in the history of English intervention in Soviet Russia" (p. 208). For another recent account, see the explanatory note in *Dokumenty vneshnei politiki*, vol. i, p. 726, n. 59.

[67] Brodski's painting is reproduced in *Istoriya grazhdanskoy voiny*, vol. iii, p. 207.

[68] Just how flimsy the charges were was indicated by the Soviet government's reply, on 12 January 1923, to the British government's denial (made 20 December 1922) of any connection with the shooting of the commissars. The Soviet note said that the

never be completely refuted. It may safely be stated that the execution of the twenty-six commissars was not the policy of the British government. Nor were the shootings ordered by the government of India or by Malleson. The puzzling element in the affair is Teague-Jones's behaviour in Ashkhabad.[69] He does not indicate that he made any effort to contradict Funtikov's statement that Malleson declined to take responsibility for the commissars. Yet he says that he knew at the time that the reverse was true. Moreover, he left the meeting of the Ashkhabad Committee before any decision had been reached. Perhaps he felt that he could exert no further influence; perhaps he was simply tired—long hours of argument, with Funtikov obviously under the influence of drink, could not have been a pleasant experience. We do not know how strongly worded Malleson's instructions to Teague-Jones were, but if the latter had chosen to make an issue over the fate of the twenty-six commissars, Funtikov and his colleagues would surely have found it difficult to refuse the British request. Upon British good-will depended British military support, and upon British military support depended the future of anti-Bolshevism in Transcaspia.

In any case, after the shooting of the twenty-six commissars, British good-will towards the Ashkhabad Committee rapidly diminished. On 9 October Malleson despairingly telegraphed to Monro:

The present committee are mainly a collection of insignificant adventurers who by distributing liberal blackmail maintain a precarious, partial and purely temporary control over the armed mob. There will probably be disturbance as soon as their funds exhausted and as soon as food position becomes acute, and this will be followed by fresh lot of adventurers procuring temporary control.[70]

"fact alone that the execution of the commissars took place during the military occupation of Transcaspia by British troops is sufficient to place the responsibility for such action on the High British Military Command. It is beyond dispute that the fate of the imprisoned commissars was in the hands of the British military authorities in the occupied territory." The inadequacy of this argument by inference is clearly seen when it is remembered that at the time of the executions, there were less than 350 British troops in "occupation" of a territory the size of western Europe. The British denial and the Soviet reply are printed in Cmd. 1846 (Russia No. 1 [1923]).

[69] For Teague-Jones's part in the incident we have only his letter, previously cited. On his return to Great Britain after the war he changed his surname to avoid publicity. He is still living, but he adamantly refuses to discuss any aspect of his experiences in Transcaspia.

[70] Malleson telegram, un-numbered, Meshed, 9 October 1918, repeated by C-i-C, India, to War Office as telegram 81351, 10 October, 12:15 a.m.; Milner MSS, box H-3.

Malleson's prediction was accurate. A month later, the Ashkhabad Committee was replaced by a "Committee of Public Safety" organised by the chief of police, Drushkin. According to Ellis, the British mission approved of the new government.[71] Drushkin included in his government those members of the former Committee who had been opposed to the execution of the Baku commissars. Funtikov was arrested and jailed.

In London, meanwhile, the Transcaspian situation was causing the Cabinet's Eastern Committee no little concern. The British government had had no warning that Malleson was going to conclude an agreement with the Ashkhabad Committee. They were then faced with the fact that Malleson had apparently led the Transcaspian government to believe that they might receive British financial assistance. When this was discussed in the Eastern Committee on 17 October, there was some feeling that since Malleson had made a promise, the government must keep it, despite the fact that Britain stood to gain nothing from financing a regime of such doubtful authority. The Treasury, however, could not take so generous a view. Malleson had entered into his obligations without Treasury approval and against Treasury warnings to exercise great care.

No decision was reached at this meeting. Malleson was told to operate for the time being with the funds he already had.[72] It was not a satisfactory situation. As the Viceroy of India, Lord Chelmsford, telegraphed on 23 October, the Ashkhabad government, although "thoroughly untrustworthy," represented at that moment the only body with whom the British could deal. The opinion of the Indian government was that the Ashkhabad Committee should continue to receive British support, on condition that they disabuse themselves of the view that Britain would do their fighting for them and cease the "barbarous methods" by which they treated their military and political prisoners.[73]

The Viceroy did not say *why* he felt that Malleson's mission should continue to support the Transcaspian government, but this question was raised in the Eastern Committee on 24 October. The war was

---

[71] Ellis, *St. Antony's Papers*, p. 142.

[72] Minutes, Eastern Committee 35th meeting, 17 October 1918, 3 p.m.; Milner MSS.

[73] Viceroy, Army Department, to Secretary of State for India, telegram 14347, 23 October 1918; Milner MSS. Despite the Viceroy's strictures on the use of British troops, British and Indian forces were as we have seen, entirely responsible for the recapture of the Merv Oasis from the Bolsheviks on 1 November.

virtually over, it was pointed out, and there was no further likelihood of Turkish or German penetration into Central Asia. In these circumstances, why should Britain retain troops in Transcaspia? One answer to this question was given immediately: Malleson's force was being maintained in Transcaspia to protect the Persian frontier against Bolshevik invasion and to keep disturbing influences out of Afghanistan.[74] Another, more detailed answer was given on 15 November, after the Armistice with Germany, in a telegram sent in reply to the Viceroy's telegram of 23 October. The Viceroy had commented that Malleson's support of the Ashkhabad Committee had brought British and Indian troops into direct conflict with the Bolsheviks. The reply, signed by the Secretary of State for India, Edwin Montagu, but probably drafted by Curzon, the Eastern Committee's chairman and its most powerful member,[75] was as follows:

It is not the policy of His Majesty's Government to embark on anti-Bolshevik campaign in Russia, but considerations both of honour and of interest demand that we should keep Bolshevism from regions East of the Black Sea. Our object is to help Russians to stand by themselves, and we should therefore do everything possible to support and strengthen existing organisations which offer hope of maintaining law and order and are working in our interests. Our support must consist ordinarily of warlike material and financial aid, and our troops must not be committed to fresh enterprises which might place them in difficult situations.[76]

This was not a very satisfactory answer. As some members of the Eastern Committee pointed out on 21 November, when the matter was next discussed, it was one thing to support Denikin, Alekseyev's successor in South Russia, and quite another thing to try to buttress so rotten a structure as the Ashkhabad government. In the end, a compromise was reached: it was decided to allocate to Malleson one lump sum so that he could fulfil his promises to the Ashkhabad Committee.[77] Accordingly, the Viceroy was informed as follows:

[74] Minutes, Eastern Committee 36th meeting, 24 October 1918, 3 p.m.; Milner MSS.
[75] As Lord Privy Seal, Curzon had no departmental responsibilities, and could devote all his time to the Eastern Committee and through it to his first love: India, Central Asia, and the Middle East.
[76] Secretary of State for India to Viceroy, Army Department, telegram 3035, 15 November 1918; Milner MSS.
[77] Minutes, Eastern Committee 38th meeting, 21 November 1918, 3:30 p.m.; Milner MSS.

While His Majesty's Government desire, in the interests of India, to keep the Askabad Government in existence as being the only organisation tending towards law and order in those parts, and appearing to work in our interest, and likely to prevent Bolshevism from penetrating Khorasan or troubling Afghanistan, they cannot meet large recurrent payments. . . . the most His Majesty's Government can undertake would be payment of a lump sum . . . in full discharge both of actual liabilities incurred by Malleson, and of any definite promises made. . . .[78]

Despite the lip service which this telegram paid in its preamble to those who favoured continued support of the Ashkhabad Committee, it effectively marked the beginning of the end of British involvement in Transcaspia. On 5 December a Treasury official admitted to the Eastern Committee that it would be possible to pay Malleson £100,000 in Persian krans at Meshed, but he expressed his opinion that such a payment would simply mean throwing the money away. Nevertheless, the Committee settled upon this sum as the "lump payment" to Malleson.[79]

A fortnight later, on 18 December, the Committee was informed that the government of India wanted to withdraw Malleson's troops across the Persian border. Malleson had telegraphed that the Ashkhabad government would certainly collapse unless British financial support were continued, which was, of course, impossible. Now that the war was over, and since the British government was not formally at war with the Bolsheviks, the government of India could find no justification for keeping British troops in Transcaspia. This view, however, was opposed by the War Office; the General Staff felt that withdrawing Malleson would mean abandoning the whole Merv-Ashkhabad-Krasnovodsk line and losing control of the Caspian, and to this the soldiers could not easily agree.[80]

The result of this conflict of views was that no decision was taken; the India Office was directed to prepare a brief on the problem for future discussion.[81] This was simply a delaying device. It was clear to all that an evacuation would have to occur. For the War Office there was the slight consolation that the withdrawal would only be into

[78] Secretary of State for India to Viceroy, Army Department, un-numbered telegram, 26 November 1918; Milner MSS.
[79] Minutes, Eastern Committee, 41st meeting, 5 December 1918, 3 p.m.; Milner MSS.
[80] Minutes, Eastern Committee 44th meeting, 18 December 1918, 3 p.m.; Milner MSS.
[81] *idem.*

Persia, and that the so-called eastern cordon could still be maintained with its apex at Meshed. The order to withdraw was finally sent to Malleson in February 1919. During the previous month his British and Indian forces had inflicted heavy losses on Red Army detachments which had attacked their positions east of Merv. Moreover, nearly all of the prisoners of war had been repatriated to Germany, Austria, and Hungary. The immediate danger to India from Bolshevik incursions, therefore, seemed much diminished. Malleson did not want to withdraw until the Transcaspian government had been able to secure some reinforcements from Denikin, and he was able to postpone the evacuation until 1 April, by which time the Russian reinforcements had started to arrive.[82] When the last British and Indian troops had left, on 5 April, the future of anti-Bolshevism in Transcaspia was linked—albeit precariously—with Denikin's fortunes in South Russia.[83]

✦

In this manner, British intervention in the troubled affairs of Transcaspia was ended. Like similar involvements in North Russia and Siberia, British presence in Transcaspia had come about not as an anti-Bolshevik measure, but as a means of stemming the threatened expansion of German arms and German influence into Russia and, in the case of Transcaspia, through Russia into British Asia. And as in North Russia and Siberia, the inevitable result of British intervention had been conflict between British and Soviet forces.

But here the similarities ceased. The scale of Britain's commitment in Transcaspia, both military and economic, was much smaller than it was in North Russia or Siberia. The Ashkhabad Committee, moreover, was scarcely worthy of the title of government. The decision to withdraw British forces from Transcaspia, therefore, was relatively easy to make. The region itself was remote; the task of supplying the British and Indian troops there was almost impossibly difficult. The country, indeed, was very largely a desert, sparsely populated and poor in resources. The only real justification for keeping British forces in the region would have been a marked threat of Bolshevik penetration into Afghanistan with its consequent danger to India. In

[82] Ellis, *St. Antony's Papers*, pp. 148-49.
[83] Britain's relations with General Denikin will be discussed in the second volume of the present work.

the winter of 1918-1919, however, this threat did not seem very great. The Bolsheviks were not much more powerful in Transcaspia and Turkestan than was the Ashkhabad Committee. Neither could really claim to govern the tribesmen who were scattered through the vast area. In the view of even the British War Office, the retention of outposts in Transcaspia would have afforded relatively little more protection to the Indian flank than that already afforded by British garrisons in Persia. Here, then, was an easy decision: Malleson's troops would leave. It was to prove much more difficult, however, to end British involvement in other parts of Russia.

EPILOGUE: INTERVENTION AND THE WAR

JUST as both Russian Revolutions were direct results of the European war, so intervention was the response of the Allied governments—particularly the British government—to Russia's departure from the war. More exactly, intervention was the reaction of the British War Office to a political situation over which they had no control and which, in the spring of 1918, after the disastrous battles of the previous autumn and the beginning of the great German offensive in March, seemed as if it would have military consequences much more grave than those which actually resulted from it. As we have seen, the War Office predicted again and again that unless the Eastern Front were restored, victory in the west would be impossible. In time of war governments too often think solely in military terms. Intervention in Russia was an attempt to apply a military solution to the political problem of the Bolshevik Revolution. As such, the surprising thing is not that its failure was so great, but that so many people allowed themselves to become convinced that it would succeed.

The British government's response to the Revolution was not, however, solely military. Through Lockhart's mission a serious attempt was made to come to terms with the Bolshevik leaders. To the British government, however, to come to terms with the Bolsheviks meant only one thing—securing their agreement to come back into the war. In the early months of 1918 few British statesmen or soldiers could face the fact that not only the Bolsheviks, but the Russian people as a whole, would not continue the war. Brest-Litovsk was seen in Britain only as a great betrayal: as Balfour told Lockhart, it was probably true that the Soviet leaders were not German agents, but if they were, their behaviour would have been no different.[1]

Underlying the British attempts to induce the Bolsheviks to come back into the war there was an assumption and a hope. The assumption was that there did, in fact, exist a community of interest between the Allies and the Soviet regime which made it advantageous to the

[1] See above, pp. 125 and 166.

latter to continue fighting the Germans; the hope was that the Bolshevik leaders could be made to see this. It was a vain hope, however, for the assumption was invalid: no such community of interest existed. To the Bolsheviks, the only thing which mattered was the immediate consolidation of their own power. It must not be forgotten that not only the Allies but the Bolsheviks themselves did not expect the infant Soviet regime to survive the dangers confronting it on every side. Through the treaty of Brest-Litovsk they had purchased a breathing space which, in the circumstances, was worth more than any amount of territory lost to the Germans. To Lenin, the certainty of freedom from further German attacks was much more valuable than the possibility of future Allied good will should the Russians be forced back into the war. A principal tenet of Bolshevik thought was that there necessarily existed an implacable hostility between themselves and the bourgeois world. Any good will which they might have bought by helping one bourgeois coalition against the other would, in the long run, have brought them little benefit and would have exposed them to the immediate risk of annihilation at the hands of the other coalition. As Lockhart discovered, the Soviet leaders would have invited Allied co-operation only if the Germans had again attacked. But the Germans, after the peace of Brest-Litovsk, were too concerned about the military situation in the west to penetrate further into Russia. Why, then, should the Bolsheviks have provoked further penetration?

The British government may perhaps be excused for so poorly comprehending the aims and interests of the Soviet regime. The Bolsheviks, after all, were Russians, and a considerable portion of Russian territory was under German occupation; to the British mind it was inconceivable that a government which claimed to be a Russian government would not do everything in its power to drive out the Germans. But the British government had no excuse for their equally poor comprehension of the factors underlying Japanese policy. The Japanese government had no reason to fight the Germans in any other area than the Far East, their own sphere of interest. To the British government it should have been obvious that Japan would not—as her leaders had indicated she would not—undertake an expedition from Siberia into European Russia. Such an expedition would have taxed her resources terribly, and would have brought her rewards scarcely commensurate with her sacrifices. Tokyo made no attempt to deceive London as to the extent to which Japanese troops might be used in Russia; in formulating grandiose plans for moving hundreds of thousands of Japanese soldiers to a new Eastern Front, the British government deceived themselves.

The idea that British interests in a restored Eastern Front were to any real degree shared by Japan was thus another of the false assumptions underlying British policy. Proceeding on the basis of this assumption, the British government was forced to mislead the American government in order to gain President Wilson's approval for intervention. The assumption was to be proved wrong only in September 1918, when 70,000 Japanese troops flooded into Eastern Siberia and made no attempt to move west.

Not only did the British government make wrong assumptions about what the Japanese government might have been prepared to do, but they were equally wrong about what Japan might have been able to do. In the existing Siberian conditions the sort of intervention envisioned by the War Office—even had Tokyo been willing—would have been impossible. The task of moving huge armies over the 6,000 miles between the Pacific and the Urals would have taken years, not months.

If there was little clear thinking in London about the objectives and resources of Japanese policy, there seems to have been no thinking at all about what Japanese troops were to do once they got to the Urals. The nearest German forces were over 1,000 miles from Chelyabinsk, which was always the point farthest west specified either in British staff papers advocating Japanese intervention or in notes on the subject to the Japanese government. These papers and notes did not state whether or how Japanese troops were to continue their journey westward until they encountered German forces. Presumably this was one of the goals of intervention. An even more important goal—indeed, a basic tenet of British interventionist policy—was that the intervening troops should serve as a nucleus around which "loyal" Russians could gather to fight the Germans. Underlying this aim was the unstated assumption that the same Russian troops who had laid down their arms in 1917 would come back into the firing lines at the side of foreign armies. Simply to state this assumption is to expose its improbability. One wonders whether it was ever so stated in the British or French war ministries during the first half of 1918.

Those months, however, were a poor time for reasoned criticism. Intervention in Russia was a policy born of a desperate feeling that something—anything—had to be done to relieve the pressure on the Allied forces in the west. Basically, it was a policy aimed at getting something for nothing—recreating an Eastern Front without sacrificing any Allied resources which might have been brought against the enemy in the west. For that very reason, it was a policy based upon so many invalid assumptions: its seeming cheapness induced a blindness to its defects.

Had the Western Allies been willing to pay a higher price, the results of intervention might have been very different. If the initial landings at Archangel could have been carried out by two or three divisions—the number which Lockhart and the military attachés at Moscow had insisted was the bare minimum necessary for success—instead of the 1,200 troops who actually occupied the port at the end of July, there is little doubt that they could have forced their way to Moscow and overthrown the Bolshevik regime. From then on, anything might have happened; the only certainty is that two or three divisions of British, French, or American troops in the heart of European Russia would have had infinitely better prospects of rallying "loyal" Russians than a Japanese force making its way across Siberia. But such was the strategy of the war that by 1918 so great a diversion of resources from the west was unthinkable.

In any event, intervention completely failed to achieve its basic purpose of restoring the Eastern Front. Nor did the threat of intervention cause the Germans to keep in the east any extra men above the amount they needed for the occupation of the conquered territories. According to Ludendorff, the only effect which intervention had upon the Central Powers was to prevent the repatriation of those of their troops who had been prisoners of war in Siberia and who could not return to their own countries, after being freed by the Brest treaty, because the Czechs were in occupation of the Trans-Siberian Railway. Ludendorff does not even give intervention full credit for this achievement: he holds the Bolsheviks equally responsible, with the Czechs, for failing to repatriate the prisoners.[2] Nor does it seem that intervention kept from the Central Powers any supplies they would otherwise have had. During the summer of 1918

[2] Erich Ludendorff, *My War Memories, 1914-1918*, London, n.d. (1919), vol. ii, p. 655.

the Germans and Austrians were busy exploiting the resources of the Ukraine; they lacked the manpower to tap the riches of Siberia.

If intervention can be said to have had any result at all, it was that it drove many Russians who were hostile to Bolshevism to support the Soviet government as a means of defending Russia against foreign invasion and preventing the restoration of a reactionary regime. There is, moreover, considerable truth in the often-repeated Soviet allegation that the Terror was a direct result of intervention. The Terror was the product of the wild desperation which followed the attempt upon Lenin's life and the murder of Uritsky in late August 1918. Much of the desperation was due to the presence of Allied forces in Siberia and in the north, and also in the Caucasus and in Transcaspia: the Bolsheviks were determined that their foreign enemies should receive no aid from their domestic enemies, and they struck out blindly against many who were innocent.

Once the Terror had begun, the Bolsheviks had burned their bridges. When Balfour declared, after the death of Cromie and the sack of the British Embassy, that there would be no "place of refuge" left to the Soviet leaders,[3] he was expressing the deep-felt anger of the British government and of the Western world. The Terror, perhaps more, even, than all of the other Soviet actions, such as the separate peace, the cancellation of the debts, the confiscation of foreign property, and the brutal murder of the Imperial family, caused the British government to resolve to continue intervention after the Armistice with Germany, in fulfilment of implicit obligations to those Russians who had remained loyal to the Allied cause.

❖

The Armistice, indeed, marked a watershed in the history of Anglo-Soviet relations, and for that reason it is appropriate that subsequent events should be left for the second volume of this study. After the Armistice, the intervention which had been conceived as a part of the war against Germany had lost its *raison d'être*. All the old arguments by which intervention had been justified were thus invalidated, and it could be continued only as an operation admittedly aimed at the destruction of the Bolshevik regime. In the future, moreover, the political aspects of British policy toward Russia were to become vastly more important than they had been during the war:

[3] See above, Chapter x.

the Armistice finally broke the strangle-hold on policy exercised by the General Staff in the form of their claim to specialised knowledge of the requirements for a victory over Germany. The decisive influence was to pass from the hands of the soldiers into those of the politicians.

Foremost among the politicians, of course, was the Prime Minister, and after the Armistice he was to become the dominant figure in Anglo-Soviet relations. During the twelve months described in the present volume Lloyd George was too preoccupied with the conduct of the war in the west to pay close attention to events in Russia. But with the end of the war, Russia was to become one of the most important problems confronting the British government, and the Prime Minister was to make it very much his own.

Along with Lloyd George, Winston Churchill, who has no part in the present volume, emerged after the war to play a commanding role in dealing with Russia. Churchill succeeded Milner at the War Office; while Milner had followed Russian events with extreme care, like Lloyd George he had been too concerned with the problems of the Western Front to be able to exert any real influence on British policy toward Russia. Churchill, however, had both more time and more energy. In large measure he was to be responsible for the transformation of intervention into an operation avowedly anti-Bolshevik in purpose.

The transformation of intervention, its failure, and the consequent British effort to come to terms with the new forces which ruled Russia, will be the subject of the second of these two volumes.

SELECTED BIBLIOGRAPHY

MANUSCRIPTS AND UNPUBLISHED DOCUMENTS

The most important original materials used in the preparation of this volume were:

The Papers of Alfred, Viscount Milner, in the Library of New College, Oxford.

The Papers of Sir William Wiseman in the Library of Yale University, New Haven.

The Documents in the following sections of the National Archives of the United States in Washington: Foreign Affairs Branch (State Department papers), Modern Army Branch (including the Records of the Supreme War Council), Naval Records Branch.

Other original materials consulted were:

The David R. Francis Papers in the Missouri Historical Society, St. Louis.
The Edward M. House Papers in the Library of Yale University.
The Robert Lansing Papers in the Library of Congress, Washington.
The Roland S. Morris Papers in the Library of Congress.
The Frank L. Polk Papers in the Library of Yale University.
The Woodrow Wilson Papers in the Library of Congress.

PUBLISHED DIPLOMATIC PAPERS

Documents on British Foreign Policy 1919-1939, Series 1, Vol. III (edited by E. L. Woodward and Rohan Butler), London: H.M. Stationery Office, 1949.

Dokumenty vneshnei politiki SSSR (Documents on the Foreign Policy of the U.S.S.R.), Moscow: Ministry of Foreign Affairs, Vol. I (7 November 1917 to 31 December 1918), 1957; Vol. II (1 January 1919 to 30 June 1920), 1958.

Papers Relating to the Foreign Relations of the United States: The Lansing Papers, 1914-1920 (two volumes), Washington: Department of State, Vol. II, 1940.

Papers Relating to the Foreign Relations of the United States: Russia, 1918 (three volumes), Washington: Department of State, 1931 and 1932.

Papers Relating to the Foreign Relations of the United States: 1918, The World War, Supplement 1, Vol. 1, Washington: Department of State, 1933.

PARLIAMENTARY PAPERS AND GAZETTED DESPATCHES

Cmd. 8587 (Misc. No. 10 [1917]), *Note from the Russian Provisional Govt. and the British Reply respecting the Allied War Aims.*

Miscellaneous No. 30 (1918), *Despatches from His Majesty's Consul-General at Moscow, August 5 to 9, 1918.*

Cmd. 1846 (Russia No. 1 [1923]), *Correspondence between H.M. Govt. and the Soviet Govt. respecting the murder of Mr. C. F. Davison in Jan. 1920.*

Despatches to the Admiralty of Rear Admiral Thomas W. Kemp on Naval Operations in the White Sea, 1917-1918, 29 April 1920, in the Fifth Supplement to the *London Gazette* of 6 July 1920.

Official Report, Parliamentary Debates: House of Commons.
Official Report, Parliamentary Debates: House of Lords.

BOOKS AND ARTICLES

Zourab Avalishvili, *The Independence of Georgia in International Politics, 1918-1921*, London: privately printed, n.d. (circa 1941).

Ray Stannard Baker, *Woodrow Wilson, Life and Letters* (8 vols.), Garden City, New York: Doubleday, Doran. Vol. VIII, *Armistice, March 1 to November 11, 1918* (1939).

Gustav Bečvar, *The Lost Legion: A Czechoslovakian Epic*, London: Stanley Paul, 1939.

Eduard Beneš, *My War Memoirs* (trans. Paul Selver), London: Allen & Unwin, 1928.

General Sir Herbert Edward Blumberg, *Britain's Sea Soldiers. A Record of the Royal Marines during the War 1914-1919*, Devonport: Swiss & Co., n.d. (circa 1927).

General V. G. Boldyrev, *Direktoriya, Kolchak, Interventy. Vospominaniya* (The Directorate, Kolchak, and the Interventionists. Reminiscences), Novonikolaevsk: Sibiraiizdat, 1925.

Bolshaya Sovetskaya Entsiklopediya (Great Soviet Encyclopedia), Moscow: Gosudarstvennii institut "Sovetskaya Entsiklopediya," First Edition, Vol. 37 (1938), Second Edition, Vol. 25 (1954).

Sir George Buchanan, *My Mission to Russia and Other Diplomatic Memories* (2 vols.), London: Cassell, 1923.

Selected Bibliography

Meriel Buchanan, *Diplomacy and Foreign Courts,* London: Hutchinson, n.d. (1928).

Meriel Buchanan (Mrs. Knowling), *The Dissolution of an Empire*, London: John Murray, 1932.

James Bunyan, *Intervention, Civil War, and Communism in Russia: April-December 1918, Documents and Materials*, Baltimore: Johns Hopkins Press, 1936.

James Bunyan and H. H. Fisher, *The Bolshevik Revolution, 1917-1918, Documents and Materials*, Stanford University Press, 1934.

Major-General Sir C. E. Callwell, *Field-Marshal Sir Henry Wilson, Bart., G.C.B., D.S.O., His Life and Diaries* (2 vols.), London: Cassell, 1927.

Edward Hallett Carr, *A History of Soviet Russia: The Bolshevik Revolution, 1917-1923* (3 vols.), London: Macmillan, 1950-1953.

William Henry Chamberlin, *The Russian Revolution 1917-1921* (2 vols.), New York: Macmillan, 1935.

G. E. Chaplin, "Dva perevorota na severe" (Two Coups d'État in the North), *Beloye delo* (White Affairs) (7 vols.), Vol. IV, Berlin, 1928, pp. 12-31.

Winston S. Churchill, *The Aftermath, being a sequel to The World Crisis,* London: Thornton Butterworth, 1929.

W. P. and Zelda K. Coates, *Armed Intervention in Russia 1918-1922,* London: Gollancz, 1935.

C. R. M. F. Cruttwell, *A History of the Great War 1914-1918*, Second Edition, Oxford: Oxford University Press, 1936.

C. K. Cumming and Walter W. Pettit, eds., *Russian-American Relations, March, 1917-March, 1920: Documents and Papers*, New York: Harcourt, Brace and Howe, 1920.

Jane Degras, ed., *Soviet Documents on Foreign Policy* (3 vols.), London: Oxford University Press for Royal Institute of International Affairs, Vol. I, *1917-1924* (1951).

I. Deutscher, *The Prophet Armed, Trotsky: 1879-1921*, London: Oxford University Press, 1954.

Blanche E. C. (Mrs. Edgar) Dugdale, *Arthur James Balfour* (2 vols.), London: Hutchinson, 1936. Vol. II.

Major-General L. D. Dunsterville, *The Adventures of Dunsterforce*, London: Edward Arnold, 1920.

C. H. Ellis, "Operations in Transcaspia 1918-1919 and the 26 Commissars Case," *St. Antony's Papers, No. 6: Soviet Affairs, Number Two* (David Footman, ed.), London: Chatto & Windus, 1959, pp. 129-53.

(C. H. Ellis) "A Correspondent," "The Revolt in Transcaspia 1918-1919," *Central Asian Review*, Vol. VII, No. 2, London, 1959, pp. 117-30.

Selected Bibliography

Louis Fischer, *The Soviets in World Affairs: A History of the Relations Between the Soviet Union and the Rest of the World 1917-1929* (2 vols.), London: Jonathan Cape, 1930 (reissued, Princeton University Press, 1951), Vol. i.

David R. Francis, *Russia from the American Embassy, April 1916-November 1918*, New York: Scribner's, 1921.

Gerald Freund, *Unholy Alliance: Russian-German Relations from the Treaty of Brest-Litovsk to the Treaty of Berlin*, London: Chatto & Windus, 1957.

Stephen Richards Graubard, *British Labour and the Russian Revolution, 1917-1924*, Harvard University Press, 1956.

William S. Graves, *America's Siberian Adventure, 1918-1920*, New York: Jonathan Cape & Harrison Smith, 1931.

L. H. Grondijs, *Le Cas Koltchak: Contribution à l'histoire de la Révolution Russe*, Leiden: A. W. Sijthoff's Uitgevermaatschappij N.V., 1939.

G. K. Guins, *Sibir, soyuzniki i Kolchak. Povorotnyi moment russkoi istorii, 1918-1920 gg: Vpechatleniya i mysli chlena Omskogo pravitel'stva* (Siberia, the Allies and Kolchak. The Turning Point of Russian History, 1918-1920: Impressions and Thoughts of a Member of the Omsk Government) (2 vols.), Peking: izd. Obschestva Vozrozhdeniya Rossii v g. Kharbin, 1921.

E. M. Halliday, *The Ignorant Armies*, New York: Harper, 1960.

Mary Agnes Hamilton, *Arthur Henderson: A Biography*, London: Heinemann, 1938.

J. L. Hammond, *C. P. Scott of the* MANCHESTER GUARDIAN, London: Bell, 1934.

History of the Communist Party of the Soviet Union (Bolsheviks), Short Course, London: Cobbett, 1943 (reprint of 1939 Moscow version).

History of the Great War Based on Official Documents, The Campaign in Mesopotamia 1914-1918 (4 vols.), Compiled at the request of the Government of India under the direction of the Historical Section of the Committee of Imperial Defence by Brig.-General F. J. Moberly, Vol. iv, London: H.M. Stationery Office, 1927.

Field-Marshal Lord Ironside, *Archangel 1918-1919*, London: Constable, 1953.

Istoriya grazhdanskoy voiny v SSSR (History of the Civil War in the USSR), Vol. iii (November 1917 to March 1919), Moscow: Marx-Lenin Institute, 1957.

Général Janin, *Ma Mission en Sibérie 1918-1920*, Paris: Payot, 1933.

Firuz Kazemzadeh, *The Struggle for Transcaucasia (1917-1921)*, Oxford: George Ronald, 1951.

Selected Bibliography

George F. Kennan, *Soviet-American Relations, 1917-1920* (2 vols.), Princeton University Press. Vol. i: *Russia Leaves the War*, 1956. Vol. ii: *The Decision to Intervene*, 1958.

Alexander F. Kerensky, *The Catastrophe*, London: Appleton Century, 1927.

Margarete Klante, *Von der Wolga zum Amur: Die tschechische Legion und der russische Bürgerkrieg*, Berlin: Ost-Europa Verlag, 1931.

Lt.-Colonel D. E. Knollys, "Military Operations in Transcaspia, 1918-1919," *Journal of the Central Asian Society*, Vol. xiii, Part ii, London, 1926, pp. 89-110.

Major-General Sir Alfred Knox, *With the Russian Army, 1914-1917* (2 vols.), London: Hutchinson, 1921.

Krasnyi Arkhiv (Red Archives) (108 vols.), Moscow-Leningrad, 1922-1941. "Anglichanie na severe" (The English in the North), Vol. 19, 1926 (No. 6), pp. 39-52.
"Nakanune peremiriya" (On the Eve of the Armistice), Vol. 23, 1927 (No. 4), pp. 195-249.

M. Ya. Latsis (Sudrabs), *Dva goda borby na vnutrennem fronte* (Two Years of Struggle on the Internal Front), Moscow: Gosizdat, 1920.

V. I. Lenin, *Sochineniya* (Complete Works), Third Edition, Moscow-Leningrad: Gosizdat, Vol. xxii (1917-1918), 1929, and Vol. xxiii (1918-1919), 1930.

David Lloyd George, *War Memoirs* (two-volume edition), London: Odhams, n.d. (originally published 1933-1936).

R. H. Bruce Lockhart, *Memoirs of a British Agent*, London: Putnam, 1932.

R. H. Bruce Lockhart, *Retreat from Glory*, London: Putnam, 1934.

Erich Ludendorff, *My War Memoirs 1914-1918* (2 vols.), London: Hutchinson, n.d. (1919), Vol. ii.

Major-General Sir Wilfrid Malleson, "The British Military Mission to Turkistan, 1918-1920," *Journal of the Central Asian Society*, Vol. ix, Part ii, London, 1922, pp. 96-110.

G. Mannerheim, *The Memoirs of Marshal Mannerheim* (trans. Count Eric Lowenhaupt), London: Cassell, 1953.

Peyton C. March, *The Nation at War*, Garden City, New York: Doubleday, Doran, 1932.

T. G. Masaryk, *The Making of a State: Memories and Observations, 1914-1918*, London: Allen & Unwin, 1927.

Arno J. Mayer, *Political Origins of the New Diplomacy, 1917-1918*, Yale University Press, 1959.

A. M. Michelson, P. N. Apostol, and M. W. Bernatsky, *Russian Public Finance during the War*, Yale University Press for the Carnegie Endowment, 1928.

[341]

Selected Bibliography

James William Morley, *The Japanese Thrust into Siberia, 1918*, Columbia University Press, 1957.

Lt.-Colonel Hon. Arthur C. Murray, *At Close Quarters: A Sidelight on Anglo-American Diplomatic Relations*, London: John Murray, 1946.

Constantin Nabokoff, *The Ordeal of a Diplomat*, London: Duckworth, 1921.

Henry Newbolt, *History of the Great War Based on Official Documents by Direction of the Historical Section of the Committee of Imperial Defence, Naval Operations*, Vol. v, London: Longmans, 1931.

Harold Nicolson, *King George the Fifth, His Life and Reign*, London: Constable, 1952.

Général Niessel, *Le triomphe des Bolchéviks et la Paix de Brest-Litovsk: Souvenirs, 1917-1918*, Paris: Plon, 1940.

Captain David Norris, "Caspian Naval Expedition, 1918-1919," *Journal of the Central Asian Society*, Vol. x, Part iii, London, 1923.

Joseph Noulens, *Mon ambassade en Russie soviétique, 1917-1919* (2 vols.), Paris: Plon, 1933.

W. J. Oudendyk, *Ways and Byways in Diplomacy*, London: Peter Davies, 1939.

Bernard Pares, *My Russian Memoirs*, London: Jonathan Cape, 1931.

Alexander G. Park, *Bolshevism in Turkestan, 1917-1927*, Columbia University Press, 1957.

Lt.-Colonel Pichon, "Le coup d'État de l'amiral Kolčak," *Le Monde Slave*, Paris, 1925, Nos. 1 & 2, pp. 1-25, 248-70.

Richard Pipes, *The Formation of the Soviet Union: Communism and Nationalism 1917-1923*, Harvard University Press, 1954.

Arthur Upham Pope, *Maxim Litvinoff*, New York: Fischer, 1943.

O. H. Radkey, *The Election to the Russian Constituent Assembly of 1917*, Harvard University Press, 1950.

John S. Reshetar, Jr., *The Ukrainian Revolution, 1917-1920*, Princeton University Press, 1952.

Lord Riddell, *Lord Riddell's War Diary: 1914-1918*, London: Ivor Nicolson & Watson, 1933.

Général J. Rouquerol, *L'Aventure de l'Amiral Koltchak, La Guerre des Rouges et des Blancs*, Paris: Payot, 1929.

Captain Jacques Sadoul, *Notes sur la Révolution Bolchevique*, Paris: Éditions de la Sirène, 1919.

Chattar Singh Samra, *India and Anglo-Soviet Relations, 1917-1947*, London: Asia Publishing House, 1959.

Charles Seymour, *The Intimate Papers of Colonel House* (4 vols.), New York: Houghton Mifflin, 1928. Vol. iii, *Into the World War*, Vol. iv, *The Ending of the War*.

Edgar Sisson, *100 Red Days: A Personal Chronicle of the Bolshevik Revolution*, Yale University Press, 1931.

Clarence Jay Smith, Jr., *Finland and the Russian Revolution, 1917-1922*, Athens, Georgia: University of Georgia Press, 1958.

Andrew Soutar, *With Ironside in North Russia*, London: Hutchinson, 1940.

J. V. Stalin, "K rasstrelyu 26 bakinskikh tovarishchei agentami angliiskogo imperializma" (On the Shooting of the 26 Baku Comrades by the Agents of British Imperialism), *Sochineniya* (Complete Works), Moscow: Gospolizdat, Vol. IV, 1947, pp. 252-5.

George Stewart, *The White Armies of Russia: A Chronicle of Counter-Revolution and Allied Intervention*, New York: Macmillan, 1933.

Leonid I. Strakhovsky, *Intervention at Archangel: The Story of Allied Intervention and Russian Counter-Revolution in North Russia 1918-1920*, Princeton University Press, 1944.

Leonid I. Strakhovsky, *The Origins of American Intervention in North Russia (1918)*, Princeton University Press, 1937.

I. Subbotovsky, *Soyuzniki, russkie reaktsionery i interventsiya; kratkii obzor (Iskliuchitel'no po offitsial'nym arkhivnym dokumentam Kolchakovskogo pravitel'stva)* (The Allies, Russian Reactionaries and Intervention: A Brief Outline [Exclusively from the Official Archive Documents of the Kolchak Government]), Leningrad: Gosizdat, 1926.

Peter S. H. Tang, *Russian and Soviet Policy in Manchuria and Outer Mongolia, 1911-1931*, Durham, North Carolina: Duke University Press, 1959.

L. Trotsky, *My Life. The Rise and Fall of a Dictator*, London: Thornton Butterworth, 1930.

Turkmenistan v period inostrannoy voyennoy interventsii i grazhdanskoy voiny 1918-1920 gg.—sbornik dokumentov (Turkmenistan in the Period of Foreign Military Intervention and Civil War, 1918-1920—Collection of Documents), Sh. Tashlieva, ed., Ashkhabad: Turkmenistan State Publishing Office, 1957.

Betty Miller Unterberger, *America's Siberian Expedition, 1918-1920: A Study of National Policy*, Durham, North Carolina: Duke University Press, 1956.

Elena Varneck and H. H. Fisher, eds., *The Testimony of Kolchak and other Siberian Materials*, Stanford University Press, 1935.

F. D. Volkov, *Krakh angliiskoi politiki interventsii i diplomaticheskoi izolyatsii sovetskogo gosudarstva (1917-1924 gg.)* (The Failure of English Interventionist Policy and the Diplomatic Isolation of the Soviet Government, 1917-1924), Moscow: State Publishing House for Political Literature, 1954.

Selected Bibliography

C. E. Vulliamy, ed., *The Red Archives: Russian State Papers and Other Documents relating to the Years 1915-1918*, London: Godfrey Bles, 1929.

Colonel John Ward, *With the "Die-Hards" in Siberia*, London: Cassell, 1920.

Robert D. Warth, *The Allies and the Russian Revolution, from the Fall of the Monarchy to the Peace of Brest-Litovsk*, Durham, North Carolina: Duke University Press, 1954.

John W. Wheeler-Bennett, *The Forgotten Peace: Brest-Litovsk, March 1918*, London: Macmillan, 1938.

John Albert White, *The Siberian Intervention*, Princeton University Press, 1950.

Sir Arthur Willert, *The Road to Safety: A Study in Anglo-American Relations*, London: Derek Verschoyle, 1952.

John Evelyn Wrench, *Alfred Lord Milner, the Man of No Illusions, 1854-1925*, London: Eyre & Spottiswoode, 1958.

INDEX

NOTE: All important page references under each main entry are grouped under sub-entries; those page numbers which follow the *last* semi-colon of each entry are less important references, and may be simply a brief mention of the index entry.

Abbeville Resolution, 155-56, 171

Admiralty: and White Sea operations, 111; sends *H.M.S. Cochrane* to Murmansk, 115; instructions to Kemp re defence of Murmansk, 117-18; instructions to Payne at Vladivostok, 146, 149

Afghanistan: map, 312; Penjdeh incident (1885), 303; and Anglo-Russian Convention (1907), 303; Turkish and German danger to, 304, 306; in British policy, 313-15, 326-27, 328; 311

Alekseyev, General M. V.: succeeds Kornilov as chief of staff, 15; in Don, 43, 47, 52, 57, 73, 265; French aid to, 56, 232; Lockhart's relations with, 232, 292; and Omsk Directorate, 269 n. 36; Balfour on, 274; death, 272-73; effect of death on British policy, 278. *See also* Volunteer Army

Alexander, *H.M.S.* (armed icebreaker): forced to leave Archangel, 181-82

Allied diplomatic corps, Russia: evacuate Petrograd, 77-78; evacuate Vologda, 234; move to Archangel, 238; close Moscow consulates, 287

All-Russian Provisional Government (Omsk), 269. *See* Directorate

Alston, B. F., British Consul at Vladivostok (replaced Hodgson), 262

Amery, Lt.-Colonel L. S., 170 n. 5

Amiral Aube (French cruiser): despatched to Murmansk, 115; in Archangel landing, 235

Amur Railway (part of Trans-Siberian): map, 97; 104, 140, 276

Amur River: map, 97; 130

Anglo-French negotiations and Convention on Southern Russia (22-23 December 1917), 53-56

Anglo-Japanese Treaty of Alliance (1902), 205

Anglo-Russian Convention (1907), 303, 313 n. 38

Archangel: map, 110; war stores at, 109, 118; situation at, 111-13, 245, 247; Bolshevik evacuation of war stores, 113, 173-74; anti-Bolshevik elements at, 112-13; Bolshevik take-over, 113; British ships bring food, 173; and Czech Corps, 178, 195, 240; Bolsheviks order departure of Allied warships, 181-82; Allied diplomats arrive from Vologda, 234; Allied landing at, 235-36; government formed, 237; Poole proclaims martial law, 237; Allied troops despatched to combat fronts, 238; diplomats establish embassies at, 238; problem of raising Russian forces, 242-43; size of

Allied forces involved, 243; military operations bog down, 245; relations between Allies and local government, 237-40, 243, 245-50; Chaplin coup, 245-48; reconstitution of government, 255; Ironside replaces Poole, 255-56; 87, 154

Archangel-Vologda Railway: map, 110; fighting on, 238, 243, 252; in Poole's orders, 240

Armenia: in British plans, 93; and Turkey, 304; 52, 84

Armenians at Baku: co-operation with British, 308-10; 306 n. 14

Armistice on Western Front (11 November 1918), effect of: on troops in North Russia, 256-57; on British policy re Siberia, 279; on British policy re Transcaspia, 326-28; on Anglo-Soviet relations, 334-35

Asahi (Japanese warship), 91-92

Ashkhabad: map, 312; situation at, 315, 324-25; 321

Ashkhabad Committee: takes power, 315; asks Malleson for help, 315; signs protocol with Malleson, 317-20; and execution of 26 Baku commissars, 320-24; Malleson on, 324; change of personnel, 325; question of British financial and military support to, 325-29

Askold (Russian cruiser): at Murmansk, 114, 118, 182; becomes *H.M.S. Glory IV*, 183 n. 50

Asquith, Herbert H., 65

Astrakhan: map, 41; 309, 321

Avksentiev, N., Chairman of Omsk Directorate: and Knox, 278, 281; kidnapped, 279

Azerbaijan: Turks establish republic of, 306; 304, 310

Baikal, Lake: maps, 97, 268; Czechs at, 212, 258-59; Bolsheviks defeated at, 262; limit of Japanese westward advance, 265; 104, 151. *See also* Trans-Baikalia

Bakhmach (Ukraine), 152

Baku: map, 41; under Bolshevik control, 306; and British policy, 306; and Dunsterville mission, 306, 309-10; Turks advance upon, 308-09; fall of Bolshevik regime at, 309, 316; falls to Turks, 310; and Malleson, 318

Baku commissars, twenty-six: arrest, imprisonment and execution of, 320-22; question of British involvement, 323-24; and Lockhart-Litvinov exchange, 294, 296 n. 37

Baku Soviet: votes to invite British aid against Turks, 308-09

Balfour, Arthur James, Foreign Secretary: expresses confidence in Buchanan, 18-19; at inter-Allied conference in Paris, November 1917, 26-28; instructions to Buchanan on Bolshevik armistice proposal, 27-28; tells Buchanan to use only consuls for dealings with Soviet regime, 30; memorandum to War Cabinet, 9 December 1917, 31-33; recommends release of Chicherin and Petrov, 33, 35; and situation in South Russia, 42-43, 45-46; reaction to dissolution of Constituent Assembly, 68-69; expounds policy to Lockhart, 74-75, 123, 125, 191-92; on Japanese intervention, 86, 95, 103, 104-05, 202; discusses intervention with Japanese Ambassador, 88, 89, 107, 108, 201, 204-05; on American policy, 88, 105, 167; discusses intervention with U.S. Ambassador, 93, 103; and Semenov, 99-101, 138, 140-41, 142, 201; discusses intervention with French Ambassador, 103; sets conditions for Japanese intervention, 107; tells Lockhart Japanese action imminent, 121-22; and Foreign Office criticism of Lockhart, 124-25; on relation of Bolshevik leaders to German policy, 125, 166; and Knox's attack on Lockhart, 132-33, 144 n. 55; orders restraint of Semenov, 140-41, 142-43; and Anglo-Japanese landings at Vladivostok, 147, 148-50; on possibility of intervention by Bolshevik invitation, 149, 165-66, 201; on ends of Bolshevik policy, 31, 161; on Allied-Soviet co-operation, 160-63, 175 n. 23; on *de facto* recognition of Soviet government, 162-63; requests U.S. participation in Siberian expedition, 162-63; justifies policy to French, 166-67; and Soviet evacuation of Archangel war stores, 173-74; instructs Lockhart to have no contacts with Savinkov's organisation, 190; on Lockhart's changing views of intervention, 191; on reasons for delay of intervention, 192; requests U.S. troops for Murmansk, 194; with Pichon and Sonnino sets conditions for Japanese intervention, 202; and question of scope of Japanese intervention, 201, 204-05; on Kerensky visit to London, 208; asks U.S. not to make decision until Supreme Council met, 211; on Wilson's decision, 218, 226-27; on probable effects of intervention on Russian internal politics, 223, 271; urges Japanese to accept U.S. decision, 226; and Lockhart's contacts with Whites, 231 n. 7; on British economic mission to Russia, 233; gives Japan free hand re additional troops to Siberia, 261; appeals to Japanese to aid Czechs on Volga front, 265; on need for temporary military dictatorship in Russia, 273-74; urges formation of strong government at Omsk, 278; tells Lockhart not to break ties with Bolsheviks, 286; and Lock-

hart-Litvinov exchange, 288, 294-95; reaction to death of Cromie, 290; receives Lockhart, 296; on Lockhart's final report, 300; member of Eastern Committee, 307 n. 16

Ballard, Brigadier-General C. R., British Military Attaché at Jassy, 46, 54

Baltic provinces, 63, 67

Barclay, Colville A. de R., Counsellor of British Embassy at Washington: warns against excessive pressure on U.S. Administration, 259; 93, 106, 248-49, 260

Barclay, Sir G. H., British Minister at Jassy, 43

Batum: map, 41; 56, 304

Beneš, Eduard: discussions with British and French re employment of Czech Corps, 153-54, 170; 152 n. 95, 262

Bereznik: map, 110; fighting at, 244

Berthelot, General, Chief of French Military Mission to Rumania, 40, 50

Bicherakhov, Colonel Lazar, leader of anti-Bolshevik force in Caucasus, 305, 308

Billing, N. P., Conservative MP, 79

Birse, Edward: assistant to Lockhart, 70; leaves Russia, 120

Bliss, General Tasker H., U.S. Military Representative to Supreme War Council: opposes British plans for North Russia, 251; 103, 154, 195

Bokhara: map, 312; 302

Boldyrev, General V. B.: in Directorate, 269; and Kolchak, 272-73; and Knox, 277-78; on Knox's role in Kolchak coup, 280

Bolshevik Party: on Stockholm conference, 10; in Constituent Assembly, 68; VII Congress, 123-24

Bolshevik seizure of power, November 1917: 16; London reaction to, 3-4, 19-20

Bolshevism: in South Russia, 94; in Siberia, 87, 144, 151; in North Russia, 111-12, 245; in Caucasus, 306; in Transcaspia, 311, 328-29; among Siberian prisoners of war, 156; collapse predicted, 3, 94; viewed as German-controlled, 56, 61, 65 n. 26, 125, 134 n. 21, 241-42; War Office troop-briefing material on, 241-42; Lockhart final report, on future of, 297-98

Brailsford, H. N., Labour journalist: on Bolshevik Revolution, 20

Brest-Litovsk negotiations: agreement on location, 22; first phase, 62-63; deadlock, 63; in Fourteen Points speech, 65; course of, 66-68, 75-76; effect of deadlock on events at Murmansk, 116

Brest-Litovsk, Treaty of: signature, 76-77; ratification, 78, 82, 119-27; effect of on Japanese policy, 104; effect of on British policy, 104-05; and Turkey, 303-04

Bridges, General, British Military Representative at Washington: on U.S. decision on Siberia, 226

British Consulate-General, Moscow: and secret intelligence operations, 134; Cheka raid and internment of staff, 286-87; closed and left in care of Netherlands Legation, 287

British Embassy, Petrograd: and Bolshevik seizure of power, 16-17; removal of most of staff from Russia, 37-39; Christmas celebration (1917), 38; issues statement on British officers in South Russia, 52-53; and Lockhart mission, 71; withdrawal of remaining staff, 77-78; left in charge of Netherlands Legation, 78; raided by mob, 31 August 1918, 288-89; alleged conspiracy involving, 289 n. 17; 11

British forces: in Caucasus, *see* Dunsterville, Major-General L. C.; in North Russia, *see* Archangel, Murmansk; in Siberia, *see* Ward, Lt.-Colonel John, and Knox, Major-General Alfred W. F.

British forces in Transcaspia: in Malleson-Ashkhabad Committee protocol, 318; combat with Bolsheviks, 316-17, 320, 325 n. 73, 328

British subjects in Russia: ordered from Archangel to Murmansk, 111; interned after start of intervention, 286-88, 293-94, 296; 33, 77, 234

Brodski, I. I., Soviet painter, 323

Brooklyn, U.S.S. (U.S. cruiser): to Vladivostok, 102

Brusilov, General: offensive (1916), 4, 11

Buchanan, Sir George W., British Ambassador at Petrograd: background, 8; Lloyd George on, 8; relations with Tsar, 9; Masaryk on, 9; and Arthur Henderson, 9-10; on Stockholm conference, 10; and Kornilov coup, 12; and warning to Provisional Government, 14; would permit Soviet to send delegate to Paris conference, 15-16; watches Bolshevik seizure of power, 16; convokes colleagues to concert action, 17-18; on Kerensky's failure to counter Bolshevik coup, 18; advice on Bolshevik armistice proposal, 21-22, 23-24; public statement, 29 November 1917, 28-30; on necessity of unofficial relations with Bolsheviks, 30; recommends release of Chicherin and Petrov, 35; on Soviet request for courier privileges, 37; instructed to withdraw Embassy from Russia when necessary, 37; receives emissaries from Don Cossacks, 42-43; and situation in South Russia, 44-48; on Brest-Litovsk talks, 63; and Bolshevik threats to Embassy, 48-49, 111 n. 85; on British evacuation of Archangel, 113-14; reaction to dissolution of Constituent Assembly, 69; sent on leave, 53; illness and departure from Russia, January 1918, 37-39

Buchanan, Lady Georgina, 17

Bukharin, N., Bolshevik leader, 67, 291 n. 25

Cadet Party (Constitutional Democrats): and Lockhart, 164

Cambon, Paul, French Ambassador at London, 26, 103

de Candolle, General, British liaison officer with Don Cossacks: on situation in South Russia, 94

Caspian Sea: maps, 41, 312; in British policy, 319; British naval control over, 320, 327; 304, 306, 311, 316

Caucasus: front, 44, 303; situation at time of Bolshevik Revolution, 50-51; British sphere of responsibility, 54; anti-Bolshevik elements in, 75, 94, 305; in British policy, 83, 84, 305-06; oil of, 96; German and Turkish penetration of, 186, 187, 203 n. 29, 303-05, 306; British mission sent to train local troops, 305; Bolshevism in, 306. *See also* Armenia; Azerbaijan; Georgia; Baku; Dunsterville, General L. C.

Cave, Sir George, Home Secretary: on Litvinov, 79-80

Cecil, Lord Robert, Under Secretary of State for Foreign Affairs: on Soviet publication of secret treaties, 21 n. 70; and recognition of Soviet regime, 32 n. 100; instructs Buchanan to aid formation of "southern bloc," 46; goes to Paris to coordinate Allied policy, 53; on policy re South Russia, 57; and Lockhart, 59, 61; on expulsion of Kamenev, 81; and Foreign Office-War Office conflict, 83-84; on intervention in Siberia, 90; discusses intervention with Japanese Ambassador, 91, 200-01; urges Japanese intervention to counter German penetration of Russia, 126; statement on Anglo-Japanese landing at Vladivostok, 149 n. 80; letter to Clemenceau on Czech Corps, 169-71; on Clemenceau's reply, 171 n. 7; on aims of British policy in Russia, 185-86; on question of scope of Japanese intervention, 206; on need for temporary military dictatorship in Russia, 273; and Kolchak coup, 284; on Lockhart's final report, 300; member Eastern Committee, 307 n. 16

Central Asia: aims of British policy, 314. *See also* Transcaspia, India, Malleson

Centro-Caspian Directorate: assumes power at Baku, 309; and Dunsterville's force, 309-10; and 26 Baku commissars, 320-21

Chaikin, Vadim, S-R journalist: alleges British ordered shooting of 26 Baku commissars

Chaikovsky, N. V.: forms government at Archangel, 237; complains against Poole's administration, 238, 245; kidnapped by Chaplin, 246-48; and Allied diplomats, 238, 245, 249; appoints Russian governor-general, 250; reconstitutes government on bourgeois lines, 255; and recall of Poole, 255-56

Chaplin, Captain Georgi E.: organises rising at Archangel before Allied landing, 236; named commander-in-chief of Russian forces at Archangel, 237; kidnaps Chaikovsky government, 245-48; 249, 250, 255

Charpentier, Captain, French military representative at Murmansk, 117

Cheka (Soviet police): suppresses anarchists in Moscow, 159; arrests 200 British and French residents of Moscow, 286-87; Terror, 288, 293, 298, 334; uncovers alleged conspiracy in British Embassy, Petrograd, 289 n. 17; arrests Lockhart and Hicks, 290, 293; uncovers "Lockhart conspiracy," 291

Chelmsford, Viscount, Viceroy of India: on support of Ashkhabad government, 325-26

Chelyabinsk: map, 268; Czech-Hungarian incident, 168, 172; 107, 129, 155, 200, 202, 203, 332

Chernov, Viktor: head of Samara government, 267; and S-R manifesto, 282, 284

Chesma (Russian battleship): at Murmansk, 114, 119

Chicherin, Georgi V., Soviet Commissar for Foreign Affairs: internment in Britain and subsequent repatriation, 33-35; acting Foreign Commissar, 71; first meeting with Lockhart, 71; summons Lockhart re Anglo-Japanese landings at Vladivostok, 147; and German protests against Allied presence in North Russia, 176-77; protests against German submarine activities off North Russia, 177; instructs Murmansk Soviet to play neutral role, 179-80; orders departure of Allied warships from North Russia, 181; and break with Murmansk Soviet, 182, 184; receives Allied protests against Soviet treatment of Czechs, 189; suspicions of Lockhart, 189; and departure of Allied embassies from Vologda, 234; reaction to start of intervention, 285-86; on internment of Allied citizens, 286; and Lockhart-Litvinov exchange, 287-88, 290, 293-94; and arrest of Lockhart, 293; and 26 Baku commissars, 322-23

China: Japanese policy toward, 86, 203; defeats Bolshevik force at Harbin, 98; question of participation in intervention, 102; and Semenov, 140; not consulted before Japanese entry into Chinese-Eastern Railway Zone, 261

Chinda, Viscount, Japanese Ambassador at London: and question of Japanese intervention, 200-01, 204-06; behaviour after conclusion of negotiations on Siberia, 229 n. 104; tells Balfour Japan sending additional troops to Siberia, 261; 88, 89, 91, 107, 108, 129, 199, 202

Chinese-Eastern Railway: map, 97; background, 98 n. 44; in British plans, 130;

in Japanese plans, 203, 228; Japanese send troops into Zone, 261; 86, 99, 102, 140

Chita: map, 97; Semenov's activities, 99, 140

Churchill, Winston S., Minister of Munitions, 65, 335

Clark, Sir William, Comptroller General of Department of Overseas Trade: leads economic mission to Russia, 232-34

Clemenceau, Georges, French Premier: opposes releasing Russia from obligations, 26; reply to Cecil's letter on Czech Corps, 171; 53, 54

Clerk, Sir George R.: on South Russia, 57

Cochrane, H.M.S. (cruiser): despatched to Murmansk, 115; in Pechenga action, 176; 116, 118 ns. 104 and 106

Cole, Felix, U.S. Consul at Archangel, 111 n. 85, 236

Congress of Soviets: II Congress (7-9 November 1917), 17; IV Special All-Russian Congress (14-17 March 1918), 122, 124-25

Constituent Assembly: dissolution of, 68-69; elections in Archangel region, 112; and Samara government, 267; and All-Russian Provisional Government, 269

Croft, Brigadier H. P., Conservative MP, 79

Cromie, Captain F. N. A., British Naval Attaché at Petrograd: killed in raid on Embassy, 288-90

Curzon of Kedleston, Marquess: chairman of Eastern Committee, 307 n. 16; and British policy re Persia and Transcaspia, 307, 326; 59, 128

Czechoslovak Corps: background and evacuation efforts, 151-52; ordered by Bolsheviks to disarm, 152; decision to resist disarmament, 153; Anglo-French discussions re employment of, 153-55, 169-71; clash with Hungarians at Chelyabinsk, 168, 172; seize control of Trans-Siberian Railway, 172; effects in Russia of rising, 181, 190; Allied diplomats in Moscow protest against Soviet measures, 189; effect of rising on British military planning, 194; question of Czechs coming to Archangel, 178, 195, 240; cause concern to Supreme War Council, 212; seize Vladivostok, 212-13; deciding factor in U.S. decision to intervene, 213-14; in U.S. *aide-mémoire*, 224; on Volga front, 234, 250, 258, 263-66; reach limit of westward advance, 250, 263; at Lake Baikal, 258-59, 262; on Ussuri front, 258-59, 262; control all railway to Urals, 262; effect of success on British and U.S. policy, 263-64; decision to retire from Volga front, 266; and Samara government, 267; and Ufa State Conference, 267-68; hostility to Kolchak, 283, 284

Czechoslovak National Council, 151-52, 172, 185, 263

Daily Express: on Litvinov, 79
Daily News: on Bolshevik Revolution, 19
Dauriya: map, 97; and Semenov, 140
debt, Russian foreign: repudiated by Bolsheviks, 69-70; Lockhart on, 73, 334
"Decree on Peace," 17, 21
Denikin, General A. I.: successor to Alekseyev in South Russia, 284, 297, 328; British support of, 326, 328 n. 83
Department of Overseas Trade mission to Russia: sent to investigate trading with Bolsheviks, 190, 232-34; Balfour on purpose of, 233
Derber, Peter, head of "Provisional Government of Autonomous Siberia," 139 n. 34, 267
Directorate (of All-Russian Provisional Government, Omsk): formation, 269; and Knox, 278, 282; and Chernov manifesto, 282
Dokhov, Ashkhabad Committee's representative with Malleson, 321, 322
Don Cossacks: 42-49, 52, 74, 232; British financial aid to, 52 n. 33; in Anglo-French Convention on Southern Russia, 54-56; Lindley on, 74 n. 50; in British intervention plans, 93. *See also* Alekseyev, General M. V.
Donets Basin: map, 41; 44
Donop, Colonel (French Army): military governor of Archangel, 237, 246; replaced, 249
Drushkin, head of government replacing Ashkhabad Committee, 325
Dukhonin, General N. N.: directed by Bolsheviks to seek armistice, 20; receives Allied protest, 22
Dunsterville, General L. C., chief of British Military Mission to Caucasus: initial terms of assignment, 305; sets out for Caspian with small force, 305-06; redefined objectives, 306-08; defence of Baku, 309-10
Durov, Colonel B. A.: appointed governor-general at Archangel, 250, 255
Dushak: map, 312; fighting at, 317
Dvina River: map, 110; fighting on, 238, 243-44, 257; 235

Eastern Committee of War Cabinet: establishment, membership and terms of reference, 307 n. 16; and Dunsterville mission, 306-07; and General Staff proposals on use of Afghan forces in Russia, 314; orders British control of Caspian, 320; and financial support of Ashkhabad government, 325-27; and maintenance of British troops in Transcaspia after war, 325-27
Eastern Front: Allied hopes to restore, 85, 128-30, 264, 271, 330, 333
Eliot, Sir Charles N. E.: appointed British High Commissioner for Siberia, 270;

Balfour's instructions to, 273-74; urges continued aid to Siberian government at Omsk, 278; warns of consequences of Kolchak coup, 284
Ellis, C. H., member of Malleson's mission, 315 n. 41, 317 n. 47, 325
Enzeli (Persia), 305, 320

February Revolution. *See* March Revolution
Finland: civil war, 77, 115 n. 96, 253; White Finn threat to Murmansk, 118, 175-76, 194-95; German landing in south, 174; Red Finn representative sees Lockhart, 175 n. 22; evacuation of German troops, 240
Foch, General (in August 1918, Marshal) Ferdinand: and Japanese intervention, 86, 213, 260; and intervention in North Russia, 195
Foreign Office: on Bolshevik Revolution, 3-4; on Ukrainian Rada, 50; on policy re South Russia, 57; and Lockhart, 61, 124-25, 130-31; Home Secretary on, 80; general approach to problem of Russia, 82-83; conflict with War Office, 83-84; and Japanese policy in Siberia, 198-99. *See also* Balfour, Arthur James, and Cecil, Lord Robert
France: role in South Russia, 54, 56; offers Bolsheviks military support, 76; and Japanese intervention, 86; reported assassination of consul at Irkutsk, 92; plan to block Trans-Siberian Railway, 92-93; willing to give Japan free hand in Siberia, 102; sends cruiser to Murmansk, 115; officers in Moscow aid Bolsheviks, 136; aid withdrawn, 164; consul at Vladivostok welcomes Japanese marines, 147; proposals for use of Czech Corps on Western Front, 151, 153, 171; refuses Soviet request for Noulens' recall, 165; worried by British policy, 168-169; general approach to problem of Russia, 171; disputes command in North Russia, 195; and Yaroslavl rising, 231; failure to recruit Russian force at Archangel, 252; French troops at Archangel, 243; at Murmansk, 252; effect of Armistice on troops at Archangel, 256-57; appoints High Commissioner in Siberia, 270; Moscow consulate-general raided, 286. *See also* Noulens, Joseph
Francis, David R., U.S. Ambassador in Russia: and Robins, 127 n. 133; on British economic mission, 233; asks Poole to hurry intervention, 235; on Poole's administration, 239; and Chaikovsky, 245, 255; and Chaplin coup, 246-48; on Ironside, 256
French Military Mission to Rumania, 40, 50, 136, 175
Funtikov, President of Ashkhabad Committee: and execution of 26 Baku commissars, 321-22, 323 n. 63, 324; jailed, 325

Garstin, Captain Dennis: joins Lockhart's mission, 120; plan for combined Northern and Siberian intervention, 193-94

General Staff, British: on intervention in Siberia, 93-94, 96, 103, 130, 304; memorandum on German use of Russian manpower, 169; plan for combined Northern and Siberian intervention, 194; on need for more troops in Siberia, 258-59; proposal to use Afghan forces in Russia, 313-14; and question of maintaining British troops in Transcaspia after Armistice, 327; influence on British policy, 334-35. *See also* War Office; Wilson, General Sir Henry; Knox, Major-General Alfred W. F.; Robertson, General Sir William

George V, King: receives Lockhart, 300; and murder of Russian Imperial family, 300 n. 44

Georgia: proclaims independence and comes to terms with Germans and Turks, 306; 84. *See also* Caucasus

Germany: transfers troops from East to Western Front, 14, 32 n. 101, 128; begins new offensive in Russia, 75; policy re Russia, 95-96; role in Finnish civil war, 115 n. 96; rumoured threat to Murmansk, 118; Lenin on capabilities of, 124; penetration and exploitation, 126, 137, 169, 186, 202, 331; offensive on Western Front of 21 March 1918, 128, 174, 197, 330; policy toward renewed war with Bolsheviks, 137, 186; troops in southern Finland, 174; concern over Allied presence in North Russia, 176-77, 181; submarine sinks ships near Pechenga, 177; evacuates troops from Finland, 240; removal of danger to Murmansk, 252; danger to India, 303-05, 311 n. 34, 327

Glory, H.M.S. (battleship): at Murmansk, 114; marines land from, 118-19

Goto, Baron Shimpei, Japanese statesman: on intervention in Siberia, 108, 150; replaces Motono as Foreign Minister, 150; reopens negotiations with British, 199; on extent of Japanese intervention, 201, 203, 205, 206, 228; refuses to aid Czechs on Volga front, 265-66; on British request for reprisals for death of Cromie, 290

Graves, Major-General William S., commanding U.S. troops in Siberia, 275

Great Britain, government of: and Kornilov coup, 12; urges inter-Allied conference to co-ordinate strategy, 14-15; and Litvinov's propaganda activities, 78-80; and making of policy re Russia, 82-84; on intervention in Siberia, 88-89, 93-95, 103, 122, 129, 227; on Chinese defeat of Bolsheviks at Harbin, 98; policy in North Russia, January 1918, 114; and Semenov, 98-100, 138-43; effect of German offensive on policy re Russia, 128-30, 174, 197, 330; view of Japanese intentions and capabilities, 129-30,

202, 204-06, 229; influence of intelligence agents on policy re Russia, 135; and Ussuri Cossacks, 145; instructions to Payne at Vladivostok; effect on policy of Anglo-Japanese landings at Vladivostok, 147; inflated estimates of prisoners of war in Siberia, 157, 158-59; policy worries French and Italians, 168-69; worries Japanese, 199; general approach to Russian problem, 171; and forcing hand of President Wilson, 167, 171; aims of policy in Russia, 185-86; and confusion of "decision" and "agreement" on intervention, 192-93; views intervention in North Russia and Siberia as one problem, 193-94; decides action in North Russia better than no action at all, 194; and Kerensky visit to London, 208; approves Japanese reply to U.S. proposal re Siberia, 228; requests U.S. approval for additional Japanese troops for Siberia, 259; and question of Japanese aid to Czechs on Volga front, 263-66; urges formation of strong government at Omsk, 278; and Kolchak coup, 279-84; does not wish to sever relations with Bolsheviks, 285-86; reaction to death of Cromie, 290; and Lockhart-Litvinov exchange, 294-95; and execution of 26 Baku commissars, 323-24 n. 68, 324; no foreknowledge of Malleson-Ashkhabad Committee protocol, 325; hopes and assumptions underlying policy, 330-32. *See also* War Cabinet; Eastern Committee of War Cabinet; War Office; General Staff; Treasury; Department of Overseas Trade; Lloyd George, David; Balfour, Arthur James; Wilson, General Sir Henry

Greene, Sir W. Conyngham, British Ambassador at Tokyo: on dangers of Japanese action in Siberia, 198-99; private talk with Goto, 201; on conclusion of Anglo-Soviet negotiations re Siberia, 229; 88, 89, 107, 108, 129, 206, 265, 271

Grenard, French Consul-General at Moscow, 189, 285

Grey, Sir Edward, 65

Guins, G. K., member Kolchak government: on British rôle in Kolchak coup, 281

Hailar: map, 97; and Semenov, 99

Hall, T. Harper, British Consul at Murmansk, 114-15, 117

Harbin: map, 97; situation at, 98 n. 44, 139, 272, 274, 275. *See also* Sly, Henry E.

Hardinge of Penshurst, Lord, permanent under-secretary at Foreign Office: on situation in South Russia, 94; and Lockhart's final report, 300; member of Eastern Committee, 307 n. 16

Henderson, Arthur, Labour Party leader: visits Russia, 8-10; resigns from War Cabinet over Stockholm conference, 10; 222

Herald (later *Daily Herald*), 20, 78

Hertling, Count von, German premier, 186

Hicks, Captain W. L.: assistant to Lock-
hart, 70, 120; reports with Webster on
Siberian prisoners of war, 157-58; War
Office asks recall of, 159; arrest and re-
patriation of, 286, 290, 295-96
Hintze, Admiral von, German diplomat, 186
historians, Soviet: on Trotsky, 21 n. 69, 115-
16 n. 102, 123 n. 118, 182 n. 48, 291 n.
25; on Anglo-French Convention on
Southern Russia, 55; on aims of British
policy, 185; on Radek, 233 n. 15; on
British role in Kolchak coup, 280, 281; on
"Lockhart conspiracy," 291 n. 25; on
Malleson-Ashkhabad Committee protocol,
319 n. 49; on execution of 26 Baku com-
missars, 323
Hodgson, Robert MacLeod, British Consul at
Vladivostok: on intervention, 91; on anti-
Japanese sentiment at Vladivostok, 107;
and Anglo-Japanese landings, 145, 146
Hoffmann, Major-General Max, German
commander on Eastern Front: at Brest-
Litovsk talks, 63, 67; 75, 127
Home Office, 80
Hong Kong: British troops from to Siberia,
90-91
Hoover, Herbert, 207, 208, 269
Horvat, General Dimitri L.: background, 98
n. 44; and Semenov, 139; and Kolchak,
272, 277; 267, 282 n. 80
House, Colonel Edward M.: on Allied war
aims, 26; confers with Balfour, 27; on
situation in South Russia, 42-43, 45; on
Japan's role in war, 86 n. 10; communications with Balfour, 95, 99-100, 161-62;
and intervention in Siberia, 101, 105-06,
129, 144, 260; discusses intervention with
Reading, 107 n. 75, 162, 211 n. 53; momentary enthusiasm for intervention, 162,
166; on War Office pressure for intervention, 211 n. 53; on U.S. government's
handling of Siberian decision

Imperial War Cabinet, 226
India: and Bolshevik propaganda, 28-29;
Turkish-German danger to, 56, 303-05,
311 n. 34, 326; and Japan, 203, 304-05;
danger of Bolshevism to, 319, 326, 327,
328-29
India, government of: concern over prisoners
of war in Transcaspia, 311; rejects General
Staff's proposal to use Afghan troops in
Russia, 314-15; and 26 Baku commissars,
322, 324; and financial support to Ashkhabad government, 325; requests Malleson's withdrawal, 327
intelligence agents: British, activities of,
134-35, 292; Allied, use of in Archangel
landing, 235-36
inter-Allied conference on conduct of war,
Paris, December 1917, 14-16, 25-27, 45
intervention: Soviet historians on, 185; lack
of agreement among Allies on aims of, 192-

93, 204-06, 214, 215, 219, 227, 229; results of lack of agreement, 264-65; assumptions underlying British policy, 330-32;
effects of, 333-34
Irkutsk: maps, 97, 268; situation in, 89-90,
212; and Semenov, 99; and Japanese plans,
104, 105; prisoners of war at, 158; limit of
Japanese penetration, 198, 211-12, 214, 215,
227, 229, 275; 172
Ironside, Major-General Edmund: background, 256; takes command of Allied
forces, Archangel, 256; on diplomats at
Archangel, 238; and Armistice on Western
Front, 256-57; 243
Ishii, Viscount, Japanese Ambassador at
Washington, 227-28
Italy: worried by British policy, 168-69; force
at Murmansk, 252
Iwami (Japanese warship), 91

Janin, General Maurice, head of French
Military Mission in Siberia and commander
of Czech Corps: on British role in Kolchak
coup, 279-80
Japan: role in World War, 85; interests in
Vladivostok, 88, 146; attitude of Army
toward intervention, 86, 87, 89, 108-09,
202-03, 227; discussions in Advisory
Council on Foreign Relations, 89, 108, 129,
202-03, 227; despatches warships to Vladivostok, 91, 108; policy re intervention in Siberia, 91, 92, 96, 102, 108-09, 129-30, 130
n. 7, 202-04, 227; in British plans for intervention, 93, 96, 100, 107, 129; policy of as
seen in London, 95, 96, 104 n. 62, 104-05,
129-30, 202-06, 314; U.S. attitude to, 92-
93, 101, 129, 193; and defence of India,
203, 304-05; question of extent of penetration of Siberia, 102, 104, 129-30, 200-06,
227-29, 264-66, 275; Soviet fear of, 121;
and Semenov, 138-42, 198, 275; aims in
Manchuria and Eastern Siberia, 96, 138-39,
198-99, 203, 227, 265-66, 272, 276, 331-
32; landing of marines at Vladivostok, 5
April 1918, 143, 146-50; marines withdrawn, 25 April, 150-51; and inflated
estimates of danger from prisoners of war
in Siberia, 158; opposed to British efforts
for intervention by Soviet invitation, 199;
conditions for intervention set by Allies,
202; likelihood of Japanese-German encounter, 202; and command of operations
in Siberia, 203, 204, 275-76; reply to Allied
proposal, 203-04; limits placed by U.S. decision re Siberia, 214-15; reply to U.S. proposal, 227-28; assumes initiative in Siberia,
229, 261; troops move into Siberia and
Manchuria, 261; troops join with Czechs to
defeat Bolsheviks on Ussuri front; refusal to
aid Czechs on Volga front, 265; Army to
handle all political aspects of intervention,
270; and Kolchak, 272; force remains east
of Harbin, 275; conduct in Siberia, 275-77.

See also Goto, Baron Shimpei, and Motono, Viscount Ichiro

Jassy (temporary Rumanian capital): map, 41; 40

Joffe, Adolf, Bolshevik negotiator at Brest-Litovsk, 62-63

Jordan, Sir John, British Minister at Peking, 138, 141

Kaakhka: map, 312; Indian troops defeat Bolsheviks at, 317, 320

Kaledin, General A. M., Don Cossack leader, 4, 42-49, 52, 53, 57, 99, 232

Kalmykov, Cossack leader in Eastern Siberia, 275, 277

Kamenev, L. B., Bolshevik leader: mission to Britain, 81; 11

Kandalaksha: map, 110; Allied-White Finn clash, 175; Maynard disarms Red Guards, 184; 235

Kaplan, Dora: shoots Lenin, 288

Karakhan, Leo, Soviet Assistant Commissar for Foreign Affairs, 189

Karymskaya: map, 97; 99, 102, 130, 140, 228

Kato, Admiral, commanding Japanese squadron at Vladivostok: orders from Tokyo, 146, 150; decides to land marines, 146-47

Kazan: maps, 41, 268; falls to Bolsheviks, 250, 263; 234

Kem: map, 110; British troops disband Soviet and kill leaders, 184, 247

Kemp, Rear Admiral Thomas W., commanding British squadron in White Sea: and evacuation of British personnel at Archangel, 111; requests force for defence of Murmansk, 115; and agreement with Murmansk Soviet, 117; instructions from Admiralty re defence of Murmansk, 117-18; lands marines at Murmansk, 118-19; requests reinforcements, 174; sends force to Pechenga, 175-76; on policy re Murmansk, 177; meets Natsarenus, 180; recommends *de facto* recognition of Soviet government, 180-81; withdraws *H.M.S. Alexander* from Archangel, 182

Kennan, George F.: on Japanese policy, 85; on British policy, 95 n. 40; on U.S. policy, 102, 208, 215, 216; on prisoners of war in Siberia, 156, 158; vii

Kerensky, Alexander F.: becomes Minister of War, May 1917, 7; and July offensive, 11; becomes Premier, 11; protests against Allied note, 14; and inter-Allied conference, 15; fails to rally forces against Bolsheviks, 18; visits London, June 1918, 208-10

Kerr, Philip, secretary to Lloyd George, 226

Khabarovsk: map, 97; Japanese conduct at, 276

Khiva: map, 312; 302

Kirsanov Resolution, 153

Kizyl-Arvat: map, 312; 315

Knight, Admiral A. N.: commanding U.S.

Asiatic Fleet, 145; orders from Washington, 146; takes no part in Vladivostok landings, 147

Knox, Major-General Alfred W. F.: and Kornilov coup, 11-12; obtains Bolshevik release of women soldiers, 17; secures guard for Embassy, 18; advises release of Russia from obligations, 23, 48; leaves Russia with Buchanan, 38; and situation in South Russia, 44, 47-48; on Ukrainian Central Rada, 50; his influence on British policy, 131; asks for recall of Lockhart, 132; Lockhart opinion of, 133; urges Japanese intervention, 132, 197-98; opposes U.S. plan for civilian commission to Siberia, 197; appointed head of British Military Mission in Siberia, 220; defended by Lloyd George against American objections, 220-21; appeals for Japanese aid to Czechs on Volga front, 263; and Kolchak, 271, 272, 277; and organising Russian army in Siberia, 271, 272, 274-75; relations with Japanese, 275-76; on Semenov, 275; relations with Siberian government, Omsk, 277-78; scorn for Directorate, 278, 282; and Kolchak coup, 279-83; on own role, 281 n. 76

Kola Inlet: map, 110; 109, 111, 114, 178

Kolchak, Admiral Aleksandr V.: background, 271-72; on need for armed force in Siberian politics, 271; and Japanese, 272; and Knox, 271, 272, 277; becomes Minister of War in Siberian government, 272-73; proclaimed Supreme Ruler of Russia after coup at Omsk, 279; British links with coup, 279-84

"Komuch," Samara government, 255, 267

Kornilov, General L. G.: attempted coup, 11-13; 4, 42 n. 4, 43

Kotlas: map, 110; 238, 263

Krasnovodsk: maps, 41, 312; in British policy, 311, 316, 317, 318, 319, 320; 315, 321

Krasnoyarsk: map, 268; and Semenov, 99

Krylenko, N. V., Soviet commissar, 22

Kühlmann, Richard von, German Foreign Minister: at Brest-Litovsk talks, 67; and German policy in Russia, 186

Kuhn, town commandant of Krasnovodsk: and 26 Baku commissars, 321, 322

Kuroki, Captain, Japanese liaison officer with Semenov, 139, 140, 141

Kushk: map, 312; 311, 313

Labour Party: declaration on war aims, 16 December 1918, 65; hears Kerensky, 208-09; 78

Lansdowne, Marquess of, 65

Lansing, Robert, U.S. Secretary of State: on Japanese intervention, 89; rejects Japanese *demarche* of 8 February 1918, 102; urges Japanese intervention on President, 105; holds North Russia and Siberia separate problems, 193; and decision on North Russia, 195; on plight of Czechs, 213-14; tells Allies of U.S. decision, 215-16; protests against British command in North Russia, 248-49; opposes British request for more Japanese troops to Siberia, 260

Lavergne, General, chief of French Military Mission in Russia: thinks Soviet-Allied military collaboration possible, 136, 164; 135, 193, 298

Law, Andrew Bonar, Chancellor of Exchequer: and giving Germany free hand in Russia, 66 n. 31; and Bolshevik debt repudiation, 69-70; 15, 295

Leeper, Reginald: and Litvinov, 60-61, 80-81; and Kamenev, 81; and Lockhart-Litvinov exchange, 294-95; xi, 83 n. 1

Lenin, V. I.: and Decree on Peace, 17; appeal (with Stalin) to peoples of East, 28-29; and Brest-Litovsk talks, 67, 76; receives Lockhart, 120-21; urges ratification at VII Congress of Bolshevik Party, 123-24; moves ratification at IV Congress of Soviets, 126-27; message to Vladivostok Soviet re Anglo-Japanese landings, 148; on situation at Murmansk, 177; denounces Yuryev, 182, 184; speech of 29 July 1918, 285; attempt on his life, 30 August, 288, 291 n. 25, 334; recovers, 293; endorses Stalin's orders to Shaumian at Baku, 308

Lindley, Francis O., Counsellor of British Embassy at Petrograd: background, 71; on Don Cossacks, 74 n. 50; on Brest-Litovsk treaty, 76; withdraws Embassy from Russia, 77-78; refuses to allow any members of Diplomatic Service to remain, 120; relations with Lockhart, 71; returns to Russia, 182, 190, 233 n. 11; on Allied control of Murmansk Soviet, 182; on dilemma faced by British in North Russia, 183; allows economic mission to go to Moscow, 233 n. 11; asks Poole to hurry intervention, 235; criticism of Poole, 239; on need for genuine Russian authority at Archangel, 239-40, 248; opposes Poole's introduction of conscription, 243; and Chaikovsky, 245, 247-48; and Chaplin coup, 245-48; threatens to resign unless given more control over British forces, 248; on after-effects of coup, 249; on Murmansk Railway strike, 254; on reconstitution of Archangel government, 255

Litvinov, Maxim: background, 59-60; appointed Bolshevik plenipotentiary in London, 60; letter introducing Lockhart to Trotsky, 61; propaganda activities, 78-80; evicted from "People's Embassy," 80-81; and Kerensky's visit to London, 208; exchanged for Lockhart, 287, 288, 293-96

Lloyd George, Prime Minister David: on British aid to Russia, 1915-1917, 5; on Buchanan, 8; on Kornilov coup and collapse of Russian war effort, 13, 19; on situation in South Russia, 43, 46; and Lock-

hart, 58-59, 61, 72, 74, 122; address on war aims, 5 January 1918, 63-66; on effect of Russia leaving war, 66 n. 22; on size of forces necessary for Siberian intervention, 201 n. 28; secret interview with Kerensky, 209-10; general attitude to problem of Russia, June 1918, 210-11; on extent of Japanese intervention, 211-12; on U.S. decision, 217-18, 226; defends Knox and British policy against U.S. criticism, 221-23; congratulates Czechs on victories, 262-63; not member of Eastern Committee, 307 n. 16; and postwar policy re Russia, 335

loans to Russian governments from British sources, 4-5, 69

Locker-Lampson, Commander Oliver: and Kornilov coup, 12

Lockhart, R. H. Bruce: background, 58-59; selected for mission, 59, 61, 127 n. 133; Litvinov on, 61; Noulens on, 61-62; reaches Petrograd, 62; on his relations with Lindley, 71; first visit to Smolny, 71-72; Chicherin on, 71 n. 45; meetings with Trotsky, 72-74, 76, 121, 122, 136-37, 159, 174; and ratification of Brest-Litovsk treaty, 78, 119-27; protests to Smolny against Litvinov's activities, 80; and Milner, 59, 61, 74, 122, 300; interview with Lenin, 120-21; urges restraint of Japanese, 121, 131, 159; and VII Congress of Bolshevik Party, 123-34; remains in Petrograd with Trotsky, 124, 131; as seen in Foreign Office, 124-25, 130-31; his influence on British policy, 130, 138, 163; recall asked by Wilson and Knox, 131-32; on Knox, 133; relations with Wardrop, 134; on British secret intelligence operations, 134; informal meetings with Allied officers, 135-36; explores possibility of Soviet-Allied collaboration, 136-38; assumes renewed German-Soviet war inevitable, 137; opposes supporting counter-revolutionary elements, 137-38, 140; and Semenov, 140, 142, 159-60; sees Chicherin and Trotsky after Anglo-Japanese landings at Vladivostok, 147; reports on Bolshevik reaction, 147-48; gives assurances to Bolsheviks re landings, 150; defends Hicks against War Office, 159; on Cheka suppression of anarchists, 159 n. 120; on strength of Soviet regime, 120-21, 124-25, 159; on possibility of Bolshevik consent to intervention, 159; on recognition of Soviet government, 163; feels Allied-Soviet co-operation no longer likely, 163; favours ultimatum to Bolsheviks, 163; contacts with anti-Bolshevik organisations, 163-64, 165, 189-90, 231-32, 292; efforts undermined by Noulens, 164-65; urges intervention with or without Bolshevik invitation, 165; protests against Soviet evacuation of Archangel war stores, 173-74; sees Red Finn representative, 175 n. 22; and Chicherin's protests against Allied presence in North Russia, 176-77;

relationship to Poole, 178; on implications of changed German policy and necessity for immediate massive intervention, 186-89; warns against reliance upon anti-Bolshevik elements, 187-88, 298-99; protests against Soviet effort to disarm Czechs, 189; Bolshevik suspicions of him, 189; threatens to resign if intervention delayed, 190; gives Kerensky visa, 209; growing precariousness of his position, 230; on French role in Yaroslavl rising, 231; assists National Centre, 231; gives aid to Alekseyev, 232, 292; and visit of British economic mission to Moscow, 233-34; sees Chicherin re Lenin's speech of 29 July 1918, 285; and his exchange for Litvinov, 287, 288, 293-96; arrested by Cheka, 290, 291, 293; and "Lockhart conspiracy," 290-93; sees Balfour, 296; final report on mission, 296-300; sees King, 300; subsequent career, 301

Low, Ivy (Mme. Maxim Litvinov), 60

Ludendorff, Field Marshal Erich von: on goals of German policy in Russia, 186; on effect of intervention, 333; 128

Lvov, Prince, first premier of Provisional Government, 7, 11, 58

MacDonald, Ramsay, Labour Party leader, 79, 81

Macdonogh, Major-General Sir G. M. W., Director of Military Operations, 307 n. 16

Malleson, Major-General Wilfred: terms of mission, 311; arrives Meshed, 315; on Transcaspian revolt and British policy, 315-16; decision to send troops against Bolsheviks, 316-17; signs protocol of aid with Ashkhabad Committee, 317-20; and 26 Baku commissars, 321-22, 324; on Ashkhabad Committee, 324; and financial support to Ashkhabad government, 325-27; forces withdrawn, 327-28

Manchester Guardian: on Bolshevik Revolution, 19

Manchuria: and Japanese, 96, 138, 272

March Revolution: British reaction to, 6-7

Marling, Sir Charles M., British Minister at Teheran, 52

Masaryk, Thomas: on Buchanan, 9; and Czech Corps, 152

Maude, General Sir Stanley, British commander in Mesopotamia: on Russian collapse, 13; 51

Maynard, Major-General C. C. M.: given command of Murmansk force, 173; on Pechenga, 175 n. 24; on Poole's relations with Russians, 179; arrives, 182; disarms Red Guards, 184; lack of success in raising Russian forces, 242; requests and receives reinforcements, 252; size of force at his disposal, 252; and railway strike, 253-54

Menshevik Party: Lockhart and, 164; in Baku Soviet, 309; 10

Merv: map, 312; 303, 313, 315, 319, 327, 328

Meshed: map, 312; Malleson's headquarters, 311, 315, 327

Mesopotamia: British army in, 13, 51, 303

Military Intelligence, Director of, 84

Milner, Alfred Viscount: at Petrograd conference, February 1917, 6; and Kornilov, 9; on Russian collapse, 13 n. 39; reaction to Bolshevik Revolution, 19; goes to Paris to coordinate Allied policy, 53; and Lockhart, 59, 61, 74, 122, 300; on use of Czech Corps, 155; requests U.S. troops for North Russia, 195-96; presses for Japanese intervention, 210; on U.S. decision, 218-19; suggests Allied political commission for Siberia, 269-70; and establishment of Eastern Committee, 307 n. 16; influence on policy, 335

Milyukov, Paul: on British role in Kolchak coup, 280-81; 7, 189

Mirbach, Count, German Ambassador at Moscow: arrives, 164; assassinated, 230; 177

Monro, General Sir C. C., Commander-in-Chief of Indian Army: gives Malleson free hand re Bolsheviks, 316; on policy in Transcaspia, 319 n. 51

Montagu, Edwin, Secretary of State for India, 307 n. 16, 326

Morley, James W., vii, 86 n. 7

Morning Post: on Bolshevik Revolution, 19

Motono, Viscount Ichiro, Japanese Foreign Minister: on intervention, 89; urges intervention on British and U.S. Ambassadors, 102; indicates Japan might act without U.S. approval, 104; ready to pledge Japanese thrust to Urals, 105; urges intervention in Advisory Council on Foreign Relations, 108; refuses to promise intervention as far as western Siberia, 129; resigns after Vladivostok landings, 150

Mudyug Island (Archangel): attacked by Allied force, 235-36

Murmansk: map, 110; construction of port, 109-11; landing of British marines, 6 March 1918, 109, 118-19; in British policy, 114, 174-75; formation of People's Collegium, 115; German attack expected, 115, 174; first fighting between Allies and White Finns, 175-76; arrival of Maynard's force, 23 June 1918, 182; communications with interior cut, 184; danger from Germans highly exaggerated, 194-95; Maynard raises Russian forces, 242; British reinforcements and total size of forces at, 252; military situation in autumn 1918, 252-53; railwaymen strike, 253; taken under political authority of Archangel, 254-55; 77, 87, 154

Murmansk Military Council: formation, 117-18; proclaims state of siege, 118

Murmansk Railway: construction, 111; German threat to, 115; cut by Bolsheviks, 184; workers strike, 253-54

Murmansk Soviet: agreement with Allies, 2 March 1918, 116-17; requests armed assistance from British, 118, 175; Chicherin's instructions to, 179-80, 181, 182; break with Moscow, 181-84; Lindley on Allied use of, 182; agreement with Allies, 6 July 1918, 184-85; dissolved, 254-55

Murray, Sir Arthur C.: background, 213 n. 62; on U.S. decision re Siberia, 219; 213, 218, 219

Nabokov, Konstantin, Russian Chargé d'Affaires at London, 15, 33, 86, 284

Nairana, H.M.S. (seaplane tender), 235

National Centre: supported by Lockhart and French, 231

Natsarenus, S. P., Bolshevik special commissar for Murmansk region: visit to Murmansk, 179-80; talks with Poole and Kemp, 180; leads force against Allies, 184

Netherlands Legation, Russia: takes charge of British interests, 78, 287

Neutral diplomatic corps, Russia, 78, 287, 289

Newbolt, Henry, 117, 118

Nicholas II, Tsar: and Buchanan, 9; executed 16 July 1918, 300 n. 44, 334

Nielson, Colonel, member British Military Mission in Siberia: on aims of Kolchak government, 283-84

Niessel, General, chief of French Military Mission in Russia until March 1918, 127 n. 133

Noel, Captain: British officer sent to report on Don Cossacks, 44-45; reports, 49

Norris, Commodore D. T., commander British naval squadron on Caspian Sea, 320

North Russia: map, 110; anti-Bolshevism in, 75; in British policy, 83, 109-19, 172-73, 194; British expeditionary force and training mission despatched, 172-73; Soviet policy re, 179; German danger eliminated, 240; formation of Provisional Government of Northern Region, 255. *See also* Archangel, Murmansk

North Russia, Russian anti-Bolshevik forces in: pay of, 178; feeding of, 184, 242-43; recruiting and conscription, 242-43, 251-52; reasons for failure, 249-50

Noulens, French Ambassador in Russia: replaces Paléologue, July 1917, 14; on Lockhart, 61-62; and evacuation of Allied embassies, 77; works against Allied-Soviet collaboration, 164-65; influence on Lockhart, 188 n. 67; and Yaroslavl rising, 231; on Allied regime at Archangel, 238-39; and Chaikovsky, 245; and Chaplin coup, 245-48; change in behaviour, 249; on British role in Kolchak coup, 280

November Revolution: *see* Bolshevik seizure of power

Novocherkassk: map, 41; 44, 47, 49, 52-53, 56

Novorossisk: map, 41; 56

Nuri Pasha, General, commander of "Army of Islam," 304

Obozerskaya: map, 110; fighting at, 243

October Revolution: *see* Bolshevik seizure of power

Odessa: map, 41, 56

Olovyannaya: map, 97; and Semenov, 100

Olympia, U.S.S. (U.S. cruiser): sent to Murmansk, 116, 178; in Archangel landing, 235

Omsk: map, 268; Hungarian war prisoners join Red Guard, 158; Siberian Provisional Government, 267, 274; All-Russian Provisional Government, 269; governments merge, 269, 277, 279; Kolchak coup, 17 November 1918, 279-84; 107, 129, 153, 155, 202

Orlando, V. E., Italian Premier, 26

Otani, Japanese general: appointed Supreme Commander of Allied forces in Siberia, 274; Knox on, 275

Oudendijk, W. J., Dutch Minister in Russia: and Lockhart-Litvinov exchange, 288-93; and death of Cromie, 289; 322

Page, Walter Hines, U.S. Ambassador at London, 93, 103

Paléologue, Maurice, French Ambassador at Petrograd: recalled April 1917, 8

Pares, Bernard, British slavicist, 13

Payne, Captain, commanding *H.M.S. Suffolk:* on situation at Vladivostok, 145; instructions from London, 146; decides to land marines, 146-47

Pechenga (Petsamo): map, 110; battle between Royal Marines and White Finns, 175-76; 175 n. 24, 177, 252

Penjdeh: incident at, March 1885, 303; 313

Penza, 152, 156, 172

Perm: map, 268; 112, 153

Persia (Iran): and Anglo-Russian Convention (1907), 303; in British policy, 307; 304

Petrograd, inter-Allied conference, February 1917, 5-6

Petrov, P.: internment in Britain and repatriation, 33-35

Phelan, Edward: assistant to Lockhart, 70; leaves Russia, 120

Pichon, Stéphane, French Foreign Minister, 26, 53, 54, 93, 202

Pichon, Lt.-Colonel, member French Military Mission in Siberia: on Knox and Kolchak coup, 280 n. 69

Poland: Lloyd George on, 66; 63

Polk, Frank L., Counsellor of U.S. State Department: and British request for additional Japanese forces for Siberia, 259; 106, 228

Ponsonby, Arthur, Labour MP, 65 n. 27
Poole, DeWitt C., U.S. Consul-General at Moscow: and "Lockhart conspiracy," 291 n. 25; 189, 285, 286
Poole, Major-General F.C.: background, 178-79; given command of North Russian expedition, 173; predicts support by Trotsky, 174; arrives Murmansk, 178; initial orders, 178; attitude toward local Russians, 179; meets Natsarenus, 180; recommends *de facto* recognition of Soviet government, 180; on break between Murmansk and Moscow, 183, 185; tells Lockhart intervention not yet prepared, 190; given command of all Allied forces, 195; asks Allied embassies to leave Vologda, 234; organises rising to precede Archangel landings, 235-36; proclaims martial law at Archangel, 237; methods of administration, 237-39; new orders from War Office, 240-41; and recruiting of Russian forces, 242-43, 252; American criticism of, 244, 248-49, 264; and Chaplin coup, 246-48; change in behaviour, 249; urges War Office to aid Czechs, 250; requests reinforcements, 251, 252; advice on Murmansk railway strike, 254; replaced by Ironside, 255-56
Porter, Captain, British Assistant Military Attaché at Peking: and Semenov, 139-40, 141-42
prisoners of war (Central Powers): in Siberia, 87, 156-58; with Semenov, 139-40; Czech-Hungarian incident at Chelyabinsk, 168, 172; reported to menace Czechs, 212; in Transcaspia, 311, 328; in Turkestan, 156
propaganda, Bolshevik: appeal to Peoples of East, 3 December 1917, 28-29, 31; British countermeasures, 29 n. 93; Balfour on, 75; and Litvinov, 78-79; Lockhart on, 122
propaganda: British in Russia, 66 n. 29; American, 66
Provisional Government: Allied pressure on, 7; and war aims, 7; and Petrograd Soviet, 7; cabinet reorganisation, May 1917, 7-8; and "July days," 11; weakened by Kornilov coup, 12
Provisional Government of the Northern Region: formation, 255

Radek, Karl, Bolshevik publicist, 67, 233, 234 n. 17; treatment by Soviet historians, 233 n. 15
Reading, Marquess of, British Ambassador at Washington: discusses intervention with House, 107, 144, 162; and Knox's attack on Lockhart, 132-33, 144 n. 55; told by Lansing of U.S. decision re Siberia, 215-16; on U.S. decision, 216; his influence, 216-17 n. 72; on U.S. opposition to Knox's

appointment, 220; 104, 161, 193, 207, 249, 260
Red Army: reorganisation by Trotsky, 135; recruitment among Siberian prisoners of war, 156; offensive against Czechs on Volga, 250
Red Guards: at Vladivostok, 146; in Pechenga fighting, 176; disarmed by Maynard, 184; in Transcaspian revolt, 315
Redl, Major, Indian Army intelligence officer: on Bolshevik policy in Transcaspia and Turkestan, 311-12
Regnault, E. L. G., French Ambassador at Tokyo: appointed French High Commissioner for Siberia, 270
Reid, Lieutenant, British intelligence agent, 134
Reilly, Sidney, British intelligence agent, 292
Richardson, Brigadier-General W. P., U.S. Army: on British command in North Russia, 244
Riddell, George, *confidant* of Lloyd George, 13
Riggs, Captain E. F., U.S. Assistant Military Attaché in Russia: works for Soviet-Allied military collaboration, 135-36
Robertson, Major D. S., British Military Attaché at Peking: and Semenov, 99, 102
Robertson, Colonel T. A., British Military Representative at Vladivostok, 262
Robertson, General Sir William, C. I. G. S. until February 1918: on effect of Russia leaving war, 40; and situation in South Russia, 46; on intervention in Siberia, 90
Robins, Raymond, chief of U.S. Red Cross mission in Russia: 126-27, 127 n. 133, 157; Knox on, 132
Rodzianko, M., President of Duma, 43
Romei, General: Italian Military Attaché in Russia, 135; thinks Allied-Soviet military collaboration possible, 136; 164, 194
Rothstein, Feodor, 60-61
Rouquérol, General J., member French Military Mission in Siberia: on British role in Kolchak coup, 280
Royal Marines: land at Murmansk, 6 March 1918, 109, 118-119; combat with White Finns, 175-176; in Archangel landing, 235; at Vladivostok, 146
Royal Navy: operations in White Sea, 111; in Caspian Sea, 320
Rumania, King of, 42
Rumanian Army, 40-42, 53, 56, 74, 86
Russia Committee (War Office-Foreign Office), 83-84, 174
Russian Embassy, London (Chesham House), 33, 60, 61
Russo-Asiatic Corporation, 232

Sadoul, Captain Jacques, member of French Military Mission in Russia: works for Soviet-Allied military collaboration, 136; 49, 127 n. 133

Samara: maps, 41, 268; government ("Ko-much"), 255, 267; Czechs evacuate, 264-65; 172

Savinkov, Boris, 43, 189-90, 230-31. *See also* Union for the Defence of Fatherland and Freedom

Scotland Yard (C.I.D.), 79

Scott, C. P., editor *Manchester Guardian*: on Lloyd George's attitude re Russia, 66 n. 31

Semenov, Gregorii, Trans-Baikal Cossack leader: background, 98; and British policy, 98, 99-100, 138, 153, 200; relations with British, 98-99, 138-43; activities of, 100, 139-42, 199-200, 275; U.S. attitude to, 101; relations with Japanese, 138-42, 198, 275; and Chinese, 140; Balfour orders restraint of, 140-41; and Kolchak, 272, 277; Knox on, 275

Serbians in Allied force in North Russia, 184, 243, 252

Shakhovski, Prince, Russian financier, 43, 52 n. 33

Shantung Peninsula (China), 85

Shaumian, Stepan, Bolshevik head of Baku Soviet: ordered to keep British out, 307, 308; appeals to Lenin, 308-09; disbands Soviet and flees, 309; executed with other Baku commissars, 322

Shore, General, chief of British Military Mission with Russian Army in Caucasus, 51

Siberia: maps, 97, 268; anti-Bolshevik governments in, 266-69, 279. *See also* Japan, Kolchak, prisoners of war, Czechoslovak Corps, Semenov, Manchuria, Vladivostok, Trans-Siberian Railway

Siberian Provisional Government (Omsk), 267-69; British representatives in Siberia on, 274; signs assistance agreement with Knox, 277

Simbirsk: maps, 41, 268; Czechs take, 233; falls to Bolsheviks, 263

Sisson, Edgar, U.S. propagandist in Russia, 71-72 n. 45; "Sisson documents," 134

Skobelev, M.: named by Petrograd Soviet to attend inter-Allied conference, 15

Slavo-British Legion, Archangel, 251-52; desertions from, 245

Sly, Henry E., British Consul at Harbin, 89-90, 100, 142

Smolny Institute, Petrograd (Bolshevik head-quarters), 17

Smuts, General J. C., South African states-man: proposed talk with Trotsky, 161 n. 126; member Eastern Committee, 307 n. 16; 59

Socialist-Revolutionary Party (S-R's): in Constituent Assembly, 68; strength in Archangel region, 112; in Trans-Baikalia, 140; Lockhart and Right S-R's, 164; Left S-R's and Mirbach assassination, 230; in Samara government, 267; in Directorate,

269; manifesto against Siberian govern-ment, 282; in Baku Soviet, 308-09; in Centro-Caspian Directorate, 309; in Ash-khabad Committee, 315

Sonnino, Baron Sidney, Italian Foreign Min-ister, 26, 27, 202

Southern Russia: map, 41; Anglo-French Convention on, 23 December 1917, 54-57; anti-Bolshevik forces in, 85, 93, 94; Bol-shevism in, 94

Soviet-Allied co-operation: discussed by Lockhart and Trotsky, 72-73, 76, 136-37, 160; Balfour on, 74-75, 123, 160-63, 175 n. 23; Allied hopes for, 82, 135-36; Lenin on, 120-21; and Robins, 127 n. 133; Lock-hart pessimistic re, 163-64; Noulens and Vologda diplomats work against, 164-65; French and Italian opposition to, 168-69, 199 n. 17; Japanese opposition to, 199

Soviet government: seeks armistice, 20-21, 25; lifts ban on Britons leaving Russia, December 1917, 35; attitude towards diplomacy, 36; demand for courier privi-leges, 36-37; dissolution of Constituent Assembly, 68-69; repudiation of foreign debts, 69-70, 334; accepts German terms, 76; fear of intervention, 82; collapse pre-dicted, 3, 94, 104; policy considerations at time of ratification of Brest-Litovsk treaty, 119-20; possibility of renewed war with Germany, 120, 137, 187; fears British landing at Archangel, 122; transferred from Petrograd to Moscow, 124; and Semenov, 140; statement on Vladivostok landings, 148; action re Czech Corps, 152, 172; activities among Siberian prisoners of war, 156; Balfour on *de facto* recogni-tion of, 162; *de facto* recognition recom-mended by Poole and Kemp, 180-81; policy re North Russia, 179, 181, 182; orders departure of Allied warships, 181-82; break with Murmansk Soviet, 181-82; Lockhart on policy of, May 1918, 187; and Mirbach assassination, 230; and Yaro-slavl rising, 230-31; urges Allied embassies to leave Vologda for Moscow, 234; and military efficiency, 249 n. 63; does not wish to sever relations with Allies, 285; initial reaction to Archangel landings, 286; and Lockhart-Litvinov exchange, 287, 288; murder of Imperial family, 300 n. 44, 334; orders Shaumian to bar Baku to British, 307; holds British responsible for execu-tion of 26 Baku commissars, 323-24 n. 68. *See also* Lenin, V. I.; Trotsky, L. D.; Chicherin, G. V.; Cheka

Soviet historians: *see* historians, Soviet

Sovnarkom (Council of People's Commis-sars): *see* Soviet Government

Soviet of Workers' and Soldiers' Deputies, Petrograd, 7

Spears, Brigadier-General Edward, British

liaison officer, Paris: urges Japanese intervention, 96

Spring-Rice, Sir Cecil, British Ambassador at Washington until January 1918, 89

Stalin, J. V.: direct wire conversation with Yuryev, 117; orders Shaumian not to seek British support, 308; on execution of 26 Baku commissars, 323; 28, 291 n. 25

Steveni, Captain, member British Military Mission in Siberia: role in Kolchak coup, 280, 282-83

Stockholm conference, 10

Strakhovsky, Leonid I., 118

Subbotovsky, I., Soviet historian: on British role in Kolchak coup, 280

submarines, German, shipment across Siberia, 87-88

Suffolk, *H.M.S.* (cruiser): to Vladivostok, 91

Supreme Administration of Northern Region (Archangel): formation, 237; kidnapped, 246-48; dissolved, 255

Supreme War Council: established November 1917, 26; Abbeville Resolution on use of Czech Corps, 155-56; and intervention in Siberia, 202, 211-12, 213; and intervention in North Russia, 241

Supreme War Council, Permanent Military Representatives to: on policy re South Russia, 56; on use of Czech Corps, 154-55; discuss Murmansk with Allied Naval Council, 174; agree to action at Murmansk and Archangel, 195; agree to divert no more forces to North Russia, 251; and Turkish-German danger to India, 305

Tashkent: prisoners of war at, 311

Tashkent Soviet: policies, 311-12; and revolt in Transcaspia, 315; and British policy, 318, 319

Teague-Jones, Captain Reginald, British liaison officer in Ashkhabad: and 26 Baku commissars, 321-22, 323, 324

Terauchi, Japanese Premier, 108

Tereshchenko, M. I.: succeeds Milyukov as Foreign Minister of Provisional Government, 7, 14, 15, 16

Terror, the: *see* Cheka

Thacher, Major Thomas D., U.S. Red Cross mission, 118-19

Thomas, Albert, French socialist leader, 8

Thornhill, Colonel, chief of British Military Intelligence in Russia: and Chaplin coup, 246; 38, 250

Tiflis: map, 41; 50, 56

Times, The: on March Revolution, 6; on Bolshevik Revolution, 19; on Lloyd George war aims address, 64; on British government's reaction to Bolshevik debt repudiation, 70

Torretta, Italian Chargé in Russia, 245

Trades Union Congress, 64

Trans-Baikalia: map, 97; activities of Semenov in, 98-101, 139-42; Japanese in, 203. *See also* Baikal, Lake

Transcaspia: map, 312; and British policy, 83, 315-16, 319, 326; German and Turkish activity in, 203 n. 29, 317; Bolshevism in 311-13, 328; Malleson mission despatched, 311; prisoners of war, 311, 328; political situation, 311-13; revolt of railwaymen, 315; 302, 304. *See also* Ashkhabad Committee; Malleson, Major-General Wilfred

Transcaspian Railway: map, 312; in British policy, 311; revolt of railwaymen, 315; 306

Transcaucasia: *see* Caucasus

Transcaucasian Commissariat: 50-51, 303, 305

Trans-Siberian Railway: maps, 97, 268; French plan to block, 92; in British plans, 130; in Japanese plans, 203, 228; Czech rising on, 172; Czechs control from Pacific to Urals, 262-63; 56, 86, 87, 88, 89, 93-94, 100, 101, 103

Treasury, British: and financial support of Ashkhabad government, 325, 327

Treaty of London (1915), 22

Trotsky, L. D.: imprisoned by British (1917), 34 n. 108; as Commissar for Foreign Affairs sends first note to Allied diplomatic missions, 20-21; on Britain and the war, 21; publishes secret treaties, 21; appeal to Russian troops, 24 November 1917, 22; note to Entente military representatives, 27 November, 23; boasts of *de facto* relations with Allies, 30-31; demands British release Chicherin and Petrov, 34-35; demands Powers admit Bolshevik couriers, 36-37; suspicions of Buchanan, 45, 48-49; appoints Litvinov Plenipotentiary in London, 60; and Brest-Litovsk talks, 63, 66-68; on Lloyd George's aims, 63; meetings with Lockhart, 72-73, 76, 121, 122, 136-37, 159, 174; tells Murmansk Soviet to cooperate with Allies, 116, 175; fears Japanese landing, 121; at VII Congress of Bolshevik Party, 124; remains in Petrograd and invites Lockhart to join him, 124; hands over foreign affairs to Chicherin, 124; questions for Robins on Allied aid, 127 n. 133; influence on Lockhart, 124, 130-31; as Commissar for War reorganises Red Army, 135; confers with Lockhart, Riggs and Sadoul on Allied-Soviet collaboration, 136-37; reaction to Vladivostok landings, 147; and Hicks-Webster mission, 157; proposes Soviet-Allied agreement, 160; Balfour on, 166; orders shooting of armed Czechs, 172; on evacuation of Archangel stores, 174; as military leader, 249 n. 63, 263; treatment of by Soviet historians, 21 n. 69, 115-16 n. 102, 123 n. 118, 182 n. 48, 291 n. 25

Index

Tsaritsin (Stalingrad), 308
Turkestan: map, 312; armed prisoners of war in, 156; and British, 279; Bolshevism in, 311-13, 328-29; 304
Turkey: danger to India, 303-05, 311 n. 34, 327; and Brest-Litovsk treaty, 303-04; capture of Baku, 308-10; 56

Ufa: map, 268; State Conference at, 268
Ukraine: situation at time of Bolshevik Revolution, 49-50; French sphere of responsibility, 54-55; and Brest-Litovsk talks, 67-68; resources of, 96; Germans continue to move into, 137, 186
Ukrainian Central Rada: Foreign Office view of, 50; joins Brest-Litovsk negotiations, 50, 67-68; separate peace with Germany, 77; 49, 51, 73, 74
Union for the Defence of Fatherland and Freedom: Lockhart's contacts with, 189-90; French relations with, 190; and Yaroslavl rising, 230-31. See also National Centre
United States: informed of Lockhart mission, 59; rejects French overture to aid Bolsheviks, 76; policy re intervention in Siberia, 55, 92-93, 101, 102, 105-06, 129, 166; orders to admiral at Vladivostok, 146; decision to intervene in Siberia, 192-93, 196, 207, 213-15, 223-25; decision to intervene in North Russia, 194-96; regards North Russia and Siberia as separate problems, 193; objections to U.S. troops under British command in North Russia, 196; opposition to Knox for Siberian post, 220; employment of forces in North Russia, 243-44; criticism of Poole and British command in North Russia, 239, 244, 244-45 n. 48; decision to send no more U.S. troops to North Russia, 251; effect of Armistice on troops at Archangel, 256-57; opposes British request for additional Japanese troops to Siberia, 259; refusal to aid Czechs on Volga front, 263-64; refusal to appoint political commissioner for Siberia, 270. See also Wilson, President Woodrow; Lansing, Robert; House, Colonel Edward M.
Uritsky, M. S., head of Petrograd Cheka: murdered, 30 August 1918, 288, 334; British blamed, 289 n. 17, 291 n. 25
Urquhart, Leslie, British businessman, 232, 233
Ussuri Cossacks: British assistance to, 145
Ussuri River front: map, 97; Czechs on, 258-59; Bolsheviks defeated, 262

Verkhneudinsk: map, 97; and Semenov, 99
Vesselago, Lt.-Commander Georgi M.: 114-15, 117, 118; Poole's relations with, 179; affirms support of Allies, 180, 183
Vladivostok: map, 97; war supplies at, 87, 89, 91, 101, 104, 145, 145 n. 57; political

situation at, 86-87, 91-92, 144-45, 274; Allied warships at, 91-92, 102; anti-Japanese sentiment, 107; landing of Japanese and British marines, 5 April 1918, 143-51; arrival of Czechs, 151; Czechs seize power, 29 June, 212-13; Allies assume formal control, 6 July, 213; Japanese conduct at, 276
Vladivostok Soviet: Lenin's message re Anglo-Japanese landings, 148; takes control of city, 2 May 1918, 151; tension with Czechs, 213; 144
Volga River front: Czechs on, 234, 250, 258, 263-66
Vologda: map, 110; Allied embassies move to, 77-78, 135; diplomats undermine Lockhart's efforts, 164-65; embassies removed to Archangel, 234; 113
Vologodsky, P. V., premier of Siberian government at Omsk, 269
Volunteer Army, 232
Vosnisensky, official in Commissariat for Foreign Affairs, 181 n. 43
Vyatka (now Kirov): maps, 110, 268; 240

War Cabinet, British: and internment in Britain of Chicherin and Petrov, 35; discusses South Russia, 42-43; decides to support Kaledin, 46; implements decision, 52; concern at lack of coordination in Allied policy re Russia, 53; memorandum on non-Bolshevik Russia, 53-54, 58; and general problem of Russia, 83; and intervention in Siberia, 90-91, 104, 169, 211; orders H.M.S. Suffolk to Vladivostok, 91; proposal for Smuts-Trotsky meeting, 161 n. 126; and employment of Czech Corps, 169-71; orders expedition to North Russia, 172-73; and Murmansk situation, 174-75, 177-78; orders 25th Middlesex Battalion to Vladivostok, 219; sends Knox to Siberia, 220; discusses U.S. opposition to Knox, 220-21; agrees to Maynard's request for reinforcements, 252; appoints Eliot as High Commissioner in Siberia, 270; decision to extend de facto recognition to merged government at Omsk, 279, 281, 284; and Lockhart-Litvinov exchange, 294-95. See also Eastern Committee of War Cabinet; Great Britain, government of; Lloyd George, David; Balfour, Arthur James
Ward, Lt.-Colonel John (Labour MP), commander 25th Middlesex Battalion: and selection of 25th Middlesex to go to Siberia, 223 n. 87; and combat on Ussuri front, 262; takes troops to Omsk for garrison duty, 276; role in Kolchak coup, 283
Wardrop, J. Oliver, British Consul-General at Moscow: receives emissary from Don Cossacks, 47; relations with Lockhart, 134; on British intelligence activities, 134;

on Cheka suppression of anarchists, 159 n. 120; escapes arrest, 286; places British interests in hands of Netherlands Legation, 287; leaves Russia, 296

War Office: general approach to problem of Russia, 83, 330; conflict with Foreign Office, 83-84; military influence over policy re Russia, 96, 101, 334-35; on necessity for intervention in Siberia, 129; on use of Czech Corps, 153-54; and inflated estimates of danger from prisoners of war in Siberia, 157; asks for Hicks' recall, 159; plan for combined Northern and Siberian intervention, 194; opposes U.S. plan for civilian commission to Siberia, 197-98; scale of operations contemplated in Siberia, 203 n. 28; memorandum predicting defeat unless Japanese intervene forthwith, 211; issues new orders to Poole, 240-41; troop-briefing material on Bolshevism, 241-42; rejects Poole's plan for offensive, 252; orders Maynard to retain his force for use against Bolsheviks, 252-53; replaces Poole with Ironside, 255-56; allows 25th Middlesex Battalion to fight on Ussuri front, 262; and Lockhart-Litvinov exchange, 295; and Dunsterville mission to Caucasus, 305, 307-08, 309-10; and policy re Caspian Sea, 319 n. 50; and question of maintaining British troops in Transcaspia after Armistice, 327-29; orders Malleson to withdraw, 328. *See also* General Staff

War Supplies: *see* Archangel, Vladivostok

Warth, Robert D., 12

Webster, Captain W. L., U.S. Red Cross: report with Hicks on Siberian prisoners of war, 157-58

Western Front: British losses on, 19; German offensive, 21 March 1918, 128; French obsession with importance of, 151, 153; diversion of troops from for intervention in North Russia, 195-96

White Guard: at Vladivostok, 145; impossibility of obtaining popular support, 249-50

White Sea: map, 110; Royal Navy operations in, 111

Wilson, General Sir Henry, C.I.G.S. from February 1918: at Petrograd conference, February 1917, 6; on compromise peace, 66 n. 31; asks recall of Lockhart, 131-32; on use of Czech Corps, 155; on proposed Smuts-Trotsky talk, 161 n. 126; on Lloyd George's attitude, June 1918, 210; will withdraw North Russian force unless action taken re Siberia, 211; on need for additional Japanese troops to Siberia, 258-59, 260; on Russia and defence of India; member Eastern Committee, 307 n. 16

Wilson, President Woodrow: Fourteen Points, 65-66; and intervention in Siberia, 105-06, 129, 144, 196; message to Russian people, 126; Balfour on, 167; decision on North Russia, 195-96; proposes civilian commission for Siberia, 196, 207; Knox on attitude of, 198; decision on Siberia, 214-15; *aide-mémoire* of 17 July 1918, 223-25, 243, 263; alarmed by Japanese response, 228; threatens to withdraw U.S. troops at Archangel unless Poole's conduct changed, 248-49; on question of additional Japanese troops to Siberia, 260; refuses aid to Czechs on Volga front, 263-64

Wiseman, Sir William: ix, 13, 106, 196; endorses U.S. plan for civilian commission for Siberia, 207; general approach re securing U.S. approval for Siberian intervention, 207-08; on U.S. policy, 213; on Wilson's decision, 218-19; on danger of trying to deceive Wilson, 260

Woodhouse, A. W. W., British Consul, Petrograd, 78

Woodroffe, Brigadier-General C. R., British Military Attaché at Tokyo: on Japanese aims in intervention, 266; 104

Wrangel, General P. N., successor to Denikin, 57

Yaroslavl: map, 110; anti-Bolshevik rising, 230-31, 291 n. 25; 112

Young, Douglas, British Consul at Archangel: on Archangel political situation, 112-13; and food relief ships, 173; warns against intervention, 236

Yuryev, A. M., President of Murmansk Soviet: asks advice from central Bolshevik authorities, 116; direct-wire conversation with Stalin, 117 n. 103; visit to Moscow, 179; final exchanges with Moscow, 182, 184; declared enemy of people, 184

Zenzinov, V. M., S-R member of Omsk Directorate, 278

Zinoviev, G. E., Bolshevik leader, 11

Zvegintsev, Major-General Nikolai I.: 114-15; Poole's relations with, 179